James K. A. Smith and Amos Yong, *Editors*

PENTECOSTAL MANIFESTOS will provide a forum for exhibiting the next generation of Pentecostal scholarship. Having exploded across the globe in the twentieth century, Pentecostalism now enters its second century. For the past fifty years, Pentecostal and charismatic theologians (and scholars in other disciplines) have been working "internally," as it were, to articulate a distinctly Pentecostal theology and vision. The next generation of Pentecostal scholarship is poised to move beyond a merely internal conversation to an outward-looking agenda, in a twofold sense: first, Pentecostal scholars are increasingly gaining the attention of those outside Pentecostal/charismatic circles *as* Pentecostal voices in mainstream discussions; second, Pentecostal scholars are moving beyond simply reflecting on their own tradition and instead are engaging in theological and cultural analysis of a variety of issues from a Pentecostal perspective. In short, Pentecostal scholars are poised with a new boldness:

- Whereas the first generation of Pentecostal scholars was careful to learn the methods of the academy and then "apply" those to the Pentecostal tradition, the next generation is beginning to interrogate the reigning methodologies and paradigms of inquiry from the perspective of a unique Pentecostal worldview.
- Whereas the first generation of Pentecostal scholars was faithful in applying the tools of their respective trades to the work of illuminating the phenomena of modern Pentecostalism, the charismatic movements, and (now) the global renewal movements, the second generation is expanding its focus to bring a Pentecostal perspective to bear on important questions and issues that are concerns not only for Pentecostals and charismatics but also for the whole church.
- Whereas the first generation of Pentecostal/charismatic scholars was engaged in transforming the anti-intellectualism of the tradition, the second generation is engaged in contributing to and even impacting the conversations of the wider theological academy.

PENTECOSTAL MANIFESTOS will bring together both high-profile scholars and newly emerging scholars to address issues at the intersection of Pentecostalism, the global church, the theological academy, and even broader cultural concerns. Authors in Pentecostal Manifestos will be writing to and addressing not only their own movements but also those outside of Pentecostal/charismatic circles, offering a manifesto for a uniquely Pentecostal perspective on various themes. These will be "manifestos" in the sense that they will be bold statements of a distinctly Pentecostal interjection into contemporary discussions and debates, undergirded by rigorous scholarship.

Under this general rubric of bold, programmatic "manifestos," the series will include both shorter, crisply argued volumes that articulate a bold vision within a field as well as longer scholarly monographs, more fully developed and meticulously documented, with the same goal of engaging wider conversations. Such Pentecostal Manifestos are offered as intrepid contributions with the hope of serving the global church and advancing wider conversations.

PUBLISHED

James K. A. Smith, *Thinking in Tongues: Pentecostal Contributions to Christian Philosophy* (2010)

Frank D. Macchia, *Justified in the Spirit: Creation, Redemption, and the Triune God* (2010)

Wolfgang Vondey, *Beyond Pentecostalism: The Crisis of Global Christianity and the Renewal of the Theological Agenda* (2010)

Amos Yong, *The Spirit of Creation: Modern Science and Divine Action in the Pentecostal-Charismatic Imagination* (2011)

Nimi Wariboko, *The Pentecostal Principle: Ethical Methodology in New Spirit* (2011)

Steven M. Studebaker, *From Pentecost to the Triune God: A Pentecostal Trinitarian Theology* (2012)

From Pentecost to the Triune God

A Pentecostal Trinitarian Theology

Steven M. Studebaker

William B. Eerdmans Publishing Company
Grand Rapids, Michigan / Cambridge, U.K.

Published 2012 by
Wm. B. Eerdmans Publishing Co.
2140 Oak Industrial Drive N.E., Grand Rapids, Michigan 49505 /
P.O. Box 163, Cambridge CB3 9PU U.K.

Printed in the United States of America

18 17 16 15 14 13 12 7 6 5 4 3 2 1

Library of Congress Cataloging-in-Publication Data

Studebaker, Steven M., 1968-
From Pentecost to the Triune God:
a Pentecostal Trinitarian theology / Steven M. Studebaker.
p. cm. — (Pentecostal manifestos)
ISBN 978-0-8028-6530-4 (pbk.: alk. paper)
1. Trinity. 2. Holy Spirit. 3. Pentecostal churches — Doctrines.
I. Title.

BT111.3.S88 2012
231′.044 — dc23

2012038521

www.eerdmans.com

To David M. Coffey, the tinder of my Trinitarian theology

Contents

Acknowledgments

The seeds of this study — completed over the last two years — were sown in my first weeks as a doctoral student. I entered Marquette University without the slightest interest in either Trinitarian theology or pneumatology. During my first semester, however, I had the good fortune of taking a course with David Coffey, whose theological acumen was and remains inspirational. In Coffey I saw for the first time how a powerful and comprehensive vision of God could shape the broader theological enterprise. Over the years, in addition to being a significant theological mentor, David has become a dear friend and reliable source of personal encouragement. As a result, my previous studies have borne the unmistakable imprint of his Trinitarian theology. Even so, those familiar with his work will recognize that the theology of this project differs from his in a number of respects. Yet, without the benefit of his insights, his published scholarship, and his dedicated attention to his students, my own contribution would never have been possible. My dedication of this book to David is an expression of personal gratitude to him as a scholar and friend.

I also want to mention D. Lyle Dabney, whose course on pneumatology proved personally and theologically formative. In the course of our first meeting after I had been appointed as his new teaching assistant, I told him that I was a Pentecostal. Dabney challenged me — perhaps provoked is a better word — to think seriously about Pentecostal theology. When I then confessed my preference for historical theology, he did not exactly rebuke me, but his response was not far from it. Specifically, he urged me to engage in theological reflection as a Pentecostal, and to do so beyond supposedly "safe" categories of historical and sociological analysis, or tired arguments over the interpretation of Spirit baptism in Luke-Acts. Pentecostals, according to Dabney, needed to develop a theology that was intrinsically *Pentecostal,* and not a weak imitation of some other position. Initially put off by this bold challenge, I nonetheless eventually saw its wisdom, embraced his call, and even continued as his TA for several more years! I hope that this project in some measure meets his challenge.

Nikola Caric, my own teaching and research assistant, also deserves recognition. I have consistently relied on him, throughout the course of this project, for help in securing sources and editing the manuscript. Bryan Dyer and Jason White have also served as my teaching assistants: although not directly involved in this study, their help with teaching and coursework freed Nick to devote his attention to support my research and writing.

It is a privilege to work with my colleagues at McMaster Divinity College, who nurture an atmosphere of scholarship and collegiality. Mark Boda, in particular, gave guidance on issues related to Old Testament pneumatology and the "wind gods." In this respect, I would be remiss not to acknowledge the contributions of Stan Porter and Phil Zylla, president and academic dean, respectively, of the Divinity College. They provided encouragement, institutional support in the form of additional teaching assistants, and a course load that allowed me the time necessary to complete this project.

I am deeply grateful to James K. A. Smith and Amos Yong for allowing me the opportunity to contribute a volume on the Trinity to the *Pentecostal Manifestos* series. They have offered valuable counsel both in the development of the proposal and later in the refinement of the scope and argument of the book. Many thanks are also due the anonymous external reviewer who, in the final stages of the project, provided important and thoughtful advice on honing the argument in respect to several historical and theological points.

Above all, I want to acknowledge my wife, Sheila, and kids, Gabrielle and Maxwell. Sheila has been a steadfast source of encouragement and has, over the years, sacrificed in many ways so that I could pursue the dream of becoming a theological academic. Perhaps putting the words into print will at least partly make up for not saying "thank you" nearly enough. Writing a book takes a lot of time. Often that meant writing when Gabby and Max were at a swim meet or another of the myriad activities that make up the life of a young person. Thank you for your patience and good humor when working on this book kept me from sharing some of those experiences in your lives.

Pittsford, New York
November 2012

Introduction

"Pentecostalism is not a theological tradition, but a religious movement," one of my professors told me when I revealed that Pentecostal theology was a long-term research agenda. Though made without condescension, the comment left me dispirited. In time, however, it spurred me on to be part of the constructive effort in Pentecostal theology. Calling it a religious movement meant that Pentecostalism is about spiritual experience, an opinion many Pentecostal scholars share. That view is true but irrelevant. All Christian movements are about experience of some kind or another. The religious experience of Catholic Christians is sacramental — of Pentecostals, charismatic. Exuberant religious experience characterizes Pentecostalism, but other Christian movements are no less about a certain kind of religious experience. My professor's comment also implied a disparity between religious experience and theology. But the distinction between them, though helpful for distinguishing theological sources, masks their inseparable relationship.

I also became intrigued with Trinitarian theology and pneumatology during my doctoral studies, but it had little to do with my background in Pentecostalism. Jonathan Edwards, an eighteenth-century Puritan Calvinist, and David Coffey, a contemporary Neo-Scholastic Catholic theologian, introduced me to the richness of the doctrine of the Trinity. D. Lyle Dabney, an exile from Pentecostalism and now a Wesleyan theologian, led me to pneumatology. Why, as a Pentecostal, had these areas of theology not captivated me? One could not be faulted for thinking that pneumatology is the central preoccupation of Pentecostal theology, and that the Trinity is but a small step away. But that is not the case. Moreover, the answer resides in the nature of Pentecostal theology itself. Though Pentecostal scholarship teems with discussions of the Holy Spirit, until recently it concentrated on a narrow range of issues. Often in conversation with evangelicals, Pentecostals have endeavored to demonstrate that Spirit baptism is a second work of grace subsequent to salvation (for Holiness Pentecostals, a third work of grace), to determine whether tongues is a necessary sign of Spirit baptism, and to validate the contemporary manifestation of the gifts of the Spirit. Thinking on fundamental pneumatology and Trinitarian theology has not been a moving part of most of Pentecostal theology.[1] I take up this task in this book.

My project has two tasks. The first shows the theological significance of the Pentecostal experience of the Holy Spirit for Trinitarian theology. The experience of the Holy Spirit — the catch phrase being "baptism in the Holy Spirit" — is the centerpiece of the Pentecostal movement. But what is the relationship between the Pentecostal experience of the Spirit and Trinitarian theology? Pentecostal theologians often avoid giving religious experience an explicit role in theology because they fear the criticism of religious subjectivism from other scholars. They should stop doing this. The outpouring of the Spirit of Pentecost and the experience of Spirit baptism is the climactic manifestation of the drama of biblical redemption. Biblical redemption begins with God's Spirit hovering over the primeval abyss in Genesis and climaxes with the outpouring of the Holy Spirit in Acts. Taking the experience of the Spirit as theologically significant is legitimate because it corresponds to the place of the Spirit in the biblical story of redemption. Pentecostal experience provides a point of orientation to the biblical narratives of the Spirit that can contribute to the traditions of Trinitarian theology.

1. The situation has changed in the last decade, but efforts are still rare. The charismatic theologian Veli-Matti Kärkkäinen's *The Trinity: Global Perspectives* (Louisville: Westminster John Knox, 2007) is probably the most well-known and comprehensive work on the Trinity; nevertheless, it is a survey of historical and contemporary figures rather than a constructive project in Pentecostal Trinitarian theology (see chapter 5 for a fuller discussion). More common are Trinitarian approaches to other areas of theology rather than a theology of the Trinity per se. A case in point is Amos Yong's use of the Trinity to develop a Pentecostal approach to theological hermeneutics: Amos Yong, *Spirit-Word-Community: Theological Hermeneutics in Trinitarian Perspective* (Eugene, OR: Wipf and Stock, 2002). Also, Frank D. Macchia uses the Trinity in his reconstructions of a Pentecostal theology of Spirit baptism and justification: *Baptized in the Spirit: A Global Pentecostal Theology* (Grand Rapids: Zondervan, 2006) and *Justified in the Spirit: Creation, Redemption, and the Triune God* (Grand Rapids: Eerdmans, 2010).

The second task mines the biblical narratives of the Spirit for their Trinitarian yield. The vital role of the Spirit in the Bible's story of salvation, however, has not led to a commensurate place in traditional Trinitarian theology. Traditional Trinitarian theology concentrates on the processions within the Godhead and christological categories. Both of these tendencies emerged in the patristic era and characterize much of the subsequent traditions of thought. In Eastern Trinitarian theology, the Spirit is a procession from the Father and sometimes also through the Son. The Western tradition portrays the Holy Spirit as the mutual love of the Father and the Son — or some other expression of divine love. The Holy Spirit has primarily a passive and derivative identity in both traditions. The activities of the Father and the Son shape the identity of the Holy Spirit and fill the content of Trinitarian theology. The result is an unintended marginalization of the Holy Spirit and ambiguity concerning the Spirit's identity. The Spirit, however, plays a prominent role in the biblical story of redemption. In fact, the outpouring of the Spirit of Pentecost is the capstone of God's redemptive work. I hold that this activity suggests that the Spirit is the divine person who fulfills God's triune identity. The Spirit fulfills the tri-unity of God not only as the third subsistent person, but as one who contributes to the identity of the Father and the Son as well. The liminal, constitutional, and eschatological work of the Spirit in the biblical drama of redemption points to the Spirit's identity in the Trinity. The implication is that the Spirit consummates the Trinitarian God and as such plays a role in the identity formation of the Son and the Father. Before outlining the way the ensuing chapters develop this theology, I will first describe the Trinitarian principle and Pentecostal orientation that is fundamental to the theological proposal in this project.

Trinitarian Principle

The theological principle "economic activity arises from immanent identity" is foundational for much of contemporary theology and serves as the methodological basis of this project's move from the Pentecostal experience of the Spirit, to the biblical narratives of the Spirit, and to the Spirit's identity in the Trinity. An early advocate of the relationship between the immanent and economic Trinity, Karl Rahner articulated the principle that the "'economic' Trinity is the 'immanent' Trinity and the 'immanent'

Trinity is the 'economic' Trinity."[2] Although this is a retrieval of ancient patristic theology rather than a new insight, it sounded novel to modern theology, which largely regarded the doctrine of the Trinity as irrelevant.[3] Rahner's principle means that economic work reveals immanent identity (doing reflects being and being informs doing). In other words, what God is in the economy is what God is from eternity.

Contemporary Trinitarian theologians widely embrace Rahner's basic assumption — with one important caveat. As David Coffey points out, since the economic Trinity does not exhaust the immanent Trinity, Rahner's formula is valid in only one direction: the economic is the immanent Trinity, but not, strictly speaking, vice versa. The transcendence of God means that the immanent Trinity surpasses the economic, even though they are harmonious.[4] With this qualification, Rahner's insight is correct: the activity and hence revelation of God in the economy of redemption corresponds to the triune identity of God. Indeed, this assumption must be granted for Christian theology to proceed at all. Without correspondence between what God does in the economy of redemption and who God is in the immanent Trinity, theological discourse cannot speak meaningfully about God. Theology has no direct access to the immanent Trinity. God's activity in the economy of redemption is the basis of theological reflection. God's economic work is the "starting point of theology."[5] Christian theology has recognized this point and historically focused on Jesus Christ as the summit and thus the primary source of knowledge of God.

2. Karl Rahner, *The Trinity,* trans. Joseph Donceel, intro. Catherine Mowry LaCugna (New York: Crossroad, 1988), p. 22.

3. E.g., the patristic logic that the sanctifying work of the Holy Spirit (doing/activity) suggests the divinity of the Spirit (being). Giulio Maspero indicates that Gregory of Nyssa developed his theology and pneumatology based on the connection between the immanent nature of God and God's economic activity (see *Trinity and Man: Gregory of Nyssa's* Ad Ablabium, Supplements to Vigiliae, 86 [Leiden: Brill, 2007], p. 170). Nyssa does not see the work of sanctification as peculiar to the Spirit, but rather that since the Spirit sanctifies, the Spirit is divine, because sanctification is a proper work of the undivided nature of the Trinitarian God (see Gregory of Nyssa, "The Lord's Prayer," in *St. Gregory of Nyssa: The Lord's Prayer, the Beatitudes,* trans. Hilda C. Graef [New York: Newman, 1954], p. 53).

4. David M. Coffey, *Deus Trinitas: The Doctrine of the Triune God* (New York: Oxford University Press, 1999), p. 151.

5. Luis F. LaDaria, *The Living and True God: The Mystery of the Trinity,* trans. Evelyn Harrison, rev. Doris Strieter and Thomas Strieter, Colección Traditio (Miami: Convivium, 2009), p. 49.

Without displacing Christology, pneumatology should also inform a Christian view of God. The title of this book, *From Pentecost to the Triune God*, assumes Rahner's theological axiom. The implications for theological hermeneutics are twofold. Expressed generally, the personal identities of the divine persons inform their economic works. More specifically, the reciprocity between identity and work means that the Spirit's work in all of its economic dimensions always bears the properties of the Spirit's personal identity. With this, the discussion reaches pneumatology proper — and this question: What is the Spirit's identity that informs the Spirit's work or, put alternatively, what does the work reveal about the Spirit's identity?

I have answered that question elsewhere in terms of the Augustinian mutual-love model.[6] This book does not disavow the mutual-love model, but pursues a different pathway for understanding the Trinity. The theological strategy developed here begins with the Pentecostal experience of the Spirit. It then moves to the biblical narratives of the Spirit, and from there to the Trinitarian God. Part of the problem of traditional pneumatology is that the Spirit's identity is often vague and derived from a theory of inner Trinitarian processions rather than the accounts of the Spirit in Scripture. Reflecting this situation, Jürgen Moltmann concludes that the Spirit has a "certain anonymity," that, vis-à-vis the Father and the Son, the Spirit's "character is . . . defined negatively rather than positively" (e.g., "not without origin . . . not generated"), and that consequently "the Holy Spirit is only presented by and in the mutual relationship of the Father and the Son."[7] A pathway to a clearer understanding of the person of the Spirit is available. The personal identity of the Spirit emerges from the personal narratives of the Spirit and especially as the Spirit of Pentecost. As Eugene Rogers highlights, the Spirit is a person, and this means, regardless of how difficult this is at times to explain, the Spirit is a "character in a story."[8] The

6. Steven M. Studebaker, *The Trinitarian Vision of Jonathan Edwards and David Coffey* (Amherst, NY: Cambria, 2011). That work is a continuation of research in Augustinian Trinitarian theology that I began during my doctoral studies, whereas the present volume approaches the Trinity from the perspective of Pentecostal theology. The two approaches are not at odds but are different from one another. I believe that multiple viewpoints enhance the Christian understanding of God.

7. Jürgen Moltmann, *The Trinity and the Kingdom: The Doctrine of God*, trans. Margaret Kohl (San Francisco: Harper & Row, 1981), pp. 168-69.

8. Eugene F. Rogers, Jr., *After the Spirit: A Constructive Pneumatology from Resources outside the Modern West* (Grand Rapids: Eerdmans, 2005), pp. 52-53.

characteristics of the Spirit that emerge from the biblical record point the way to the identity of the Holy Spirit and its implications for Trinitarian theology.

I use several terms to refer to the person of the Holy Spirit. "Subsistence" means that the Spirit is a distinct instantiation of the divine nature and has a distinct identity relative to the Father and Son, though without dividing the nature. The Spirit also has unique agency. The identity of the Spirit emerges in the Spirit's agency or activity. My understanding of the Spirit as a person is in many respects consistent with the traditional Western notion that a divine person is a unique subsistence of the divine nature. Where I differ from traditional theology is in the degree of agency I attribute to the Spirit, which I believe the biblical narratives about the Spirit warrant. I also think that it is worthwhile to recognize that the language of "person" is not biblical per se, but philosophical and theological. Nevertheless, the Spirit, as well as the Father and the Son, act in the biblical accounts of redemptive history in ways that are best described as personal: for example, they are distinct from one another, act as agents, and relate and respond to human persons. Thus I believe that theology properly applies the term "person" to the Father, the Son, and the Holy Spirit. This book focuses on what pneumatology — the person of the Spirit as the Spirit of Pentecost — has to offer Trinitarian theology. But why should the Spirit of Pentecost serve as the navigating point to the biblical narratives of the Spirit?

Pentecostal Orientation

If the economic Trinity is the source of the Christian understanding of God, with what economic activity should we begin? The conventional answer is Jesus Christ.[9] However, I suggest that a Pentecostal contribution to

9. E.g., Allan Coppedge, *The God Who Is Triune: Revisioning the Christian Doctrine of God* (Downers Grove, IL: InterVarsity, 2007), p. 14. Although integrating pneumatology, Wolfhart Pannenberg also takes Jesus and his relationship to the Father as the starting point of the Christian doctrine of the Trinity (see Pannenberg, *Systematic Theology*, vol. 1, trans. Geoffrey W. Bromiley [Grand Rapids: Eerdmans, 1991], pp. 259-68). Pannenberg's Trinitarian theology can be characterized as Patrocentric, since the glorification of the Father and his kingdom is the *telos* of the Son and the Spirit. However, his epistemology of the Trinitarian God is Christocentric because the revelation of the Father occurs principally in Christ (see Pannenberg, *Systematic Theology*, 1: 313-17). LaDaria's excellent work on the Trinity also reflects Christocentrism (see *The Living and True God*, p. 49).

Trinitarian theology should begin with the Holy Spirit and especially the Spirit of Pentecost, though without ignoring Christ. I agree with Amos Yong that theology cannot initially operate from a comprehensive viewpoint. Theology begins from a particular point and then seeks comprehensiveness from that standpoint.[10] Furthermore, recognizing a starting point is not a methodology of blinkered idiosyncrasy. For a Pentecostal approach to Trinitarian theology, the entry and navigating point to the biblical narratives of the Spirit is the outpouring of the Spirit in the book of Acts — the Spirit of Pentecost and Spirit baptism.

Why begin with the outpouring of the Spirit of Pentecost in Acts 2? The Pentecostal experience of the Spirit, or Spirit baptism, is the initial catalyst for this return to Scripture to find the Spirit. Pentecostal experience is about the Holy Spirit, and the Pentecostal experience of the Spirit suggests that the Spirit is not ornamental but indispensable to Christian life and theology. The link between the Pentecostal experience of the Spirit and theology is similar to the one in Lutheranism between its theology and its practice of the sacraments of baptism and Lord's Supper. I address the oft-assumed unilateral relationship between theology and experience in chapter 1, but for now I posit the reciprocal and mutually determining relationship between them. The vital nature of the experience of the Spirit to the Pentecostal movement means that pneumatology is fundamental to Pentecostal theology.

When I argue that Spirit baptism has theological significance, I do not have in mind the classical Pentecostal doctrine. Indeed, classical Pentecostal theology, by construing Spirit baptism as a *donum superadditum* to salvation and the work of Christ, confounds progress toward a fundamental theology of the Holy Spirit. "Spirit baptism" is a biblical and comprehensive term that takes in the charismatic experience of the Spirit that typifies the various forms of the Pentecostal movement. If the Pentecostal movement is a work of the Holy Spirit, then we should expect the Spirit to play as significant a role in biblical redemption as it does in the Pentecostal movement. But is that the case?

The vital place of the Holy Spirit in Pentecostal experience resonates with the Spirit's role in the biblical account of redemption. Scripture frames Jesus' salvation as baptism in the Spirit. In each of the Gospels, John the Baptist declares, "He will baptize in the Holy Spirit." Jesus en-

10. Amos Yong, *The Spirit Poured Out on All Flesh: Pentecostalism and the Possibility of Global Theology* (Grand Rapids: Baker Academic, 2005), p. 27.

courages his disciples: "Do not leave Jerusalem, but wait for the gift my Father promised . . . in a few days you will be baptized with the Holy Spirit" (Acts 1:4-5). The outpouring of the Spirit on the day of Pentecost fulfilled Jesus' promise to baptize his disciples with the Holy Spirit. The Spirit of Pentecost and the experience of Spirit baptism, therefore, are cumulative and consummative because they fully express earlier biblical images and themes of the Spirit and the Trinitarian nature of redemption. The paramount place of the outpouring of the Spirit in Acts and the economy of redemption confirms the Pentecostal experience of the Spirit. Moreover, its eminent location in the canon of redemption means that it can serve as a gateway to an exploration of the biblical narratives of the Spirit. "From Pentecost to the Triune God" does not imply that Trinitarian theology will consider references to the Spirit of Pentecost in exclusion to other biblical accounts of the Spirit. Rather, it means that the eschatological place of Spirit baptism in Luke-Acts and the broader biblical drama of redemption provides a point of orientation for pneumatology and Trinitarian theology — much as texts about Christ often become the lens with which we can understand other parts of Scripture.

One might wonder whether this approach backs a Pentecostal bias that discounts alternative theological topics (e.g., Christology). That danger needs to be avoided, but that is the case for all traditions and theological orientations. For example, when evangelicals define the essence of Christianity as a "personal relationship with Jesus Christ," they tilt toward Christocentrism. Moreover, allowing the unique character of a particular tradition of Christianity to guide the approach to theology and the Bible is not problematic. As Amos Yong points out,

> A distinctive Pentecostal perspective would highlight a Lukan hermeneutical approach, a pneumatological framework and orientation . . . [and] I see as unavoidable such an open acknowledgement of approaching the whole of Scripture through a part of the whole: no one can be merely and fully biblical in the exhaustive sense of the term.[11]

Therefore, engaging the theological task and the approach to Scripture, based on the Pentecostal experience of the Spirit, is not distinct from other theological traditions in a formal sense, but in a material one, because it

11. Yong, *The Spirit Poured Out*, p. 27.

begins with the Spirit of Pentecost. This starting point gives it ecumenical potential to speak to other Christian traditions.

What does the Spirit of Pentecost offer to historical Trinitarian theology? The biblical narratives of the Spirit — and especially the Spirit's eschatological identity as the Spirit of Pentecost — suggest that the Spirit both completes the economic work of redemption and the immanent fellowship of the Trinitarian God.[12] Rather than primarily having a derivative and passive identity and function in the immanent Trinity, the Spirit's eschatological nature means that the Spirit consummates and constitutes the fellowship of the triune God. In doing so, the Spirit not only participates in fellowship with the Father and Son but also contributes to the constitution of their personal identities. The chapters in this volume detail the theological approach and content of this Pentecostal contribution to Trinitarian theology.

Overview

The chapters organize around three tasks. Chapters 1 and 2 are constructive in nature. They lay the foundational theological hermeneutic and content of a Pentecostal approach to Trinitarian theology. The first chapter makes the theological and hermeneutical case for taking the Pentecostal experience of Spirit baptism as theologically significant and as a point of orientation to Scripture. Taking its lead from the Pentecostal experience of the Holy Spirit, the second chapter examines the biblical narratives of the Spirit. It lays the central theological and biblical argument for a Pentecostal contribution to Trinitarian theology. Based on the Holy Spirit's liminal, constitutional, and consummational roles in the history of redemption (including creation-redemption, Christology, and Pentecost), it argues that the Holy Spirit should be understood as the divine person who completes the fellowship of the Trinitarian God.

Chapters 3-5 have an ecumenical focus and engage historical and contemporary figures in Trinitarian theology. Chapter 3 begins with historical figures in Eastern and Western Trinitarian theology — for example, the Cappadocians, Augustine, Thomas Aquinas, and Richard of Saint Victor —

12. Amos Yong also suggests that the Spirit completes the relationship of the Father and the Son, but does so for the most part within the categories of the mutual-love model. See Yong, *Spirit-Word-Community*, pp. 67, 74.

and then moves to contemporary representatives, for example, John Zizioulas and Thomas Weinandy. Turning to Reformed evangelical theology, chapter 4 assesses the Trinitarian theology of Jonathan Edwards, Donald Bloesch, Millard Erickson, and Myk Habets. These figures span the history of modern evangelicalism and provide voices from its North American colonial beginnings to its dominant form in the twentieth century and its emergent expressions at the beginning of the new millennium. Chapter 5 examines the work on the Trinity among charismatic theologians — Kilian McDonnell, Frank Macchia, and Clark Pinnock. The goal throughout these three chapters is to enter into a conversation with figures and trajectories of Trinitarian theology and thereby engage the broader ecumenical field of contemporary Trinitarian theology. Though I write as a Pentecostal and for Pentecostals, my primary goal is not parochial, but ecumenical.

The last two chapters bring Trinitarian theology to bear on important issues of contemporary Christian thought and life. Theology should speak, at least at some point, to the circumstances of life. With that in mind, chapter 6 proposes a Trinitarian and pneumatological theology of religions that can help Christians embrace a more inclusive attitude and relationship toward people in other religions. Chapter 7 develops a Trinitarian theology of creation that supports the practice of creation care as an activity of Christian formation.

1 A Pentecostal Approach to the Trinity

"My experience is my creed," declared the early Pentecostal J. H. King.[1] But what did he mean? Does this statement substantiate the popular fear that Pentecostal hermeneutics are effusive extrapolations from overheated religious experience? At first glance it appears so, but a closer inspection reveals that King is not naively writing off theology from his experience. King assumes that his Christian experience is an experience of God and that, as such, "[d]ivine experience is the basis of theology or classified knowledge of God, [and the] Christian Creed is not an arbitrary formulation, but the outgrowth of the conscious work of God in the heart."[2]

For King, theology and doctrinal formulation, or "creed," arise out of the church's experience of Christ's redemptive work. Since this work grounds Christian experience and theology, theology is neither bare abstract speculation nor rhapsodic religious subjectivism. Theology and doctrine specify the meaning of what the Christian community takes as the revelation and work of God in its midst. Pentecostals have intuitively sensed that their experience and theology are interrelated, but they have not always effectively identified the theological rationale for that interrelationship or drawn out its theological implications. Indeed, many Pentecostals deny that Pentecostalism can be defined in theological terms and must

1. Joseph H. King, "The Foundation Eternal," *The Pentecostal Holiness Advocate,* May 27, 1937; reprinted in B. E. Underwood, ed., *Christ — God's Love Gift: Selected Writings of Joseph Hillery King,* vol. 1 (Franklin Springs, GA: Advocate Press, 1969), p. 155.

2. King, *Christ — God's Love Gift,* p. 154.

rather be understood in experiential categories. According to this view, Pentecostals are about religious experience and not theology.[3]

I prefer a different approach to the role of religious experience in Pentecostalism. Pentecostal experience, which includes both individual and collective — but primarily the collective, or common, type of experience within the Pentecostal movement — should inform Pentecostal theology. I agree with Veli-Matti Kärkkäinen, who says: "I am convinced that a proper way to assess and describe the state of Pentecostal pneumatology is to take a close look at Pentecostal spirituality and its implications for theologizing."[4] Pentecostals should give theological significance to what they take as the manifestation and experience of the Holy Spirit within their incipient tradition.[5] This chapter makes a case for seeing Pentecostal experience, and especially the Pentecostal experience of the outpouring of the Holy Spirit — Spirit baptism — as a legitimate and fertile source of theology in general and Trinitarian theology in particular.

Why should the experience of Spirit baptism inform Trinitarian theology? Spirit baptism, despite its variety of interpretations, should play a key role in Trinitarian theology because it is central (1) to the practice and experience of the Pentecostal movement and (2) to the biblical narratives of the Spirit. This raises the methodological and hermeneutical issue of the role that Christian practice and experience plays in theology, particularly for practices and experiences informed by biblical categories. Accordingly, this chapter first establishes the theological rationale for letting Pentecostal practice and experience lead theology to the biblical narratives of the Spirit. Substantiating the theological, indeed the pneumatological, ground for the place of experience in the theological task sets the stage for the second part, which suggests that the experience and biblical metaphor of Spirit baptism provide a navigating point for Trinitarian theology.

3. E.g., Keith Warrington, *Pentecostal Theology: A Theology of Encounter* (New York: T&T Clark, 2008), pp. 18-27; and Allan Anderson, *Pentecostalism: An Introduction* (New York: Cambridge University Press, 2004), pp. 9-15, 60.

4. Veli-Matti Kärkkäinen, "Pneumatologies in Systematic Theology," in *Studying Global Pentecostalism: Theories and Methods*, ed. Allan Anderson, Michael Begrunder, André Droogers, and Cornelius van der Laan (Berkeley: University of California Press, 2010), pp. 223-44 (esp. p. 227).

5. Amos Yong makes a similar appeal to Pentecostals in *The Spirit Poured Out on All Flesh: Pentecostalism and the Possibility of Global Theology* (Grand Rapids: Baker Academic, 2005), and *Hospitality and the Other: Pentecost, Christian Practices, and the Neighbor* (Maryknoll, NY: Orbis, 2008).

The following points summarize the logic and plan of this chapter: the biblical metaphor and promise of Spirit baptism is foundational to and formative of the practice and experience of Pentecostalism; and the Pentecostal experience of the Spirit is just that, and thus the experience of Spirit baptism within the Pentecostal tradition can inform the nature of theology in general, and of Trinitarian theology in particular. In order to support these two theological principles, I begin this chapter, first, with a discussion of the interrelationships between experience-practice, tradition, Scripture, and theology; second, I outline the historical ways Pentecostals have engaged these issues; third, I present the theological hermeneutics at work in the Jerusalem Council as biblical support for a theological method that gives theological significance to the experience of the Holy Spirit; fourth, by drawing on the Pentecostal Kenneth J. Archer and the once Lutheran but now Catholic Reinhard Hütter, I propose a constructive and pneumatological rationale for allowing the experience of Spirit baptism within the Pentecostal movement to play an informative role in Trinitarian theology; finally, I present the case for taking the biblical metaphor of Spirit baptism as representative of Pentecostal experience-practice and theology.

Experience, Practices, Tradition, and Scripture

How do Christian experience, practice, tradition, and Scripture relate to one another?[6] Should they be arranged hierarchically — Scripture, tradi-

6. My use of the four terms is not an attempt to replace what is often called the Wesleyan quadrilateral of Scripture, tradition, reason, and experience. According to Albert Outler, who coined the term "quadrilateral" (it does not appear in Wesley's writings), Scripture is the preeminent source of revelation. Tradition and reason assist in the interpretation of Scripture. Experience, though listed in the quadrilateral, is not a source of biblical understanding. Rather, Outler argues, "experience refers to Wesley's conviction that genuine faith is always vital faith or the reception of biblical revelation in the heart (e.g., Wesley's emphasis on 'heart religion') in contrast to mere doctrinal orthodoxy. Moreover, Wesley deferred from establishing a normative theological model, which the term the 'Wesleyan Quadrilateral' can imply." See Albert C. Outler, "The Wesleyan Quadrilateral in John Wesley," *Wesleyan Theological Journal* 20, no. 1 (1985): 7-18; W. Stephen Gunter et al., *Wesley and the Quadrilateral: Renewing the Conversation* (Nashville: Abingdon, 1997); and Donald A. D. Thorsen, *The Wesleyan Quadrilateral: Scripture, Tradition, Reason, and Experience as a Model of Evangelical Theology* (Grand Rapids: Zondervan, 1990), pp. 98-100.

Like Wesley, I am not attempting to establish a normative model of revelation and the-

tion, practice, and experience? Or are the distinctions less hard and more a perspective of historical time and place? Today, Nicene Trinitarian theology is unquestioned orthodoxy. But in the early churches of the first and second century no one had ever heard of it. Although the differences between these categories are real, at another level the categories are very much integrated and reciprocal.

The Nexus of Experience, Practices, Doctrine, and Tradition

A common practice in theological hermeneutics and method is to treat Christian experience and church practices as distinct.[7] They are different in theory, but according to the cultural-linguistic approach, experience, doctrine, and church practices cannot be separated in the concrete realities of church life. Water baptism, for instance, can be discussed abstractly as a church doctrine and practice, but the actual practice of water baptism always includes the particular experience of an individual who is baptized and the church family that celebrates the event. Christian experience, then, is the particular appropriation of church practices by specific individuals of faith; church practices do not exist concretely other than in the experience of individual believers and communities of faith. On the role of experience in theology, an appropriate theological method can recognize and draw on the interrelationship between Christian experience, church practices, and doctrine. Theology does not need to be bound to a view that reifies these elements into hermetically sealed hermeneutical categories and applies a top-down hermeneutic in which practice and doctrine carry theological freight and inform experience, but not vice versa.

---

ology. Moreover, as will become clear below, these four distinctions, though helpful in some respects, can confuse the fluid connections between them. I affirm the preeminence of Scripture because, as a written canon, it is the most solid source of revelation available to the church. Yet Scripture is a record of the experiences and evolving traditions of the ancient Hebrews and early Christians and thus not categorically different from Christian experience and tradition today. Moreover, Christian "experience" can serve as a source of theology and is not simply a term for vital faith.

7. E.g., Vanhoozer distinguishes four "sources and norms" of theology: biblical propositions, the person of Christ, Christian piety, and church practices. See Kevin J. Vanhoozer, *The Drama of Doctrine: A Canonical-Linguistic Approach to Christian Theology* (Louisville: Westminster John Knox, 2005), pp. 4-7.

The place of Spirit baptism in the Pentecostal movement illustrates the interrelationship between experience, tradition, and doctrine: it is central to the Pentecostal tradition. In this respect, Spirit baptism may be similar to the practice and experience of the sinner's prayer in the evangelical tradition. The sinner's prayer is the conversion paradigm through which people experience being "born again" and the forgiveness of sins. Embedded in the practice of the sinner's prayer is a theology of conversion and salvation. Moreover, here the concern is not about which came first, the experience or the theology that makes sense of the experience, but only with their reciprocal relationship.

In Pentecostalism, reciprocity likewise characterizes the experience and doctrine of Spirit baptism. The early Pentecostals formulated their doctrine of Spirit baptism as a work of grace subsequent to salvation on the basis of theological tradition and Christian experience. Borrowing from their backgrounds in the Wesleyan Holiness and Reformed revival movements, the early Pentecostals understood the doctrine of Spirit baptism as a second or third work of grace. Moreover, since they experienced Spirit baptism as believers, they naturally believed that it was an experience subsequent to salvation. Therefore, the Pentecostal doctrine of Spirit baptism is the product of the dynamic interplay of tradition and experience — along with biblical reflection. The Pentecostal doctrine of Spirit baptism in turn became the framework for Pentecostal preaching and teaching, which in turn funded the practice of inviting people to first receive Jesus as savior and then Spirit baptism for empowered ministry and life. In summary, experience, practice, and doctrine, though separable at a purely abstract level, are not so in the life of Christian communities. For this reason, when I use the term "experience," it is shorthand for the complex interrelationships of practice, experience, and tradition that are shaped by the unique appropriation of the biblical witness within the Pentecostal movement, which characterizes corporate and individual participation in and experience of the Christian faith. Based on the interrelationships among experience, practice, and doctrine, I want to address the tendency to prioritize practices and doctrine over experience.

Experience and Tradition

Theological hermeneutics frequently elevates tradition, or "community," over experience as a theological source. The problem is that what we consider tradition was once experience. When does personal and collective experience make the transition to tradition and become regulative for Christian faith and practice? In other words, what now serves as the normative ecclesiastical context for the individual's understanding of Christian thought and life was, at an earlier time, the viewpoints, practices, and experiences of individuals whose theology and practices may have seemed bizarre or even heretical to their contemporaries. The doctrine and experience of Spirit baptism was both a new experience and a doctrine that was deemed aberrant by many outside early Pentecostalism, but became the distinctive doctrine for many Pentecostals. In this respect, more established traditions could have an advantage over younger ones.[8] For example, Lutherans can appeal to a tradition of Christian thought that spans nearly five centuries. The longevity of such a tradition can seem to trump the more ephemeral experiences of an upstart one. The situation is similar to parents giving advice to children based on the accumulated wisdom of their years of experience. In many respects, their parental wisdom is correct, but at times the younger generation's experience, since it is more reflective of contemporary life, may in fact be wiser. In other words, a twenty-something's understanding of the culture — and hence her action in light of it — may be wiser than her parents' understanding because it is more in tune with the contemporary world. The point is that traditional longevity can be a boon and a bane. A long-established tradition, by virtue of its age, has demonstrated its viability. Yet it also can inhibit new insights and practices because of its tendency to ossify and its inability to adapt to the dynamic circumstances of the Christian life.

One solution is to identify a certain era of the church, say the patristic one, or a confessional tradition, such as the Westminster Confession, as definitive for Christian thought and practice. Tradition in this sense plays a normative role in theology. The role of tradition has had a renaissance in non-Catholic theological contexts in the past three decades. Lutheran George Lindbeck's cultural-linguistic approach to doctrine helped to show that church doctrine, sacred texts, and practices (i.e., tradition) provide the framework and data for individual experience and theological reflection.[9] In this sense, tradition plays a normative function because, as an ob-

8. Veli-Matti Kärkkäinen remarks that, "[u]nlike established Christian traditions such as Roman Catholicism, Pentecostalism cannot build on tradition for the simple reason that it came into existence only a century ago" ("Pneumatologies in Systematic Theology," p. 225).

9. George A. Lindbeck, *The Nature of Doctrine: Religion and Theology in a Postliberal Age* (Philadelphia: Westminster, 1984).

jective framework, it shapes the structure for individual practice. This insight is important, but it tends to be unilateral in the way it understands the relationship between (1) the beliefs and practices of the church and theology, and (2) the beliefs and practices and Christian experience.

A better option is to recognize that, though it bears a degree of normativity, tradition is dynamic. For example, Luther critiqued and proposed an alternative to the medieval church's view of grace in the sixteenth century, which in time produced a new normative tradition — the Lutheran and, more broadly, the Protestant one. Furthermore, Protestant theology cannot be separated from Luther's experience and the theology he produced or from the similar experiences of many of his contemporaries with whom his theology resonated. Lindbeck discerns a unidirectional movement from Luther's doctrine of justification by faith to his tower experience.[10] It may well be true that Luther made his exegetical discoveries and theological formulation of justification by faith prior to the tower experience, but certainly his frustration *(Anfechtung)* with late-medieval spirituality fueled his quest for a biblical and theological new way. The problem is that the cultural-linguistic approach, when taken as an exclusive model, becomes unidirectional and forestalls the reciprocal influence between experience, church practices, and theology.

A century after the worldwide emergence of the Pentecostal movement, Pentecostals can draw on their own emerging tradition. Moreover, the emerging Pentecostal tradition cannot be neatly separated from Pentecostal experience. For this reason, the Pentecostal experience-tradition can be taken as a unit. When we refer, then, to Pentecostal experience, it is not just to the scintillating subjective experience of Pentecostals (though it does not discount it); rather, it has in mind the broader and common character of the Pentecostal experience and thus invokes the notion of tradition — the practice and experience of Spirit baptism within the Pentecostal movement. From this standpoint, Spirit baptism can be understood as a constitutive experience within Pentecostalism. Even granting the varied interpretations of Spirit baptism among Pentecostals, Spirit baptism is a biblical metaphor for an experience that many Pentecostals have in common and as such is an experience that characterizes the movement and not just certain individuals within it. "Experience" in this sense includes traditional practices and the attendant experiences they engender. Moreover, though church practices can be contemplated in the abstract, in reality

10. Lindbeck, *The Nature of Doctrine,* p. 39.

they provide the structure for the concrete ways specific communities and persons of faith experience the Christian faith. Taken together, the particular practices and beliefs of a Christian community and the way they structure Christian experience form a tradition. "Experience" is roughly equivalent to "tradition." The experience of Spirit baptism thus refers to the common experience of Spirit baptism and charismatic practices within the Pentecostal movement.

Text, Tradition, and Experience

Because of the close historical and theological affinities between Pentecostals and evangelicals, I also need to address the tendency to give precedence to the biblical text over tradition and experience. Evangelicals — and Pentecostals along with them — have been people of the Bible. This is, of course, appropriate since Scripture is in principle the clearest testimony to the revelation and redemptive work of God. However, the writers of Scripture were more comfortable drawing on past experience and tradition than contemporaneous biblical, text-driven theologies. When the Hebrew prophets, for instance, appeal to the Exodus, they are not referring primarily to a text, but to an event, to the meaning ascribed to that event, and to the attendant religious and social practices that developed from it. They looked back to the experience of their ancestors, an experience that included deliverance, journey and provision in the wilderness, and revelation of the law in order to understand God's work and their appropriate response to God in their changing circumstances.

The tradition of the Exodus includes experiences both individual (e.g., Moses and the burning bush) and corporate (e.g., the people of Israel passing through the sea). The prophets refer to the earlier experience of their forebears and what became their religious tradition in time. Scripture, therefore, recognizes the role of experience (both of individuals and of a community of faith) that eventually becomes tradition in the process of developing religious identity. The experience of the Exodus was formative not only for the identity of the people who experienced it, but also for the subsequent generations of Israelites who recalled it in order to understand their origins and contemporary experience of God. Moreover, the Exodus experience became the basis for theology: that is, God saved us then and can do so again; God saved us, so we should be faithful.

The significance of this for Pentecostals is that formative experiences within the Pentecostal tradition, such as Azusa Street, can inform Pentecostal identity and theology. Since the ancient Israelites reflected on their formative religious experiences, so can contemporary Pentecostals (and all Christians). Just as the witnesses on the day of Pentecost asked, "What does this mean?" (Acts 2:12), so the early Pentecostals asked of their experience, "What Meaneth This?" Contemporary Pentecostals should continue to ask, "What meaneth this?"[11] Before developing the case for the reciprocity between Pentecostal experience and theology, I will first chart the primary ways Pentecostals have dealt with the role of experience in theology.

Pentecostal Experience and Theology

The Pentecostal understanding of the relationship between experience and theology has not been static. The dynamic understanding of the interrelationship between experience and theology reflects the broader and changing theological context of Pentecostalism. Pentecostalism emerged and developed during the heyday of the movements of modern theology — liberalism, evangelicalism, and neo-orthodoxy. Pentecostalism, though sharing certain features with each of these movements, does not fit easily into any one of them. However — and notwithstanding significant differences — the Pentecostals remained closest theologically and culturally to the evangelicals. In this section I briefly canvass the history of theological hermeneutics in Pentecostalism in order to highlight the way Pentecostals have dealt with the relationship between experience and theology.

Pentecostal Theology in Conversation with Evangelical Theology

Although Pentecostals and evangelicals shared significant historical and theological connections, their differing views on spiritual gifts and hermeneutics led to tensions between them. Pentecostals also were caught in an internal conundrum. On the one hand, they wanted to defend their exegetical conclusions from Luke-Acts in terms that their evangelical colleagues found respectable and, on the other hand, wanted to honor their experience of the Spirit. These needs were intimately interrelated because

11. Carl Brumback, *"What Meaneth This?" A Pentecostal Answer to a Pentecostal Question* (Springfield, MO: Gospel Publishing House, 1947).

the former gave the biblical justification for the latter. Two central hermeneutical issues characterize the interactions between Pentecostal and evangelical biblical scholarship: (1) the role of historical narrative in the formation of doctrine and theology, and (2) the place and role of religious experience in theology. These two points are important because they showcase the reciprocal relationship between Pentecostal experience, narratives of the Spirit, and Pentecostal theology.

The use of narrative sections of the Bible for doctrine and theology is the first point of tension between Pentecostal and evangelical hermeneutics. Pentecostal scholarship through the late 1980s focused largely on defending the classical Pentecostal doctrine that Spirit baptism is subsequent to conversion, is evidenced by speaking in tongues, and is for the purpose of charismatic empowerment. Vital to this doctrinal apologetic was the legitimacy of basing doctrine on historical narratives. Traditional evangelical hermeneutics insisted that historical narrative is not the primary basis for normative Christian doctrine and that "didactic" material or texts that make clear definitive statements about Christian thought and life should serve as the basis for normative Christian doctrine. The result was that evangelicals gave precedence to specific genres of biblical literature, especially the Pauline epistolary corpus of the New Testament.[12] The debates became reduced down to Paul versus Luke. An example of this traditional evangelical hermeneutic is Graham Cole's recent contribution to evangelical pneumatology. Cole draws on a wide range of biblical sources, but in the end he still subordinates historical narratives in general, and Luke-Acts in particular, to epistolary literature.[13] Furthermore, though some of the recent evangelical contributions to hermeneutics recognize that narrative is as valuable as epistolary literature for normative Christian instruction, the earlier perspective framed the parameters of the majority of Pentecostal biblical scholarship through the 1980s.[14]

12. William W. Menzies and Robert P. Menzies, *Spirit and Power: Foundations of Pentecostal Experience* (Grand Rapids: Zondervan, 2000), p. 38.

13. Graham A. Cole, *He Who Gives Life: The Doctrine of the Holy Spirit* (Wheaton, IL: Crossway, 2007), pp. 203-7.

14. E.g., William W. Klein, Craig L. Blomberg, and Robert L. Hubbard, Jr., *Introduction to Biblical Interpretation* (Dallas: Word, 1993), pp. 349-50; Grant R. Osborne, *The Hermeneutical Spiral: A Comprehensive Introduction to Biblical Interpretation* (Downers Grove, IL: InterVarsity, 1991), p. 172. I avoid using the "narrative-didactic" categories and in their place use "narrative-epistolary" because the terminology of "didactic" presupposes that it is intentionally setting forth normative Christian teaching, whereas "narrative" is not doing so.

Illustrative of this era of Pentecostal scholarship is the work of Roger Stronstad and Robert P. Menzies.[15] Pentecostals such as Stronstad argued for the legitimacy of historical narrative and of taking Luke as a theologian with a unique theological voice — particularly vis-à-vis Paul — for good reasons. First, late-twentieth-century biblical critical methods, especially redaction and narrative criticism, showed that narrative carries theological intent and meaning no less than so-called didactic texts. Second, the narratives of the Spirit in Luke-Acts were formative for Pentecostal experience. Abandoning — or at least muting — the theological importance of Luke-Acts would be forsaking the stories that defined the formative stages of their movement. As William and Robert Menzies maintain, Spirit baptism "has given definition . . . [and] cohesion to the movement."[16] Therefore, Pentecostals should tap their experience of the Holy Spirit for sound reasons of both theological method and tradition.

The second point of tension between Pentecostal and evangelical theologians is the place or the problem of Christian practice and experience in theology. Evangelicals are wary of granting experience a significant role in theology. Walter C. Kaiser Jr., for instance, conveys misgivings toward Stanley Horton's use of Pentecostal experience in the interpretive task, when he asks, "Should we give experiential evidence the pride of place over the Scriptures in places where Scripture does not give us a direct statement?" Then he rhetorically answers, "Must we not as Evangelicals declare that experience cannot be its own authority but must rest on the clear teaching of the Word of God if we are to build a doctrinal case for a particular teaching?"[17] Kaiser and other evangelicals are suspicious of the role of experience in theology because of the historic conflict between evangelical

15. Roger Stronstad, *The Charismatic Theology of St. Luke* (Peabody, MA: Hendrickson, 1984); see also Stronstad, *The Prophethood of All Believers: A Study in Luke's Charismatic Theology* (Sheffield, UK: Sheffield Academic, 1999), and Robert P. Menzies, *The Development of Early Christian Pneumatology with Special Reference to Luke-Acts,* Journal for the Study of the New Testament Supplement Series, 54 (Sheffield, UK: Sheffield Academic Press, 1991). I should note that some Pentecostal scholars accept the evangelical hermeneutical principle that narrative and Luke should be subordinate to epistolary texts in formulating theology. Gordon Fee is a well-known Pentecostal who advocated the evangelical principle, but more recently Keith Warrington adopts this view as well, in Warrington, *Pentecostal Theology: A Theology of Encounter* (New York: T&T Clark, 2008), p. 127.

16. Menzies and Menzies, *Spirit and Power,* pp. 9-10.

17. See Kaiser's response to Horton, in Stanley M. Horton, "Spirit Baptism: A Pentecostal Perspective," in *Perspectives on Spirit Baptism: Five Views,* ed. Chad Owen Brand (Nashville: Broadman and Holman, 2004), pp. 96-97.

and liberal approaches to theology.[18] In contrast to liberalism, which saw theology as a symbolic articulation of a common religious experience and tended to locate the essence of Christianity in ethics and morality, evangelicals affirmed that objective and "timeless truths" or doctrines define Christianity.[19] The second issue with respect to the role of experience in theology is the fear that recourse to religious experience invariably leads to theological relativism and subjectivism. Articulating this concern, Kevin J. Vanhoozer warns, "Christian experience on its own terms is too varied and unreliable to serve as the ultimate criterion for our knowledge of God."[20] Indeed, even Pentecostals share this concern and are ambivalent on the role of experience in the theological task. I will propose a solution to this problem later in this chapter, but at this point I want to discuss a common way Pentecostal theology has addressed the issue.

Taking recourse to the Bible as the final authority and adjudicator of religious experience, Pentecostals often followed evangelicals in resolving the relationship between religious experience and theology. For example, James Railey Jr. and Benny C. Aker recommend that "theology is done best when the Bible is acknowledged as the authority and the Holy Spirit is allowed to mediate the revealed Word of God to us," and "[t]he Bible alone is the sufficient rule of faith and practice."[21] Yet, reflecting the tension within Pentecostal theology to take experience of the Spirit as just that — experience of the Spirit — they later affirm that "a rational knowing or simple memorizing of Scripture does not take the place of a personal experience of regeneration and baptism in the Holy Spirit. . . . Pentecostals believe it is counterproductive to downplay these experiences. . . . Without this experience, one cannot know God."[22] Railey and Aker endeavor to affirm in tandem the regulative authority of the Bible and the necessity of personal

18. Indeed, even among the more progressive or postconservative evangelicals, such as Stanley Grenz and John R. Franke, suspicion endures toward giving experience a significant role in theology because of its historical association with the liberal approach to theology. See Grenz and Franke, *Beyond Foundationalism: Shaping Theology in a Postmodern Context* (Louisville: Westminster John Knox, 2001), pp. 48-49; see also John R. Franke, *The Character of Theology: An Introduction to Its Nature, Task, and Purpose* (Grand Rapids: Baker Academic, 2005), pp. 84-87.

19. Millard J. Erickson refers to Christian doctrine as "timeless truth" in *Christian Theology* (Grand Rapids: Baker, 1987), p. 73.

20. Vanhoozer, *The Drama of Doctrine*, p. 6.

21. James H. Railey, Jr., and Benny C. Aker, "Theological Foundations," in *Systematic Theology*, rev. ed., ed. Stanley M. Horton (Springfield, MO: Logion, 1998), pp. 45-46.

22. Railey and Aker, "Theological Foundations," p. 59.

experience for correct biblical understanding, or what they call an "experience-certified theology, a theology that through faith and obedience becomes a Bible-based 'experience-reality.'"[23]

However, they are not so much calling for Pentecostals to draw on their experience in the formulation of theology as suggesting that genuine Christian faith is more than an intellectual exercise of accumulating doctrinal knowledge. Faith is embracing and living what is believed. In this respect they reflect a similar one-way relationship between doctrine and experience to that expressed by the evangelical Graham Cole, who maintains that "any evidence provided by contemporary Christian experience needs to be viewed through the grid of Scripture and not the other way around, especially when the question of how best to describe the experience is under examination."[24]

I agree in principle that Scripture ultimately serves as the highest authority of Christian thought and life, but I disagree with the marginalization of experience in the theological task. Experience can sometimes point to a better understanding and embodiment of biblical truth than can the received interpretation of Scripture. A case in point is Seymour's inclusive worship experience at the Azusa Street Mission, which better reflects the promise and results of Spirit baptism in Acts as a social-, ethnic-, and gender-transcending experience than does an exclusive focus on the classical Pentecostal doctrines of subsequence and initial evidence. The purpose is not to relativize Scripture to experience, but to recognize that Pentecostal experience of the Spirit can be a venue for seeing and interpreting Scripture and thus a significant source for (1) Pentecostal theology and (2) Pentecostals to make a contribution to the other Christian theological traditions. Pentecostals have correctly sought to recognize the theological significance of the narratives of the Spirit in Luke-Acts and have done so precisely because those texts have shaped their Christian experience, and yet they have been reluctant to press home the importance of their experience of the Spirit for the task of articulating a Pentecostal theology in general and a Trinitarian theology in particular. What is the way forward for

23. Railey and Aker, "Theological Foundations," p. 59. They borrow the term "experience-reality" from Stronstad, *Charismatic Theology,* p. 81. Their emphasis on the importance of spiritual experience for proper apprehension of biblical truth follows earlier Pentecostals, such as Howard M. Ervin, *"These are not drunken as Ye suppose" (Acts 2:15)* (Plainfield, NJ: Logos, 1968), pp. 1-3.

24. Cole, *He Who Gives Life,* p. 27; see also Kaiser's response to Horton, in Horton, "Spirit Baptism," p. 97.

Pentecostals with respect to the interrelationship between Pentecostal experience and Pentecostal theology?

Recent Pentecostal Proposals on the Role of Experience in Theology

In the 1980s and 1990s, Pentecostal scholarship began to move beyond the bounds of evangelical approaches to theology and the biblical-theological issues related to the Pentecostal interpretation of Luke-Acts, doctrines of Spirit baptism, and speaking in tongues. However, these new efforts in hermeneutics still mainly focused on Pentecostal approaches to biblical interpretation rather than theological hermeneutics as such. A few examples illustrate the point.

Howard M. Ervin proposes a pneumatic epistemology that overcomes subjectivism and rationalism. Ervin sees biblical hermeneutics arising out of the immediacy and work of the Spirit in the interpreter.[25] He observes that "it is only as human rationality *joined* in ontological union with 'the mind of Christ' (1 Cor. 2:16) is *quickened* by the Holy Spirit that the divine mystery is understood by man."[26] Ervin also insists that, when an interpreter's charismatic experience dovetails with the apostolic experience, he or she is better suited "to come to terms with the apostolic witness in a truly existential manner."[27] Drawing on postmodern and postcritical hermeneutical theory, Timothy B. Cargall maintains that the Pentecostal notions that the Spirit illuminates the text and fuses the dialogical relationship between Pentecostal experience and biblical interpretation are consistent with a postmodern (postcritical) approach to biblical interpretation. He also maintains that Pentecostals should transcend the modernist assumptions of the priority of historical objectivity that have characterized their interactions with evangelicals over the interpretation and use of Acts.[28]

25. Howard M. Ervin, "Hermeneutics: A Pentecostal Option," *Pneuma: The Journal of the Society for Pentecostal Studies* 3 (1981): 11-25.

26. Ervin, "Hermeneutics: A Pentecostal Option," p. 18.

27. Ervin, "Hermeneutics: A Pentecostal Option," p. 22. Those embracing this view include French L. Arrington, *Encountering the Holy Spirit: Paths of Christian Growth and Service* (Cleveland, TN: Pathway, 2003), p. 87; and Mark D. MacLean, "Toward a Pentecostal Hermeneutic," *Pneuma* 6 (1984): 35-56. In each of these proposals, the unique Pentecostal experience of the Spirit serves as the basis for a distinct Pentecostal ability to interpret the biblical text.

28. Timothy B. Cargall, "Beyond the Fundamentalist-Modernist Controversy: Pentecostals and Hermeneutics in a Postmodern Age," *Pneuma* 15 (1993): 163-87.

Richard D. Israel, Daniel E. Albrecht, and Randal G. McNally ask this question: "How does a Pentecostal experience of the Holy Spirit impact one's appropriation of Scripture?"[29] They warn that calls for a Pentecostal hermeneutic, on the one hand, can be a veiled power play to justify Pentecostalism and the notion of an epistemology of the Spirit, and on the other hand, can imply elitism or a Docetic approach to Scripture. They suggest that Pentecostals can appropriately bring the horizon of their experience of the Spirit into interaction with the horizon of the biblical text and use the occasion of interaction to discern divergences between the two horizons.[30] Although each is unique, the above scholars share a focus on Pentecostal strategies of biblical hermeneutics and not on the broader field of theological hermeneutics or the theological role of Pentecostal experience for Pentecostal theology per se.

The Eclipse of Pentecostal Theology by Charismatic Experience

In recent years, the most popular perspective advanced by Pentecostal and non-Pentecostal scholars alike is that Pentecostalism cannot be defined doctrinally or theologically, but experientially. Consider Harvey Cox, who defines Pentecostalism as a potent expression of primal religion.[31] Keith Warrington suggests that encountering God and not doctrine is fundamental to Pentecostalism.[32] Mark J. Cartledge defines charismatic spirituality in terms of "encountering the Spirit." Although he bases charismatic spirituality on the experience of the Spirit, he discusses it in terms of the categories of spiritual experience and worship practices.[33] Steven Land keeps the emphasis on an experiential essence of Pentecostalism, when he argues that the distinctive feature of Pentecostalism is its unique fusion of eschatological passion for the kingdom of God and Christian practice.[34]

29. Richard D. Israel, Daniel E. Albrecht, and Randal G. McNally, "Pentecostals and Hermeneutics: Texts, Rituals, and Community," *Pneuma* 15 (1993): 137-61 (esp. p. 144).

30. Israel, Albrecht, and McNally, "Pentecostals and Hermeneutics," pp. 144-45.

31. Harvey Cox, *Fire from Heaven: The Rise of Pentecostal Spirituality and the Reshaping of Religion in the Twenty-First Century* (Reading, MA: Addison-Wesley, 1995), pp. 81-83.

32. Warrington, *Pentecostal Theology*, pp. 20-21.

33. Mark J. Cartledge, *Encountering the Spirit: The Charismatic Tradition*, Traditions of Christian Spirituality Series, Philip Sheldrake, gen. ed. (Maryknoll, NY: Orbis, 2007), pp. 19-32.

34. Steven J. Land, *Pentecostal Spirituality: A Passion for the Kingdom*, Journal of Pente-

These theologians draw the common conclusion that a unique charismatic experience rather than a specific doctrine or theology defines Pentecostalism. Their point is not that Pentecostals are bereft of theology, but rather that charismatic experience is the essence of Pentecostalism and that the diversity of Pentecostal theologies precludes defining the movement in terms of one theological paradigm, such as the classical Pentecostal one. Veli-Matti Kärkkäinen concludes: "The best thing to do is to acknowledge and live with the lack of consensus. Diversity is the hallmark of this Spirit movement."[35] I do not disagree with them regarding the diversity of Pentecostal theologies and experiences, or regarding the centrality of the experience of the Holy Spirit to the Pentecostal movement. However, the central place of charismatic experience and the diversity of theology do not mean that experience should be privileged over theology. The effort to define the "essence" of Pentecostalism seems to reflect the reductionist method of modern theology, namely, that a religious movement can be stripped down to its bare essence. The downside of this analytical technique is that it reduces the actual beliefs and practices of Pentecostals to epiphenomena of its fundamental nature, for example, charismatic experience.[36] In contrast to this approach, the Pentecostal experience of the Holy Spirit can fund Pentecostal theology in general, and a Pentecostal Trinitarian theology in particular. In other words, the choice is not between giving experience or doctrine precedence over the other, but rather of letting the experience-tradition of the Pentecostal movement inform Pentecostal theology.

The Jerusalem Council: A Case Study for Pentecostal Experience and Theology

What does Scripture indicate on the place of experience in theological reflection? Does Scripture support the notion that experience is a source not only for theology but also for reappropriating the biblical data? I think it does. In order to demonstrate the dynamic interplay of experience, theology, and church practices, in this section I examine the Jerusalem Council in Acts 15.

---

costal Theology Supplement Series, John C. Thomas, Rick D. Moore, and Steven J. Land, gen. eds. (Sheffield, UK: Sheffield, 1993).

35. Kärkkäinen, "Pneumatologies in Systematic Theology," p. 232.

36. Frank D. Macchia makes a similar critique of Hollenweger's dismissive attitude toward Pentecostal theology. See Macchia, *Baptized in the Spirit: A Global Pentecostal Theology* (Grand Rapids: Zondervan, 2006), p. 55.

The role of the early Christians' experience of the Spirit in the theological deliberation of the council can illuminate the interrelationship between these issues and thus support this project's method of drawing on the Pentecostal experience of the Spirit for a Pentecostal Trinitarian theology.

The Context of the Council

The Jerusalem Council in Acts 15 is a major turning point in the book of Acts. It is the climax of the text's focus on Peter's ministry and the development of the Christian communities associated with Jerusalem, and it sets the stage for the spotlight to turn toward Paul and the rise of the Gentile churches across Asia Minor.[37] The controversy that led to the council concerned whether Gentile converts should be required to be circumcised and should adhere to certain requirements of the Torah. F. F. Bruce points out that the expectations the Jewish Christians wanted to place on the Gentile converts were essentially those required of proselytes to Judaism.[38] As reports of Peter's ministry among the Gentiles (e.g., Cornelius's household, Acts 10:23a-48) and of Gentile conversions in Antioch arrived in Jerusalem, some Jewish Christians "who belonged to the party of the Pharisees" (Acts 15:5a) began to teach that "'the Gentiles must be circumcised and required to obey the law of Moses'" (Acts 15:5). To set matters straight, a group of Jewish Christians "came down from Judea to Antioch and were teaching the brothers: 'Unless you are circumcised, according to the custom taught by Moses, you cannot be saved'" (Acts 15:1).

Paul and Barnabas protested the teaching and afterward were appointed by the church in Antioch to resolve the matter with the leadership in Jerusalem. The result was the Jerusalem Council. The council is an example of the early church's communal discernment of God's work and production of theology (salvation is by faith), interpretation of Scripture (the community of faith is inclusive and not limited to the Jews), and

37. See Darrell L. Bock, *Acts*, Baker Exegetical Commentary on the New Testament, Robert W. Yarbrough and Robert H. Stein, gen. eds. (Grand Rapids: Baker, 2007), p. 486; Luke Timothy Johnson, *The Acts of the Apostles*, Sacra Pagina, vol. 5, Daniel J. Harrington, gen. ed. (Collegeville, MN: Liturgical Press, 1992), p. 268; I. Howard Marshall, *The Acts of the Apostles: An Introduction and Commentary* (Grand Rapids: Eerdmans, 1983), p. 242.

38. F. F. Bruce, *The Book of Acts*, New International Commentary on the New Testament, R. K. Harrison and Robert L. Hubbard, Jr., gen. eds. (Grand Rapids: Eerdmans, 1989), p. 286.

church practices (Gentile believers do not need to adopt certain aspects of Judaism). The structure of the council's deliberative process consists of testimony by Peter, Paul, and Barnabas, biblical argument by James in favor of Gentile inclusion in the Christian community, and the promulgation of a letter for the Gentile churches stipulating some minimal moral and ritual guidelines that could enable the Gentile and Jewish Christians to remain in fellowship.

Theological Hermeneutics at the Council

The Jerusalem Council has been used in missiology to provide a model for contextualizing the gospel to specific cultural circumstances and in theological hermeneutics to support various strategies for coordinating the relationship between religious experience, the community of faith, and Scripture.[39] I want to focus on theological hermeneutics and look primarily at the role Peter's experience — and, secondarily, Paul and Barnabas's experience — as it played out as a source for theology relative to Scripture's function at the council. In fact, I suggest that Peter's experience illuminates the Jerusalem leadership's understanding of Scripture.[40] The Jerusalem Council illustrates three points for theological hermeneutics: (1) experience is a legitimate source of theology; (2) theological insights drawn from experience can lead to a clearer understanding of Scripture; and (3) this new perspective can lead to a revision of tradition and practice.

Peter's testimony before the Jerusalem Council in Acts 15 recounts his experience of the outpouring of the Holy Spirit on Cornelius's household.[41] Peter draws on his experience with the Gentile Cornelius to encourage the early Christian leaders in Jerusalem to adopt a more inclusive practice toward Gentile Christians (Acts 15:7-11).[42] Prior to this experience,

39. For a survey of approaches to the Jerusalem Council among biblical interpreters, missiologists, and theologians, see Timothy Wiarda, "The Jerusalem Council and the Theological Task," *Journal of the Evangelical Theological Society* 46 (2003): 233-48.

40. Though, as Yong's trialogic method shows, theology can begin with the experience of the Spirit, Scripture, or church because they are triadically related in the hermeneutical process. See Amos Yong, *Spirit-Word-Community: Theological Hermeneutics in Trinitarian Perspective* (Eugene, OR: Wipf and Stock, 2002), pp. 270-71.

41. Marshall, *Acts,* p. 249.

42. F. Scott Spencer, *Journeying Through Acts: A Literary-Cultural Reading* (Peabody, MA: Hendrickson, 2004), p. 165.

his belief, reflecting a traditional first-century Jewish attitude, seems to have been that the gospel was for the Jews. Though he does not explicitly make the claim, the vision he receives while relaxing on Simon the Tanner's rooftop makes sense only when it is presupposed (Acts 10:9-22). His declaration to Cornelius also implies it: "'I now realize how true it is that God does not show favoritism but accepts men from every nation who fear him and do what is right'" (Acts 10:34-35). At the Jerusalem Council he announced that "God, who knows the heart, showed that he accepted them [i.e., Cornelius's household, symbolizing the Gentiles] by giving the Holy Spirit to them, just as he did to us. He made no distinction between us and them, for he purified their hearts by faith" (Acts 15:8-9). James, the principal leader of the Christian community in Jerusalem, concludes the discussion by agreeing with the inclusive attitude toward the people of God drawn from Peter's experience with Cornelius.[43] Concluding his reasoning, James cites Amos 9:11-12 as biblical support for a theology of Gentile inclusion in the Christian community.

The important point for theological hermeneutics is that Peter's experience with Cornelius's household — and, secondarily, the testimony of Paul and Barnabas — is the starting point and decisive source for settling the theological question of the council.[44] Scripture is important, too, but Peter's experience is the primary basis for the inclusive interpretation of Scripture, theology, and practices advocated by the Jerusalem Council.[45] Furthermore, the theological fruit of Peter's experience with the Gentiles is the basis of James's understanding of Scripture, specifically the scope of redemption described in Amos 9:11-12. Finally, the council's theological conclusion leads the Jerusalem church to reject the practice of insisting that Gentile converts adhere to Jewish social and religious customs and to adopt more minimalist expectations that reflect its more inclusive theology. The lag time between the work of the Spirit and the theology of the

43. Bruce, *Acts,* p. 293.

44. Johnson, *Acts,* p. 271; see also Finny Philip, *The Origins of Pauline Pneumatology: The Eschatological Bestowal of the Spirit upon Gentiles in Judaism and in the Early Development of Paul's Theology,* Wissenschaftliche Untersuchungen zum Neuen Testament, Jörg Frey, gen. ed. (Tübingen: Mohr Siebeck, 2005), pp. 208-9. Gordon D. Fee makes a similar case for the role of Paul's experience in Pauline pneumatology and Trinitarian theology, in Fee, *God's Empowering Presence: The Holy Spirit in the Letters of Paul* (Peabody, MA: Hendrickson, 1994), p. 843.

45. On the Jerusalem Council, Mark J. Cartledge concludes that "the Church begins with experience before moving to Scripture" (Cartledge, *Encountering the Spirit,* p. 123).

church should also be noted. The Christian leadership in Jerusalem takes ten years to ratify the Spirit's inclusion of the Gentiles. As Stephen Fowl notes, "What comes as no real surprise to readers of Luke/Acts, however, is cloaked in mystery to the central characters of the narrative, particularly Peter."[46] Through Peter's rooftop vision, the outpouring of the Spirit on Cornelius's household, and Peter's commentary on these events, the narrative of Acts 10–11 shows that the Spirit has already included the Gentiles, though the official church leadership does not do so until Acts 15.

The suggestion that Peter's experience took precedence over — and indeed provided the hermeneutical lens for — the council's understanding of Scripture is contentious. A number of objections could be, and have been, raised against such an interpretation. First, one could object that Peter's experience with Cornelius followed the revelation he received on the rooftop. In other words, a "word" of revelation preceded and provided the foundation for this experience, and thus also the conclusions of the council. True, but the task here is not to argue for the precedence of experience to all theological and doctrinal positions and developments, but rather to show their interrelationship. Moreover, Peter's vision, the revelation on the rooftop, was an experience that began to open his mind to the universal and inclusive scope of the gospel of Jesus Christ. To classify that vision as "revelation" and not "experience" is beyond credulity. Furthermore, Peter does not fully grasp the theological significance of the revelation until the experience with Cornelius (Acts 10:34-48). Charles Van Engen observes: "This is the moment that becomes the hermeneutical, theological, and missiological key to the eventual acceptance by the Jewish Christians of the Gentile Christians in their midst."[47]

In addition, my point is not that experience was the sole theological source in the deliberations of the Jerusalem Council. As Richard I. Pervo notes, the proof presented at the council consisted of "experience, miraculous attestation, and Scripture."[48] Yet the theological determination of the

46. Stephen E. Fowl, *Engaging Scripture: A Model for Theological Interpretation* (Oxford: Blackwell, 1998; Eugene, OR: Wipf and Stock, 2008), p. 105. Luke Timothy Johnson elucidates it this way: "The human church now catches up with the divine initiative, and formally declares itself on the side of God's plan to save all humanity" (Johnson, *Acts*, p. 268).

47. Charles E. Van Engen, "Peter's Conversion: A Culinary Disaster Launches the Gentile Mission: Acts 10:1–11:18," in *Mission in Acts: Ancient Narratives in Contemporary Context*, ed. Robert L. Gallagher (Maryknoll, NY: Orbis, 2004), pp. 133-43 (esp. p. 138).

48. Richard I. Pervo, *Acts: A Commentary*, Hermeneia — A Critical and Historical Commentary on the Bible, Harold W. Attridge, gen. ed. (Minneapolis: Fortress, 2009), p. 370.

council — that is, the inclusion of the Gentiles in the Christian community — originated not in biblical exegesis or an objective body of doctrine but in the work of the Spirit in the midst of the Christian community.[49] Finally, Peter refers explicitly to his experience of seeing Cornelius's household receive the Spirit as the source of his theological insight regarding the Gentiles when he addresses the leaders at the council.

A second objection, made by David K. Strong and Cynthia A. Strong, is that, though the hermeneutical process of the council includes recourse to Scripture, the work of the Holy Spirit, and the Christian community, Scripture is the final and primary authority.[50] They reject the notion that Peter's testimony was determinative for James's interpretation of Scripture, and thus they declare, conversely, that James "evaluated Peter's testimony in light of Scripture."[51] However, Peter's experience at Cornelius's household is the turning point for the theological breakthrough and understanding of Scripture embraced by James and the council in Acts 15. Peter's sequence of reasoning in Acts 15 illustrates the formative and illuminative power of his experience at Cornelius's household for understanding the scope of the gospel. John Christopher Thomas points out that Peter "reasons that to place the yoke (of the Law?) upon these Gentiles would be tantamount to testing God." Then Thomas notes: "It is particularly significant that the church seems to have begun with its experience and only later

49. I am not suggesting a hermeneutical model that trades on the priority of Spirit-experience to Scripture. As Stephen Fowl maintains, these are "false alternatives," and Scripture no doubt influenced the apprehension, even if unconsciously, of the experience as a work of the Spirit (Fowl, *Engaging Scripture,* pp. 114, 132-33). But I am saying that, in Acts 10–15, Peter draws specifically on his experiences surrounding the outpouring of the Spirit on Cornelius's household to adjudicate the question of Gentile inclusion and religious/cultural standards and that his experience becomes the primary lens for James's interpretation of Scripture before the Jerusalem Council. Furthermore, Pentecostals will resonate with Fowl's notions that Christians need (1) to learn to "read Scripture with the Spirit"; (2) to grant the Spirit "hermeneutical significance" by using the experience of the Spirit as a lens through which to read Scripture; and (3) to rely on testimony regarding the work of the Spirit by those recognized as "people of the Spirit" within the Christian community for discerning the work of the Spirit and the interpretation of Scripture. I agree with all three points, but I think in the end, Fowl's emphasis on testimony runs the risk of reducing the "voice" of the Spirit to the voice of the church community and particularly its leadership, who are identified as the "people of the Spirit" (see Fowl, *Engaging Scripture,* pp. 114-15).

50. David K. Strong and Cynthia A. Strong, "The Globalizing Hermeneutic of the Jerusalem Council," in *Globalizing Theology: Belief and Practice in an Era of World Christianity,* ed. Craig Ott and Harold A. Netland (Grand Rapids: Baker Academic, 2006), pp. 127-39.

51. Strong and Strong, "Globalizing Hermeneutic," p. 129.

moves to a consideration of the Scriptures."[52] Peter draws the theological conclusion that "we *believe* it is through the grace of our Lord Jesus that we are saved, just as they are," from the *experience* that "God . . . [gave] the Holy Spirit to them, just as he did to us" (Acts 15:8-9; italics added).

Moreover, Luke Timothy Johnson argues that the syntax of James's statement that "'the Prophets agree with *this*' rather than that 'this agrees with *the prophets*'" (Acts 15:15) suggests that "it is the experience of God revealed through narrative that is given priority in this hermeneutical process: the text of Scripture does not dictate how God should act. Rather, God's action dictates how we should understand the text of Scripture."[53] Both Peter and James give Peter's experience of the outpouring of the Holy Spirit on the Gentiles hermeneutical leverage in their understanding of the nature of the gospel and Scripture.[54] The implication is that Peter's experience at Cornelius's house carried theological freight. His experience taught him that the promise of the outpouring of the Spirit "on *all* people" includes the Gentiles (Acts 2:17). Van Engen also notes that the narrative focus of Acts 10 is not Cornelius, but Peter: Peter is the one who experiences

52. John Christopher Thomas, "Reading the Bible from Within Our Traditions: A Pentecostal Hermeneutic as Test Case," in *Between Two Horizons: Spanning New Testament Studies and Systematic Theology,* ed. Joel B. Green and Max Turner (Grand Rapids: Eerdmans, 2000), pp. 108-22 (esp. p. 112). Thomas suggests that the church leaders of the Jerusalem Council used a hermeneutic of the Christian community, the work of the Holy Spirit, and Scripture (pp. 117-20). Although Thomas recognizes the value of religious experience, he ultimately seems to see experience more as something to be evaluated by Scripture than as a source for theology and biblical hermeneutics (Thomas, "Reading the Bible," p. 119).

53. Johnson, *Acts,* p. 271 (italics in original); see also David Lertis Watson and Warren S. Brown, "Tuning the Faith: The Cornelius Story in Resonance Perspective," *Perspectives in Religious Studies* 33 (2006): 449-65 (esp. p. 463).

54. Pentecostal scholar James Shelton makes the point even more strongly: "James defers to Peter's experience as being *definitive* . . . [and] [t]he Scripture James quotes is interpreted in the light of the God event that has occurred in the apostolic end-time community. James does *not* say that God's act agrees with and is accountable to Amos the prophet but that the prophets resonate . . . with God's saving act related and explained by Peter!" See James B. Shelton, "Epistemology and Authority in the Acts of the Apostles: An Analysis and Test Case Study of Acts 15:1-29," *The Spirit and Church* 2 (2000): 231-47 (esp. p. 243). Shelton's point that "Pentecostals and Charismatics must insist on the continued activity of the Holy Spirit as epistemologically essential" is well taken, but I do think he overreaches when he says, "It is not the text of Scripture that is our normative authority, but the Holy Spirit-filled Church living in the now in connection with the apostolic Tradition" (pp. 246-47). He is correct that tradition informs and the Spirit-filled community helps adjudicate and appropriate Scripture, but I think Scripture remains in principle a normative authority for Christian thought and life.

a conversion of sorts.[55] He embraces the full reality of the "all" in the promised outpouring of the Spirit on "all people" (Acts 2:17). Peter realizes that Christ's grace extends to the Gentiles.

What is more, Peter's testimony to the council is the second recorded instance of his recourse to his experience with Cornelius for theological purposes and, as David Watson and Warren Brown note, does not include a reference to Scripture to substantiate his new theological view.[56] In Acts 11:1-18, Peter has returned to Jerusalem, and some believers there question him about his ministry among the Gentiles. He answers their concern by sharing the two experiences, the vision on the rooftop of Simon the Tanner and the subsequent reception of the gospel and the Holy Spirit by Cornelius's household, showing that "God gave them the same gift as he gave us, who believed in the Lord Jesus Christ" (Acts 11:17). Thus, with respect to the relationship between experience and Scripture, Peter's experience in Acts 10–11 and 15 illuminates Scripture rather than Scripture ratifying his experience. Of course, Scripture sanctions the inclusive posture toward the Gentiles that Peter assumed after his experience with Cornelius. Nevertheless, his arrival at this viewpoint was the product of his experience: that is, "while Peter was still speaking these words, the Holy Spirit came on all who heard the message. The circumcised believers who had come with Peter were astonished that the gift of the Holy Spirit had been poured out even on the Gentiles. For they heard them speaking in tongues and praising God" (Acts 10:44-46). Peter's theological judgment that the Gentiles are now included does not arise from a process of biblical exegesis, but from his reflections on his experience of the Holy Spirit — the rooftop vision, the Spirit's instruction to show hospitality to the messengers from Cornelius, and the outpouring of the Spirit on Cornelius's household. Peter briefly mentions Scripture in Acts 10:43: "'[A]ll the prophets testify about him that everyone who believes in him receives forgiveness of sins through his name'"; and he expressly repudiates what was for him the "biblical" understanding on the issue of Jew-Gentile inclusion. The reason his experiences are theologically informative is that they are the product of the work of the Holy Spirit. Therefore, Peter's appeal to ex-

55. Van Engen, "Peter's Conversion," pp. 136-37.

56. They suggest that Peter does not refer to Scripture because his theological conclusion that the Gentiles are included in God's salvation just as the Jews are would have seemed contrary to the accepted understanding of Scripture. See Watson and Brown, "Tuning the Faith," pp. 458 and 460.

perience for developing theology at the Jerusalem Council was not a one-off strategy, but a repeated pattern.

Finally, Timothy Wiarda suggests that the Jerusalem Council is historically sui generis and thus should not serve as an ongoing model for contextualizing the gospel and theological decision-making. He maintains that the ongoing relevance of the council should relate to (1) the theological message of the conference that Gentiles are saved by faith in Christ and the clear implications of that theological message, and (2) the theological process characterized by harmony and unity.[57] To support the unique character of the council, he points out that the council convened within a few years of Jesus' death, resurrection, and ascension. The council sits within a brief and unique eschatological time horizon that saw the establishment of the church of Jesus Christ. According to Wiarda, "the Spirit's hermeneutical guidance, fresh and context-related though it was, may have been decisively tied to the eschatological change brought about by the once-for-all (all times and all communities) work of Christ."[58] He also argues that Peter, Paul, Barnabas, and James are unique leaders in the history of the church. These leaders — with the possible exception of Barnabas — bear the title "apostle" and thus possess unique authority relative to subsequent Christian leaders. He concludes that the unique place of the council in the redemptive work of God and apostolic authority of its key players should caution its use as a model for contemporary church leaders and theologians.

Wiarda is certainly correct that the council and its leaders played a unique role in the history of the church, and that the purpose of the story of the council is not to provide a universal paradigm for church leadership decision-making.[59] But his argument is a recycled version of the cessationist one. In other words, certain functions and gifts were necessary during the emergence and development of the Christian church; but they lost their utility in the postapostolic era and thus ceased to be operative in the life of the church. The result is that, since the circumstances and leadership of the Jerusalem Council were unique to the apostolic era, so were its practices. Still, one can grant the unique features of the council and its leadership and also see its practices as instructive for the ongoing life of the church. Faith in the Trinity, as it is known today, was not stipulated until

57. Wiarda, "The Jerusalem Council," pp. 245-48.

58. Wiarda, "The Jerusalem Council," p. 238.

59. Wiarda, "The Jerusalem Council," pp. 244-45.

the councils of Nicaea (325 CE) and Constantinople (381 CE) and did not arise purely from reading Scripture. "Faith in the Trinity arose not from learned speculation but out of the experience of Christian life, especially worship," says Kilian McDonnell.[60] Finally, I do not contend that the express purpose of Acts 15 is to present a model of theological hermeneutics. Nevertheless, in the theological deliberations of the council, Peter's experience played a key role in the council's understanding of Scripture and the nature of the work of God in their midst, which is suggestive of the nature of the ongoing theological task.

In summary, the Jerusalem Council and the role that experience played in its theological reasoning is not the only "biblical" way of addressing theology. Acts 10–11 and 15 show that Christian experience can be the source of (1) theology, (2) a clearer understanding of Scripture, and (3) a revision of tradition and practices. Furthermore, the reason that the experience is fruitful for theology is that it arises from the work of the Holy Spirit. Pentecostals, along with all Christians, should neither shy away from drawing on what they believe is the work of the Spirit for theological purposes nor allow the fear of religious subjectivity and relativism to keep them from giving their experience of the Spirit theological significance. Discernment is important because not all of the religious experience that takes place within Christian communities is a product of the Holy Spirit.[61] So far I have highlighted from biblical sources the theological hermeneutical principle that the experience of the Spirit can inform the theological task. But what is the theological rationale for the role of the experience of the Spirit beyond the fact that it is simply in the Bible?

60. Kilian McDonnell, *The Other Hand of God: The Holy Spirit as the Universal Touch and Goal* (Collegeville, MN: Liturgical Press, 2003), p. 21. Amos Yong also argues that early Christian Trinitarian theology both emerged from and shaped Christian practice; thus he affirms the codeterminacy of orthodoxy and orthopraxis. See Yong, *Hospitality and the Other,* pp. 42-46.

61. I admit that setting forth principles for the discernment of the Spirit is a gap in this project. My goal is to think through the implications of the Pentecostal experience of the Spirit and the biblical narratives of the Spirit for Trinitarian theology. I recommend that readers look to Amos Yong's work for criteria for discerning the Spirit: *Discerning the Spirit(s): A Pentecostal-Charismatic Contribution to Christian Theology of Religions* (Sheffield, UK: Sheffield Academic Press, 2000).

Pentecostal Theological Hermeneutics

The theological rationale for taking the Pentecostal experience of the Spirit as the navigating point for Trinitarian theology comes to shape through a constructive conversation with a contemporary Pentecostal, Kenneth J. Archer, and a non-Pentecostal, Reinhard Hütter. First, my suggestion that Pentecostal experience of the Spirit can orient the nature of Pentecostal theology is very similar to Archer's proposal for taking the Pentecostal narrative tradition as the source of Pentecostal theology. However, Archer needs pneumatological supplementation, and for this I proceed to Hütter's pneumatological understanding of the *doctrina* and core practices of the church. Hütter argues that church practices and beliefs are key sources of theological reflection because they are a product of the Holy Spirit. The extension of this idea to Christian experience and theology establishes a pneumatological foundation for taking the Pentecostal experience of the Spirit as a starting point for a Trinitarian theology.

Kenneth J. Archer and the Pentecostal Narrative Tradition

In *A Pentecostal Hermeneutic: Spirit, Scripture, and Community,* Archer proposes that a particular doctrine or exegetical method is not what makes Pentecostalism unique, but its narrative tradition, or story.[62] The Pentecostal narrative tradition arose from its unique spirituality, history, and way of interpreting Scripture, and understanding itself and its place in the world. "The Pentecostal narrative tradition," Archer suggests, "is the hermeneutical horizon of the community and the means of articulating its identity."[63] According to Archer, the Latter Rain motif and the restoration of the Full Gospel are the primary plot lines of the Pentecostal narrative.

The Latter Rain motif derives from the weather cycle of Palestine, in which a heavy rain period, or latter rain, follows an earlier rain season. The Pentecostals believed that the outpouring of the Holy Spirit in Acts 2 was

62. Kenneth J. Archer, *A Pentecostal Hermeneutic: Spirit, Scripture, and Community* (Cleveland, TN: CPT Press, 2009); see also Archer, "A Pentecostal Way of Doing Theology: Method and Manner," *International Journal of Systematic Theology* 9 (2007): 301-14, and "Pentecostal Story: The Hermeneutical Filter for the Making of Meaning," *Pneuma* 26 (2004): 36-59.

63. Archer, "Pentecostal Story," p. 42; see also Archer, *A Pentecostal Hermeneutic,* pp. 128-36; Archer, "A Pentecostal Way of Doing Theology," p. 306.

the early rain, and the eruptions of revival and charismatic manifestations in their midst were the first drops of the latter rain. They believed that they were on the cusp of the great outpouring of the Spirit that would precede and prepare the world for the second coming of Christ.[64] Following the initial outpouring of the Spirit in the apostolic period, a great drought of the Spirit came upon the church. Now, in the Pentecostal movement, the latter rain of the Spirit has brought renewal to the parched landscape of the church. Thus did the latter rain provide a narrative framework for Pentecostal self-understanding. The Latter-Rain theme dovetailed with the second key feature of the Pentecostal narrative tradition: the restoration of the Full Gospel (pp. 150-56). The Full Gospel is a Christocentric paradigm of grace that portrays Jesus Christ as the one who saves, sanctifies, baptizes in the Holy Spirit, heals, and will soon return.[65] The Pentecostals believe that they are recovering the original Full Gospel, which includes the charismatic experiences and practices of the church described in Acts (p. 155).

Kenneth Archer's work is important because it recognizes that Pentecostal theology arises out of the peculiar Pentecostal narrative tradition, but that it sequesters theology too much in "community" and "Scripture." Archer declares that the Holy Spirit is "dependent upon the community and Scripture. The Holy Spirit does have a voice, but the Spirit's voice is heard 'horizontally' in and through the individuals in community and in and through Scripture" (p. 247). He wants to avoid conflating the Spirit's voice with Scripture and the community's discernment; but he does not provide a clear pneumatological basis for distinguishing them (p. 248). He is right that the discernment of the Spirit's work happens through Scripture and the community of faith, and that the Pentecostal narrative shapes the identity of Pentecostals and the way Pentecostals read Scripture. But Archer's contribution needs to be supported with pneumatological content.

Without a pneumatological ground, why should the Pentecostal story have theological significance? One might respond that it has significance because Pentecostals, like all other Christians, read Scripture and under-

64. Archer, *A Pentecostal Hermeneutic,* pp. 136-50 (hereafter, page references to this work appear in parentheses in the text).

65. Archer is part of a Pentecostal-Holiness tradition (the Church of God) and thus the "Full" Gospel consists of the fivefold Gospel, whereas non-holiness Pentecostals affirm the fourfold "full" gospel of salvation, Spirit baptism, healing, and second coming of Christ. For background on the development and distinctions between these two forms of the Full Gospel, see Donald Dayton, *The Theological Roots of Pentecostalism* (Grand Rapids: Francis Asbury Press, 1987), pp. 15-23.

stand reality from within the narrative horizon of their community of faith. Yes, but from a theological perspective, the discussion of the Pentecostal narrative tradition or hermeneutical horizon is not simply one of religious history and sociology; it is also one of *theology,* indeed, of *pneumatology.* A modification of the work of Reinhard Hütter helps provide the pneumatological rationale for taking the Pentecostal narrative tradition as a resource for theology.

Reinhard Hütter and the Pneumatological Pathos of Doctrine and Church Practices

Reinhard Hütter is a former Lutheran, now a Roman Catholic, professor of Christian theology at Duke Divinity School. Hütter critiques both the theologies of modernism and postmodernism, but he draws on their insights (e.g., Karl Barth and George Lindbeck) and retrieves traditional (premodern) theology (Luther) in an effort to promote a vision of theology that altogether surpasses them. Covering a variety of theological subjects, such as ecclesiology, pneumatology, and Christian rationality, Hütter has an overall project that seeks to articulate the nature of theology and to do so on pneumatological and ecclesiological grounds. He believes that theology should be understood as a distinct church practice, and, as such, theology receives its pathos from the Holy Spirit and church practices. However, he is successful in only the latter respect, because pneumatology grounds theology in only a derivative way. Nevertheless, his understanding of theology has much to offer Pentecostals. With modification, it provides a pneumatological foundation for using the Pentecostal experience of the Spirit and narrative tradition for a Pentecostal theology in general and a Trinitarian theology in particular.

Pathos is the most important concept in Hütter's theology: pathos is a passive and receptive notion that stands in contrast to doing. It means to be affected or determined by something else. Pathos does not imply total inaction; it does imply that a being's activity derives from receiving its orientation toward certain activity from another: that is, its activity is determined by another. The companion term and concept to pathos is *poiesis.* Poiesis is productive: it produces pathos. Poiesis is the productive power that determines or shapes the pathos of another. Moreover, the pathos received from the poiesis of another includes an intrinsic poiesis. The recipient of pathos acts out of the pathos received. In this sense, even active agency is *pathic,* because the ability to act in certain ways derives from the pathos received. Pathos and its correspondent poiesis function as the systematic and philosophical principle of Hütter's theology, whereas the doctrine of the Trinity is the more purely theological foundation of his work. The concepts of pathos and poiesis run through the multiple layers of his theology, which begins with the Trinity and concludes with his view of theology as a distinct church practice.

With respect to the Trinity, the divine persons have their identity in a pathic way. The divine persons receive their personal identities through their relationships with the others, which is "the pathos of relationality."[66] Consequently, the persons of the Trinity are what they are only through their relationships with each other; they are constituted as persons through their mutual relationships. Moreover, their personal activity (their poiesis) in the economy of redemption flows out of their relational constitution and identity (their pathos) in the immanent Trinity. The Holy Spirit facilitates the believer's — and collectively the church's — induction into the communion of the Trinity and thus informs the pathos of the church and her doctrines and core practices.

Within the economic mission, the primary work, or poiesis, of the Holy Spirit is the constitution of the church's *doctrina,* which is the doctrinal expression of the gospel, and the core church practices.[67] The *doctrina* and the core practices have a pneumatological pathos because they are the concrete ways the Spirit enacts the salvific-economic mission of the triune God. *Doctrina* and core church practices mediate the salvific-economic mission of the triune God precisely because they are the locus for the work of the Holy Spirit. The *doctrina* and the core practices are the *poiemata* of the Holy Spirit: that is, they are the products of the Spirit's poiesis and as such they have their pathos, their determinative character, from the Spirit's poiesis/productive activity. Church doctrine and core practices (e.g., baptism and Lord's Supper) form the pathos of theology.

66. Reinhard Hütter, *Suffering Divine Things: Theology as Church Practice,* trans. Doug Stott (Grand Rapids: Eerdmans, 2000), p. 117.

67. He refers to the gospel with the technical term *doctrina evangelii.* See Steven Studebaker, "The Pathos of Theology as a Pneumatological Derivative or a Poiemata of the Spirit? A Review Essay of Reinhard Hütter's *Pneumatological and Ecclesiological Vision of Theology,*" *Pneuma* 32 (2010): 269-82. Hütter does not explicitly delineate the core practices, but he presents Luther's seven practices — preached Word, baptism, Lord's Supper, office of the keys of church discipline, ordination and offices, public worship, and discipleship in suffering — as an illustrative paradigm (Hütter, *Suffering Divine Things,* p. 129).

Hütter maintains that the pathos of theology is ecclesiological and pneumatological. By locating the pathos of theology in *doctrina* and church practices, Hütter's proposal attains his goal of delineating an ecclesiological basis for theology. It does so because theology as a church practice has its horizon of discourse precisely in the *doctrina* and core practices of the church. Notwithstanding the success of his ecclesiological program, his proposal undermines the constructive role of theology and Christian experience and does not provide a pneumatological basis for theology.

On the ecclesiological basis, Hütter's pathic understanding of theology reflects the cultural-linguistic method, which suggests that theology is a second-order reflection on the first-order data of religion — practices and doctrine. In this respect, theology receives its pathos from the first-order data. In terms of Christian experience, theology is a third-order task. The reason is that experience is a second-order phenomenon because the first-order data of doctrines and practices provides the structure and informs the texture of Christian experience. Subjective experience is derivative of the external features of religion and thus cannot be, strictly speaking, a first-order phenomenon.[68] Insofar as theology takes account of Christian experience, it does so as third-order reflection because it reflects on experience, which is a second-order phenomenon. As Kathryn Tanner points out, the cultural-linguistic approach assumes a modernist notion of culture, according to which culture provides the objective structure that shapes the individual.[69] Consequently, the cultural-linguistic nature of doctrine and practices form the individual, and thus the individual's experience is always a second-order phenomenon relative to the "cultural-linguistic" aspect of religion. The problem is that an exclusive emphasis on the pathic nature of theology and Christian experience obscures their poietic or constructive capacities. Showing that religious systems provide the structure for Christian experience, and that theology and experience are second-order categories, is the strength of the cultural-linguistic theory. However, it needs a pneumatological supplementation that recognizes the active, dynamic, and transformative role of experience and theology.

Hütter's approach to theology does not easily allow for the dynamic theological insight that can arise from emergent Christian practices, beliefs, and experiences — such as the Pentecostal movement. His focus is on

68. See Lindbeck, *The Nature of Doctrine,* pp. 32-41.

69. Kathryn Tanner, *Theories of Culture: A New Agenda for Theology,* Guides to Theological Inquiry (Minneapolis: Fortress, 1997), pp. 72-74.

Christian traditions with long and venerable histories, which is understandable given his background in Catholic and Lutheran churches and his desire to give theology objective criteria and to avoid the theological vicissitudes and subjectivism of appeals to religious experience. Hütter dismisses spiritual experience as the place of the salvific-economic mission of the Spirit (or at least as something that should be understood as a resource for theology) and restricts it to *doctrina* and church practices, which he calls the "mediate forms" of the Holy Spirit.[70] His reluctance to see experience and theology as "mediate forms," or direct *poiemata,* also arises from his desire to avoid the subjectivist tendency of modern theology. Despite the fear of subjectivism, Pentecostal theology should locate its foundation in pneumatology and the experience and manifestation of the Spirit within the movement, or what Amos Yong calls the "confessional location" of Pentecostal theology, by which he means the actual experiences and practices of Pentecostals.[71] Moreover, why limit the mediate forms to *doctrina* and church practices? Why not see religious experience, emergent Christian traditions, and theological reflection as mediate forms, or sacramental means, of the grace of the Spirit? Although not using Hütter's concepts of pathos and *poiemata,* Simon Chan maintains that the Spirit constituted the church as the body of Christ, and then the Spirit facilitated its dogmatic definitions. Moreover, the Spirit continues to actualize the church as the body of Christ, and in doing so "the Spirit gives to present salvation history its distinctive character."[72]

Hütter's fear of subjectivism leads to a restriction of the Holy Spirit to what are essentially the familiar Protestant notions of Word and Sacrament, which in Hütter's presentation become *doctrina* and core church practices. Moreover, the text of Scripture and the practice of the sacramental rites should not be treated as something abstract from the experiences of the early Christians who produced them. I am not suggesting that a contemporary Christian's religious experience should be consulted as a source of religious authority equivalent with Scripture and historical

70. Hütter, *Suffering Divine Things,* p. 127.

71. Yong, *The Spirit Poured Out,* p. 29.

72. Here Chan pulls together the transcendent and dynamic and contextual nature of the church. The church and her dogmas, as the body of Christ constituted by the Spirit, transcend any one particular cultural location. Yet, at the same time, the Spirit manifests the normative nature of the church in ways that are unique and appropriate to its given cultural location. See Simon Chan, "Mother Church: Toward a Pentecostal Ecclesiology," *Pneuma* 22 (2000): 177-208 (esp. pp. 190-93, 195).

church practices. Yet what we now treat as a nonexperiential norm (e.g., a "core practice" or tradition) was at an earlier time novel, concrete, and experiential. Hütter's tendency to treat *doctrina* and core practices as fixed is convenient for established traditions; but it neither recognizes the role of experience and theological innovation in these traditions nor provides the categories to articulate the pneumatological pathos of the dynamic emergence of new core practices and doctrines among more recent Christian groups and movements, such as the Pentecostal movement. I believe that Hütter's notion of pathos can be applied more directly to emerging Christian experience, practices, and beliefs that may not have the benefit of a staid tradition and can be understood as conditioned by the Holy Spirit in a similar way to that of Hütter's doctrines and core church practices. My goal is to articulate the pneumatological rationale for taking the Pentecostal experience-tradition as a source for theology.

The account of Peter at Cornelius's home detailed earlier in this chapter illustrates the way that experience of the Spirit provides the basis for new beliefs (Christ's redemption includes the Gentiles) and new practices (withdrawing the expectations that Gentile converts adhere to elements of Jewish religious and social customs). Peter's experience on the rooftop, and later at Cornelius's home, were experiences of the Holy Spirit and thus were legitimate sources of theology, as his recourse to them at the Jerusalem Council illustrates. An unintended consequence of drawing on what are thought to be the experience and manifestation of the Holy Spirit might be to cast off theology's mooring to doctrine and core practices and set it adrift to the whim of the theologian, who could claim the directive from the Holy Spirit. This concern is legitimate, but positing a direct pneumatological pathos for Christian experience and the theological insight that may arise from it does not necessarily lead to unhinged theological subjectivism and relativism.

One of the problems with the role of experience in Christian theology is the false alternative that theology is either about God or the way Christians talk about and experience God.[73] In point of fact, theology is both. Why? Theology is — at least though not exclusively — talk about the Christian experience *of God*. When Christian theologians talk about Christian practices, interpretation of Scripture, and experience, are they not talking about their experience of God and about what the Spirit of God is doing in their midst? As Jürgen Moltmann points out, "Anyone who stylizes revela-

73. Vanhoozer, *The Drama of Doctrine*, p. 7.

tion and experience into alternatives ends up with revelations that cannot be experienced, and experiences without revelation."[74] I do not think that we should allow the fear of unbridled religious subjectivism and religious relativism to prevent us from recognizing that the Spirit is at work in the churches and in the lives of individual Christians and, therefore, based on the Spirit's work, draw on individual and corporate Christian experience for theology. Moreover, Christian experience — and Pentecostal experience in particular — is not a theological loose cannon. The voice of the Spirit, heard through Scripture, tradition, and received practices, plays a key role in evaluating the diverse and new tongues and gifts of the Spirit.

The proposal to take contemporary Christian experience and emergent Christian movements as a resource for theology does not mean that they are equivalent in authority with the biblical sources. But it does mean that Christians should be open to hearing the voice of the Spirit within their lives and their traditions, even if they are relatively young traditions within the larger history of the church. And the youth of traditions is a matter of perspective. In the early sixteenth century, Lutheranism was an upstart and a novelty; now it is a historic Christian tradition. Furthermore, the Spirit's work at Cornelius's household and the Antioch church was not at variance with Scripture. The viewpoint of the established church was the problem. The Jerusalem church's understanding of Scripture missed the inclusive nature of the gospel, and James's new apprehension put it in step with the Spirit. Scripture did not change, but the Jerusalem church's interpretation did, and the work of the Spirit funded that alteration in biblical understanding. Indeed, the experience at Cornelius's home, and Peter's interpretation of it, eventually became part of Scripture. Amos Yong's trialectic hermeneutic protects the theological use of experience and more recent Christian practices and beliefs from slipping into subjectivism and theological relativism. Recourse to experience does not occur in a silo of intrapersonal subjectivity, but in conversation with contemporary experience in the church and the broader traditions of the church and Scripture.[75]

The Holy Spirit is the basis for the constructive role of Christian experience and theology vis-à-vis received doctrines and practices. Christian experience and theology have poietic power precisely because they are (at least potentially) *poiemata* of the Spirit. Christian experience can em-

74. Jürgen Moltmann, *The Spirit of Life: A Universal Affirmation,* trans. Margaret Kohl (Minneapolis: Fortress, 1992), p. 7.

75. See Part 3 of Yong's *Spirit-Word-Community,* pp. 221-310 (esp. pp. 219-20).

power new theological apprehensions that in turn fund new insight and the transformation of first-order doctrines and practices. Theology is not only a passive discipline or commentary on the received tradition and experience. The promise of theological reflection is that it can transform and not only articulate, clarify, and defend the received tradition. Furthermore, Christian experience, both individual and collective, is a resource for theology's constructive task. Lindbeck recognized the reciprocal influence religious traditions and experience have on one another, but he gave primacy to tradition in the cultural-linguistic model. That is, the external or objective features of religion take precedence over the inner or subjective experience of religion in terms of causal interaction.[76] Without discounting the objective influence on the subjective, we can say that doctrines and traditional practices are not closed systems; rather, an inverse order of influence is at play. The objective features of religion — beliefs and practices — can be transformed by the outpouring of the Spirit, as Acts 10-11 and 15 demonstrate. Moreover, the source of theological insight does not exclusively arise out of biblical exegesis; it also comes from the experience of the Holy Spirit by individual humans (e.g., Peter) and by the Christian community (e.g., the Jerusalem Council).

Drawing on one of Hütter's central concepts, I propose that the Pentecostal movement is a *poiemata* of the Spirit, and central to the Pentecostal movement is the experience of baptism in the Holy Spirit. Making the claim that the Pentecostal movement — and, more specifically, the experience of Spirit baptism within the movement — is a *poiemata* of the Spirit does not sanction all of a movement's experiences, beliefs, and practices. All movements have practices and beliefs that reflect their lunatic fringe, and Pentecostalism is no different. However, Spirit baptism, despite the diversity of its doctrinal and theological articulations, is a central experience within the movement, and it has clear biblical foundations. Moreover, the experience of Spirit baptism can be theologically fecund, even if historically it has been underharvested.

A case in point is the experience of ethnic, confessional, and social diversity fostered by the experience of Spirit baptism in the Azusa Street revivals. This experience was more a *poiemata* of the Spirit than the segregation that marked the developing Pentecostal denominations and much of the other Christian churches. In this case, the experience of a small congregation and incipient movement was more revelatory, and thus regulative,

76. Lindbeck, *The Nature of Doctrine*, pp. 33-34.

than the more prevalent church practice of the time, because it embodied a promise of Pentecost: that the outpouring of the Spirit transcends social prejudices. Thus, in the history of the Pentecostal movement, while the "biblical" discussions focused on defining Spirit baptism as a second work of grace, the practice of segregation was clearly not biblical because it missed the fundamental promise of the Spirit, which is to make one community of Christ from the old and young, male and female, and maidservants. The promise of Pentecost, the baptism in the Spirit, was not a second work of grace per se, but a community of unity and love that transcends the bigotries of the prevailing social context.

With the above modifications and qualifications, Hütter's account of pathos points a better way forward for Pentecostals to articulate a pneumatological foundation for Pentecostal theology than do the proposals that (1) suggest that charismatic experience and not theology defines Pentecostalism, or (2) locate the essence of its theology in a specific narrative tradition. As discussed above, Kenneth Archer proposes that the distinguishing feature of Pentecostal theology is its unique story.[77] However, locating the essence of Pentecostalism there does not provide a pneumatological foundation for Pentecostal theology. From this "Archerian" viewpoint, the foundation for theology is the church's sociological metanarrative, not pneumatology. With extension, Hütter's concept of poiesis and pathos opens up a way to specify a pneumatological basis for Archer's use of Pentecostal story in Pentecostal theology. It does so because the experiences that led to the formation of the Pentecostal narrative tradition can be understood as having their pathos from the Holy Spirit; they are *poiemata* of the poiesis of the Spirit actualizing the salvific-economic mission of the triune God among Pentecostal Christians.

Since the Holy Spirit imbues charismatic experience within the Pentecostal movement, what Archer calls the Pentecostal narrative tradition, with its unique pathos (just as is the case in alternative Christian traditions that have unique experiences and manifestations of the Spirit), it makes theological sense to let the Pentecostal narrative tradition inform the theological task. Therefore, I am affirming Archer's theological method, but giving it a foundation in pneumatology. Theological reflection on Pentecostal experience-tradition is something that occurs in the power of the Spirit, and it is reflection *on something* that has arisen from the work of the Spirit. In other words, both the process of theological interpretation and

77. Archer, "The Pentecostal Story," p. 42.

its object — Pentecostal experience-tradition, Scripture, and the broader Christian traditions — are pneumatologically conditioned.

Pentecostal Experience and Spirit Baptism

With the case set forth for taking the Pentecostal experience-tradition as a source of theology, what biblical and theological category best captures the nature of the Pentecostal experience of the Spirit? I agree with Pentecostals, such as Simon Chan and Frank Macchia, who argue that Spirit baptism plays this role in the Pentecostal movement.[78] Spirit baptism is a principal biblical metaphor that both informs and characterizes the Pentecostal movement. The outpouring of the Spirit of Pentecost is also a clear pivot point in the story of biblical redemption. Therefore, it can serve as an orienting theological source and category for Pentecostal theology — as well as other traditions. The selection of Spirit baptism as a representative doctrine for Pentecostalism needs qualification.

First, taking Spirit baptism as an archetype for Pentecostalism does not mean that all charismatics and Pentecostals identify Spirit baptism as central. For example, the Third Wave, or neo-charismatic, movement emphasizes spiritual renewal through the Holy Spirit — sometimes with and other times without the classical Pentecostal doctrine of Spirit baptism. The neo-charismatic movement also replaced the classical Pentecostal emphasis on Spirit baptism for empowerment for witness and church growth with charismatic manifestations — for example, "Signs and Wonders" — and took charismatic spirituality to the evangelical churches. Without sidelining obvious points of diversity, Spirit baptism has nonetheless historically been, and remains today, a widespread and central experience for many people within the Pentecostal and charismatic movements.[79] Scholars sometimes use Charles Fox Parham's and William J. Seymour's divergent views on the signs of Spirit baptism (Parham preferred tongues, and the later Seymour preferred love expressed in community) to argue for doctrinal diversity in early Pentecostalism; but they both believed that Spirit baptism was central to the movement.[80] Moreover, though my con-

78. Simon Chan, *Spiritual Theology: A Systematic Study of the Christian Life* (Downers Grove, IL: InterVarsity, 1998), p. 47; Macchia, *Baptized in the Spirit*, p. 26.

79. Chan, *Spiritual Theology*, p. 47.

80. Douglas Jacobsen, *Thinking in the Spirit: Theologies of the Early Pentecostal Movement* (Bloomington: Indiana University Press, 2003), pp. 78-79; Jacobsen, *A Reader in Pente-*

text here is North America, and I do not pretend to speak globally for all Pentecostals, among North American Pentecostals and charismatics — and for those groups worldwide influenced by the North American Pentecostal churches — Spirit baptism has been a primary doctrine and term used to describe their experience.[81] The history of the Pentecostal movement in North America indicates that the doctrine of Spirit baptism has provided a theological paradigm for the Pentecostal experience of the Spirit, and that it has played a key role in defining the theological distinctive of two of the movement's three primary forms, to wit, classical Pentecostalism and the charismatic movement.

Second, the status of Spirit baptism as the defining doctrine of Pentecostalism has fallen out of favor among Pentecostal scholars. Frank Macchia delineates four reasons for the eclipse of Spirit baptism. The first is the Pentecostal propensity to see Spirit baptism as a work distinct from Christian initiation. Second, recent scholarship has shied away from Spirit baptism because of the diversity within both the early and contemporary global Pentecostal movement.[82] Representing this trend, Douglas Jacobsen suggests that the fluidity and variety within early Pentecostalism belies the notion of an original unified theology and set of practices.[83] Diversity on the understanding of the doctrine of Spirit baptism and especially the role of tongues in the experience is beyond question.[84] Nevertheless — and without dismissing the variety of views on the doctrine of Spirit baptism — Pentecostals across

---

costal Theology: Voices from the First Generation (Bloomington: Indiana University Press, 2006), pp. 53-54; Cecil M. Robeck, Jr., "William J. Seymour and 'The Bible Evidence,'" in *Initial Evidence: Historical and Biblical Perspectives on the Pentecostal Doctrine of Spirit Baptism*, ed. Gary B. McGee (Peabody, MA: Hendrickson, 1991), pp. 76-87.

81. Many scholars note that Pentecostals and charismatics, both from the beginning of the movement and in their diverse manifestations worldwide, use the term "Spirit baptism" to describe their experience of the Spirit. See Allan Anderson, *An Introduction to Pentecostalism: Global Charismatic Christianity* (New York: Cambridge University Press, 2006), p. 189; Steve Durasoff, *Bright Wind of the Spirit: Pentecostalism Today* (Englewood Cliffs, NJ: Prentice-Hall, 1972), p. 4; Michael P. Hamilton, ed., *The Charismatic Movement* (Grand Rapids: Eerdmans, 1975), p. 7; Richard Quebedeaux, *The New Charismatics: The Origins, Development, and Significance of Neo-Pentecostalism* (Garden City, NY: Doubleday, 1976), p. 128; and Warrington, *Pentecostal Theology*, p. 95.

82. Macchia, *Baptized in the Spirit*, pp. 28-29, 33-38.

83. Jacobsen, *Thinking in the Spirit*, pp. 10-12.

84. For a survey of the variety within the charismatic movement alone, see Henry I. Lederle, *Treasures Old and New: Interpretations of "Spirit-Baptism" in the Charismatic Renewal Movement* (Peabody, MA: Hendrickson, 1988), pp. 217-41.

the diverse spectrum of their movement have described their experience of the Spirit in terms of Spirit baptism, which lends credibility to Macchia's claim that it is the central theological distinctive of Pentecostalism.[85]

Third, the turn to eschatology as the defining theological character of Pentecostalism has resulted in the subordination of the doctrine of Spirit baptism.[86] Macchia highlights a fourth tendency, inspired by Walter J. Hollenweger: to locate the uniqueness of Pentecostal theology in its oral and narrative theological method rather than in a particular doctrine.[87] We could add a fifth tendency, related to the fourth, and also influenced by Hollenweger, along with the recognition of theological diversity within Pentecostalism: the current trend among scholars is to move away from defining Pentecostalism in terms of doctrine and theology and toward seeing experience or the encounter of the Holy Spirit as the characteristic mark of Pentecostalism.[88]

Pentecostal theology that takes the experience and biblical category of Spirit baptism as a fundamental starting point is legitimate because large segments of the historical and contemporary Pentecostal movement identify it as vital to their experience of God and theology, even though not all Pentecostals and charismatics worldwide understand it in the same way. A Pentecostal theology does not need to be a metatheology that speaks for all Pentecostal experience. Achieving a universal or one-size-fits-all theology is no more possible for Pentecostalism than any other religious movement. There is no "Lutheran theology," for example; rather, there are Lutheran theologies. They no doubt have common characteristics, such as an appeal to Luther and the Lutheran confessions and a unique understanding of grace inspired by Luther's doctrine of justification by faith. However, the various forms of Lutheranism around the world are not the same. Identifi-

85. Macchia, "Baptized in the Spirit: Towards a Global Pentecostal Theology," in *Defining Issues in Pentecostalism: Classical and Emergent,* ed. Steven M. Studebaker (Eugene, OR: Pickwick, 2008), pp. 13-28 (esp. p. 27).

86. Macchia, *Baptized in the Spirit,* pp. 38-49. For this view of Pentecostalism, see D. William Faupel, *The Everlasting Gospel: The Significance of Eschatology in the Development of Pentecostal Thought* (Sheffield, UK: Sheffield Academic Press, 1996).

87. Macchia, *Baptized in the Spirit,* pp. 49-57. Kenneth J. Archer's work, discussed earlier in this chapter, is a variation on Hollenweger's reorientation of the essence of Pentecostal theology to its narrative method.

88. E.g., Anderson, *An Introduction to Pentecostalism,* pp. 10, 188, and Wonsuk Ma, "Asian (Classical) Pentecostal Theology in Context," in *Asian and Pentecostal: The Charismatic Face of Christianity in Asia,* ed. Allan Anderson and Edmond Tang (Oxford: Regnum, 2005), pp. 59-91 (esp. p. 74).

able characteristics of Lutheran theology do exist, so theologians may appropriately pursue Lutheran theology, as long as they recognize the limitations of any one of its representative voices. In a similar way, Spirit baptism is a representative doctrine. As Macchia maintains, "Despite the diversity of distinctive doctrines among Pentecostals, a survey of Pentecostal literature especially in the early years of the movement (but even beyond) reveals that the favored doctrine is definitely the baptism in the Holy Spirit. . . . Neglecting the doctrine as merely one minor component of a plethora of Pentecostal ideas is neither convincing as a historical thesis nor to my mind fruitful as a theological option at the ecumenical table."[89]

Several points of evidence support this position. A review of the major North American Pentecostal confessions illustrates that they identify Spirit baptism as their defining doctrine.[90] Furthermore, the identification of Spirit baptism as a focal point of Pentecostalism is not limited to its North American expressions. Commenting on Korean Pentecostalism, Myung Soo Park declares that "[t]he essence of Pentecostal spirituality is found through the baptism in the Holy Spirit."[91] Pentecostal biblical scholarship, by both its supporters and critics, concentrated — at least through the 1980s — on the issue of Spirit baptism, which suggests its preeminent place in the movement. Pentecostals have routinely turned to the biblical metaphor of Spirit baptism to describe their experience of the Spirit despite the fact that they may disagree over the doctrinal formulation, purpose, and the signs of Spirit baptism.[92]

89. Macchia, *Baptized in the Spirit*, pp. 37-38.

90. See the official websites of the Assemblies of God, USA: http://ag.org/top/Beliefs/index.cfm (accessed Aug. 7, 2009); the Pentecostal Assemblies of Canada, http://www.paoc.org/about/what-we-believe (accessed Aug. 7, 2009); International Pentecostal Holiness Church, http://arc.iphc.org/theology/artfaith.html (accessed Aug. 7, 2009); Church of God, Cleveland, TN, http://churchofgod.org/declaration-of-faith/ (accessed August 7, 2009); the Foursquare Church, http://www.foursquare.org/landing_pages/4,3.html (accessed Aug. 7, 2009).

91. Myung Soo Park, "Korean Pentecostal Spirituality as Manifested in the Testimonies of Believers of the Yoido Full Gospel Church," *Asian Journal of Pentecostal Studies* 7 (2004): 35-56 (esp. p. 44).

92. Simon Chan puts it this way: "Pentecostals themselves are not in agreement over the precise nature of their distinctives. But what comes through over and over again in their discussions and writings is a certain kind of spiritual experience of an intense, direct and overwhelming nature centering in the person of Christ which they schematize as 'baptism in the Holy Spirit'" (Chan, *Pentecostal Theology and the Christian Tradition* [Sheffield, UK: Sheffield Academic Press, 2000], p. 7).

When we use "Spirit baptism" as a representative term for Pentecostal experience, we should avoid a confessional conception of it (e.g., the classical one). Rather, we can use the term in a more comprehensive way to capture the unique spirituality and experience that more broadly characterizes the Pentecostal movement. Although I am less convinced that speaking in tongues can serve as a representative concept, I agree with Simon Chan that Spirit baptism is one of "the most significant symbols of the Pentecostal movement," but that it "is far bigger than the classical Pentecostal conceptualization of it."[93] Thus, in the end, I do not reject the popular opinion among Pentecostal scholars that what is distinctive to Pentecostalism is an emphasis on the charismatic experience of the Spirit; but I do want to draw on that experience of the Spirit, encapsulated in the theological term "Spirit baptism," to propose a Pentecostal contribution to Trinitarian theology. My contention that the Pentecostal experience of the Spirit can contribute to Trinitarian theology is consistent with Amos Yong's principle that "Pentecostal theology should be rooted in the experiences of the worshiping community."[94] Furthermore, the use of Spirit baptism as an orienting biblical and theological notion is not a continuation of North American theological imperialism, because it does not presuppose the classical Pentecostal understanding of the term.[95]

The theological-hermeneutical principle of this project can be stated succinctly: the experience of Spirit baptism is a defining feature of the Pentecostal movement and thus should shape the content of Pentecostal theology and, more specifically, of its contribution to Trinitarian theology.[96] Al-

93. Chan, *Pentecostal Theology,* p. 13.

94. Yong, *The Spirit Poured Out,* p. 79. He adds: "A distinctive Pentecostal theology would also be confessionally located, in the sense of emerging from the matrix of the Pentecostal experience of the Spirit of God" (p. 29).

95. Indeed, I have critiqued the classical Pentecostal doctrine of Spirit baptism and specifically noted its inability to serve as a defining doctrine of worldwide Pentecostalism precisely because it is representative neither of the worldwide movement nor even of all Pentecostals in North America. See Studebaker, "Beyond Tongues: A Pentecostal Theology of Grace," in Studebaker, ed., *Defining Issues in Pentecostalism,* pp. 46-68; and "Globalization and Spirit Baptism," in *Pentecostalism and Globalization: The Impact of Globalization on Pentecostal Theology and Ministry,* ed. Steven M. Studebaker (Eugene, OR: Pickwick, 2010), pp. 87-108. For a critique of the tendency to discuss Pentecostalism from a Western and especially North American bias, see Allan Anderson, "Revising Pentecostal History in Global Perspective," in Anderson and Tang, eds., *Asian and Pentecostal,* pp. 147-73.

96. Paul M. Collins also affirms that the doctrine of the Trinity is rooted in the "activity of God in the Christ event and the event of Pentecost," as well as the Trinitarian language

though defending the classical Pentecostal doctrine of subsequence is not the purpose of this project, it shares its theological assumption that the Pentecostal experience of the Spirit has theological implications. The classical doctrine of Spirit baptism was an attempt to articulate theologically what the Pentecostals knew from their experience of the Holy Spirit, specifically that the Holy Spirit is central to the Christian life and that soteriologies that are primarily christological are insufficient. The role of the doctrine of Spirit baptism within Pentecostalism is, therefore, to give the recovery of the experience and manifestation of the Spirit a commensurate theological articulation. Although Douglas Jacobsen is correct that theological categories informed the Pentecostal experience of the Spirit, he is also right to note that Pentecostal theology as such was (and continues to be) an attempt on the part of the Pentecostals to make theological sense of their charismatic experience.[97] In this respect, the Pentecostal experience of the Spirit is the source of Pentecostal theological (inclusive of biblical) reflection. Furthermore, the Pentecostal movement has an intentional reforming impulse. The early Pentecostals, the charismatics, and more recently the Third Wavers sought to bring reform through a recovery of a fuller experience and manifestation of the Holy Spirit in the lives of Christians and Christian churches. Since Pentecostal experience has a renewal dimension, Pentecostal theology should, too. Pentecostal theology should reflect the renewal nature of the movement and thus offer a unique theological contribution to alternative Christian theologies. This book endeavors to pursue this renewal impulse in terms of Trinitarian theology by allowing the Pentecostal experience of the Spirit to orient an approach to the biblical narratives of the Spirit and from there to the traditions of Trinitarian theology.

Conclusion

In this chapter I have presented a case for taking the experience of Spirit baptism within Pentecostalism as a point of orientation for Pentecostal theology — not as a call toward effervescent religious subjectivism, but

---

that is central to Christian worship and liturgy. However, the ramifications of the Pentecost event are more suggested than developed in his discussion (Collins, *The Trinity: A Guide for the Perplexed* [New York: Continuum, 2008], pp. 8-26).

97. Jacobsen, *Thinking in the Spirit*, pp. 2-12.

one that takes the experience of the Spirit within the Pentecostal tradition as theologically meaningful. I have established this position on biblical and theological grounds. The Jerusalem Council's reliance on Peter's experience to form the early church's theology — that the gospel includes the Gentiles — provided biblical support for treating the Pentecostal experience as theologically significant. Kenneth Archer and Reinhard Hütter offer a basis in contemporary theological hermeneutics. The extension of Hütter's pneumatological view of the pathos of theology provides the pneumatological foundation for Archer's proposal for the Pentecostal narrative tradition as the source of Pentecostal theology. Finally, this chapter has argued that the experience of Spirit baptism is the defining characteristic of the Pentecostal tradition. In chapter 2, I will connect the experience of the Spirit in the Pentecostal tradition to the biblical narratives of the Spirit, which come to thematic climax in the Spirit of Pentecost.

2 The Holy Spirit and the Trinity

Pentecostal experience is about the Holy Spirit, but is it the biblical vision of redemption? The answer of this chapter is yes. In the first chapter I presented a case for letting Pentecostal experience provide the orientation for Pentecostal theology. This chapter moves from the Pentecostal experience of the Spirit to the biblical narratives of the Spirit, which confirm the centrality of the Spirit in Pentecostal experience. The move to Scripture grounds a Pentecostal Trinitarian theology in the canonical tradition. But what is the entry point to Scripture for a Pentecostal theology?

Pentecostal theology traditionally looks to Luke-Acts to articulate the theological fruit of its experience of the Spirit in terms of the doctrine of Spirit baptism. In a similar way, a Pentecostal Trinitarian theology can turn to the locus classicus of Pentecostal theology: the outpouring of the Spirit of Pentecost. However, more than its favored status recommends turning to the Spirit of Pentecost. The Spirit's identity and work is manifested most expressly as the Spirit of Pentecost. The Spirit of Pentecost has three characteristics: liminal, constitutional, and consummative (or eschatological). Liminal refers to the Spirit's presence and activity at critical threshold stages in creation and redemption. Constitutional relates to the central and substantial role of the Spirit in creation and redemption. Consummative, or eschatological, indicates the Spirit's role in enabling something to achieve and fulfill its divine goal. Moreover, these three characteristics reveal the Spirit's role and identity in the Trinitarian God. This connection between economic activity and immanent identity recalls a foundational hermeneutical and methodological premise: a reciprocal relationship pertains between the Spirit's identity and work in the economy and the Spirit's identity and role in the Trinity.

To develop the content of a Pentecostal contribution to Trinitarian theology, in this chapter I first address the appropriateness of taking both the Old and New Testaments as sources for constructing a theology of the Holy Spirit. I then examine the Spirit's work as Spirit of creation and redemption, Spirit of Christ, and Spirit of Pentecost. A thematic continuity in the Spirit's work emerges from these episodes in the drama of biblical redemption. Finally, it shows what the personal character of the Spirit's work in redemption adds to Trinitarian theology. In short, since the Spirit is the eschatological fulfillment of the economy of redemption, the Spirit completes the immanent fellowship of the Trinity. The purpose of the following is to set forth the fundamental content of a Pentecostal Trinitarian theology, not to distinguish it from other approaches, though differences are implied. I will do the dialogical and distinguishing work in chapters 3 through 5.

The *Ruach* of God as the Holy Spirit?

The paramount issue here is this: Can theology legitimately interpret Old Testament references to God's Spirit (Spirit of Elohim/Yahweh) as the Holy Spirit? Can "Spirit of God" in certain creation and re-creation stories serve as sources for Christian pneumatology and Trinitarian theology? The biblical canon begins with two creation narratives. The first account opens with cosmic bedlam: Genesis 1:2a declares that "the earth was formless and empty, darkness was over the surface of the deep," describing the formlessness and disorder of the primordial state. It was cosmic anarchy. The key for pneumatology is the second part of Genesis 1:2: "[T]he Spirit of God was hovering over the waters." The word translated as "Spirit" is the Hebrew word *ruach,* which has the semantic range of wind, breath, God's life-giving power and wisdom, God's S/spirit(s), and human emotions, psychological states, and will.[1]

1. "Holy Spirit," in *Anchor Bible Dictionary,* ed. David N. Freedman, 6 vols. (New York: Doubleday, 1992), vol. 3; "רוח," in Ludwig Koehler and Walter Baumgartner, *The Hebrew and Aramaic Lexicon of the Old Testament,* 5 vols. (New York: E. J. Brill, 1996); "רוח rûah spirit," in Ernst Jenni and Claus Westermann, *Theological Lexicon of the Old Testament,* 3 vols., trans. Mark E. Biddle (Peabody, MA: Hendrickson, 1997), vol. 3; Hans Walter Wolff, *Anthropology of the Old Testament* (Philadelphia: Fortress, 1974), pp. 32-39.

Wonsuk Ma distinguishes six traditions of meaning for "divine spirit." These are the

The second creation story is in the second chapter of Genesis. Genesis 2:7 describes the creation of human beings this way: "God formed man from the dust of the ground and breathed into his nostrils the breath of life, and man became a living being." The Hebrew word for "breath" is *neshamah*, but it functions as a synonym for *ruach*.[2] "Breath" does not indicate the Holy Spirit, at least in any direct sense; but the breath that animates the human is clearly a gift from and — in some sense — a participation in the life of the Spirit of God.[3] The texts reflect a common theme. They portray a transition from lifelessness to life, and they describe the agent/agency of that transition in pneumatological images. In this segment I will develop a theological and canonical-hermeneutical rationale for seeing the Spirit of God operative in passages such as Genesis 1:2, 2:7, and other texts that use pneumatological language to describe God's presence and activity in creation and redemption in the Old Testament.

Theological Rationale

The first reason to understand the *ruach*/breath of God as the Spirit of God in the creation stories is the Ancient Near Eastern sacral view of the world. Readers of Genesis 1 in contemporary North America understand "wind" according to the myth of modern science. ("Myth" does not mean some fanciful and unscientific way of seeing the world, but rather a perspective that provides the fundamental way a group of people understands the world, how it works, and the way to act in it.) The myth of science and its various subcults dominates twenty-first-century North America. The modern myth assumes the secular hubris that human beings can solve all of their problems through the sheer strength of their own ingenuity, technological talent, therapeutic treatments, and pharmacological palliatives.

---

leadership spirit, prophetic spirit, creation spirit, spirit as God's independent agent (e.g., angelic messenger of Yahweh), spirit as an aspect of God's person and sign of God's presence, and spirit as synonym for God. See Wonsuk Ma, *Until the Spirit Comes: The Spirit of God in the Book of Isaiah,* Journal for the Study of the Old Testament Supplement Series, 271 (Sheffield, UK: Sheffield Academic Press, 1999), pp. 29-32.

2. Wilf Hildebrandt, *An Old Testament Theology of the Spirit of God* (Peabody, MA: Hendrickson, 1995), p. 58; John H. Walton, *Genesis,* New International Version Application Commentary Series (Grand Rapids: Zondervan, 2001), p. 166; Walter R. Wifall, "The Breath of His Nostrils, Genesis 2:7b," *The Catholic Biblical Quarterly* 36 (1974): 238.

3. Gerhard von Rad, *Genesis: A Commentary* (Philadelphia: Westminster, 1972), p. 77; John R. Levison, *Filled with the Spirit* (Grand Rapids: Eerdmans, 2009), pp. 30-31.

Different myths shaped the mind of the Ancient Near East. One of its key elements was the sacral nature of the world. People believed that "[t]he gods had purposes, and their activities were the causes of what humans experienced as effects."[4] The Ancient Near Eastern person did not inhabit a dialectical world of the natural and the supernatural.[5] The heavens above were distinct from the earth below; nevertheless, they were not hermetically sealed realms of reality, but existed in seamless relationship. As John H. Walton remarks, "Our modern 'dilemma' of trying to discern what happens naturally and what is the result of God's intervention would seem to ancient Israelites, at best ludicrous and, at worst, heretical."[6] In the religions of the Ancient Near East, the wind and the four winds were often understood to be ruled by the gods and/or personified as the gods' servants.[7] Ancient Egyptians perennially identified the fours winds as gods and, according to one creation account, a deified wind brought arable land out of the primeval waters.[8] The Assyrian king Adad-Nerari II appropriated to himself the

4. Walton, *Genesis,* p. 27.

5. My argument for the natural world as the place and manifestation of divine presence shares affinity with John R. Levison's case that in Israelite literature the spirit of human life given by God was both a continuing endowment from and intimately connected to God, even though uniquely possessed by each person. See Levison, *Filled with the Spirit,* pp. 14-86. I also share with Levison the view that the Spirit who gives life is intrinsic to all human life and continuous with the Spirit of grace. Pentecostal biblical scholars have, for the most part, sharply rejected Levison's thesis about the relationship between Israelite and early Christian pneumatologies. The fundamental problem for these Pentecostals is that they believe Levison's thesis invalidates the doctrine of Spirit baptism as a second work of grace. But that is not the case. One can affirm that the Spirit is an intrinsic and abiding presence throughout human life and that human beings have evolving and dynamic relationships with the Spirit, and I make the case for that below in this chapter. For Pentecostal assessments of Levison's *Filled with the Spirit,* see the review essays and Levison's response in *Pneuma: The Journal of the Society for Pentecostal Studies* 33, no. 1 (2011): 29-78; see also the *Journal of Pentecostal Theology* 20, no. 2 (2011).

6. Walton, *Genesis,* p. 50; see also John H. Walton, *The Lost World of Genesis One: Ancient Cosmology and the Origins Debate* (Downers Grove, IL: InterVarsity Academic, 2009), p. 20.

7. "Wind-gods," in K. van der Toorn, Bob Becking, and Pieter Willem van der Horst, *Dictionary of Deities and Demons in the Bible,* rev. ed. (Leiden: Brill; Grand Rapids: Eerdmans, 1999); see also "Whirlwind," in *Dictionary of Biblical Imagery,* ed. Leland Ryken, James C. Wilhoit, and Tremper Longman III (Downers Grove, IL: InterVarsity, 1998).

8. Susanne Woodhouse, "The Sun God, His Four Bas and the Four Winds in the Sacred District at Saïs: The Fragment of an Obelisk (BM EA 1512)," in *The Temple in Ancient Egypt: New Discoveries and Recent Research,* ed. Stephen Quirke (London: British Museum Press, 1997), pp. 132-51 (esp. pp. 136-37); Hans-Peter Hasenfratz, "Patterns of Creation in Ancient Egypt," in *Creation in Jewish and Christian Tradition,* ed. Henning Graf Reventlow and Yair

sun god and likened and associated his power with the "onslaught of the wind" and "the gale."[9]

Nor did the Hebrews construe the wind and air as mere natural elements. Rather, as Theodore Hiebert points out, "air as both atmospheric winds and breath is described in the Hebrew Scriptures as possessing a divine character. . . . For the biblical theologian, [*ruach*] is sacred."[10] Moreover, the association of God's breath with the wind and tempest cannot be reduced to poetry and metaphor.[11] T. John Wright suggests that "for the ancients, 'wind' and 'breath' were not distinguished, neither from each other, nor distinct from the ghostly specter or numinous presence."[12] The ancients did not separate the world into neat categories of physical and spiritual forces. In some sense, Yahweh was both in and beyond the storm wind.[13] The tenth chapter of Exodus (vv. 13, 19) provides a sense of the intimate interrelationship between the divine and the world, when Yahweh

---

Hoffman, Journal for the Study of the Old Testament Supplement Series, 319 (London: Sheffield Academic Press, 2002), pp. 174-78 (esp. p. 175); Lászlo Kákosy, "The Ptah-Shu-Tefnut Triad and the Gods of the Winds on a Ptolemaic Sarcophagus," in *Essays on Ancient Egypt in Honour of Herman te Velde,* ed. Jacobus van Dijk, Egyptological Memoirs, 1 (Groningen: Styx, 1997), pp. 219-29. Furthermore, the Egyptian high god Shu, who was associated with the air and ultimate source of the winds and reigned with his sister-goddess, Tefnut, ultimately controlled the four winds and was a chief actor in ancient Egyptian cosmology. See "רוח rûah," in *Theologisches Wörterbuch zum Alten Testament,* ed. G. J. Botterweck and Helmer Ringgren, 10 vols. (Stuttgart: W. Kohlhammer, 1973-2000), vol. 7.

9. Albert Kirk Grayson, *Assyrian Royal Inscriptions: From Tiglath-pileser I to Ashurnasir-apli II,* 2 vols. (Wiesbaden: Otto Harrassowitz, 1976), 2: 85-86.

10. Theodore Hiebert, "Air, the First Sacred Thing: The Conception of [*ruach*] in the Hebrew Scriptures," in *Exploring Ecological Hermeneutics,* ed. Norman C. Habel and Peter L. Trudinger (Leiden: Brill, 2008), pp. 9-19 (esp. p. 13).

11. "רוח rûah spirit," in *Theological Lexicon of the Old Testament,* vol. 3.

12. T. John Wright, "The Concept of *RUACH* in Ezekiel 37," in *Seeing Signals, Reading Signs: The Art of Exegesis; Studies in Honour of Antony F. Campbell, SJ, for His Seventieth Birthday,* ed. Mark A. O'Brien and Howard N. Wallace (New York: T&T Clark, 2004), pp. 142-58, 175.

13. Friedrich Baumgärtel emphasizes that Hebrew theology excludes pantheistic ideas and that "nature is stripped of power and de-deified." Although I agree with the first point, on the latter point this is the case only with respect to stripping the natural world of divine powers other than Yahweh. See Baumgärtel, "Spirit in the Old Testament," in *Theological Dictionary of the New Testament,* ed. Gerhard Friedrich, trans. Geoffrey W. Bromiley, 10 vols. (Grand Rapids: Eerdmans, 1968), 6: 366. Commenting on the historical writing of the Hebrew Bible, Daniel I. Block maintains that "ancient Israel has a sophisticated and complex view of God who was both transcendent and present in their midst" ("Empowered by the Spirit of God: The Holy Spirit in the Historiographic Writings of the Old Testament," *The Southern Baptist Journal of Theology* 1 [1997]: 42-61 [esp. p. 53]).

commands an east wind to bring the plague of locusts upon Egypt and then changes its direction to a west wind to blow them out to sea.

Storm theophanies are another example of the manifestation of divine presence in terms of atmospheric phenomena. For instance, God speaks to Job from the "whirlwind" (Job 40:6; see also Ps. 29; Ps. 50:3; Ps. 97; Ps. 107:25; Amos 1:2).[14] The "wind," weather, and storm do not contain God, but they are also inseparable from God. The ancient Israelites demythologized the wind in one sense, since they did not deify and worship it (i.e., they rejected the Baalism of Canaan); yet, in another sense, they retained the sacral understanding of the world as the place of — and perhaps even indistinguishable from — Yahweh's presence and manifestation.[15]

The relationship between God and human breath also reflects this inseparable relationship between what moderns might think of as the material — in contrast to the divine or spiritual. Ecclesiastes indicates that "the dust returns to the ground it came from, and the spirit returns to God who gave it" (Eccles. 12:7). The text conceives of the breath or spirit of the human as something that is in one sense irreducible to God — it is the breath of a human being — yet in another sense inseparable from God. The breath of life is life from God that "returns" to God at death. Hebrew Scripture portrays God's presence as life giving breath, and when that breath leaves, the human returns to dust. Reflecting the continuity between the wind, the Spirit of God, and the animating power of life, Yahweh declares to the prophet Ezekiel, "Prophesy to the breath; prophesy, son of man, and say to it, 'This is what the Sovereign Lord says: Come from the four winds, O breath, and breathe into these slain, that they may live'" (Ezek. 37:9). Here *ruach* is "breath," the "four winds," and the divine power that will bring new life to the people of Israel. Thus, the breath that revivifies the dry bones of the nation is the four winds that Ezekiel 37:14 clarifies as the Spirit of Yahweh. The theology of the ancient Hebrews makes distinctions between wind, breath, and the Spirit of God, but it also sees them possessing a relationship of continuity.[16]

14. Hiebert, "Air, the First Sacred Thing," p. 13.

15. "Storm" and "Weather," in Ryken, Wilhoit, and Longman, eds., *Dictionary of Biblical Imagery.*

16. Block suggests that the juxtaposition of these terms in Ezekiel 37:9 is "intentionally ambiguous." However, to consider their use "ambiguous" seems to assume their ontological distinction. If wind, breath, and Spirit of God are understood in a more organic relationship rather than in terms of ontological dualism — e.g., physical wind and breath in contrast to immaterial Spirit — then the use of these terms is less opaque. Breath is concomitant with

Regarding Genesis 1, even if the *ruach* of God is interpreted as the "wind of God," the Hebrews would not have understood the "wind of God" as a brute natural force, but as one of God in the world that is active to achieve God's purposes.[17] The God of the Hebrews neither can be reduced to the "wind," nor can the active power of God in the world be separated from it.[18] In his study of Pauline pneumatology, which interprets it in relationship to its Jewish background, Mehrdad Fatehi concludes that the *ruach* of Yahweh is the objective expression of Yahweh, yet that Yahweh remains transcendent to his manifestation.[19] Hiebert suggests, with respect to Genesis 1:2, that "the atmospheric wind blowing over the primordial sea . . . is pictured here not just as created matter but as divine, and, as the first aspect of the world so described, the first sacred thing."[20] Indeed, divine agency as the source of creation is the central point of Genesis 1. Therefore, the *ruach* of God in Genesis 1:2 was likely understood as the manifestation of God's power in the creation of the world — thus the translation of the *ruach elohim* as Spirit or wind of God is appropriate.[21] Of course, the first readers of Genesis 1:2 did not think, "Oh hey, the *ruach* of God is the Holy Spirit." The Christian notion of the Holy Spirit is one that emerges from the early Christian experience of God, Scripture, and the efforts of early church theologians to come to terms with these two phenomena.[22]

The theological hermeneutical question is this: Is it appropriate to read Genesis 1:2 in light of the New Testament revelation of God as Trin-

---

life; breath is the same stuff of the wind; both the breath and the wind are from God, who gives life and controls the meteorological rhythms. See Daniel I. Block, "The Prophet of the Spirit: The Use of *RWH* in the Book of Ezekiel," *Journal of the Evangelical Theological Society* 32 (1989): 27-49 (esp. p. 38).

17. John P. Peter, "The Wind of God," *Journal of Biblical Literature* 30, no. 1 (1911): 44-54 (esp. p. 53); Block, "Empowered by the Spirit of God," pp. 43-44.

18. Ma, *Until the Spirit Comes,* pp. 15, 25-26.

19. Mehrdad Fatehi, *The Spirit's Relation to the Risen Lord in Paul: An Examination of Its Christological Implications,* Wissenschaftliche Untersuchungen zum Neuen Testament, 128 (Tübingen: Mohr Siebeck, 2000), pp. 57-58.

20. Hiebert, "Air, the First Sacred Thing," p. 15.

21. For more detailed syntactical and semantical reasons for interpreting *ruach elohim* as Spirit or wind of God, see Victor P. Hamilton, *The Book of Genesis, Chapters 1–17* (Grand Rapids: Eerdmans, 1990), pp. 111-15. On *ruach elohim* in Genesis 1:2, Gordon J. Wenham concludes: "I have adopted the rendering 'Wind of God' as a concrete and vivid image of the Spirit of God" (*Genesis 1–15,* Word Biblical Commentary [Waco, TX: Word, 1987], p. 17).

22. George T. Montague, *The Holy Spirit: Growth of a Biblical Tradition* (New York: Paulist, 1976), p. viii.

ity? I agree with Colin E. Gunton when he says, "While we cannot say categorically that this refers to the Spirit we know as the Holy Spirit, we should not be afraid to understand it trinitarianly in the light of later thought."[23] I argue (1) that the Old Testament establishes a precedence for understanding creation and redemption in pneumatological terms, and (2) that when the Old Testament work of God's Spirit correlates with work attributed to the Holy Spirit in the New Testament, then one can legitimately identify the Hebrew Bible *ruach* of God as the Holy Spirit.

Canonical Rationale

The Old Testament displays a hermeneutical trajectory that interprets God's activity in creation and redemption in terms of the agency of God's Spirit. First, the Hebrew Bible interprets the *ruach* of God in creation as the creative presence of God's Spirit. Echoing Genesis 1, Psalm 33:6-7 declares that the "word of the LORD" and the "breath of his mouth" are the dynamic power of creation and that through which God rules over creation.[24] In this psalm, the *ruach* of Yahweh has displaced the pantheon of the Ancient Near East. The Babylonians and Egyptians identified the sun with a god (e.g., the Babylonian god Shamash); the Canaanites associated the god Yam with the sea, and Baal, the storm god, with the earth and its seasonal cycles.[25] In place of these gods, the *ruach* of Yahweh reigns supreme as he creates and orders the sun, moon, and stars.[26] Job 26:10, 12-13

23. Colin E. Gunton, *The Triune Creator: A Historical and Systematic Study,* Edinburgh Studies in Constructive Theology (Grand Rapids: Eerdmans, 1998), p. 17.

24. John Goldingay, *Psalms,* vol. 1: *Psalms 1–41,* Baker Commentary on the Old Testament Wisdom and Psalms (Grand Rapids: Baker Academic, 2006), p. 467. Yair Hoffman maintains that Psalm 33 does not refer to Genesis 1:2 because it does not include the six-day pattern of creation, the central creation verb ברא, and the creation of the heavenly lights. Yet, even if the psalm does not have the Genesis 1 creation story in its background, it does combine the images of the divine word and spirit as the active power of creation. See Hoffman, "The First Creation Story: Canonical and Diachronic Aspects," in Reventlow and Hoffman, eds., *Creation in Jewish and Christian Tradition,* pp. 32-53 (esp. p. 40).

25. Mark J. Boda, *Haggai, Zechariah,* New International Version Application Commentary (Grand Rapids: Zondervan, 2004), pp. 318-19; Christopher J. H. Wright, *Knowing the Holy Spirit through the Old Testament* (Downers Grove, IL: InterVarsity Academic, 2006), pp. 17-19.

26. Jesus embodies Yahweh's presence in a similar way when he exercises power over evil spirits. In Matthew 12:28, he declares, "If I drive out demons by the Spirit of God, then the kingdom of God has come upon you." Jesus' activity stands in continuity with the pneumatology of Psalm 33:6; the Spirit of God is the source of God's rule in the world.

incorporates pneumatological imagery and elements of Ancient Near Eastern cosmological beginnings when it describes creation in the following way: "[God] marks out the horizon on the face of the waters for a boundary between light and darkness. . . . By his power he churned up the sea; by his wisdom he cut Rahab to pieces. By his breath the skies became fair; his hand pierced the gliding serpent." Both the Babylonian and Canaanite creation myths depict a primordial battle between dragon-like chaos gods (e.g., Rahab) and the god/s that bring order to the world.[27] The use of *ruach*/breath here correlates with the *ruach's* activity in the Genesis 1 creation story and the receding waters of the flood — *ruach* brings order to chaos — and thus connects God's Spirit to cosmic origins.[28]

Second, Isaiah connects the Spirit of God's work in creation and redemption. In Isaiah 40:12-17, the Spirit of God is the power and wisdom of God displayed in creation.[29] Isaiah 63:10-14 specifies God's presence among the people of Israel during the Exodus from Egypt as "the Holy Spirit" and "the Spirit of the Lord." Now, certainly that reference to "Holy Spirit" does not carry the theological content of its use in the New Testa-

27. Norman C. Habel, *The Book of Job: A Commentary,* Old Testament Library (Philadelphia: Westminster, 1985), p. 192. The extent to which Genesis 1:2 draws or does not draw on Canaanite and Mesopotamian creation myths or whether Genesis 1:2 and Job 26 adapt common mythic themes and/or synthesize them is not important for my theological project, though the biblical creation accounts and association of Yahweh with the forces of nature appear to amalgamate Ancient Near Eastern myths. For example, in the Old Testament, Yahweh is both God of the storm, which correlates with the Canaanite god Baal, and the God of creation, which correlates with the supreme Canaanite god El. The significant point for my theological project is the role of God's *ruach* in these various biblical creation accounts and associations of Yahweh with the forces of nature. For a detailed investigation of the relationship between the Genesis 1 and 2 creation stories and alternative Ancient Near Eastern ones, see David Toshio Tsumura, *The Earth and the Waters in Genesis 1 and 2: A Linguistic Investigation,* Journal for the Study of the Old Testament Supplement Series, 83 (Sheffield, UK: Sheffield Academic Press, 1989).

28. John Goldingay, "Was the Holy Spirit Active in Old Testament Times? What Was New about the New Testament Experience of God?" *Ex Auditu* 12 (1996): 14-28. Hoffman again sees no connection between the creation stories in Genesis 1 and Job 26 and suggests they are alternative creation accounts embedded in the canonical tradition (Hoffman, "The First Creation Story," p. 45). I think he may very well be correct, especially since Genesis 1 demythologizes the *Chaoskampf* relative to Job. Nevertheless, the common attribution of creation as a work of the Spirit of God supports my canonical-hermeneutical case to interpret *ruach* as "the Spirit" of God.

29. Ma, *Until the Spirit Comes,* pp. 72-74; Claus Westermann, *Isaiah 40–66: A Commentary,* trans. David M. Stalker, Old Testament Library (Philadelphia: Westminster, 1969), pp. 50-51.

ment; but it is a pneumatological description of the redemptive presence and work of God in the Exodus.[30] Isaiah also presents the Spirit of God as the activity of God that restores the nation of Israel from exile; in other words, the Spirit re-creates the nation. The Spirit of God's restoration of the nation of Israel presupposes the Spirit's work in creation (Isa. 34:16; 41:22-29).[31] The theological logic is that since the Spirit of God established the heavens and the earth, then the same Spirit trumps all other gods, can restore the national fortunes of Israel, and is sovereign over all history.[32]

Third, the Old Testament suggests that God's Spirit is the animating vitality of human life. In Genesis 2:7, God's breath makes dirt become a living human being. It is not a picture of a living body getting a soul or spirit, but of dirt animated by God's breath. The passage suggests that the entirety of human life is from the Spirit of God and not only its inner spiritual dimension. The dirt is not a living human being until the Spirit vivifies it.[33] The breath of God animates the dust, and the dust then becomes living by the presence of the breath of life. Genesis 2:7 presents a pneumatological anthropology: to be human is to be a creature uniquely vitalized by God's Spirit for a unique relationship with God and creation.

The flood narrative both deepens the association of breath that animates human life with God's Spirit and expands it as the source of life for all living creatures (Gen. 6:3, 17; 7:15, 22). Intensifying — though in a negative way — the pneumatological anthropology of Genesis 2:7, Genesis 6:3 describes death as the moment when Yahweh's Spirit no longer abides with human beings as the sustaining power of their lives.[34] The book of Job shares the pneumatological anthropology of Genesis. In Job 27:3, the

30. "Holy Spirit" became a common way to refer to God's Spirit in Palestinian and Diaspora Judaism (Sang Meyng Lee, *The Cosmic Drama of Salvation: A Study of Paul's Undisputed Writings from Anthropological and Cosmological Perspectives,* Wissenschaftliche Untersuchungen zum Neuen Testament, 276 [Tübingen: Mohr Siebeck, 2010], p. 177).

31. Ma, *Until the Spirit Comes,* pp. 98, 191, 207; John W. Yates, *The Spirit and Creation in Paul,* Wissenschaftliche Untersuchungen zum Neuen Testament, 251 (Tübingen: Mohr Siebeck, 2008), pp. 28-31.

32. Klaus Baltzer, *Deutero-Isaiah: A Commentary on Isaiah 40–55,* trans. Margaret Kohl, Hermeneia: A Critical and Historical Commentary on the Bible (Minneapolis: Fortress, 2001), pp. 71-72; see also Ben C. Ollenburger, "Isaiah's Creation Theology," *Ex Auditu* 3 (1987): 54-71 (esp. pp. 64-66).

33. Levison, *Filled with the Spirit,* pp. 14-15; Montague, *The Holy Spirit,* p. 5; Walton, *Genesis,* p. 166.

34. Walton, *Genesis,* p. 295; Von Rad, *Genesis,* pp. 77, 115; Yates, *Spirit and Creation in Paul,* pp. 25-27.

breath of the Almighty is the animating principle of human life. Job 32:8 reaffirms and extends the Spirit's work to include giving wisdom to those to whom the Spirit has given the breath of life.[35] Job 33:4 and 34:14 use *ruach* and *neshamah* in a poetic parallelism to affirm that the Spirit or breath of God constitutes and is the animating power of human life and that, "if . . . he withdrew his spirit and breath, all mankind would perish together and man would return to the dust."[36] To be human is to be imbued with the breath of life, the Spirit of God. The Spirit of God's life-giving power is not a zap that merely initiates life, but an enduring presence that sustains it. Psalm 104:27-30 draws on similar pneumatological images when it affirms that Yahweh's Spirit is the divine power of creation and life.[37] Its imagery of breath infusing life into creatures coheres with the description of the creation of human life in Genesis 2:7 and the source of animal life in the sixth and eighth chapters of Genesis. Furthermore, the passage affirms "that when you send your Spirit, they are created, and you renew the face of the earth."[38] The first clause clearly connects with the creation of human beings in Genesis 2, and the second, which attributes the renewal of the earth to the Spirit, coheres with the *ruach* that drives away the floodwaters from the earth in Genesis 8:1. Finally, the Spirit's role in animating life in Adam in Genesis 2:7 parallels the Spirit's role in the creation of the world in Genesis 1. Just as the Spirit is the presence of God that emancipates the cosmos from the primordial maelstrom, so also the Spirit is the divine presence that enables the dust to become a living human being.[39]

35. Habel, *Job*, pp. 380, 450-51, 464; John E. Hartley, *The Book of Job*, New International Commentary on the Old Testament (Grand Rapids: Eerdmans, 1988), pp. 434, 438.

36. Hartley, *Job*, pp. 438, 454. Levison points out that, though Job and Elihu share a common pneumatological anthropology, Elihu's use of it is more sycophantic and anthropocentric, whereas Job understands the Spirit of God as the source of life for all living creatures (Levison, *Filled with the Spirit*, pp. 18-23). Moreover, the words *ruach* and *neshamah* function as interchangeable synonyms (Yates, *Spirit and Creation in Paul*, pp. 25-28).

37. Goldingay, *Psalms*, vol. 3: *Psalms 90–150*, Baker Commentary on the Old Testament Wisdom and Psalms (Grand Rapids: Baker Academic, 2008), p. 194; Konrad Schaefer, *Psalms*, Berit Olam Series (Collegeville, MN: Liturgical Press, 2001), p. 258.

38. For Pentecostal explorations of this theme in terms of the dialogue between theology and science, see Amos Yong, ed., *The Spirit Renews the Face of the Earth: Pentecostal Forays in Science and Theology of Creation* (Eugene, OR: Pickwick, 2009).

39. Second Temple Jewish literature continued the hermeneutical trajectory of interpreting the *ruach* of Genesis 1:2 as the Spirit of God and more than just a natural wind from God. For background on this, see Marie E. Isaacs, *The Concept of Spirit: A Study of Pneuma*

While one may recognize the limited explicit Trinitarian-pneumatological implications of Old Testament references to God's Spirit, the New Testament nonetheless personalizes divine activity in the world in terms of a Trinitarian God and further clarifies the Spirit of God as the Holy Spirit.[40] Furthermore, the New Testament writers associate the Holy Spirit with the same images and activities attributed to God's Spirit in the Old Testament. The Gospel of John completes the canonical trajectory of the Spirit's work in creation and redemption (or new creation). John 3:8 uses the uncontainable nature of the wind to illustrate the freedom of the Spirit to renew human life. John's portrayal of the Spirit in terms of wind and as the source of new life likely draws on Ezekiel's vision of God's Spirit putting a new heart in the people of Israel (Ezek. 36:24-28). In John 20:22-23, Jesus gives the Holy Spirit to the disciples by breathing on them. The impartation of the Holy Spirit through the act of breathing coheres with God's giving the breath of life to Adam in Genesis 2:7 and breathing new life into the dead bones of the nation of Israel (Ezek. 37:1-14).[41] John 1:3 begins with the declaration that all things were created through the Word, who then becomes incarnate in Jesus Christ (John 1:14) and who promises a new birth through God's Spirit (John 1:12-13; 3:1-8; 7:37-39); and John 20:21-22 completes the creation to new creation trajectory through the giving of the Holy Spirit.

Connecting the themes of creation and new creation has now been completed for both testaments. The Gospel of John also clarifies the promise of the presence of God's Spirit among the people of God in terms of the presence of the Holy Spirit. Ezekiel promises that God's Spirit will dwell among the people of Israel (Ezek. 37:26-28; 29:29). Jesus encourages his disciples by saying that, though he will leave, they should take heart that he and the Father will come to them through the Holy Spirit (John 14:15-26).

in Hellenistic Judaism and Its Bearing on the New Testament, Heythrop Monographs, 1 (London: H. Charlesworth, 1976), pp. 43-45; John R. Levison, *The Spirit in First-Century Judaism* (Boston: Brill, 2002), and *Filled with the Spirit;* Robert P. Menzies, *Empowered for Witness: The Spirit in Luke-Acts* (New York: T&T Clark, 2004).

40. Max Turner, "Holy Spirit," in *New Dictionary of Biblical Theology*, ed. T. Desmond Alexander and Brian Rosner (Downers Grove, IL: InterVarsity, 2008), pp. 551-58 (esp. p. 558).

41. James D. G. Dunn, *Baptism in the Holy Spirit: A Re-examination of the New Testament Teaching on the Gift of the Spirit in Relation to Pentecostalism Today*, Studies in Biblical Theology, 2nd ser., 15 (London: SCM, 1970), p. 180. For the connection of John 20:22 with Ezekiel, see John Pretlove, "John 20:22 — Help from Dry Bones?" *Criswell Theological Review* 3 (2005): 93-101.

John's Gospel refines biblical pneumatology by specifying the promise of divine indwelling and transformation of human life by the Spirit of Yahweh in Ezekiel in terms of the Holy Spirit.

Acts 2 describes the outpouring of the Holy Spirit on the Day of Pentecost in terms of wind and tongues of fire. The manifestation of God's presence, specified with respect to the Holy Spirit in Acts 2:2 as wind and fire, has significant precedent in the Hebrew religious tradition.[42] As I have noted above, "wind" is the visible manifestation of the presence and activity of God's Spirit in creation, the receding floodwaters, the path made through the waters during the Exodus, and the restoration of the exiles to their homeland in Ezekiel's vision. The use of "wind" to describe the tangible presence of the Holy Spirit on the Day of Pentecost links the experience with the ancient Hebrew way of understanding the dynamic and powerful presence of God's Spirit, which "both animates and moves all things toward their fulfillment in God."[43] Fire was also the vehicle for the visible manifestation of God's presence in the Old Testament. The angel of the Lord (Yahweh) appears to Moses in the burning bush (Exod. 3:1-3). Yahweh's presence appears in the pillar of fire to guide the Israelites in the wilderness (Exod. 13:21). Nehemiah directly associates the pillar of fire among the Israelites with God's Spirit (9:19-20 ; see also Haggai 2:5). On Mount Sinai, Moses encounters and hears God in the midst of billowing clouds of smoke (Exod. 19:16-19). The fire that consumes the offerings on the tabernacle altar comes out "from the presence of the Lord" (Lev. 9:24; 1 Kings 18:38). Joel 2:28-32 sees "wonders in the heaven above and signs on the earth below, blood and fire and billows of smoke" attending the promised outpouring of the Holy Spirit, which Peter declares as transpiring on the day of Pentecost (Acts 2:16).

42. Darrell L. Bock, *Acts*, Baker Exegetical Commentary on the New Testament (Grand Rapids: Baker, 2007), pp. 96-97; F. F. Bruce, *The Book of Acts*, rev. ed., New International Commentary on the New Testament (Grand Rapids: Eerdmans, 1989), p. 50; I. Howard Marshall, *The Acts of the Apostles: An Introduction and Commentary*, Tyndale New Testament Commentaries (Grand Rapids: Eerdmans, 1980), pp. 68-69; Montague, *The Holy Spirit*, p. 277; and F. Scott Spencer, *Journeying through Acts: A Literary-Cultural Reading* (Peabody, MA: Hendrickson, 2004), pp. 41-42. Levison presents the case for seeing the context of the manifestation of the Spirit in terms of fire and for the purpose of inspired speech in Acts 2:1-4 as the broader late first century BCE through the fourth-century CE Greco-Roman religious setting (Levison, *Filled with the Spirit*, pp. 325-31, 363-65). I do not disagree that Luke's imagery resonates with his contemporary religious context, but I also maintain that it has deeper traditional antecedents within the religious literature and history of Israel.

43. Ronald W. Young, "The Mission of the Church in Accord with the Mission of the Holy Spirit," *Theoforum* 37 (2006): 287-323 (esp. p. 313).

The canonical hermeneutic that I propose here affirms that the Spirit of Pentecost completes the revelation and work of the Spirit of creation. Biblical pneumatology evolves from the language of the Spirit of God to the Holy Spirit; nevertheless, it bears remarkable consistency with respect to the range of the Spirit's activities. Consequently, one can read the Old Testament references to the Spirit of God as the Holy Spirit when that activity is consistent with the work associated with the Holy Spirit in the New Testament.[44] Since the New Testament uses the same imagery (e.g., wind) and attributes the same kind of work to the Holy Spirit (e.g., creative-redemptive work) that the Old Testament attributes to the Spirit of God, then from a canonical-hermeneutical perspective, reading the Old Testament references to "Spirit of God" as the Holy Spirit is acceptable. Theology can read passages such as Genesis 1:2 in light of later and clearer Trinitarian notions of God that are found in the New Testament; but it should avoid anachronistically insinuating those ideas into the minds of their original compilers.[45] The Spirit of God in Genesis 1:2, with respect to the theology of ancient Israel, is not the Holy Spirit of later Christian theology. "Spirit of God" is probably the presence of God in creative action.

While recognizing the limited original pneumatological meaning of Genesis 1:2, the New Testament personalizes divine activity in the world in terms of a Trinitarian God and further clarifies the Spirit of God as the Holy Spirit.[46] As Graham Cole insists, since Jesus saw himself in the Old Testament — and other New Testament writers did as well — contemporary Christian readers should "travel past Pentecost too" to understand the Old Testament's discussion of God's activity in the world.[47] Thus, even though the later Christian notion of the Holy Spirit was not part of the theological vision of the Old Testament texts, one can legitimately associ-

44. I agree with Colin Gunton's recommendation of interpreting *ruach* in Genesis 1:2: "We can thus discern a measure of continuity between New Testament usage and this mysterious prolegomenon. . . . Only with the benefit of hindsight can we read this whole passage in a Trinitarian way, and yet surely we may and must" (Gunton, "The Spirit Moved Over the Face of the Waters: The Holy Spirit and the Created Order," *International Journal of Systematic Theology* 4 [2002]: 190-204 [esp. p. 191]).

45. Amos Yong proceeds in a similar way in "*Ruach,* the Primordial Chaos, and the Breath of Life: Emergence Theory and the Creation Narratives in Pneumatological Perspective," in *The Work of the Spirit: Pneumatology and Pentecostalism,* ed. Michael Welker (Grand Rapids: Eerdmans, 2006), pp. 183-204 (esp. p. 192).

46. Turner, "Holy Spirit," p. 558.

47. Graham A. Cole, *He Who Gives Life: The Doctrine of the Holy Spirit* (Wheaton, IL: Crossway, 2007), p. 110.

ate their pneumatological images with the later revelation of the Holy Spirit in the same way that one can understand the revelation of God as Yahweh to Moses in Exodus 3:14 as the Trinitarian God, though it may have been the furthest thing from Moses' mind.

Spirit of Creation as Spirit of Redemption

The next three sections describe three narrative roles of the Holy Spirit: the Spirit of creation/redemption, the Spirit of Christ, and the Spirit of Pentecost. Though it is common to think of creation and redemption as distinct movements in the drama of biblical redemption, Scripture coordinates the Spirit's work in these two areas. Creation and redemption are distinct in the sense that God redeems creation. But they are not distinct concerning their economic program and end. The economic order is one: the redemption of creation. Therefore, creation and redemption are not two separate orders, spheres, or modalities of divine activity in Scripture; rather, they are one program in that God's acts of redemption *redeem* creation.[48] In short, the Spirit of creation is also the Spirit of redemption. Wolfhart Pannenberg puts it this way: "The life-giving activity of the divine spirit determines the horizon for all other functions that the Old Testament attributes to the spirit of God."[49]

Creation and redemption should not be thought of as unrelated activities of the Spirit, but rather as two modalities of a unified work. The Spirit's role in creation and the significance that work had for the Hebrew prophets' vision of salvation demonstrate the continuity between the Spirit of creation and redemption. Though most fully displayed in the discussion of the Spirit of Pentecost, the Spirit's work in creation-redemption

48. A unified theology of God's redemptive program is at odds with Reformed theology's covenant of works and grace. Covenantal theology holds that God first entered into relationship with Adam based on his obedience. After Adam breached the covenant of works, God established the covenant of grace, which, though it had various permutations, ultimately consists in salvation by faith in Christ. The fundamental problem with covenant theology, aside from the ostensible positing of two ways for relationship with God (works versus grace), is that there is no grace in it. The covenant of grace is in fact a covenant of works. Christ fulfills the law or provides the work that fulfills the original covenant of works. True, those who put their faith in Christ do not need to work. But the necessity of Christ fulfilling the law in their place means that keeping the law is the basis for the human relationship to God.

49. Wolfhart Pannenberg, *Toward a Theology of Nature: Essays on Science and Faith,* ed. Ted Peters (Louisville: Westminster John Knox, 1993), p. 124.

in the Old Testament has three primary characteristics. The Spirit is a liminal agent who operates at the threshold between death and life and chaos and order; the Spirit is the principal actor and content of God's redemptive activities; and the Spirit consummates or eschatologically fulfills God's work of creation and redemption. In the next section, I wish to articulate, first, a unified theology of creation and redemption: creation and redemption are one creative-redemptive program. Second, I wish to enunciate the liminal, constitutional, and eschatological character of the Spirit's work. The structure of the discussion follows the three characteristics of the Spirit with the theme of creation-redemption integrated throughout.

Liminal

Before I describe the liminal Spirit of creation and redemption, I need to draw the reader's attention to the theological significance of the Genesis creation account. Canonical and historical reasons recommend the interpretation of the *ruach* in Genesis 1:2 as the Spirit of God and the correlation of the Spirit's creative and redemptive work. The Hebrew prophets drew a connection between the Spirit's work of creation and redemption.[50] Coming to shape in the exilic and postexilic period, the Genesis 1 creation narrative served a religious and liturgical function for the people of Israel during their Babylonian captivity and repatriation.[51] Genesis 1 is primarily a theological account — not a blow-by-blow account — of cosmological beginnings in a modern scientific sense, although the original audience likely believed it was a true account. Its theological function was to support the hope that the God of Israel could restore the exiles to their land. The razing of Jerusalem and the temple, along with the Israelites' exile in Babylon, was a national and religious crisis. Yahweh appeared impo-

50. Bernhard W. Anderson, *Understanding the Old Testament,* 3rd ed. (Englewood Cliffs, NJ: Prentice-Hall, 1975), p. 451. Elke Toenges similarly points out that Scripture has an inner coherence between creation and redemption. The final vision of salvation in Revelation 21 indicates that "the eschatological theology of creation . . . is intended to demonstrate the inner connection between creation and salvation, redemption as perfection of the creation" ("'See, I Am Making All Things New': New Creation in the Book of Revelation," in Reventlow and Hoffman, eds., *Creation in Jewish and Christian Tradition,* p. 139).

51. Walter Brueggemann, *Theology of the Old Testament: Testimony, Dispute, Advocacy* (Minneapolis: Fortress, 1997), pp. 153-54; Winfried Thiel, "God as the Creator and Lord of Nature in the Deuteronomistic Literature," in Reventlow and Hoffman, eds., *Creation in Jewish and Christian Tradition,* pp. 54-71 (esp. pp. 54-55).

tent before the might of Babylon's pantheon of gods, as did his people before the Babylonian military juggernaut.[52]

Speaking to their hopeless situation, Genesis 1 portrays the God of Israel as the supreme master of creation, the one who brings forth the world with no need for — or even the company of — other gods.[53] Contrary to alternative Ancient Near Eastern creation stories, Yahweh does not brawl with other gods in the beginning, but is there alone as the one true God.[54] Isaiah shows the theological significance of the creation stories when he promises: "He who created the heavens and stretched them out, who spread out the earth and all that comes out of it . . . I, the Lord, have called you in righteousness; I will take hold of your hand . . . to free the captives from prison and release from the dungeon those who sit in darkness" (Isa. 42:5-7). The theological logic is that, since Yahweh created the heavens and the earth and the people of Israel, Yahweh can redeem them from their exile.[55] In addition, Isaiah 32:15 supports the connection of the Spirit of God with creative activity. In this text, the Spirit poured out from on high transforms the "desert" into a "fertile field" and also empowers the people to live in justice and righteousness. The Spirit's restoration of the people and the land are inseparable, which suggests the synthesis of the Spirit's creative and redemptive work.

Genesis 1:2 reveals the Spirit's liminal character in creation-redemption. The structure of Genesis 1:2 looks like this:

> "Now the earth was formless and empty . . .
> Darkness was over the surface of the deep . . .
> *and* the Spirit of God was hovering over the waters."

52. Brueggemann, *Theology of the Old Testament*, pp. 149-51.

53. John Goldingay, *Old Testament Theology*, vol. 1: *Israel's Gospel* (Downers Grove, IL: InterVarsity, 2003), p. 44.

54. Interestingly, Job 24:12-13 also incorporates pneumatological imagery and elements of Ancient Near Eastern cosmological beginnings. The use of *ruach*/breath in the passage correlates with the *ruach's* activity at creation and the receding waters of the flood: that is, *ruach* brings order to chaos.

55. Brevard S. Childs notes the connection between Yahweh in Isaiah 42 and the "creator God" in Genesis 1; see *Isaiah*, Old Testament Library (Louisville: Westminster John Knox, 2001), p. 326. The development of biblical pneumatology in the context of exile has a possible point of correspondence with the experience of many early Pentecostals in North America and of many around the world today. The early Pentecostals — and even many contemporary ones — are "exiled" people; they do not operate in the centers of cultural and ecclesiastical power, but on the political, social, economic, and religious margins.

A key interpretive question is whether the third nominal clause — "*and* the Spirit of God was hovering over the waters" — continues to modify the formless and empty space of the first part of the verse or contrasts with them and issues in the creative presence of God, which complements 1:3: "And God said, 'Let there be light.'" According to Wilf Hildebrandt, the *waw* ("and") introducing the third clause is adversative; that is, it separates the third clause from the preceding two in a contrasting way.[56] Understood in this way, the Spirit of God hovering over the waters diverges with the disorder of "formless and empty" and "darkness . . . over the surface of the deep." Thomas L. Brodie submits that the "striking picture — God's spirit amid the darkness — is like an intimation, a nucleus, of the vast drama that is about to unfold."[57] The hovering Spirit of God sets the stage for and initiates the creation process.[58] Genesis 1:2b is a pneumatological transition from cosmic chaos to God's creation. The Spirit of God is the pneumatological threshold across which primordial pandemonium gives way to a pastoral creation.[59]

56. Hildebrandt, *An Old Testament Theology of the Spirit of God*, pp. 32-35. For similar interpretations, see also Tuvia Freedman, "רוח אלחים — and a Wind from God, Genesis 1:2" (trans. Aviva Wolfers-Barazani), *Jewish Bible Quarterly* 24 (1996): 9-13; John H. Sailhamer, *The Pentateuch as Narrative: A Biblical-Theological Commentary* (Grand Rapids: Zondervan, 1992), pp. 32, 87.

57. Thomas L. Brodie, *Genesis as Dialogue: A Literary, Historical, and Theological Commentary* (New York: Oxford University Press, 2001), p. 133.

58. Pentecostal biblical scholar Scott A. Ellington argues that Genesis 1:2 does not entail a notion of the Spirit of creation, but says rather that one should look to later biblical writings that associate God's "spirit" with God's "face" (e.g., Ps. 104) for a developed theology of the Spirit of creation. See Ellington, "The Face of God as His Creating Spirit: The Interplay of Yahweh's *panim* and *ruach* in Psalm 104:29-30," in Yong, ed., *The Spirit Renews the Face of the Earth*, pp. 3-16 (esp. pp. 7, 13-16).

59. For an interpretation of Genesis 1:2 as the Spirit's superintendence of Big-Bang cosmology, planetary formation, and biological evolution, see Paul Elbert, "Genesis 1 and the Spirit: A Narrative-Rhetorical Ancient Near Eastern Reading in Light of Modern Science," *Journal of Pentecostal Theology* 15 (2006): 23-72. Amos Yong interprets Genesis 1 in terms of a canonical-pneumatological approach and brings the Spirit's role in the creation narrative into dialogue with Philip Clayton's theory of emergence; see Yong, "*Ruach*, the Primordial Chaos, and the Breath of Life: Emergence Theory and the Creation Narratives in Pneumatological Perspective," in Welker, ed., *The Work of the Spirit*, pp. 183-204. Yong finds Elbert's prophetic reading of Genesis 1 (according to which it presages the discoveries of modern science) problematic because it misses the point of the creation stories. They invite the reader to live in harmony with God and creation and not detail a scientific report of cosmic origins. See Amos Yong, "Reading Scripture and Nature: Pentecostal Hermeneutics and Their Implications for the Contemporary Evangelical Theology and Science Conversation," *Perspectives on Science and Christian Faith* 63 (2011): 3-15 (esp. pp. 7-8).

The work of the Spirit of God in Genesis 1:2 establishes the fundamental nature of the Spirit's work throughout Scripture with regard to both creation and redemption. The Spirit's work in creation suggests that the Spirit of God is a liminal agent — liminal because, through the activity of the Spirit, creation crosses over from darkness and chaos to light and ordered life. In this light, Karl Barth's understanding of the Spirit's role in creation is unsatisfactory. Barth maintains that the "'Spirit of God' who . . . hovers or broods over [the nothingness of Genesis 1:2a] — a divine power which is not that of the creative Word — cannot make good this lack but can only reveal it more sharply . . . 'the Spirit of *Elohim*' who is not known in his reality therefore hovers and broods over it impotently because wordlessly."[60] Even if we grant the necessity of the Spirit and the Word working in tandem to bring forth creation, we also need to recognize that, if the Spirit is impotent without the Word, then so is the Word without the Spirit. Without breath, a word cannot be spoken. In the narrative structure of creation, the Spirit hovering over the waters is the liminal stage between lifeless cosmic tumult and the days of creation that bring forth a creation bursting with life. Thus the Spirit is the Spirit of creation because the Spirit is the divine agent of creation. The Spirit leads the primordial elements from chaos to ordered cosmos.

Talking about the Spirit as the agent of liminal transformation from primordial bedlam to a fertile earth raises questions of philosophical theology. For instance, since Genesis 1 begins with a world in cosmic anarchy, does that mean that the world existed originally in a fallen state or that it deteriorated from a previous pristine condition? These kinds of questions are appropriate, but simply not the concern of the Genesis creation story. The Genesis story speaks to the principal problem on the minds of the people of Israel: How do we get out of Babylon and go back home? The answer of Genesis is that since Yahweh — not one of the gods of Babylon — freed the world from the primordial abyss, Yahweh can deliver Israel from Babylon. Genesis 1 speaks in terms of the religious and cosmological assumptions of the Ancient Near East. The story begins with darkness and cosmic morass and then moves toward a world in which life can flourish.

60. Karl Barth, *Church Dogmatics,* III/1, Part 2: *The Doctrine of Creation,* ed. G. W. Bromiley and T. F. Torrance (Edinburgh: T&T Clark, 1958), p. 108. Biblical scholars are just as prone to prefer Word/christological categories to the complementary pneumatological ones in the text. See, e.g., Bruce Waltke, who describes the Genesis 1 creation account in terms of "Creation by Word" (Waltke, *Genesis: A Commentary* [Grand Rapids: Zondervan, 2001], p. 69).

The movement is from a condition that is decidedly negative to one that is felicitous. When I refer to creation as a redemptive activity of the Spirit, my assertion must be understood in light of the imagery of Genesis 1. I do not dismiss the value of questions posed by philosophical theology with respect to cosmic origins. But, since Genesis 1 does not delve into such questions, neither will I. The theological point is that creation and redemption are not two divine programs. Genesis 1 does not present a picture of "creation" followed by "redemption." Genesis 1 portrays the Spirit's liminal activity in creation as a redemptive one. For this reason I refer to the Spirit's work as creative-redemptive.

Constitutional

Creation is a redemptive act of God, and the Spirit is its constitutive agent. The Spirit of God initiates the divine work that frees the primordial forces from darkness and formlessness. The Ancient Near Eastern myths of cosmic origins often portray the pre-creation state of things as churning waters welling up from an unfathomable abyss. The thrall of the antediluvian elements is the cosmological context for the Spirit's creative work, and within this worldview the process of creation is an act of deliverance. The creative process that begins with the Spirit of God hovering over the waters and proceeds through the six days of creation should be understood as a redemptive act of God and not purely as an act of "creation," because God delivers the primeval elements from the abyss and produces an earth that is harmonious and fruitful. Psalm 74 captures the redemptive nature of the Hebrew theology of creation, declaring:

> But you O God . . . bring salvation upon the earth. It was you who split open the sea by your power; you broke the head of the monster in the waters. . . . It was you who opened up springs and streams; you dried up the ever flowing rivers . . . you established the sun and moon. It was you who set all the boundaries of the earth. (Ps. 74:12-17)

Yahweh's creative work is understood as one that brings harmony, order, and life in place of the swirling and frightening waters of the deep. Creation, therefore, is the first act of divine deliverance and redemption, and it begins with the *ruach* of God. The Spirit's creative-redemptive work reveals the constitutive role of God's Spirit.

The redemptive nature of creation is the reason that similar pneumatological images found in Genesis 1 appear in other redemptive moments in the Pentateuch, such as the flood and Exodus stories. In Genesis 8:1-5, a *ruach* from God delivers Noah and the world from the floodwaters. The descriptions of the pre-creation abyss and the floodwaters that covered the earth are very similar. The flood effectively returns the earth to the murkiness of Genesis 1:2a.[61] The floodgates of the heavens and the earth spew forth, and the waters again flood the earth except for those stowed away in Noah's ark. In both stories dark and destructive waters engulf the earth; moreover, in both stories a *ruach* from God initiates the deliverance of the earth from its peril. Genesis 8:1 states: "But God remembered Noah and all the wild animals and the livestock that were with him in the ark, and he sent a wind *(ruach)* over the earth and the waters receded." The *ruach* from God closes the "springs of the deep and the floodgates of the heavens" (Gen. 8:2).

The two parallelisms of Genesis 1 and 8 with respect to the state of the earth and the activity of the *ruach* suggest the constitutive character of the *ruach* of God. First, the floodwaters signify chaos, like the darkness over the deep in the creation story. Second, the role of wind/*ruach* sent by God to deliver the ark and the world from its watery abyss cohere. In both stories, the *ruach* of God and the *ruach* sent by God are divine agents of redemption. Therefore, the movement of God's Spirit initiates creation — that is, deliverance from chaos — and the *ruach* of God is what frees the earth from the desolation of the floodwaters. The ascription of "Spirit" of God in Genesis 1 seems clearer than in Genesis 8. In Genesis 8, *ruach* is more literally "wind," but a wind sent by God. The Exodus story provides a textual and theological rationale for seeing the wind that blows the floodwaters from the land as the personal agency of God's Spirit (as well as the sacral understanding of the world developed earlier in the chapter).

Exodus 14:1–15:21 contains a narrative (Exod. 14:10-31) and a poetic account (Exod. 15:1-18) of the liberation epic of the people of Israel: the escape from the threat of annihilation by Pharaoh's oncoming army through the Sea of Reeds. In both descriptions of the event, the divine agency that causes the water to pile up and to provide safe passage for the Israelites, and to come crashing down to destroy the Egyptian forces, is the *ruach* of God. In the prose account, "the Lord drove the sea back with a strong east

61. Walther Eichrodt, *Theology of the Old Testament,* 2 vols. (Philadelphia: Westminster, 1961-67), 2: 93-94.

wind and turned it into dry land" (Exod. 14:21). The poem (the Song of Moses) intensifies the personal connection of the wind that drives back the water of the sea. Exodus 15:8 and 10 declare: "[B]y the blast of your nostrils the waters piled . . . you blew with your breath and the sea covered them." The song attributes both the act of restraining the waters for the Israelites (deliverance) and of swamping Pharaoh's army (judgment) to the *ruach*/ Spirit of God.[62] Taken together, the texts interpret the physical phenomenon that caused the sea to recede for the Israelites and cascade over the Egyptians as the direct intervention of Israel's God — and describe that activity in pneumatological terms.

Isaiah makes the connection between the divine agency in the redemption through the sea with the Spirit of God even more telling: "Then his people recalled the days of old, the days of Moses and his people, saying: 'Where is he who brought them through the sea, with the shepherd of his flock? Where is he who set his Holy Spirit among them, who sent his glorious power to be at Moses' right hand, who divided the waters before them . . . who led them through the depths?' [T]hey were given rest by the Spirit of the Lord" (Isa. 63:11-14). Walther Eichrodt sees that passage as an "enlarged and deepened" understanding of the Spirit of God as "the medium through which God's presence in the midst of his people becomes a reality, and in which all the divine gifts and powers which work within that people are combined."[63] Deuteronomy 32:10 correlates the theophanic glory of the Exodus with the hovering Spirit of God in Genesis 1:2. The creation and Exodus stories also possess parallel images. The light that shines in the primordial darkness, the division of the waters, and the appearance of the dry land compares with the glory of the Lord that guides the Israelites through the darkness and the receding waters and that opens up the dry seabed for the Israelites.[64]

In other words, in the theological tradition of Israel, pneumatology developed and became an important category for understanding the presence and redemptive work of God in the history of Israel. Moreover, the redemp-

62. Al Wolters argues that Exodus 15:8 does not refer to the deliverance of the Israelites, but that Exodus 15:8 and 10 both refer to the flood of water that destroyed the Egyptian forces. Although I agree with Wolters that the song primarily showcases the destruction of Pharaoh and his army, Exodus 15:8 and 10 appear to connect the two aspects — deliverance and judgment — of the one event. See Wolters, "Not Rescue but Destruction: Rereading Exodus 15:8," *Catholic Biblical Quarterly* 52 (1990): 223-40.

63. Eichrodt, *Theology of the Old Testament,* 2: 60-61.

64. Meredith G. Kline, *Images of the Spirit* (Grand Rapids: Baker, 1980), pp. 14-15.

tive work of the Spirit has strong associations with the Spirit's work in creation, and the Spirit's creative work corresponds to the Spirit's formation of the people of Israel. Thus the Spirit emerges as the vital agent of God's creative-redemptive work, which points to the Spirit's constitutive character.

Eschatological

"Eschatological" does not mean end-time cataclysm, as it often does in evangelical and Pentecostal theology. Though eschatology entails a future element, it primarily deals with the fulfillment of God's designs for the world. The eschatological character of the Spirit refers to the Spirit's crucial role in consummating God's plan for creation. Passages from Joel, Isaiah, and Ezekiel highlight the eschatological character of the Spirit.

Joel 2:28-32 is a classic Pentecostal passage. Pentecostals quote this, along with Acts 2:1-4, to support their experience of Spirit baptism and self-understanding of being an end-time movement of the Spirit. Frank Macchia observes that in recent years eschatology has gained favor among Pentecostals (e.g., William Faupel and Steven Land) as an overarching category for defining the essence of Pentecostalism. From this perspective, Spirit baptism and the Pentecostal revivals are indicators of the coming kingdom of God. Macchia, however, argues that this view is upside down: it subsumes Spirit baptism under eschatology. "[E]schatology is an aspect of Spirit baptism — and not the other way around," he says.[65] I agree with Macchia, because the alternative confuses cause and effect. In Joel, the Spirit of God is the agent of eschatological renewal. The charismatic manifestations in the people and the "wonders in the heavens" are the result of the Spirit's activities. Moreover, the Spirit is the primary content of the eschatological promise of Joel. The prophet encourages the people of Israel to look toward the outpouring of God's Spirit that will bring a "fullness . . . and democratization of the Spirit."[66] Moreover, according to Peter, the pouring out of the Spirit of Pentecost is unambiguously eschatological: "'In the last days,' God says, 'I will pour out my Spirit on all people'" (Acts 2:17). Finally, the Spirit in Joel 2 is eschatological because the pouring out

65. Frank D. Macchia, *Justified in the Spirit: Creation, Redemption, and the Triune God*, Pentecostal Manifestos, James K. A. Smith and Amos Yong, gen. eds. (Grand Rapids: Eerdmans, 2010), p. 94.

66. Douglas Stuart, *Hosea-Jonah*, Word Biblical Commentary (Waco, TX: Word, 1987), p. 260.

of the Spirit completes the restoration of the people of Israel. The Spirit of God fulfills God's redemptive program.

Isaiah has additional links between Yahweh's creative and redemptive activity.[67] Isaiah 51:9-11 draws on Yahweh's creative activity and redemptive work in the Exodus from Egypt to offer the exiles hope of a new exodus and restoration to Jerusalem. What is significant is that the work of creation is redemptive and eschatological. Reflecting the Babylonian creation accounts, Yahweh cuts "Rahab to pieces" and pierces the "monster through" (Isa. 51:9). Furthermore, Yahweh, who saved the world from the "mythical dragons of chaos," is the one who "dried up the sea, the waters of the great deep, who made a road in the depths of the sea so that the redeemed might cross over" (Isa. 51:10).[68] Isaiah concludes this summary of redemptive history with the promise that "the ransomed of the Lord will return. They will enter Zion with singing; everlasting joy will crown their heads" (Isa. 51:11). Thus does Isaiah provide the textual and theological basis to tie together the creative and redemptive activity of God and to associate that activity with the Spirit of God: the redemption from primeval chaos is a creative action; exodus as redemption from the threat of military annihilation by the same God who tamed the primeval waters leads to the creation of the people of Israel, to a new exodus as the return from exile in Babylon, and to restoration of the land, or a re-creation of the people of Israel. The Spirit thus operates as an eschatological agent. The Spirit liberates creation and the people of God from doom and achieves God's intended life for them.

Ezekiel also draws on pneumatological creation images to develop the promise of Israel's restoration from exile. Ezekiel's eschatological view of the Spirit's work in redeeming Israel from exile also coheres with the liminal and constituting nature of the Spirit's work in creation. Ezekiel promises that Yahweh will put the Spirit of God in them and that the Spirit will restore the people of Israel to their homeland. Ezekiel uses the vivid imagery of the Spirit of God revivifying a valley of dry bones to portray the restoration of Israel to her homeland (Ezek. 36–37). His use of pneumatological images to describe Yahweh's fulfillment of the promise to restore the people of Israel coheres with Genesis 1:2.[69] The Spirit of God, whom Ezekiel sees as the divine power who emancipates the people of Is-

67. Anderson, *Understanding the Old Testament,* pp. 449-50.

68. John D. W. Watts, *Isaiah 34–66,* Word Biblical Commentary (Waco, TX: Word, 1987), p. 211.

69. James Robson, *Word and Spirit in Ezekiel,* Library of Hebrew Bible/Old Testament Studies, 447 (New York: T&T Clark, 2006), p. 269.

rael from their desolation in captivity and returns them to Jerusalem as the faithful covenant people of God, is the same Spirit who restrained the primordial chaos and ushered in the creative process that concludes with a planet teeming with life.[70]

Just as the Spirit moved over the antediluvian mayhem of Genesis 1:2 and brought forth a lush creation, so will the Spirit of God breathe new life into the dead bones of exiled Israel in Ezekiel 37:1-14. Redemption is thus creation. The dry bones infused with new life by the Spirit of God is also a clear parallel to Genesis 2:7, where God breathes life into the lifeless dirt, and the dirt becomes a living human being through the breath of God,[71] The creation narrative of Genesis 1 and Isaiah's and Ezekiel's promises of restoration to and revitalization in the land of Israel portray the Spirit as the agency of God that facilitates the transition from disrepair and despair to life and flourishing.[72] Ezekiel and Isaiah draw on the creation narratives and images to buttress faith in God's power to redeem the people of Israel. In other words, the creation story supports soteriology.[73] On the human and cosmic level, creation and redemption are thus intrinsically related through the Spirit, who gives life to and renews the life of both of them.[74]

To summarize this point: first, in both the creation of the world and the redemption of the people of Israel from exile and their reestablishment in the land of Israel, the Spirit is the liminal agent who facilitates the transition from chaos to the realization of God's purposes — from cosmic

70. Bruce Vawter and Leslie J. Hoppe, *A New Heart: A Commentary on the Book of Ezekiel,* International Theological Commentary (Grand Rapids: Eerdmans, 1991), pp. 166-67.

71. R. Jerome Boone, "The Role of the Holy Spirit in the Construction of the Second Temple," in *The Spirit and the Mind: Essays in Informed Pentecostalism,* ed. Terry L. Cross and Emerson B. Powery (Lanham, MD: University Press of America, 2000), pp. 49-63 (esp. pp. 52-53); Paul M. Joyce, *Ezekiel: A Commentary,* Library of Hebrew Bible/Old Testament Studies, 482 (New York: T&T Clark, 2007), p. 209; Yates, *Spirit and Paul in Creation,* pp. 32-33.

72. George Montague does not think that the pneumatological themes in the Exodus and Genesis 1 stories are related; rather, he sees Genesis 1 connected with the exilic and postexilic pneumatology of Second Isaiah and Ezekiel (George T. Montague, "The Fire in the Word: The Holy Spirit in Scripture," in *Advents of the Spirit: An Introduction to the Current Study of Pneumatology,* ed. Bradford E. Hinze and D. Lyle Dabney [Milwaukee: Marquette University Press, 2001], pp. 35-65 [esp. p. 39]). Without disagreeing with the historical-critical connection of Genesis 1 with exilic and postexilic pneumatology, I would say that reading the texts canonically is also appropriate. When they are read canonically, a theological consistency with regard to the images and activity of the *ruach*/Spirit of God emerges. Hebrew Scripture describes God's redemptive presence in pneumatological categories.

73. Von Rad, *Genesis,* pp. 45-46.

74. Yates, *Spirit and Creation in Paul,* pp. 151-54.

chaos to creation and from exile to restoration. The Spirit inhabits the liminal space between chaos/exile and creation/redemption; and the Spirit enables creation and the people of Israel to cross the threshold from chaos and exile to creation and restoration. The Spirit also plays a central role in God's creative-redemptive work: the Spirit is not supplemental, but essential. Furthermore, the Spirit emerges as an eschatological agent. God's salvation finds fulfillment in the outpouring of the Spirit. Second, as I have observed above, continuity characterizes the work of the Spirit in creation and redemption. Creation itself is a form of redemption, and the Spirit's work of redemption parallels the Spirit's creative work. Creation and redemption, therefore, are not two programs, but one. God redeems creation, and pneumatology is a key category for that redemption.

With the continuity between the Spirit's work of creation and redemption established, the next step in the argument is to show that this continuity informs the identity and work of the Spirit — as Spirit of Christ and Spirit of Pentecost. That is, the Spirit's work as Spirit of creation and redemption has the Spirit's work as Spirit of Christ and Pentecost as its *telos.* Moreover, the identity of the Spirit emerging in these biblical narratives supports a pneumatological contribution to Trinitarian theology.

Spirit of Christ

What is the role of the Holy Spirit in the life of Jesus Christ? According to traditional theology, not much. Theologians usually treat Christology and pneumatology as separate theological categories. Beyond admitting that Luke 1:35 shows the Spirit creating Jesus' human nature, Christology is often pursued with little thought of the Spirit. However, a complete Christology must take into consideration the Spirit's work in the life of Jesus Christ. Moreover, the Holy Spirit's work in Christ shares continuity with the Spirit's creative-redemptive work in the Hebrew Scriptures. The Holy Spirit plays a liminal, constitutional, and eschatological role in the life and ministry of Jesus Christ.

Liminal

The Spirit is the liminal and constituting agent of the incarnation. The Spirit who precedes and initiates the redemption of the primordial chaos in the creation account of Genesis 1:2 is the same Spirit who precedes and instantiates the union of the humanity of Jesus and the Son in the incarnation. Furthermore, Genesis 2:7 describes God breathing the breath of life into the dirt and thereby creating living human persons. The creation story then portrays the purpose of the creative act. The text describes Adam and Eve living in sublime harmony with each other (i.e., the significance of their "nakedness"), creation, and their God, who comes walking to them in the garden during the cool of the day. God's Spirit breathes life into the dirt so that human beings can live in loving relationship with their creator and each other.

In Matthew 1:20, the angel of the Lord assures Joseph: "Do not be afraid to take Mary home as your wife, because what is conceived in her is from the Holy Spirit." And in Luke 1:35 the angel Gabriel comforts Mary with these words: "The Holy Spirit will come upon you, and the power of the Most High will overshadow you. So the holy one to be born will be called the Son of God." The Spirit's work is the threshold of the union of the humanity of Jesus with the eternal Son of God. The Holy Spirit facilitates the incarnation of the Son of God and achieves the Spirit's original purpose of animating the dirt (i.e., the creation of the human beings in Genesis 2:7). Matthew and Luke present the Spirit as the liminal agent of the incarnation, because, just as the Spirit of God led the primordial elements from darkness through the dawn of creation, the dirt across the threshold to living creature, so the Spirit is the divine agent that precedes and facilitates the incarnation. Colin Gunton emphasizes that the Spirit creates the humanity of Jesus for its union with the divine Son.[75] Though I agree with Gunton on that point, the role of the Spirit in the incarnation extends beyond the creation of Jesus' human nature. The Spirit is the primordial agent who makes a barren womb the bosom of the incarnate Son. Matthew and Luke show that what transpires between John 1:1 and John 1:14 (Logos Christology) occurs through the agency of the Holy Spirit (Spirit Christology). The Spirit not only creates but also brings the humanity of Jesus into union with the eternal Son of God.

The work of the Spirit in Jesus retains its liminal character throughout his life. At his baptism, the Spirit comes upon Jesus and ushers him into his messianic ministry (Matt. 3:3-17; Mark 1:9-11; Luke 3:21-22; John 1:29-34). The descent of the Spirit at his baptism should not be understood as a new reception of the Spirit in the sense that the Spirit was not previously pres-

75. Gunton, "The Spirit Moved Over the Face of the Waters," p. 197.

ent with Jesus. Rather, the descent of the Spirit is a public manifestation of his messianic identity. The event was public in two senses. First, it undoubtedly confirmed Jesus' sense of a unique relationship with and mission from God; thus, as a public event, it helped Jesus embrace his identity and calling. Second, it was a public announcement to all who witnessed the event and would later testify about him, especially John the Baptist (John 1:35-36). The Spirit also leads Jesus into the wilderness and empowers him to forswear Satan's temptations, which verifies his messianic identity (Matt. 4:1-11; Mark 1:12-13; Luke 4:1-14). In Luke 4:14-30, the Spirit solidifies this identity. On the Sabbath, in a synagogue in Nazareth, the Spirit leads Jesus to identify himself as the Spirit-anointed messiah by reading Isaiah 61:1-2. Therefore, the Holy Spirit is a principal factor in the key threshold moments of Jesus' life. The Spirit operates in the pivotal events of Jesus' evolving messianic consciousness and ministry.

Constitutional

The Spirit also has a constitutional role in Christology. "Constitutional" means taking part in making something what it is. Traditional theology reduces the Spirit to an instrument of distributing the blessings of Christ, but does not give the Spirit a role in the incarnation as such. In contrast, to say that the Spirit is constitutive of Christ means that the Spirit plays a vital function throughout the life of Christ. Unfortunately, traditional theology habituates us to think of Christ as constituting the ministry of the Spirit. Gordon Fee exemplifies this outlook when he insists that "Christ gives definition to the Spirit" and then endorses Christocentrism.[76] In one sense, this mindset is correct. Christ does define the Holy Spirit. But it is one-sided: it does not acknowledge the Spirit's contribution to Christology. To address this issue, I turn to the notion of "the Spirit of Christ."

Thinking about the Holy Spirit as "the Spirit of Christ" is common. In fact, it is so pervasive that one would expect to find a prolific use of the term throughout the New Testament. But, in fact, it appears only twice: in Romans 8:9 and 1 Peter 1:11. Christocentrism is so embedded in our minds that we naturally assume that Christ defines the Spirit's work and thus we do not pause to reflect on whether the relationship is reciprocal. I suggest

76. Gordon D. Fee, *God's Empowering Presence: The Holy Spirit in the Letters of Paul* (Peabody, MA: Hendrickson, 1994), p. 837.

that it is. "The Spirit of Christ" has a christological and a pneumatological meaning, and only when they are both taken together do they yield a biblical Christology. I propose that we think of the "of" in "Spirit of Christ" in two ways: "of" can mean from, but it can also carry the connotation of "the source or starting point of action" and "indicating the creator of a work" *(Oxford English Dictionary)*. From the first meaning arises the popular way of thinking about the Spirit of Christ; the second meaning provides a more pneumatological perspective.

First, the most familiar usage is to refer to the Spirit as "Spirit of Christ" in the sense that the risen Christ pours out or sends the Holy Spirit on the Day of Pentecost. In this respect, the Spirit is *of* Christ because the Spirit is *from* Christ and enacts in the believer the redemptive work that occurred in Christ. Acts 2:33 supports this imagery when it portrays the risen Christ receiving the "promise of the Father" (see Luke 11:13; 24:49; Acts 1:4) and then giving the Spirit at Pentecost. "If anyone does not have the Spirit of Christ, he does not belong to Christ" (Romans 8:9) suggests that the indwelling Spirit mediates the presence of the risen Christ: to have the Spirit is to have Christ.[77] However, even in Romans 8:9, the meaning of "Spirit of Christ" is not entirely determined by Christology. The new life effected by the Spirit — as the Spirit of Christ — is the life the Spirit brought throughout the life of Jesus Christ.

This first way of thinking about the Spirit as "the Spirit of Christ" also reflects the influence of the Gospel of John and the Logos Christology that derives from it. John portrays the Father sending the Son, and the Father and the Son sending the Holy Spirit. Reading that back into the immanent Trinity, Western theology interpreted that as the Holy Spirit originating or proceeding from the Father and the Son (e.g., the *filioque*). The Orthodox tradition is similar, except that it rejects the *filioque.* But with respect to processions establishing divine personal identity, the Eastern tradition is in agreement with the West because the Holy Spirit is from the Father and in some expressions through the Son. Furthermore, the influence of the Gospel of John and the traditional tendency to derive the identities of the divine persons from the processions has meant that Trinitarian theology has relied on christological data: that is, the relationship between the Father and the Son has provided the primary content for Trinitarian theol-

77. Fatehi, *The Spirit's Relation to the Risen Lord in Paul,* pp. 206-15; see also Robert Jewett, *Romans: A Commentary,* Hermeneia: A Critical and Historical Commentary on the Bible (Minneapolis: Fortress, 2007), pp. 490-91.

ogy in general and the identity of the Spirit in particular. For instance, Wolfhart Pannenberg assumes Christocentrism when he says that the "differentiation of Father and Son is grounded in one and the same event, in the message of Jesus concerning God and his coming kingdom. What is said about the Holy Spirit also relates to this event."[78] The content of pneumatology, therefore, is a byproduct of Christology.

The second meaning of "of" also applies to the Spirit of Christ. Moreover, though often overlooked, it expresses the fundamental nature of the Spirit's work in Christ. It also carries forward the nature of the Spirit's liminal and constituting work in creation-redemption. Moreover, this second sense of "of" reveals an important facet of the Spirit's identity in the Trinity. "Of" in this second sense refers to the source of something. For example, the description of the Spirit as the Spirit of creation means that the Spirit is the source and author of creation. In a similar way, the Spirit can be understood as the source of the incarnation of Jesus Christ. Not that the Spirit creates the eternal Son of God; but the Spirit facilitates his incarnation. The Spirit of Christ in this sense means that the Spirit is the divine person who unites the humanity of Jesus Christ with the eternal Son of God (Luke 1:35 and Matt. 1:18-21). The technical term for this understanding of the incarnation is "Spirit Christology." The theological insight of Spirit Christology is that the Spirit plays a constitutional role in the incarnation.[79] The incarnation — the union of the humanity of Jesus with the eternal Son of God — was as much an event of the Holy Spirit as of the Son. The Son becomes incarnate, but the Spirit is the catalyst of the hypostatic union.[80] Moreover, as James D. G. Dunn points out, the Holy Spirit, as the Spirit of Christ, is "that power which determined Christ in his ministry and in so doing provided a pattern of life in the Spirit."[81]

Christocentrism correctly emphasizes the importance of the revela-

78. Wolfhart Pannenberg, *Systematic Theology,* 3 vols., trans. Geoffrey W. Bromiley (Grand Rapids: Eerdmans, 1991), 1: 272.

79. For background on and approaches to contemporary Spirit Christology, see Ralph Del Colle, *Christ and the Spirit: Spirit-Christology in Trinitarian Perspective* (New York: Oxford University Press, 1994); see also Myk Habets, *The Anointed Son: A Trinitarian Spirit Christology,* Princeton Theological Monographs Series, 129 (Eugene, OR: Pickwick, 2010), pp. 188-227.

80. See Steven M. Studebaker, "Integrating Pneumatology and Christology: A Trinitarian Modification of Clark H. Pinnock's Spirit Christology," *Pneuma* 28 (2006): 5-20.

81. James D. G. Dunn, *Romans 1–8,* Word Biblical Commentary (Waco, TX: Word, 1988), p. 446.

tion of God in Jesus Christ, but neglects the significance of pneumatology for understanding the Trinitarian God. Wolfhart Pannenberg reflects this tendency when he maintains that "a systematic grounding and development of the doctrine of the Trinity must begin with the revelation of God in Jesus Christ" and, as I have mentioned above, that "[w]hat is said about the Holy Spirit also relates to this event."[82] However, relying exclusively on Christology misses the fact that the Spirit's work is constitutive of Christology. The conception narratives of Matthew and Luke, which portray the Holy Spirit as the active divine agent who instantiates the incarnation, as well as Paul's identification of the Holy Spirit as the agent of the resurrection in Romans, help fill this gap in traditional Trinitarian theology. Pneumatology conditions Christology. Consequently, theology can also start with pneumatology on its path to the Trinitarian God.

Though marginal to nonexistent in traditional Trinitarian theology, the Holy Spirit's work in Christ is fundamental for an understanding of the Spirit's identity. Moreover, the Spirit's work in the incarnation as "the Spirit of Christ" shares continuity with the Spirit's creative-redemptive work in the Old Testament. First, the work of the Spirit in the creation-redemption episodes discussed in the Old Testament provides a paradigm for the Spirit's work in the incarnation. The Spirit's work, which begins in Genesis 1:2 with the redemption of creation from chaos, which is carried on further in breathing life into the dirt in Genesis 2:7, and which revivifies the valley of dry bones in Ezekiel 37:1-14, finds its historical zenith in Christ and especially his resurrection by the Spirit (Rom. 8:11).[83] As Dunn remarks, "The double resurrection — initially of Christ, at the end, of believers — thus completing God's proper work as creator [and] this life-giving work of God is characteristically understood as wrought through his Spirit."[84] In other

82. Pannenberg, *Systematic Theology,* 1: 300, 272.

83. 1 Peter 1:11 expresses this sense of Spirit of Christ. It affirms that the Spirit's inspiration of the Old Testament prophets had Christ's work in mind. David M. Coffey argues that this passage indicates that Christ is the entelechy of the Spirit; Christ is an intrinsic orientation of the Spirit's work. For more on Coffey's theology of the entelechy of the Spirit, see my discussion in chapter 7 below, pp. 253ff., under the subheading "The Trinitarian Spirit of Creation." See also Coffey, "The Spirit of Christ as Entelechy," *Philosophy and Theology* 13 (2001): 363-98.

84. Dunn, *Romans 1–8,* p. 432. Though it should be noted that Dunn clarifies it by saying that Paul seems "to avoid attributing the resurrection of Jesus to the Spirit" (Dunn, *Romans 1–8,* p. 433). However, it makes little sense to suggest that the resurrection of Jesus was "through" the Spirit, but then to deny its attribution of the Spirit. Peter Stuhlmacher is clearer on this point: "After his passion and burial, God brought about, in fulfillment of his promise, the realization of the eschatological resurrection of the dead by the creative power

words, the union of creation with Creator attains its highest possible concrete manifestation and fulfillment in Jesus Christ. Although Christ is the definitive historical instance of the Spirit's work to bring creation into union with its Creator (i.e., he is the incarnation of the eternal Son of God), the work of the Spirit in Christ is in continuity with the preceding creative-redemptive work of the Spirit; indeed, the latter is the historical journey of the Spirit that culminates in the incarnation and the coming of the Spirit of Pentecost. The second sense of the Spirit of Christ thus means that Christ is of the Spirit. The work of the Spirit makes Christ the incarnate Son of God. Spirit Christology both safeguards the distinction of the divine persons and integrates their respective roles in the incarnation.

Eschatological

If the Spirit's work is the threshold in key transition points in Jesus' life and constitutes him as the Messiah, what about the resurrection of Christ? The New Testament writers believed that Christ was an eschatological figure. Hebrews 1:1-2 announces: "In the past God spoke to our forefathers through the prophets at many times and in various ways, but in these last days he has spoken to us by his Son" (see also Heb. 9:26 and 1 Pet. 1:20). But what is the Spirit's relationship to the eschatological Christ? The Spirit is there with Christ on the cross and raises him from the dead. D. Lyle Dabney proposes a *pneumatologia crucis*. He argues that the "Spirit of the Cross is the presence of God with the Son in the eschatological absence of the Father."[85] Though inspired by Dabney's work, my proposal looks to the Spirit's function in the resurrection of Christ. The Spirit who remains with Christ in the death and darkness of the cross is the Spirit who unleashes the power of new life in him and ushers him forth from the tomb. The Spirit's role in the resurrection further unveils the Spirit's liminal, constitutional, and especially eschatological character.

---

of the Holy Spirit." Stuhlmacher further declares: "The Spirit of God, who raised Jesus from the dead, fills the Christians [from Rome] with the certainty of faith . . . that God will also make alive their mortal bodies by the power of his Spirit and will cause them to partake of the same resurrection glory which has already been granted to the Christ of God in the present." See Peter Stuhlmacher, *Paul's Letter to the Romans: A Commentary,* trans. Scott J. Hafemann (Louisville: Westminster John Knox, 1994), pp. 19, 122.

85. D. Lyle Dabney, "*Pneumatologia Crucis:* Reclaiming *Theologia Crucis* for a Theology of the Spirit Today," *Scottish Journal of Theology* 53 (2000): 511-24 (esp. p. 524).

Paul opens his letter to the Christians in Rome by defining Jesus Christ in terms of two of the messianic expectations of the Hebrew Scripture. Jesus was "as to his human nature a descendant of David, and through the Spirit of holiness was declared with power to be the Son of God by his resurrection from the dead" (Rom. 1:4). Though unknown whether Paul had it in mind, his affirmation correlates with the promises of Isaiah 11:1-2 that the future messiah will be a "shoot . . . from the stump of Jesse . . . [t]he Spirit of the Lord will rest on him." Paul also makes the Holy Spirit the agent of Jesus' resurrection in Romans 8:11: "And if the Spirit of him who raised Jesus from the dead is living in you, he who raised Christ from the dead will also give life to your mortal bodies through his Spirit, who lives in you."[86] Paul also cites a hymn, or confessional piece, in 1 Timothy 3:16: "He appeared in a body, was vindicated by the Spirit." Here again, the Spirit is the agent of the resurrection.[87] John W. Yates argues that Ezekiel 36–37 (the new life from the Spirit and the animation of the dead bones) is the backdrop of Paul's resurrection theology.[88] Moreover, as in

86. For biblical scholars who interpret this passage as the Spirit raising Jesus from the dead, see Jewett, *Romans,* pp. 106-7, 492; Grant R. Osborne, *Romans,* IVP New Testament Commentary (Downers Grove, IL: InterVarsity, 2004), pp. 32, 201; Stuhlmacher, *Paul's Letter to the Romans,* p. 122.

87. Not all agree that the Spirit is the agent of Christ's resurrection. On the Spirit in Romans 8:11, Douglas Moo says that "[t]he reference, of course, is to God the Father . . . but the focus is on the Spirit." How the term "the Spirit" refers to the Father and focuses on the Spirit defies comprehension. See Douglas J. Moo, *The Epistle to the Romans,* New International Commentary on the New Testament (Grand Rapids: Eerdmans, 1996), p. 493. Fee also rejects the notion that the Holy Spirit is the agent of the resurrection. Rather, he argues: "For Paul the presence in our lives of the Spirit of the God who raises the dead does not imply agency, but rather expresses certainty about our future, predicated on the Risen Christ and by the already present Spirit: that, after all, is quite the point of the repeated 'who dwells in you.'" The Spirit certainly assures believers about their future resurrection, but precisely because the Spirit also raised Christ from the dead. I wonder if a lingering Christocentrism lurks behind Fee's exegesis. Does he fear that if the Spirit is an agent in the life of Christ and not merely "effects" Christ's work, it will subvert Christology? See Fee, *God's Empowering Presence,* pp. 553, 484.

Fee argues that through the resurrection Jesus entered the "spiritual/supernatural realm, the realm of the Spirit." Moreover, he recognizes that, while "in the flesh," Jesus "ministered in the power of the Spirit." I find it bewildering that Fee can argue that the Spirit empowered Jesus' life while in the flesh and that, "vindicated by the Spirit," Jesus is ushered into the resurrected "spiritual realm" of the Spirit, but that the Spirit had no role in the resurrection. In other words, he recognizes the agency of the Spirit during Jesus' time in the flesh, but not so for the resurrection. See Fee, *God's Empowering Presence,* p. 766.

88. Yates, *The Spirit and Creation in Paul,* pp. 143-51.

Ezekiel, Paul sees the Spirit as the principal agent of resurrected life. Ezekiel's vision of God's *ruach* breathing new life into the desiccated bones resounds with Genesis 2:7. Paul presents a similar connection between the resurrected life of the Spirit and creation. The Spirit raises Christ and believers, and "liberates creation from its bondage to decay" in Romans 8:21.

Romans reveals that the Spirit's role in the resurrection of Christ resonates with the Spirit's eschatological work throughout the history of biblical redemption. When Jesus was moldering in the tomb, the Spirit breathed new life into him and raised him from the dead. The Spirit functions in the liminal space between decay and renewal. Through the Spirit, Christ crosses the threshold from death to life. Moreover, Dunn notes, "for Paul the resurrection marked a decisive stage in Christ's divine Sonship — not as marking its beginning . . . but certainly as marking a significant 'heightening' or enlarging of its scope."[89] The existential nature of the evolution of Jesus' consciousness of divine Sonship follows from the theology of the incarnation: Jesus Christ was the incarnation of the eternal Son, but his awareness of that reality emerged in the concrete experiences of his life. Moreover, the Holy Spirit led him across the key thresholds of his messianic consciousness and ministry.

The Spirit's role in the resurrection is eschatological. If Jesus were to be left in the tomb, his ministry would remain unrealized. Jesus can rise from the dead, return to the Father, and pour out the Spirit only after the Spirit renews his life. Without the Spirit, there is no salvation in Christ. Since the resurrection "declares" that Jesus is the Son of God (Rom. 1:4), the activity of the Spirit completes Christ's work. Moreover, the Spirit's work in Jesus Christ reaches its fullness when the Spirit raises him from the dead. Finally, the Spirit also plays a part in constituting Christ's work: the resurrection is the capstone of Christ's work, and the eschatological activity of the Spirit sets it in place.

First Peter 3:18 also affirms the Spirit's agency in the resurrection of Jesus Christ: "He was put to death in the body but made alive by the Spirit." This further establishes the Spirit's eschatological character (see also 1 Tim. 3:16). Verses 19-20 — "through whom also he went and preached to the spirits in prison who disobeyed long ago when God waited patiently in the days of Noah" — are difficult, but unrelated to the case made here. The ba-

89. Dunn, *Romans 1–8*, p. 23. Osborne also sees the Holy Spirit's resurrection of Christ as "the turning point from the earthly messianic ministry of Jesus to the eschatological lordship of Jesus as the Son of God" (Osborne, *Romans*, p. 32).

sic point of the text is the affirmation of the early Christian faith that Christ was crucified and raised from the dead. Christ died on the cross ("put to death in the body"); the Spirit resurrected him. Subsequently, through the same Spirit, he "preached to the spirits in prison who disobeyed long ago when God waited patiently in the days of Noah while the ark was being built" (1 Pet. 3:19-20) — whoever and wherever they were.[90] Alone, the reference to "Spirit" does not directly refer to the Holy Spirit. Yet, taken with Romans' and 1 Timothy's clear identification of the Spirit as the agent of the resurrection, "Spirit" here can be understood as the Holy Spirit.[91] Also noteworthy is that the resurrection is key to salvation in Christ. Drawing an analogy between the water that carried Noah to safety and the faith that leads to the water of baptism, Peter clarifies that "[i]t saves you by the resurrection of Jesus Christ" (1 Pet. 3:21). Here is the eschatological role of the Spirit again. Not simply that the Spirit is at work in an eschatological — that is, "end-time" — event, but that the Spirit's activity is eschatological or consummational. The Spirit completes Christ's work by raising him from the dead. Without the Spirit, Christ's work remains incomplete.

Spirit of Pentecost

The outpouring of the Holy Spirit on the Day of Pentecost is an eschatological work of the Spirit. The Spirit's work that is the foundation of the creation of the cosmos, which breathes life into all living creatures and which brings forth the incarnation of the Son of God, attains its fullness in the outpouring of the Spirit of Pentecost: Spirit baptism. As an eschatological event, the outpouring of the Spirit of Pentecost is also a critical threshold in the history of redemption. As such, it comprehends the liminal and constitutive activity of the Spirit and the two senses of the Spirit as the Spirit of Christ: that is, Christ *sends* the Spirit, and the Spirit is the divine person who *establishes* the community of believers, the body of Christ. The follow-

90. For support for the above interpretation of 1 Peter 3:18, see Paul J. Achtemeier, *A Commentary on First Peter*, Hermeneia: A Critical and Historical Commentary (Minneapolis: Fortress, 1996), pp. 246-53; Karen H. Jones, *1 Peter*, Baker Exegetical Commentary on the New Testament (Grand Rapids: Baker Academic, 2005), pp. 237-42; J. N. D. Kelly, *A Commentary on the Epistles of Peter and Jude* (Grand Rapids: Baker, 1977), pp. 150-53.

91. J. Ramsey Michaels, *1 Peter*, Word Biblical Commentary (Waco, TX: Word, 1988), pp. 204-5.

ing discussion illustrates that the Spirit of Pentecost fulfills the liminal, constitutional, and eschatological character of the Spirit's creative-redemptive work.

Liminal

The outpouring of the Spirit on the Day of Pentecost is an eschatological event.[92] The outpouring of the Spirit as the Spirit of Christ draws the disciples into union with the risen Christ. Pentecost is not primarily about the disciples' charismatic experience in the upper room, but a climactic point in redemptive history, and in this sense it is liminal and eschatological. Calling Pentecost an eschatological event does not mean that salvation history comes to an abrupt end in Acts 2.[93] What it means is that at Pentecost salvation history crosses a critical threshold no less than at the moment of the incarnation, the cross, and the resurrection of Jesus Christ.

92. On the basis of Pauline literature and Jürgen Moltmann's theology, T. David Beck develops a pneumatological eschatology around six ideas: inauguration, eschatological tension, universality, historical character, advent, and *novum* (*The Holy Spirit and the Renewal of All Things: Pneumatology in Paul and Jürgen Moltmann,* Princeton Theological Monograph Series, 67 [Eugene, OR: Pickwick, 2007], p. 234).

93. My description of Pentecost as an eschatological event is distinct from the characterization of the Pentecostal movement in terms of an eschatological harbinger of the Second Coming of Christ within a broader premillennial eschatological framework. For example, D. William Faupel presents a case for Pentecostalism as primarily an eschatological or end-time mission movement with Spirit baptism and charismatic manifestations serving as its principal signs (David W. Faupel, *The Everlasting Gospel: The Significance of Eschatology in the Development of Pentecostal Thought,* Journal of Pentecostal Theology Supplement Series, 10 [Sheffield, UK: Sheffield Academic Press, 1996]); and, more recently, Allan Anderson and Wonsuk Ma emphasize Pentecostal eschatological identity as a key motivating factor of Pentecostal missions (Anderson, *Spreading Fires: The Missionary Nature of Early Pentecostalism* [Maryknoll, NY: Orbis, 2007], pp. 219-23; Ma, "'When the Poor Are Fired Up': The Role of Pneumatology in Pentecostal/Charismatic Mission," in *The Spirit in the World: Emerging Pentecostal Theologies in Global Contexts,* ed. Veli-Matti Kärkkäinen [Grand Rapids: Eerdmans, 2009], pp. 43-44). I agree with Amos Yong that Pentecostals should understand their eschatological identity not as a halfway house between the previous history of the church and the second coming of Christ, but as the possibility that the present dimensions of life can participate in the grace of the Spirit of Pentecost. See Yong, *In the Days of Caesar: Pentecostalism and Political Theology,* Cadbury Lectures 2009, Sacra Doctrina: Christian Theology for a Postmodern Age, Alan G. Padgett, gen. ed. (Grand Rapids: Eerdmans, 2010), pp. 331-32. Frank D. Macchia also understands Spirit baptism as an eschatological event, one complete only "when God inhabits all things" (Macchia, *Justified in the Spirit,* p. 97).

The work of the Spirit in creation and in the incarnate Christ achieves its fullest historical expression as the Spirit of Pentecost. The redemptive event that occurs through the particular and historical mediation of the person of Christ becomes universally available through the Spirit of Pentecost as the Spirit of Christ. The eschatological and culminating nature of the Spirit's work questions Alan Coppedge's statement that "[a]ll that God reveals through the history of Israel finds its culmination in the person of Jesus."[94] The outpouring of the Spirit is not only a revelation and work of Jesus Christ, but one of the Spirit as well. Moreover, it is not an addendum to the work of Christ, but the goal of Christ's work. The Spirit of Pentecost, therefore, fulfills the work of redemption, even though the historical actualization of that redemption remains penultimate until the coming of the everlasting kingdom.[95]

The eschatological nature of Pentecost is similar to that of the crucifixion. Jesus' cry "it is finished" is eschatological because it expresses the fact that on the cross he fulfilled humanity's devotion to the Father, even though that devotion is penultimate in historical terms, because the everlasting kingdom and the concrete realization of Jesus' devotion to God in the lives of believers remain in the future. Graham Ward uses the term "eschatological remainder" to describe the eschatological nature of Christian discipleship. The eschatological remainder means that the Christian participates in the future kingdom of God because that kingdom is operative in the present.[96] Although Ward primarily uses "the eschatological remainder" in terms of Christology, the notion has usefulness for understanding the liminal and eschatological nature of the Spirit of Pentecost. The Spirit of Pentecost is eschatological because, on the one hand, it culminates the previous creative-redemptive work of the Spirit; on the other hand, it has not ended, because the Spirit is still being poured out on all

94. Allan Coppedge, *The God Who Is Triune: Revisioning the Christian Doctrine of God* (Downers Grove, IL: InterVarsity Academic, 2007), p. 13.

95. Frank D. Macchia argues that Spirit baptism is eschatological in the sense that it proleptically provides the believer with an experience of the future kingdom of God (Macchia, *Baptized in the Spirit: A Global Pentecostal Theology* [Grand Rapids: Zondervan, 2006], pp. 42-49, 85-88). I agree with Macchia that Spirit baptism is a proleptic experience of the everlasting kingdom, but also affirm that it is eschatological in the sense that it consummates God's work of redemption.

96. Graham Ward, *The Politics of Discipleship: Becoming Postmaterial Citizens,* The Church and Postmodern Culture, James K. A. Smith, gen. ed. (Grand Rapids: Baker Academic, 2009), pp. 167-80.

people — hence, the eschatological and, I suggest, the *pneumatological* remainder. Therefore, although the Day of Pentecost achieved certain eschatological expectations, it also has a surplus of pneumatological potential. Pentecost remains a liminal reality. The outpouring of the Spirit continues evermore. The Christian life is an ongoing reception of the Spirit of Pentecost and journey into the horizon of the Spirit. As people of faith participate in the Spirit, they cross the threshold from death to life that will ultimately yield the everlasting kingdom of God.

Constitutional

The Spirit of Pentecost is a creative agent because the Spirit establishes the community of believers both on individual and corporate levels. With respect to the individual, the Spirit "creates" and actualizes redemption in the believer (John 3:1-8 and 7:37-39). Spirit baptism is a central biblical metaphor for describing the experience of participation in the Spirit of Pentecost that enables the human person to cross the threshold from being dead in sin to new life in Christ (Rom. 8:1-1). The New Testament imagery of the Holy Spirit as the one sent to bring new life in Christ connects with the Old Testament movement and work of the Spirit of God. For example, Psalm 104:27-30 affirms that, "when you send your Spirit, they are created, and you renew the face of the earth." The sending of the Spirit creates and renews. Similarly, the sending of the Spirit of Pentecost creates the community of faith (Acts 2) and renews the believer (John 3:3-8).

Spirit baptism can be understood as a comprehensive metaphor for participating in the Spirit of Pentecost. The biblical justification for seeing Spirit baptism as a comprehensive metaphor is its canonical position. Scripture frames Jesus' redemption in terms of Spirit baptism: John the Baptist promises, "He will baptize in the Holy Spirit" (Matt. 3:11; Mark 1:8; Luke 3:16; John 1:33), and Jesus promises the fulfillment of that promise on the Day of Pentecost: "Do not leave Jerusalem, but wait for the gift my Father promised. . . . For John baptized with water, but in a few days you will be baptized with the Holy Spirit" (Acts 1:4-5). On the Day of Pentecost, the Spirit also creates the body of Christ. As the Spirit was the divine presence that preceded and brought the humanity of Jesus into union with the divine Son, so the Spirit of Pentecost goes before and instantiates what Scripture refers to as the body of Christ. The body of Christ, in the ecclesiological sense, is not the physical human body of Jesus of Nazareth but the extended "body" of all those united to the risen Christ by the Spirit of Pentecost.

Eschatological

The Spirit of Pentecost completes the Spirit's creative-redemptive work in the drama of biblical redemption. It stands in continuity with and brings to full expression the liminal and constitutional nature of the Spirit's creative-redemptive work in two ways. First, the Spirit's work as Spirit of Pentecost is in continuity with the Spirit's activity in creation-redemption, and this is true not only with respect to the larger history of redemption, but also in the individual human. In the macro-plot of biblical redemption, the Spirit is the divine agent who empowers and fosters the transition from one existential plane to another: a transition from darkness to light, from a cosmic morass to a garden bursting with life, and, as the Spirit of Pentecost, the formation of the church of Jesus Christ. In the initial historical moment of the church of Jesus Christ, the outpouring of the Spirit enables the disciples to make the transition from being a scared band hiding in the upper room to a bold community that spreads the gospel in Jerusalem. Moreover, in short time they take it throughout the Roman Empire. The Spirit's work in the individual bears the same continuity. The eschatological goal (both cosmic and individual) of Genesis 1:2 and 2:7 is Acts 2:1-4, which ultimately leads to the new heaven and new earth (Rev. 21:1).[97] The Spirit who initiates creation and breathes life into all human persons is the Spirit who liberates creation from its bondage to decay (Rom. 8:21) and brings new life to all those drawn into the fellowship of the Trinitarian God. The Spirit of Pentecost is thus the eschatological culmination of the Spirit's creative-redemptive work.[98]

Second, a similarity marks the ways the Spirit is the pneumatological threshold or liminal point in the biblical history of creation-redemption:

97. For the eschatological nature of the Day of Pentecost, see Graham H. Twelftree, *People of the Spirit: Exploring Luke's View of the Church* (Grand Rapids: Baker Academic, 2009), pp. 75-79.

98. As noted, Frank D. Macchia also sees the outpouring of the Spirit and the experience of Spirit baptism as an eschatological event that inaugurates the kingdom and enables all of creation to participate in the new life of God's kingdom. See Macchia, *Baptized in the Spirit,* pp. 101-2, 106, 110, 116, 130, 138-39; see also *Justified in the Spirit,* pp. 93-98. I discuss Macchia's work at more length in chapter 5.

the emergence of life and of the living creatures in Genesis 1 and 2; the promise of the restoration of Israel in Isaiah and Ezekiel; the incarnation of the Son of God; and the formation of the church of Jesus Christ through the union of all those who participate in the Spirit of Pentecost. At each of these critical liminal moments, the Spirit of God is active, and this activity of the Spirit has a common pattern. In each of these creative-redemptive events the movement of the Spirit precedes and then empowers the transition of creation into a pneumatological horizon of redemption. The Spirit is the divine agent who takes something or someone and enables it to achieve God's purposes for it. In the Spirit's ultimate liminal and constitutional work, the Spirit will redeem creation by liberating it from its bondage to decay (Rom. 8:21) and raising it to new life in the everlasting kingdom of all those drawn into fellowship with the Trinitarian God (Rom. 8:11). Therefore, the Spirit of Pentecost fully manifests the personal work of the Holy Spirit in the biblical drama of creation-redemption. The eschatological kingdom is but the final stage of the Spirit of Pentecost's redemption of creation.

Paul also draws on Old Testament pneumatological images and develops them in terms of the Holy Spirit. First, Paul interprets the Old Testament promise of a new covenant, which entails an eschatological outpouring of God's Spirit, in terms of the Holy Spirit.[99] Ezekiel 39:29 promises: "I will no longer hide my face from them, for I will pour out my Spirit on the house of Israel" (see also Ezek. 36 and 37).[100] The giving of the Spirit is the sign and seal of Yahweh's covenant relationship with the people of Israel.[101] Paul portrays the Spirit's dwelling in the believer along similar lines, and likely as the eschatological fulfillment of the promise of the outpouring of God's Spirit in his religious tradition, when he says, "He anointed us, set his seal of ownership on us, and put his Spirit in our hearts as a deposit guaranteeing what is to come," and "having believed, you were marked in him with a seal, the promised Holy Spirit, who is a deposit guaranteeing our inheritance until the redemption of those who are God's possession" (2 Cor. 1:22; Eph. 1:14; see also 2 Cor. 5:5; Eph. 4:30).[102] Here, ac-

99. Fee, *God's Empowering Presence,* pp. 812-13.

100. Joyce, *Ezekiel,* p. 204.

101. Daniel I. Block, "Gog and the Pouring out of the Spirit: Reflections on Ezekiel 39: 21-9," *Vetus Testamentum* 37, no. 3 (1987): 259-70 (esp. pp. 267-69); see also Walter Zimmerli, *Ezekiel,* vol. 2: *A Commentary on the Book of the Prophet Ezekiel, Chapters 25–48,* Hermeneia: A Critical and Historical Commentary on the Bible (Philadelphia: Fortress, 1983), pp. 320-21.

102. Fee, *God's Empowering Presence,* pp. 670-71 and 806-8.

cording to Gordon Fee, Paul interprets the gift of the Holy Spirit as the "*certain evidence* that the future has dawned, and the *absolute guarantee* of its final consummation."[103] Paul's description of salvation as the washing away of sin and the sanctification and justification in Jesus Christ and the Holy Spirit also captures the heart of the new covenant promise that God's Spirit will give the people a new heart and empower covenantal faithfulness.[104] Paul clarifies the Spirit of Yahweh/Spirit of God who will enable the fulfillment of the new covenant among the people of God with the more specific designation of the Holy Spirit.

Paul's pneumatology has additional continuities with that of the Hebrew Bible. The description of the church as the temple of the Holy Spirit in 1 Corinthians 3:16-17 has Old Testament precedent. In ancient Israel the Tabernacle and then the Jerusalem Temple was the place where Yahweh's presence was most manifest. The Hebrew prophets also foretold of an eschatological outpouring of God's Spirit that would surpass their traditional expectations of the Spirit of God's presence among them (Isa. 61:1 and Joel 2:28).[105] In the New Testament, Jesus becomes the place where the presence of God is visible. After the resurrection and the outpouring of the Spirit on the Day of Pentecost, the community of believers becomes the body of Christ or the place that displays God's presence. Ephesians 2:21-22 explicitly portrays the people of God as the temple that God raises and "in which God lives by his Spirit."[106] Although — as in the Hebrew tabernacle and temple theology — God's presence is not limited to the church, the community of the believers is the temple or "the building" of the Holy Spirit because the Spirit of God dwells and is manifest in them in a unique and redemptive way.[107]

Benjamin D. Sommer argues that the manifestation of God's presence in the tabernacle in Exodus 39–40 culminates the Genesis 1 creation story. He goes on to say that creation stories in the Ancient Near East often conclude with the "construction of the high god's temple," and until this takes place the creation story is incomplete. The Exodus tabernacle story closes the creation narrative because, at that point, the God who creates becomes

103. Fee, *God's Empowering Presence,* p. 806 (italics in original).

104. Walter Eichrodt, *Ezekiel: A Commentary* (Philadelphia: Westminster, 1970), p. 499.

105. Vawter and Hoppe, *A New Heart,* p. 168; see also Douglas Stewart, *Hosea-Jonah,* Word Biblical Commentary (Waco: Word, 1987), pp. 260-62.

106. Fatehi, *The Spirit's Relation to the Risen Lord in Paul,* pp. 167-68.

107. J. A. Draper, "The Tip of an Ice-Berg: The Temple of the Holy Spirit," *Journal of Theology for Southern Africa* 59 (1987): 57-65 (esp. pp. 58-60).

fully present within creation, and creation itself is complete.[108] This line of interpretation can be applied to the continued manifestation of God's presence and creation activity attributed to the Spirit of God. The manifestation of the Spirit in terms of tongues of fire has a clear connection with the demonstration of Yahweh's presence as fire in the tabernacle. In the canonical trajectory of biblical revelation, the Spirit of God, who initiates creation, forms the people of Israel, and constitutes the union of the Son in Jesus Christ, becomes fully manifest as the Spirit of Pentecost. The christological point is vitally important because the incarnation is the fullest manifestation of God's presence in history. Moreover, Luke and Matthew attribute this presence to the work of the Spirit of God. Through the Spirit's work, God "tabernacles" in Christ (John 1). Additionally, the historical presence and manifestation of God in Christ becomes available to all people through the outpouring of the Spirit of Pentecost. For this reason, believers are collectively called the temple of the Holy Spirit. The presence and work of God is fully revealed and has its most intimate presence and manifestation in creation within the individual human and the community of believers as the Spirit of Pentecost and, therefore, finally completes the Spirit's work of creation.

The Spirit of Pentecost and a Pentecostal Trinitarian Theology

The climactic nature of the Spirit of Pentecost in the biblical drama of redemption provides the biblical corroboration for the theological fruitfulness of the Pentecostal experience of the Holy Spirit. However, what does it mean for Trinitarian theology? The final section of this chapter applies the insight drawn from the exploration of biblical pneumatology more directly to Trinitarian theology. It moves from economic to immanent pneumatology and thereby to Trinitarian theology. This section maintains that the economic work of the Spirit, characterized as liminal, constitutional, and consummational or eschatological, reveals the Spirit's immanent identity. In short, only in the Holy Spirit does the triune nature of God find fullness of fellowship.

First, the Trinity is a *Trinitarian* fellowship of the Father, the Son, and the Holy Spirit. The Trinity is not a set of unilateral relationships (proces-

108. Benjamin D. Sommer, *The Bodies of God and the World of Ancient Israel* (New York: Cambridge University Press, 2009), pp. 111-12.

sions from the Father) nor bilateral relationships *(filioque)*, but a triune community in which the Spirit plays a liminal and constitutional role. The Spirit's eschatological role in the biblical drama of redemption suggests that the Spirit has a constitutional role in the immanent Trinity (see the discussion of Rahner and the relationship between the economic and immanent Trinity in chapter 1 above). In the person of the Holy Spirit the immanent Godhead becomes a Trinitarian fellowship. In the economy of redemption the Spirit functions as a liminal agent at the threshold between chaos and creation, sin and forgiveness, creation and new creation. This economic characteristic suggests the immanent liminality of the Holy Spirit. Regardless of the way one describes the nature of the immanent divine subsistences, only in the subsistence of the Holy Spirit does the Godhead cross the Trinitarian threshold and "become" the fellowship of the Father, the Son, and the Holy Spirit. The Holy Spirit, therefore, constitutes the triune Godhead.

When I use the term "become," it does not connote temporal sequence in the Godhead. The distinction of speaking of the immanent Trinity in terms of *in facto esse* and *in fieri* is helpful here. In *in facto esse*, the divine persons are equally divine and subsist eternally. However, human beings have no direct access to the divine being, and human language cannot exhaust the richness of the divine life. Consequently, theology speaks of the subsistence of the Son and the Holy Spirit in terms of "becoming," or *in fieri.*[109] For example, traditional Trinitarian theology refers to the Son as being begotten from the Father and the Spirit as proceeding from the Father (Eastern) or from the Father and the Son (Western). Taken literally, this language sounds as though the Father exists before the Son, and only after the Son is the Holy Spirit brought into existence. Yet the temporal connotation of the language is not characteristic of the subsistence of the Son and the Holy Spirit, considered *in facto esse.* The relative order and dependence of the subsistence of the Son on the Father and of the Holy Spirit on the Father and the Son does not entail ontological inferiority or temporal succession. Trinitarians, who begin with the Father in the order of immanent subsistence, assume that, though theological language describes the Trinity as becoming — that is, the generation of the Son and procession of the Spirit — that language does not imply

109. David Coffey alerted me to these distinctions. See Coffey, *Deus Trinitas: The Doctrine of the Triune God* (New York: Oxford University Press, 1999), pp. 51-52. Vladimir Lossky also recognizes this way of speaking as inevitable given the constraints of human thought vis-à-vis the ineffable Trinity (Lossky, *The Mystical Theology of the Eastern Church* [Crestwood, NY: St. Vladimir's Seminary Press, 1976], p. 45).

a temporal order or ontological hierarchy because God exists eternally as the Father, the Son, and the Holy Spirit.

Second, the focus on the Holy Spirit does not displace Christology in either the economic or immanent Trinity. As Bradford E. Hinze and D. Lyle Dabney insist, "the more recent interest in Pneumatology is not a move away from the center of Christian worship and witness in Jesus Christ. It is, rather, a search for a mode of witness to and worship of Christ that is more true to the biblical witness."[110] They correctly advise against a move from Christocentrism to pneumacentrism. Nevertheless, the Christian tradition, at least the Western one, has tended to privilege christological categories over pneumatological ones. Traditional Trinitarian theology privileges the biblical accounts that describe the Son (and the Father) sending the Holy Spirit (e.g., John 14).

Consider the following examples. Protestant theologian Colin Gunton maintains: "We may explore the theology of the Spirit only through the lens provided by Jesus Christ."[111] Catholic theologian Luis F. LaDaria portrays the Son as the "source" of the Holy Spirit and the gift of the Holy Spirit as an "inseparable consequence" of the glorification of Christ.[112] Reformed theologian Jürgen Moltmann, even though revitalizing pneumatology, retains a christological focus. For Moltmann, the risen Christ mediates the Holy Spirit. The Holy Spirit's chief objective is to glorify the Son, and through the glorification of the Son to glorify the Father. Thus, though Moltmann sees the Spirit as an active agent and not merely as an activity of the Father and the Son, he orients the work of the Spirit to the Son and the Father.[113] In other words, the Spirit's activity is instrumental for achieving the work of the Father and the Son. Wolfhart Pannenberg states that Moltmann

> showed convincingly that the glorifying of the Son and the Father by the Spirit is the personal act which most decisively expresses the subjectivity

110. Bradford E. Hinze and D. Lyle Dabney, "Introduction," in *Advents of the Spirit: An Introduction to the Current Study of Pneumatology,* ed. Hinze and Dabney (Milwaukee: Marquette University Press, 2001), pp. 11-34 (esp. pp. 20-21).

111. Gunton, "The Spirit Moved Over the Face of the Waters," p. 195.

112. Luis F. LaDaria, *The Living and True God: The Mystery of the Trinity,* trans. Evelyn Harrison, rev. Doris Strieter and Thomas Strieter, Colección Traditio (Miami: Convivium Press, 2009), pp. 125-26.

113. Jürgen Moltmann, *Trinity and the Kingdom: The Doctrine of God,* trans. Margaret Kohl (San Francisco: Harper & Row, 1981), pp. 122-27.

> of the Spirit over against the other two persons, and above all that we must regard this doxological activity of the Spirit as an intratrinitarian relation because it is not directed outward but to the Son and the Father.[114]

These views are right to see Christ and his relationship with the Father as informative for pneumatology, but they overlook the fact that pneumatology is also instructive for the identity of the Father and the Son and thus for Trinitarian theology.

Traditional Trinitarian theology's tendency to emphasize the way Christology and the Son's relationship to the Father conditions pneumatology rather than to see these relationships as mutually conditioned is a problem. However, Scripture shows that the relationship between the Holy Spirit and Jesus Christ is reciprocal and not unilateral.[115] In Luke 1:35, the Holy Spirit is the divine agent of the incarnation, which is the concrete realization of Isaiah's promise that the Spirit will define the identity and ministry of the Messiah (Isa. 11:1-9; 42:1-9; 61:1-3). The Holy Spirit is the foundation and horizon of Jesus' life and ministry. The Spirit inaugurates Jesus' public ministry at his baptism (Mark 1:9-11; Matt. 3:16-17; Luke 3:21-23); leads him into the desert and empowers him to resist Satan's temptations (Mark 1:12-13; Matt. 4:1-11; Luke 4:1-13); empowers his public ministry (Luke 4:14-21); is the power through which Jesus heals and casts out demons (Matt. 12:9-28); and finally raises Jesus from the dead (Rom. 8:11).[116] The risen Christ's ability to the send the Holy Spirit is thus made possible by the work of the Holy Spirit throughout the life of Jesus. Moreover, the outpouring of the Spirit of Pentecost suggests that the work of the Father and the Son is directed toward the Spirit; indeed, their work is eschatologically complete only in the coming of the Spirit of Pentecost.

The Spirit's identity then, contrary to Pannenberg and the views implied in the other scholars mentioned above, does not reside exclusively in an orientation to the Father and the Son, but includes the orientation of the Father and the Son to the Spirit. The implication for the immanent Trinity is that the Spirit is the recipient or object of interpersonal relation-

114. Pannenberg, *Systematic Theology,* 1: 330.

115. Although LaDaria's work reflects Christocentrism, it also recognizes that the Spirit should not be subordinated to Christ and that the missions of the Son and the Spirit have a "mutual implication" (LaDaria, *The Living and True God,* p. 135).

116. John W. Yates argues that in Romans 8 Paul consciously draws on Ezekiel's notion of the Spirit as the agent of creation and new creation. The resurrection of Christ is the "inaugural act of the new creation" (Yates, *Spirit and Creation in Paul,* pp. 143-46, 151).

ship from the Father and the Son and not more minimally one who only facilitates their fellowship. The fellowship of the Trinitarian God is a Trinitarian one in which the Father, the Son, and the Spirit equally receive and give love, and not a binitarian communion of the Father and the Son identified as the Holy Spirit — for example, the Holy Spirit as the mutual love of the Father and the Son. My goal, based on a pneumatological reading of Scripture and sensitized by the Pentecostal experience of the Spirit, is to coordinate Christology and pneumatology and give them both constitutional roles in place of the traditions' tendency to treat pneumatology as a derivative doctrine of the theology of the Father and the Son. In other words, the Trinity is primarily neither a set of relationships derived from the Father nor a binary relationship between the Father and the Son. Moreover, the Spirit is not only a product of a unilateral procession from the Father or bilateral procession from the Father and the Son. The Spirit is the divine person who constitutes and consummates the immanent fellowship of the Trinitarian God.

Third, Pentecost is an eschatological work of the Spirit. Two points follow from the eschatological nature of Pentecost. On the one hand, it completes or consummates the biblical sequence of redemption — incarnation, cross, resurrection, and Pentecost. In certain ways it culminates the promises of the Old Testament of a new age of the outpouring of God's Spirit (e.g., Ezekiel, Isaiah, and Joel) and of Jesus to send the Spirit; but also it is a day that has not ended because the Spirit is still being poured out on all flesh — that is, the pneumatological remainder. The Spirit does not only realize or actualize the work of Christ by making Christ's grace available to human beings, but rather the Spirit of Pentecost is the *telos* of the work of the Father in sending the Son. On the other hand, it most fully reveals the identity of the Holy Spirit. Since economic work reveals immanent identity, the liminal, constitutive, and consummative work of the Spirit of Pentecost unveils not only something of the Spirit's work in redemption, but also something of the Spirit's identity in the Trinitarian God.

Based on the above hermeneutical point, since the Spirit of Pentecost culminates the work of redemption (economic Trinity), the Spirit brings the triune life of the Godhead to fulfillment (immanent Trinity). The Spirit is, therefore, eschatological in that "eschatological" means to bring the divine life and community to fullness. Because the Spirit completes the fullness of the triune God, the Spirit's work in the economy of redemption is eschatological. The Spirit consummates redemption, in the sense that Christ's life, death, and resurrection lead to the Pentecostal outpouring of the Holy Spirit. The economic work of the Spirit shows that the Spirit is not a *donum superadditum,* an ornament to something more or less already given and complete. I am arguing that Pentecost has exactly the opposite theological implication one sometimes finds in Classical Pentecostal interpretations. Representing the Classical Pentecostal reading of Pentecost, William W. and Robert P. Menzies maintain that the gift of the Spirit of Pentecost "is not a soteriological necessity; rather, it is a *donum superadditum* (or a charismatic gift)."[117] This reading reduces the primary work of the Holy Spirit in the biblical drama of redemption to an epiphenomenon of God's redemptive work. My case is that Pentecost discloses the centrality and essential nature of pneumatology to God's redemptive work. Rather than being supplementary and extraneous to salvation, the Spirit's work in the economy — creation, incarnation, Pentecost — is constitutional. To be sure, the eschatological consummation of the kingdom of God remains outstanding. However, the coming of the kingdom is not something in addition to the work of Christ and the Spirit narrated in the Gospels and Acts, but the eschatological fulfillment of their work. The eschatological nature of the Spirit of Pentecost's work in the biblical narrative of redemption (outpouring of the Spirit/Spirit baptism) means that the Spirit fulfills the economic work of the Father and the Son.

The Spirit's eschatological role in the economic Trinity points to the Spirit's role in the fellowship of the Trinitarian God.[118] The implication for the immanent Trinity is that the Holy Spirit constitutes the fullness, or fulfills the fellowship of, the Trinitarian God. Just as the outpouring of the Holy Spirit on the day of Pentecost is a threshold and eschatological moment in the economy of redemption, so the coming forth of the Spirit in the immanent Trinity is a liminal and consummational moment. Without the Spirit, the Trinitarian fellowship is incomplete. In the person of the

117. William W. Menzies and Robert P. Menzies, *Spirit and Power: Foundations of Pentecostal Experience* (Grand Rapids: Zondervan, 2000), p. 89.

118. Wolfhart Pannenberg also speaks of the Spirit playing a consummative role in the economy of redemption. He suggests that the Spirit "completes the revelation of the Father by the Son" (Pannenberg, *Systematic Theology,* 1: 315). However, his point is quite different from mine. The work of the Spirit has nothing to do with the Spirit per se, but is entirely oriented to the revelation of the Father. The Spirit — and the Son, for that matter — are subservient to and the dutiful servants of the Father. The Spirit's economic subordination to the Father occurs through the Spirit's obeisance to the Son as the vice-regent of the Father's kingdom. The Holy Spirit completes the revelation *of the Father* by the Son and does so by glorifying the Son. Pneumatology is ultimately subordinate to patrology via its penultimate subordination to Christology (Pannenberg, *Systematic Theology,* 1: 321-25).

Spirit, the divine fellowship crosses the threshold to full Trinitarian love. Not by simply adding a third to a fellowship otherwise had between the Father and the Son. In the person of the Holy Spirit, the personal fellowship of the Godhead transcends a binary relational dynamic and achieves a Trinitarian one. In the following chapters I will bring this Pentecostal insight into ecumenical dialogue with traditional and contemporary forms of Trinitarian theology.

Conclusion

Chapter 1 built a case for taking the Pentecostal experience of the Spirit as theologically significant. It also recommended taking the outpouring of the Spirit of Pentecost as a starting point to investigate the biblical narratives of the Spirit. This chapter followed through on that proposal and detailed the character of the Spirit's work in terms of creation-redemption, Spirit of Christ, and Spirit of Pentecost. The biblical narratives of the Spirit reach their dramatic apex in the outpouring of the Holy Spirit in Acts. The implication for Trinitarian theology is that the Spirit brings the fellowship of the Trinitarian God to fullness. The Spirit does not merely facilitate the relationship of the Father and the Son. The Holy Spirit is a distinct divine person who exists in relationship with the Father and Son, contributes to their identities, and constitutes the fullness of the triune God.

3 Eastern and Western Trinitarian Theology

Two approaches to the Trinity shaped the Christian theological tradition. Although the periodically contentious debates between Eastern and Western Trinitarian theology give the impression that they are vastly different theologies, they are actually remarkably similar. Both Trinitarian traditions rely on the doctrine of processions to define the divine persons. Moreover, in both approaches the Holy Spirit has an ambiguous and passive identity. In this chapter I engage both historic figures (Cappadocians, Augustine, Thomas Aquinas, and Richard of Saint Victor) and contemporary figures (John D. Zizioulas and Thomas G. Weinandy) in these two traditions of Trinitarian theology from a Pentecostal Trinitarian perspective. I propose that the Spirit plays a role in the formation of the personal identities of the Son and the Father — and thus constitutes the Trinity as the Trinity. I initially develop this notion in conversation with the Eastern doctrine of the monarchy of the Father; later I examine the Western doctrine of the *filioque* and mutual-love model of the Trinity. Since Eastern and Western Trinitarian theologies are similar on the basic issue of the processions and the identities of the divine persons, the interactions with both the historical and contemporary expressions of them have some overlap, so I will seek to avoid tedious repetition.

Historical Traditions

The major figures in Eastern Trinitarian theology are Gregory of Nazianzus, Gregory of Nyssa, and Basil of Caesarea — known as the Cappadocians. Their counterpart in Western theology is Augustine. Though a medieval figure, Thomas Aquinas is also representative and formative for Western Trinitarian theology because he gave Augustinian Trinitarian theology scholastic precision. Richard of Saint Victor did not initiate a distinct Trinitarian tradition; but he did develop a unique contribution that has been popular in the contemporary renaissance of Trinitarian theology. This first section outlines the contours of these historic forms of Trinitarian theology and interacts with them from a Pentecostal perspective.

Eastern Trinitarian Theology

The context for Cappadocian Trinitarianism is the development of pro-Nicene theology. Pro-Nicene theology is a mid- and late-fourth-century set of theological arguments and grammar that were for (or *pro*) the theology of Nicaea.[1] Lewis Ayres identifies three "central principles" of pro-Nicene theology. The first is a clear distinction between nature and person, along with "the principle that whatever is predicated of the divine nature is predicated of the three persons equally and understood to be one." The second principle is that the eternal generation of the Son in no way compromises the unity and ineffable nature of divine being. The third notion is that the divine persons work inseparably.[2] Entailed in these three doctrines was a grammar, or rules, for thinking about the nature of God and the possibility of differentiation within that nature. This grammar includes two doctrines: (1) the divine nature is unique and indivisible (divine simplicity); and (2) differentiation within the divine nature according to relationships of origin does not divide the divine nature or admit to a hierarchy in the divine being.[3] These theological principles

1. For the development of pro-Nicene Trinitarian theology, see Lewis Ayres, *Nicaea and Its Legacy: An Approach to Fourth-Century Trinitarian Theology* (New York: Oxford University Press, 2004), pp. 167-68, 236-37; see also Michel René Barnes, *The Power of God: Δύναμις in Gregory of Nyssa's Trinitarian Theology* (Washington, DC: The Catholic University of America Press, 2001), pp. 125-72 (esp. pp. 169-72).

2. Ayres, *Nicaea and Its Legacy,* p. 236. See, e.g., Basil of Caesarea, *On the Holy Spirit,* in *A Select Library of the Nicene and Post-Nicene Fathers of the Christian Church,* Second Series (hereafter *NPNF*²), 14 vols., ed. Philip Schaff and Henry Wace (Edinburgh, 1886-1900), 8: 28; see also, e.g., Gregory of Nyssa, *On the Holy Spirit, and of the Godhead of the Holy Spirit* (*NPNF*² 5: 328-29).

3. Lewis Ayres, "On Not Three People: The Fundamental Themes of Gregory of Nyssa's

and doctrinal grammar provided several benefits. They enabled pro-Nicene theologians, such as the Cappadocians, to affirm that the Father, the Son, and the Holy Spirit are real subsistences of the divine nature and that their subsistence does not divide or compound the divine essence — thus the distinction between *essence* and *hypostases*. They also provided a way to speak of an order of relationships or processions that provided a rationale for the personal distinctions of the Father, the Son, and the Holy Spirit.

A consistent feature of Cappadocian Trinitarianism, and more broadly of Eastern theology in general, is the doctrine of the monarchy of the Father. The monarchy of the Father refers to the Father's priority in the order of the processions of the Son and the Holy Spirit. Gregory of Nyssa is representative of this view.[4] While maintaining the inseparability of God's activities and nature, Gregory makes room for a differentiation within the nature according to "cause" and "caused" (or "of the cause"). Gregory explains these distinctions in the following way:

> We apprehend that one Person is distinguished from another; — by our belief, that is, that one is the Cause, and another is of the Cause, and again in that which is of the Cause we recognize another distinction. For one is directly from the first Cause, and another by that which is directly from the first Cause.[5]

The original cause of the diversification of the divine persons is the Father. Gregory defines the Father as "without generation," "without origination," and "without a cause." The Son is "of the cause" — that is, generated, or begotten, by the Father. The Holy Spirit comes forth from the Father — third in the order of processions.[6]

The doctrine of the monarchy of the Father served several important roles in Cappadocian theology. According to Ayres, it is a "prophylactic against charges that pro-Nicenes teach a plurality of Gods or that the God-

---

Trinitarian Theology as Seen in *To Ablabius: On Not Three Gods*," in *Re-Thinking Gregory of Nyssa*, ed. Sarah Coakley (Malden, MA: Blackwell, 2003), pp. 15-44 (esp. p. 20).

4. For this theology in other Eastern theologians, see John of Damascus, *Exposition of the Orthodox Faith* 8, *NPNF*[2] 9: 9; Basil of Caesarea, *Letter 120*, *NPNF*[2] 8: 250, and *On the Holy Spirit* 16.38 and 18.45-46, *NPNF*[2] 8: 23 and 28-29; Gregory of Nazianzus, *The Third Theological Oration*, *NPNF*[2] 7: 301, and *The Fifth Theological Oration* 8, *NPNF*[2] 7: 320.

5. Gregory of Nyssa, "On 'Not Three Gods,'" *NPNF*[2] 5: 336.

6. Gregory of Nyssa, *Letter 38*, *NPNF*[2] 8:138; "On 'Not Three Gods,'" *NPNF*[2] 5:336, 5:138.

head is divided."[7] It provided a way to maintain the unity of divine operations in the economy of redemption and did so in a way that was consistent with the biblical description of that work and with the notion of the indivisibility of the divine nature. Gregory indicates the interconnection of these themes when he says, "Every operation which extends from God to the Creation, and named according to our variable conceptions of it, has its origin from the Father, and proceeds through the Son, and is perfected in the Holy Spirit. . . . [W]hatever comes to pass . . . comes to pass by the action of the Three, yet what does come to pass is not three things." The origin from the Father means that the Son and the Spirit are inseparable from the Father in operation and nature. For example, Gregory notes that, according to Scripture, human beings have their life from God and more specifically from the Father, the Son, and the Holy Spirit. Yet this does not mean that human beings have three lives; no, human beings have one life. Gregory makes clear that the acts of the divine persons are united in action so that human beings receive one life "from the Father through the Son to the Spirit" or, as he declares later in the same text, "the power is one, in Father, Son, and Holy Spirit . . . issuing from the Father as from a spring, brought into operation by the Son, and perfecting its grace by the power of the Spirit."[8] Therefore, divine activity is from the Father, through the Son, and in the Spirit.

The doctrine of the monarchy of the Father has significant consequences for pneumatology and the formation of the personal identities of the divine persons. First, the Father's personal identity derives from his status and activity as the cause of the procession of the Son and the Holy Spirit. Gregory puts it this way: "God [i.e., the Father], who is over all, alone has, as one special mark of His own hypostasis, His being Father, and His deriving His hypostasis from no cause; and through this mark He is peculiarly known."[9] John of Damascus emphatically says:

> For the Father is without cause and unborn: for He is derived from nothing, but derives from Himself His being, nor does He derive a single quality from another. . . . All then that the Son and the Spirit have is from the Father, even their very being.[10]

7. Ayres, *Nicaea and Its Legacy*, p. 206.
8. Gregory of Nyssa, "On 'Not Three Gods,'" *NPNF*^{2} 5: 334-35.
9. Gregory of Nyssa, *Letter 38*, *NPNF*^{2} 8: 139.
10. John of Damascus, *Exposition of the Orthodox Faith* 8, *NPNF*^{2} 9: 9 and 11.

Softening this unilateralism, Ayres notes that pro-Nicene theology also affirmed that the identity of the Father is correlative with the Son's.[11] Nevertheless, the doctrine of the monarchy portrays the Father's identity in a unique way as independent of the generation of the Son and the procession of the Holy Spirit. The second consequence that follows from the monarchy of the Father is that, compared to the Father, the Son and the Holy Spirit have passive and derivative personal identities.[12] Since the Father's identity derives solely from his own hypostasis and being the unbegotten and origin of the Son and the Spirit, the Son and Holy Spirit's identities derive from being begotten and proceeding from the Father.

Disagreement exists over whether the Eastern tradition assigns the Son a role in the procession of the Holy Spirit. Vladimir Lossky insists that the Holy Spirit proceeds from the Father alone. However, Giulio Maspero shows that Gregory of Nyssa believed that since Scripture describes the Spirit as "the Spirit of Christ," the Spirit is from the Son in the eternal Trinity.[13] Gregory does appear to give the Son a role in the procession of the Holy Spirit. In the *Lord's Prayer,* Gregory suggests, "the Holy Spirit is also said to be from the Father, as is testified to be the Son's. . . . Hence the Spirit that is from God is also Christ's Spirit; but the Son, who is from God, neither is nor is said to be from the Spirit."[14] Here Gregory recognizes that the Spirit is from the Son in some way; but he also maintains that the relationship should not be inverted so that theology should not say that Christ is of the Spirit.[15] Never-

11. Ayres, *Nicaea and Its Legacy,* p. 207.

12. As Wolfhart Pannenberg remarks, the passive identities of the Son and the Spirit as products of processions are common to the Eastern and Western Trinitarian theologies (Pannenberg, *Systematic Theology,* 3 vols., trans. Geoffrey W. Bromiley [Grand Rapids: Eerdmans, 1991], 1: 305).

13. Maspero also shows that Gregory of Nyssa believed that since Scripture describes the Spirit as the Spirit of Christ, it means the Spirit is from the Son in the eternal Trinity. See Giulio Maspero, *Trinity and Man: Gregory of Nyssa's* Ad Ablabium, Supplements to Vigiliae, 86 (Leiden: Brill, 2007), pp. 175-80.

14. Maspero, *Trinity and Man,* pp. 158 and 175-80. Gregory of Nyssa, "The Lord's Prayer," in *St. Gregory of Nyssa: The Lord's Prayer, the Beatitudes,* trans. Hilda C. Graef (New York: Newman, 1954), p. 55. Lossky could correctly note that Gregory draws this imagery of the Spirit being from the Son from the economic relations described in Scripture (e.g., Romans 8:9) and that as such it reflects the order of personal origins and economic relations and activities, but does not indicate the source of "hypostatic procession." See Lossky, "The Procession of the Holy Spirit in Orthodox Trinitarian Theology," in *Eastern Orthodox Theology: A Contemporary Reader,* ed. Daniel B. Clendenin (1995; reprint, Grand Rapids: Baker Academic, 2003), pp. 163-82 (esp. pp. 180-81).

15. Gregory of Nyssa, "Lord's Prayer," p. 55.

theless, the primary identity of the Son, even if he has an active role in the procession of the Holy Spirit, is as the "only-begotten," which accentuates his derivative identity as being from the Father. What is unequivocal in Eastern pneumatology is that the Holy Spirit's identity is thoroughly passive and derivative.

The preceding chapter maintained that "Spirit of Christ" has two senses. The first is that the Son sends the Spirit; thus the "Spirit is of Christ." The second is that Christ is constituted the Christ by the work of the Holy Spirit, because the Spirit is the active agent of the union of the humanity of Jesus with the eternal Son; therefore, the "Spirit of Christ" in the active or constitutional sense; Christ is "of" the Spirit. The first sense of the "Spirit of Christ" is uncontroversial and recognized as an economic relationship between Christ and the Spirit by both the East and West. The second sense, however, stands in tension with the monarchy of the Father — especially as it relates to pneumatology.

A basic theological principle invoked throughout this project is that the economic work of the divine persons informs their personal identity. I have been focusing particularly on the implications of the Spirit's economic work to develop a Pentecostal contribution to pneumatology and Trinitarian theology. They suggest that the Son is from the Holy Spirit. The biblical narratives of the Spirit portray the Spirit's playing a central role in Christ from the initial moment of the incarnation to the resurrection. Jesus Christ is, therefore, "of" the Holy Spirit. Jesus would not be the incarnate, faithful, and finally resurrected Christ without the Holy Spirit's presence and activity in his life. Since the economic Trinity reflects the immanent Trinity, then the eternal Son must be in some sense from the Holy Spirit as well. But in what way is the Son's eternal identity from the Holy Spirit? I answer that question in the context of making a second case for the Spirit's formation of personal identity in the Trinity, one that directly engages the centerpiece of Eastern Trinitarian theology: the Spirit constitutes the Father as the Father.

The two senses of "of" apply to the Spirit's relationship to the Father. In the first sense, Jesus indicates that the Father sends the Holy Spirit (John 14:25). In the second sense, the Holy Spirit contributes to the Father's identity. The Christian doctrine of the Trinity does not affirm an amorphous or abstract Father, but confesses a very particular understanding of the Father. The doctrine affirms a Father who exists in communion and loving fellowship with the Son. The Father, as the Father who is in loving communion with the Son, is only Father as such by the Holy Spirit who facilitates their fellowship and completes the triune community.

The biblical and economic data that support this point is John 14–17. In John 17:21 and 26, Jesus prays to the Father for his disciples, "'that all of them may be one, Father, just as you are in me and I am in you . . . in order that the love you have for me may be in them and that I myself may be in them.'" Based on Jesus' promise that he will not abandon the disciples as orphans, but that he and the Father will make their home with them (John 14:18, 23) — and the clear implication that he and the Father will come to the disciples through the Holy Spirit, whom they both will send — the mutual indwelling between Jesus and the Father and the disciples is also through the Holy Spirit. Moreover, Jesus is not only talking about his and the Father's relationship to the disciples, but also about his relationship with the Father. He promises that the love the Father has for him will be received by the disciples, and that the disciples will participate in their fellowship. Since the Holy Spirit is the divine person in whom the Father and the Son come to dwell in the disciples (John 14:18, 23, 25), a legitimate conclusion is that the Spirit is also the person who facilitates the fellowship Jesus promises his disciples in John 17:18-26. Furthermore, since the economic relationships reflect the immanent relationships, Jesus indeed promises that if the disciples' economic experience of fellowship with him and the Father is a participation in their immanent fellowship, then the Holy Spirit can be understood as the one who constitutes both the fellowship between the disciples and the Father and the Son, as well as the fellowship between the Father and the Son. Consequently, the Holy Spirit's activity is co-constitutional of the Father's and the Son's personal identities. Since the Holy Spirit constitutes the fellowship of the Father and the Son, a fellowship that defines their eternal identities, the Spirit plays an active role in defining the identities of the Father and the Son.

The Father and the Son are not "of" the Spirit in the sense that they proceed from the Spirit. Gregory of Nyssa exhibits this perspective: "[T]he Spirit that is from God is also Christ's Spirit; but the Son, who is from God, neither is nor is said to be from the Spirit; and this relative sequence is permanent and incontrovertible. Hence the sentence cannot properly be resolved and reversed in its meaning so that, as we say the Spirit to be of Christ, we might also call Christ the Spirit's."[16] Gregory is correct that, in the order of procession, the relations of origins are not invertible. But that does not mean that the processions and relations of origins provide the totality of the divine persons' eternal identities. Traditional Trinitarian theol-

16. Gregory of Nyssa, "Lord's Prayer," p. 55.

ogy, with its emphasis on the processions as the source of the divine persons' identities, has assumed that the processions exclusively define their identities. Thus, though the order of processions is real — as pointed out by Gregory — and is informative of divine personal identity, and cannot be inverted, the processions do not wholly account for the personal identities of the divine persons. The Holy Spirit, by facilitating and contributing to the full fellowship of the divine persons, completes their divine personhood.

The Father and the Son are "of" the Spirit in the sense that the Spirit's activity within the Godhead contributes to their personal identity; they would not be who they are without the Spirit. The biblical accounts show that the Holy Spirit plays a constitutional role with respect to the incarnation and Jesus' identity as the incarnate Son of God. John's presentation of the relationship between the Father and the Son also suggests that the Holy Spirit's activity is co-constitutional of the Father's and the Son's personal identities. Since their fellowship is formative for their identities, the Spirit's role in facilitating their relationship means that the Spirit contributes to the formation of their divine personhood. Thus, though the doctrine of the Father's monarchy can explain the order of processions, it does not fully account for the Father's and the Son's personal identities, because it does not incorporate the mutual and dynamic interrelationship of the divine persons, which is intrinsic to their personal identities.

Western Trinitarian Theology

I will begin this section by outlining the key features of Western Trinitarian theology using Augustine and Aquinas as representatives. Richard of Saint Victor also comes under consideration as a creative development within the Western approach to the Trinity. The next step is a critical dialogue with this material from a Pentecostal perspective.

The stature of Augustine in the Western theological tradition is perhaps unmatched by anyone who preceded or followed him in postapostolic Christianity. His influence in Western Trinitarian theology is a case in point. His credits include the establishment of the psychological model, the doctrine of the *filioque,* and the mutual-love model as the primary conceptual categories for Western Trinitarianism. As with my discussion of the Eastern doctrine of the monarchy of the Father, my goal is not to comprehensively canvass Augustine's Trinitarian theology, but to highlight aspects of his thought that have influenced the subsequent Western traditions of

Trinitarian theology and to engage those patterns of thought from the perspective of Pentecostal pneumatology and Trinitarian theology.

Augustine has the nefarious reputation of being the source of the psychological analogy of the Trinity, which is the telltale sign of Western Trinitarianism's capitulation to Hellenistic philosophy. Indeed, in this narrative of Western Trinitarianism, Augustine's penchant for psychological analogies or mental triads proves that he started with a Platonic emphasis on the absolute oneness of the divine nature and thus necessarily subordinated the divine persons to the divine essence.[17] Moreover, the God of Augustine is a self-related monad. Despite this popular perspective, rather than evidence of the overriding influence of Neo-Platonism, the mental triads allow Augustine to illustrate individuation within an essence without dividing or multiplying the essence.[18]

Augustine's understanding of the Father and the Son bears striking similarity to Cappadocian theology. Augustine describes the Father as the "source of all godhead, or if you prefer, of all deity," and thus the Father is unbegotten. The Father is God, who begets and from whom the Son and

17. For examples recent and past of this narrative of Augustine and Western Trinitarian theology, see Allan Coppedge, *The God Who Is Triune: Revisioning the Christian Doctrine of God* (Downers Grove, IL: InterVarsity Academic, 2007), pp. 108-9; Edmund J. Fortman, *The Triune God: A Historical Study of the Doctrine of the Trinity* (Philadelphia: Westminster, 1972), pp. 140-41; Colin Gunton, "Augustine, the Trinity, and the Theological Crisis in the West," in *The Promise of Trinitarian Theology* (Edinburgh: T&T Clark, 1997), p. 32; and Christoph Schwöbel, "Introduction," in *Trinitarian Theology Today: Essays on Divine Being and Act*, ed. Christoph Schwöbel (Edinburgh: T&T Clark, 1995), pp. 1-30 (esp. pp. 4-5).

18. St. Augustine, *The Trinity*, trans. Edmund Hill, vol. 5 of *The Works of Saint Augustine: A Translation for the 21st Century*, ed. John E. Rotelle (Brooklyn: New City, 1991), 9.2-8 (pp. 272-75); 9.18 (p. 282); 14.15 (p. 383); and 14.25 (pp. 390-91). He also used the mental triads to illustrate the pro-Nicene doctrine of inseparable operations and nature. Lewis Ayres and Michel René Barnes show that this understanding of Augustine is part of the Cappadocian/Eastern-Augustinian/Western paradigm popular in contemporary theology. They argue that it emerges from nineteenth-century patristic theology (principally, Theodore de Régnon's) and not the primary texts of patristic theology. For theirs and others' evaluation of the threeness-oneness paradigm in light of patristic theology, see Ayres, *Nicaea and Its Legacy*, pp. 364-83 and "'Remember That You Are Catholic' (Serm. 52.2): Augustine on the Unity of the Triune God," *Journal of Early Christian Studies* 8 (2000): 39-82; Barnes, "Rereading Augustine's Theology of the Trinity," in *The Trinity: An Interdisciplinary Symposium on the Trinity*, ed. Stephen T. Davis, Daniel Kendall, and Gerald O'Collins (New York: Oxford University Press, 1999), pp. 145-76; Mary T. Clark, "Augustine's Theology of the Trinity: Its Relevance," *Dionysius* 13 (1989): 76-77 (esp. pp. 71-84); and Basil Studer, *The Grace of Christ and the Grace of God in Augustine of Hippo: Christocentrism or Theocentrism?* trans. Matthew J. O'Connell (Collegeville, MN: Liturgical, 1997), pp. 104-6.

Spirit proceed, but who is not from another.[19] Like the Cappadocians, Augustine implies no temporal sequence or ontological hierarchy based on the Father's identity as the unbegotten. He also describes the Son as the divine person begotten by the Father's act of generation. Although not absent from Cappadocian Trinitarian theology, the portrayal of the generation of the Son in terms of the procession of the intellectual capacity of rational nature is more common in Augustine.[20] In this view, a rational nature has two operations: the acts of understanding and will. The Son corresponds to the generation of a mental word by the understanding. A mental word — one formed by the understanding — corresponds exactly to the knowledge contained in the memory.[21] The generation of the Son as Word does not correspond to a human mind remembering one item contained within the memory; rather, it is similar to a human mind recalling its being or essence. This nuance is important because the Son is identical in being with the Father. For God to know Godself by a Word entails the being or existence of the Word as precisely that which it represents; therefore, the Son as the divine Word is a subsistence of the divine nature (15.22-24 [pp. 414-16]).

The Holy Spirit proceeds as the love or the will of God (15.38 [p. 426]; 15.41 [p. 427]). However, whereas the Father alone begets the Son, the Holy Spirit proceeds from both the Father and the Son, though *principally* from the Father (15.29 [p. 419]; 15.47 [pp. 432-33]). This does not imply that the Spirit's procession is a linear movement through the Son and away from the Father; rather, the Spirit proceeds simultaneously from the Father and the Son (15.48 [p. 433]). Augustine's turn to the double procession of the Holy Spirit from the Father and the Son as a way to distinguish the distinct manner of the Spirit's procession vis-à-vis the Son's became the basis for the doctrine of the *filioque*, even though Augustine himself was not the first to propose it.[22] Lewis Ayres notes: "[F]or all pro-Nicenes, further progress in describing the nature of the Spirit's procession (beyond simply

19. Augustine, *The Trinity* 4.29 (p. 174); 4.32 (p. 177); 15.47 (p. 432).

20. For instances of the Cappadocians using the intellectual capacities of the soul as a way to understand the relationships among the divine persons, see Basil of Caesarea, *On the Holy Spirit* 16.40 (*NPNF*^{2} 8: 25-26); see also Gregory of Nyssa, *The Great Catechism*, ch. 1 (*NPNF*^{2} 5: 474-76); Ayres, *Nicaea and Its Legacy*, pp. 207-8 and 290-91.

21. Augustine, *The Trinity* 15.19-20 (p. 409). Hereafter, references to this work appear in parentheses in the text.

22. Ambrose of Milan described the Holy Spirit as proceeding "from the Father and the Son" (Ambrose, *Of the Holy Spirit*, 1.3.44 and 1.11.120 [*NPNF*^{2} 10: 99 and 109]).

saying that it is different from that of the Son) is difficult."[23] Gregory of Nazianzus exhibits the impasse of pro-Nicene theology in describing the difference between the generation of the Son and the Holy Spirit when he offers this question:

> The Holy Ghost, which proceedeth from the Father; Who, inasmuch as He proceedeth from That Source, is no Creature; and inasmuch as He is not Begotten is no Son; and inasmuch as He is between the Unbegotten and the Begotten is God. . . . What then is Procession? Do you tell me what is the Unbegottenness of the Father, and I will explain to you the physiology of the Generation of the Son and the Procession of the Spirit.[24]

Augustine understood the procession of the Spirit from the Father and the Son in terms of love, which is the highest expression of the will. By virtue of the double procession of the Spirit as love, the Spirit unites the Father and Son in a communion of mutual love (*The Trinity* 15.27 [p. 418]). The Holy Spirit's identity as the love of God derives from the Spirit's unitive function (15.31 [p. 420]). The mutual-love model receives its name from the Spirit's identity as the immanent mutual love that unites the Father and the Son.

Aquinas is the second most important influence on the development of Western Trinitarianism. His relationship to Augustine is more that of a refiner than an originator of a new Trinitarian theology.[25] Like Augustine, Aquinas understood the Father as the unbegotten and as the unoriginate principle of the personal relationships in the Godhead. The common feature between Augustine's and Aquinas's theories of the Father is that the Father is the absolute origin of the generation of the Son and the principal origin of the procession of the Spirit.[26] Aquinas also operates with a similar ontology of a spiritual or rational nature. A spiritual nature has two fundamental acts or processions: understanding and will. The act of the understanding produces a word or idea. The act of the will issues forth the

23. Ayres, *Nicaea and Its Legacy,* p. 370.

24. Gregory Nazianzus, *Fifth Theological Oration, On the Holy Spirit* 8 (*NPNF*[2] 7: 320).

25. For the development and nuances of Aquinas's Trinitarian theology, see D. Juvenal Merriell, *To the Image of the Trinity: A Study in the Development of Aquinas' Teaching,* Studies and Texts, 96 (Toronto: Pontifical Institute of Mediaeval Studies, 1990).

26. Thomas Aquinas, *Summa Theologiae* (Oxford: Blackfriars, 1964), 1a.33.1, 4 (pp. 5, 7, and 17-23). Hereafter, references to this work appear in parentheses in the text.

subsistence of love, which joins the mind and the idea conceived by the understanding (1a.93.5-6 [pp. 61-71]; 1a.27.1-5 [pp. 3-21]). The result is that relationships of opposition pertain between the source and product(s) of procession. As Aquinas says at one point, "[R]elations result from actions" (1a.34.3 [p. 41]). The principle is that an act of procession is productive, and thus the act of procession produces relationships of opposition between the source of procession and the product of procession.

The acts of procession and their productions are central to Aquinas's Trinitarian theology because they are the basis of the personal identities of the divine persons. "Person" refers to what is distinct within a nature (1a.29.4 [p. 61]); in the Godhead, personal distinctions derive from acts or processions of the divine nature. "Procession" is a general term that refers to the act of a spiritual nature that yields a subsistent relationship. More specifically, the procession of the intellectual capacity is called "generation," and the procession of the volitional capacity is called "procession." The processions in the divine nature produce relationships of opposition — and thus individuation — within the divine nature and the divine persons (1a.29.4 and 1a.93.7 [pp. 57-63, 73]).

The Son is begotten by the intellectual procession of the Word. By virtue of being a product of divine intellectual procession, the Son is also called the image of God. The Word is the begotten, and that from which the Word comes, the Father, is the unbegotten (1a.28.4 [p. 37]). Furthermore, since the term "person" refers to a distinction within a nature, the generation of the Word and the distinction of relationships of opposition — that is, unbegotten and begotten — introduced by the Son's generation manifests personal distinctions in the divine nature. The Word is properly called the Son of God because it is of the nature of the divine understanding to beget a word, and it is of the nature of a son to be begotten (1a.27.2 [pp. 9 and 11]; 1a.34.2 [p. 35]). The Holy Spirit corresponds to the procession of the will. The association of the Holy Spirit with the procession of will is a necessary one given Aquinas's ontology of a spiritual nature. Since the Son is the product of the generation of the understanding, the Holy Spirit must match up with the procession of the will. More specifically, Aquinas portrays the Holy Spirit as the mutual love of the Father and the Son. As the mutual love of the Father and the Son, the Holy Spirit unites the Father and the Son in a bond of love (1a.37.1 [p. 83]).

A problem arises with naming the relationship that subsists by the procession of the will. The terms "spiration" and "procession," which describe the manner in which the Holy Spirit subsists, denote origin and acts, not relationships (1a.37.1 [p. 81]). Specifying the difference between the Spirit's procession and the Son's generation has bedeviled theologians from the patristic era and was the problem the *filioque* sought to solve. Aquinas admits that a proper term for the procession of will and its constituting relationships of opposition is unavailable (1a.28.4 [pp. 37 and 39]). Due to the ambiguous nature of the relationships constituted by the procession of the will, Aquinas concludes that the name of the Holy Spirit is indistinct — that is, it does not signify relationship. He follows Augustine and suggests that Scripture adopted the name *Holy Spirit* to refer to the third divine person because, by virtue of belonging to both the Father and the Son, he is what they both are — that is, *Holy* and *Spirit*. In addition, the term "spirit" denotes movement toward something, and "love" denotes the propulsion of will toward another; therefore, the compound name *Holy Spirit* captures the meaning of the immanent procession of love within the Godhead (1a.36.1 [pp. 53 and 55]).[27]

The second problem Aquinas addresses is the nature of the distinction between the procession of the Holy Spirit and of the Son. His solution presupposes the principle that personal distinctions within the Godhead rest on relationships of opposition, which, in turn, arise from processions. He concludes that the double procession of the Holy Spirit from the Father and the Son — *filioque* — is the only viable answer. The only way the Spirit can be distinct from the Son is to have a unique relational status. Since relationships derive from processions, the Spirit cannot proceed from the Father alone, for then the Spirit would be indistinct from the Son. The only alternative is for the Spirit to proceed from the Father and the Son (1a.36.2 [pp. 59, 61, 65]; 1a.37.1 [p. 83]). The doctrine of the double procession of the Holy Spirit from the Father and the Son is the backdrop for Aquinas's teaching that the Holy Spirit is the mutual love of the Father and Son.

The procession of the Holy Spirit as the *mutual* love of the Father and the Son is necessitated by the assumption that the Father and Son are the indeterminate principle of the procession of the Holy Spirit. If the Holy Spirit were not the mutual love of the Father and the Son, he would proceed from either one determinate principle (i.e., as the Father's love for the Son alone) or two determinate principles (i.e., first, the Father's love for the Son, and second, the Son's love for the Father). The former is inconsistent with the principle of relative opposition constituting personal distinc-

27. For Augustine, see *The Trinity* 5.3.12 (p. 197).

tion, since the Spirit would be, like the Son, from the Father alone. The latter introduces two subsisting processions of love; namely, the subsistence of the Father's love for the Son and the Son's love for the Father. By positing that the Spirit proceeds as the mutual love of the Father and the Son, Aquinas maintains the notion that the Spirit proceeds from one principle — the Father and the Son (1a.36.4 [pp. 73-77]). The Father and Son love each other, but the love subsisting between them is one by virtue of its mutuality. The Spirit is not conceived as two separate loves proceeding from two subjects, but as the mutual love of the Father and the Son subsisting as one love uniting them (1a.36.4 [p. 75]).

The problem of the mutual-love model is not so much that it portrays the Holy Spirit uniting the Father and the Son in eternal communion; indeed, that is its greatest strength. The issue is that it is often inextricable from the theory that the divine persons are products of processions, and that problem is threefold. First, a philosophical notion of spiritual being and not the biblical narratives of the Spirit shape its fundamental understanding of the Spirit. Second, it portrays the Son — and especially the Holy Spirit — in passive terms. Third, it conceives of the divine persons' identities as complete at the point of their procession and thus does not allow for a reciprocal dynamic of personal identity formation.

First, my contention that the mutual-love model does not derive primarily from the biblical narratives of the Spirit needs clarification. Augustine and Aquinas obviously read Scripture and saw their theology as an explication of Scripture; but that's the case for most Christian theologians. For example, a reading of the Gospel of John that describes the Father as sending the Son, and the Father and the Son as sending the Holy Spirit, does not immediately invoke the idea of eternal processions of the divine understanding (producing the subsistence of the Word) and will (producing the subsistence of love) and the notion of an unbegotten ontological ground of the processions (the Father). But those are the categories Augustine and Aquinas used to articulate the relationships between the divine persons described in the Bible. Ontological assumptions of the nature of rational or spiritual being were presupposed and served as the conceptual categories to interpret the biblical texts. In this sense, the biblical narratives of the Spirit were not the primary source of their articulated theology of the Holy Spirit in particular or the Trinity in general. This point does not mean that their views are unbiblical, but simply that a priori assumptions about the nature of spiritual beings, in this case God, shaped their interpretation of the Bible. Moreover, I am not piling on to the popular disparagement of Augustine;

indeed, my previous work has used and defended his theology.[28] But the baseline conceptual categories of the mutual-love model emerge more from philosophical assumptions about the nature of spiritual being than from the biblical narratives about the Spirit.

The widespread use of the psychological analogy to articulate the mutual-love model indicates that a philosophical notion of spiritual being is the model's *Urbegriff.* The psychological analogy relies on the psychological operations of a human being's rational or spiritual soul as a conceptual category to understand the nature of the immanent processions of the divine persons. Although Augustine based his turn to the rational structure and capacities of the human soul for a way of understanding the way God could be both one and three persons on the notion that human beings bear the image of God, the primary problem with this assumption is twofold: (1) it likely misinterprets Genesis 1:26-27 and, based on this problematic exegesis, (2) it proceeds to develop an account of the immanent Trinity that does not draw much from the biblical narratives of the Holy Spirit presented in chapter 2 above. I am not saying that either Augustine's or Aquinas's pneumatology and Trinitarian theology are unbiblical. For example, Augustine's interpretation of 1 John 4 and Romans 5:5, and the way he identifies the presence and love of God dwelling in the saints, is insightful and, I believe, basically correct. Yet that does not mitigate the fact that his way of understanding the divine persons — and particularly the Holy Spirit — in terms of processions derives from a particular way of understanding the structure of a rational soul. The interpretation of the Spirit's activity in 1 John 4 and Romans 5:5 as "love" does not at the same time necessitate the interpretation of love in terms of the mutual-love model. So the point here is not that Augustine's view of the Holy Spirit's role in the immanent Trinity as one who facilitates the union of the Father and the Son was misguided, but that his view of the Spirit's identity as love in terms of the theory of processions presupposes the rational structure and operations of the "soul" as informative for the immanent distinctions and relationships of the divine persons.

David Coffey convincingly shows that the mutual-love model is, in fact, distinct from the psychological analogy. The critical difference is that

28. See Steven M. Studebaker, *The Trinitarian Vision of Jonathan Edwards and David Coffey* (Amherst, NY: Cambria, 2011); see also Studebaker, *Jonathan Edwards' Social Augustinian Trinitarianism in Historical and Contemporary Perspectives* (Piscataway, NJ: Gorgias, 2008), pp. 67-88, 113-17.

the psychological model portrays the divine persons in terms of the processions of knowledge and will/love of one subject, whereas the mutual-love model does so in terms of giving and receiving between subjects. The mutual-love model is interpersonal, not just intrapersonal. The mutual-love model does not need to propose that the Son proceeds by knowledge, but only that the Father generates or begets the Son from eternity. The psychological and mutual-love models agree that the Son originates from the Father, but they do not necessarily affirm equivalent modes of procession. Moreover, the models reflect differing goals. The psychological model asserts essential unity: the distinction within but without division of the divine essence. The mutual-love model posits personal unity: the union of divine persons through love.[29] At the level of systematic theology, I concur with Coffey; but if one is to view it from the perspective of historical theology, the psychological analogy often functions as the template for the articulation of the mutual-love model. Furthermore, even when decoupled from the psychological analogy, the mutual-love model defines the Son and especially the Holy Spirit in terms of their mode of procession and does not portray their personal identities as products of dynamic and reciprocal relationships.

Second, the result of relying on the processions of the divine persons as the source of their personal identities is to conceive of the Spirit in derivative and passive terms.[30] The Father and the Son are clearly active in the immanent Trinity, but the Spirit's identity as the bond of love is amorphous. I have used the mutual-love model elsewhere and have sought to deal with the passive nature of the Spirit's identity entailed in it, but while doing so have been unsatisfied with its portrayal of the Spirit.[31] One objection could be that in the mutual-love model the Father and the Son are dynamically related, and so relational reciprocity is achieved in their mutual love. True, but the Son's primary identity is not as the one who assists in the procession of the Holy Spirit, but as the Father's begotten Son; and the Holy Spirit provides no functional contribution to the Trinity. As mutual love, the Spirit's identity is primarily passive and derivative. Mutual love is

29. David Coffey, "A Proper Mission of the Holy Spirit," *Theological Studies* 47 (1986): 227-50 (esp. pp. 233-35).

30. I am not the only theologian to make the claim. Wolfgang Vondey, e.g., notes the same in "The Holy Spirit and the Physical Universe: The Impact of Scientific Paradigm Shifts in Contemporary Pneumatology," *Theological Studies* 70 (2009): 3-36 (esp. pp. 32-33).

31. See, e.g., Studebaker, *The Trinitarian Vision of Edwards and Coffey* and *Jonathan Edwards' Social Augustinian Trinitarianism.*

not something that one does (i.e., the Holy Spirit), but something two others do (i.e., the Father and the Son). The Spirit is the mutual act of the Father and the Son.

Patristic and Augustine scholar Lewis Ayres argues that the Spirit plays an active role in constituting the communion of the Trinity. In the following quotation Ayres summarizes Augustine's mature theology of the Spirit's identity in relation to the Father and the Son:

> The complementarity of Augustine's mature accounts of Son and Spirit suggests with even greater force a vision of the divine communion as constituted by the intra-divine acts of the divine three. . . . While Augustine does not simply identify the Spirit with the act of loving or self-giving . . . the equation is clear enough. . . . Thus . . . Augustine presents the Spirit as the agent identical to the act of communion between Father and the Son. . . . It seems true to say then both that the Son loves the Father and that the Spirit is the love and communion which joins Father and Son in love — the Son both loves (being himself love itself) and the Spirit is the love with which he loves.[32]

Ayres's point is that in begetting the Son, the Father gives the Son all that he is, including the capacity to love. The love that adheres in the Son as the gift of the Father has an intrinsic agency to love the Father in return. The "agency" of the Spirit resides in the orientation of the Son and Father's love to one another.[33] What is clear, however, is that the Spirit is not an agent in the same way as are the Father and the Son. The agency of the Spirit is *their* intrinsic orientation to love one another. The Spirit remains an act of the Father and the Son. The Spirit does not love. The Father and the Son love each other. The Spirit is their love.

Furthermore, the Spirit does not constitute a *Trinitarian* communion. The procession of the Spirit as the mutual love of the Father and the Son constitutes the communion of the Father and the Son. A communion, however, of three persons is not in the picture. The Spirit is their mutual act. The Spirit is their communal love. The Father and the Son have communion, but not the Holy Spirit. The Holy Spirit is their communion. As mutual love, the Spirit, therefore, does not constitute Trinitarian, but

32. Lewis Ayres, *Augustine and the Trinity* (New York: Cambridge University Press, 2010), p. 258.

33. Ayres, *Augustine and the Trinity,* p. 258.

binitarian, fellowship. The mutual-love model effectively makes a triune distinction within the Godhead. The Spirit, as mutual love, has a distinct subsistence; nonetheless, the Spirit is neither an agent, as the Father and the Son are, nor one with whom they have relationship. The Spirit is their mutual act of love. In the end, the important question is not whether Augustine attributed agency to the Spirit. As Ayres shows, he did. The reason he did is that Scripture describes the Spirit doing things and not merely as the act of the Father and the Son. The question is: Do the conceptual categories of the mutual-love model adequately allow for the articulation of the Spirit's activity found in Scripture? I do not think they do. The Western tradition also recognizes this tension, and it has not been able to find a clear way of identifying the personhood of the Holy Spirit, as it has been better able to do for the Father and the Son.

The emphasis on the processions is also the result of relying on the relationships described between the divine persons in the Gospel of John. John portrays the Father sending the Son, and the Father and the Son sending the Holy Spirit (John 14:25 and 15:26). This sent-from pattern is taken to reveal not only the relationships among the divine persons in the history of salvation, but their eternal interrelationships. If the Father sends the Son, or, put alternatively, the Son is from the Father in the economic Trinity, then the Son is eternally from the Father. If the Father and the Son send the Holy Spirit, then the Holy Spirit must be from them from eternity — hence the *filioque.* Of course, John's Gospel reveals something about the divine persons' eternal relations. Moreover, I am not dispensing with the theology of processions, or even of the *filioque.* The *filioque* is not inherently problematic, but it does not adequately integrate into Trinitarian theology implications from the Spirit's work in redemption.[34] The biblical narratives of the Spirit should be consulted, and these accounts suggest that the passive and derivative themes of the procession models do not account for the nature of the Spirit's work revealed in the biblical record.

34. After coming to this conclusion about the *filioque* and pneumatology, I discovered that David Bentley Hart had also done so. He observes: "If one is seeking a theological argument against the *filioque* clause . . . it would be better to point out that it fails adequately to account for other aspects of what is revealed in the economy of salvation: that the Son is begotten in and by the agency of the Spirit as much as the Spirit proceeds through the Son, inasmuch as the incarnation, unction, and even mission (Mark 1:12) of the Son are works of the Spirit, which must enter into our understanding of the Trinitarian *taxis*" (Hart, "The Mirror of the Infinite: Gregory of Nyssa on the *Vestigia Trinitatis*," in Coakley, ed., *Rethinking Gregory of Nyssa*, p. 129, n. 11).

Third, the divine persons arise from dynamic reciprocal relationships.[35] The doctrine of the *filioque*, as an immanent *taxis* of the procession of the Holy Spirit, implies that the Spirit's personal identity is derived from the Father and Son's act of co-*spiration*. The consequence of this theology has been a functional subordination of pneumatology to Christology both with respect to the development of theology and the way of understanding the relationship between Christ's and the Spirit's respective work in redemption. Historically, the *filioque* can be seen as a continuation of a theological habit, rather than something new. The historical development of Trinitarian theology concentrated on the relationship between the Father and the Son and the incarnation of the Son in Jesus Christ. The formative councils of Nicaea (325) and Chalcedon (451), for example, affirmed, in turn, the *homoousios* of the Son and the Father and the hypostatic union of the divine and the human natures in Jesus Christ. Nicaea's brief confession — "we believe . . . in the Holy Spirit" — illustrates the pneumatological neglect, addressed by an added statement on the Holy Spirit in the later Constantinopolitan Creed of 381. Accordingly, during the patristic era the doctrine of the Trinity was primarily the product of discussions about the nature of the relationship of the Son to the Father and secondarily of the Spirit's relationship to the Son and the Father.

Christological emphases continued in the Western tradition and were accentuated in the modern era.[36] The theological categories of incarnation

35. Based on pneumatology and the traditional doctrines of *perichoresis/circuminsession*, and subsistent relations, Amos Yong maintains that the divine persons have their personal characteristics formed through their mutual relationships (Yong, *Spirit-Word-Community: Theological Hermeneutics in Trinitarian Perspective* [Eugene, OR: Wipf and Stock, 2002], pp. 56-59).

36. The Western tradition, however, is not without proponents of pneumatology. The theology of the Holy Spirit was a significant resource for the creative medieval mystics, such as Catherine of Siena and Julian of Norwich. Though often using Augustinian Trinitarian theology, they also developed alternative images of the Holy Spirit, which enriched their vision of the Spirit's work in the world, the Christian life, and the church. For a survey of alternative pneumatologies during the medieval period, see Elizabeth A. Dreyer, *Holy Power, Holy Presence: Rediscovering Medieval Metaphors for the Holy Spirit* (New York: Paulist, 2007). Albert Hernández also shows that pneumatology and the feast of Pentecost were useful points of connection with the rural and agrarian people of medieval Europe. The new life of the Spirit and Pentecost's celebration during early spring harmonized with the nature and fertility cycles that were central to the religious beliefs and practices of pre-Christian Europe (Hernández, *Subversive Fire: The Untold Story of Pentecost*, Asbury Theological Seminary Series in World Christian Movements in Medieval and Reformation Studies, 1 (Lexington, KY: Emeth, 2010).

and Christology fit well with the methodological concerns of the theologies of modernism that focused on issues of religious epistemology. In this context, pneumatology remained sidelined from making a contribution to the doctrine of the Trinity. Though laments that the Spirit is the "Cinderella" of theology no longer ring true, christological emphases still dominate Trinitarian theology.[37] For instance, affirming a christological criterion for pneumatology, Colin Gunton says, "We may explore the theology of the Spirit only through the lens provided by Jesus Christ. . . . There is no Spirit without the Son."[38] Yet the inverse is no less true: no Spirit, no Son, and no Christ.

The biblical account of redemption implies that dynamic and reciprocal relationships define the identities of the divine persons. The doctrine of the *filioque* overlooks the biblical data that portrays the Holy Spirit involved as much in constituting the Son as the Son is in sending the Spirit: for example, conception, baptism, empowerment in temptation and ministry, and raising Christ from the dead. The *filioque* is not problematic per se; indeed, the doctrine has strong support based on the sent-from relationships portrayed between the Father, the Son, and the Holy Spirit in the Gospel of John. However, traditional Trinitarian theology needs supplementation with input from pneumatology. Biblical redemption is the yield of the Father's, the Son's, and the Holy Spirit's work. Since the biblical record of the economy of redemption is the primary source of knowledge of God, the relations and activities of the divine persons in that record are the basis for constructing a Christian understanding of God. If theology takes the Johannine sent-from relationships between the Father, the Son, and the Spirit as informative for their eternal relationships, then it also needs to factor the Spirit's work in Christ and the facilitation of his relationship to the Father in the same way. The result is a Trinitarian theology in which the identities of the divine persons are tri-conditioned.

The implicit assumption of traditional Trinitarian theology is that the

37. Contributions to Trinitarian theology on the basis of pneumatology are still fairly rare; explorations in various forms of pneumatological theology are more common (e.g., Denis Edwards, *Breath of Life: A Theology of the Creator Spirit* [Maryknoll, NY: Orbis, 2004]). The oft-cited nomenclature of the Spirit as the "Cinderella" of theology comes from G. J. Sirks, "The Cinderella of Theology: The Doctrine of the Holy Spirit," *Harvard Theological Review* 50 (1957): 77-89.

38. Colin Gunton, "The Spirit Moved Over the Face of the Waters: The Holy Spirit and the Created Order," *International Journal of Systematic Theology* 4 (2002): 190-204 (esp. pp. 195-97).

divine persons' identities are complete at their point of procession and the relations produced by the procession.[39] The Father is primordially the Father, who, as Father, begets the Son. The Son's identity as begotten is complete at the stage of his generation from the Father. In other words, according to the sequence of the immanent order of processions, the Son's identity is complete at the moment of his generation from the Father — and thus before the procession of the Holy Spirit. Even though the Son is active in the procession of the Holy Spirit, this activity derives from his personal status as begotten or generated from the Father. The Spirit's identity is realized as a procession of the Father and Son's mutual love. However, since the divine persons' work in redemption reflects their immanent interrelationships, the Father's and the Son's identities are not complete without the Holy Spirit. The last stage of the immanent *taxis* brings to completion the formation of the personal identities of the divine persons. Why is this the case? Just as the Spirit is the eschatological fulfillment of the Trinitarian God's work of redemption, so the Spirit brings to completion the fellowship of the Trinitarian God. The Father and the Son are not in communion until the Holy Spirit brings them into loving communion. That is, the identities of the Father and the Son described in John 17 are not realized in the immanent *taxis* "until" the third stage of the *taxis* — the subsistence of the Holy Spirit.

The unavoidable temporal sound of this description — that is, "until" — reflects the limitation of human language and does not introduce a temporal sequence into the Godhead any more than does the traditional discussion of the immanent order of the processions of the divine persons. The dynamic processions in traditional Trinitarian theology are atemporal. When theologians use temporal language to describe the generation of the Son and the procession of the Spirit, they do not imply that the Father existed before the Son, or that the Father and the Son existed before the Holy Spirit. Yet what this way of speaking shows is that traditional Trinitarian theology allows for sequential and some degree of dynamic development of the identities of the divine persons via the order of the immanent processions of the divine persons. For example, the relationship between the Father and the Son combines the sequential nature of the processions and, to a lesser degree, reciprocal relationality between the Father

39. For an excellent statement of this viewpoint, see Luis F. LaDaria, *The Living and True God: The Mystery of the Trinity,* trans. Evelyn Harrison, rev. Doris Strieter and Thomas Strieter, Colección Traditio (Miami: Convivium Press, 2009), pp. 290-92, 300-301.

and the Son, as the Father cannot be the Father without the Son. Yet, even here, the Father's identity derives more from his activity of begetting than from being in relationship to the Son. However, the same cannot be said of the Holy Spirit. The Spirit is the relationship between the Father and the Son and does not possess a distinct personal identity.

Rather than halting the formation of the identities of the divine persons at the moment of the double procession of the Holy Spirit, I want to expand the dynamic development of the divine persons' identities beyond the processions. In doing so, I am simply drawing on the principle that dynamic development of the divine persons through the processions is atemporal and thus does not violate the eternal nature of the Godhead. The extension of the process that shapes the divine persons' identities permits a contribution from pneumatology to Trinitarian theology. More specifically, the activity of the Holy Spirit in the immanent Godhead contributes to the personal identity of not only the Father and the Son, but also of the Holy Spirit.

The Spirit's activity shapes the identity of the Son because the Son, who is defined as the one who exists in eternal communion with the Father, is constituted as such by the Holy Spirit. The Holy Spirit also shapes the identity of the Father, since the Spirit facilitates the Father's fellowship with the Son. Without the Holy Spirit, the Father and the Son would not be what they are; therefore, the Spirit plays a constitutional role in the formation of their personal identities. Moreover, since the Spirit's activity plays a role in the formation of their identities, the Godhead crosses the Trinitarian threshold only in the subsistence and personal activity of the Holy Spirit. The persons of the Trinity achieve their full personhood in the subsistence of the Holy Spirit and the fellowship that the Spirit constitutes.

The importance of this point for pneumatology is that the Spirit's identity in the immanent Trinity is not entirely derivative vis-à-vis the Father and the Son. The Spirit's activity in the immanent Trinity contributes to the formation of the Father's and the Son's eternal identity. The Spirit's activity in relationship with the Father and the Son, drawing them into and constituting the eternal fellowship of the Trinitarian God, also contributes to the Spirit's identity. The formation of the personal identities of the Father, the Son, and the Holy Spirit is complete only when the Spirit achieves the fullness of the eternal fellowship of the Trinitarian God. The Spirit's identity does not derive from being the mutual act of love, but from the Spirit's activity of bringing to completion the communion of the Trinitarian God. Hence, the Spirit's personal identity arises from a unique activity of the Spirit and is not purely derivative from the processive activities of the Father and the Son. Finally, the case for the Spirit's substantive role in the formation of the Father's and the Son's identity is not a rejection of the role of the Spirit in the mutual-love model; yet it does imply that it is incomplete. The mutual-love model underscores the Spirit's role in uniting the Father and the Son in loving fellowship. However, based on a pneumatology informed by the biblical accounts of the Spirit, the Spirit can be seen to contribute to the Father's and Son's identity in a way that gives the Spirit an active role in the immanent Trinity and an identity that arises from that activity.

Richard of Saint Victor is sometimes called on to provide historical support for contemporary social Trinitarianism.[40] Although Richard does possess a distinct approach to the Trinity in the Western tradition, his is not a protosocial Trinitarianism, because he does not start with the three divine persons or give divine plurality preeminence over divine oneness, as do contemporary social Trinitarians.[41] In fact, Christopher P. Evans affirms this: "Like the entire western tradition before him, Richard's point of departure is the divine substance . . . [and] his arguments are . . . thoroughly entrenched in the theological traditions of the Latin West."[42] Richard's Trinitarian theology, according to Evans, is an effort "to prove through reason the church's profession of the triune God as depicted in the so-called Athanasian Creed or *Quicumque*."[43] The recitation of the creed was central to the faith and worship of the Abbey at Saint Victor. Though Richard's theology of the Trinity has unique features, it also expresses insights that were part of his contemporaneous and past tradition.[44] Driven by "a burning

40. Graham A. Cole, *He Who Gives Life: The Doctrine of the Holy Spirit* (Wheaton: Crossway, 2007), pp. 75-76; Veli-Matti Kärkkäinen, *The Trinity: Global Perspectives* (Louisville: Westminster John Knox, 2007), pp. 60-61.

41. For a comprehensive discussion of Richard's Trinitarianism and its relationship to social Trinitarianism, see Nico den Bok, *Communicating the Most High: A Systematic Study of Person and Trinity in the Theology of Richard of St. Victor (†1173)*, Bibliotheca Victorina, 7 (Paris: Brepols, 1996).

42. Christopher P. Evans, introduction to "Richard of St Victor's *On the Trinity*," trans. Christopher P. Evans, in *Trinity and Creation: A Selection of Works of Hugh, Richard, and Adam of St Victor*, ed. Boyd Taylor Coolman and Dale M. Coulter (Turnhout: Brepols, 2010), pp. 197-208 (esp. pp. 204, 207).

43. Evans, introduction to "Richard of St Victor's *On the Trinity*," pp. 202-3.

44. Evans details the connections between Richard's thought and that of other theologians such as Anselm of Canterbury, John of Salisbury, Gilbert of Poitiers, Achard of St. Victor, and Augustine. See Evans, introduction to "Richard of St Victor's *On the Trinity*," p. 207;

mind," Richard endeavored to set forth a reasoned account of the faith confessed in the creed, not for knowledge's sake, but because "rational comprehension" of "eternal things" instead of mere belief in them is necessary for mature Christian spirituality.[45]

Richard's treatise on the Trinity contains six books, but only one (Book Three) receives much attention in contemporary theology. The reason for this focus seems twofold. On the one hand, Book Three contains what is unique in Richard's Trinitarian theology, and, on the other hand, it was the only part of his treatise available in English translation until the recent full English translation by Christopher Evans in *Trinity and Creation* (2010).[46] Richard's theology of divine plurality outlined in Book Three is also a creative development within the Western tradition and has served as a resource for contemporary Trinitarian theology. For these reasons, it is my focus as well.

Richard argues for the threeness of God from the concept of perfect goodness, or *benevolentia*. Self-sharing love is the chief nature of divine goodness.[47] He provides a Trinitarian application of Anselm's "greatest conceivable being" argument for the existence of God. According to Anselm, the existence of God is intrinsic to the very notion of God.[48] Likewise, Richard argues that the notion of perfect goodness and love entails three divine persons. Richard begins with the idea that God is supremely good. Since goodness that includes love is superior to that which lacks love, it follows that God must be love. Since interpersonal love is better than self-love, then God must be a plurality of persons. Moreover, love requires not only two persons, but also three for its full expression. The love

---

see especially the detailed text-critical notes in his translation of *De Trinitate*, which set out the intellectual landscape for Richard's Trinitarian theology.

45. Richard of St. Victor, *On the Trinity*, trans. and intro. by Christopher P. Evans, in Coolman and Coulter, eds., *Trinity and Creation*, 3.1 (p. 247); *Prologue* (p. 211); 1.1 (p. 213).

46. For the earlier translation of Book 3 of *The Trinity*, see Richard of St. Victor, *The Trinity*, in *Richard of St. Victor: The Twelve Patriarchs, the Mystical Ark, and Book Three of the Trinity*, trans. Grover A. Zinn, Classics of Western Spirituality (New York: Paulist, 1979), pp. 371-97.

47. Richard of St. Victor, *On the Trinity* 3.14 (p. 259). For a fuller discussion of the centrality of benevolence to the theology developed at St. Victor, see Boyd Taylor Coolman, "General Introduction," in Coolman and Coulter, eds., *Trinity and Creation*, pp. 23-48 (esp. pp. 37-42).

48. Zachery Hayes, "Introduction," in *The Works of St. Bonaventure*, ed. George Marcil, vol. 3: *Disputed Questions on the Mystery of the Trinity*, trans. Zachery Hayes (St. Bonaventure, NY: The Franciscan Institute, St. Bonaventure University, 2000), p. 19.

between two, or mutual love, is better than self-love because a giving and receiving of love occurs between the two. However, a higher manifestation of love happens when two who experience mutual love share this love with a third. The third person becomes the recipient of the shared love of the first two. The love between two that they share with a third *(condilectus)* is the zenith of love.

Richard maintains that love only attains the level of utter donation — and thereby perfection — when the Holy Spirit receives the mutual love of the Father and the Son. Therefore, the perfection of love transcends mutual love by sharing mutual love with a third. Since no greater form of love is imaginable, divine goodness and love requires no less than and no more than three divine persons. Richard portrays the Spirit as the divine person who shares in — as the recipient of — the mutual love of the Father and the Son. The Spirit is not the mutual love of the Father and Son itself; therefore, the Father and the Son conjointly love the Spirit, and the Spirit shares in this mutual love between the Father and the Son. The Spirit's sharing in the mutual love of the Father and the Son satisfies the gratuitous nature of love — that is, giving without receiving. Furthermore, in order to share or enjoy the mutual love between the Father and the Son, the Spirit, too, loves the Father and the Son. Each divine person gives and receives the three modes of love: love of another, the reception of returned love from the one loved (mutual love), and the reception of shared love *(condilectus)*, or the inclusion in the happiness of the mutual love of the other two.[49]

Several factors distinguish a Pentecostal approach to the Trinity from Richard's. First, whereas he draws explicitly on a principle of philosophical theology, this project draws on the Pentecostal experience of the Spirit and biblical narratives of the Spirit. His argument is sensible and has a certain compelling logic to it, but its primary categories are those of medieval theology and not the biblical accounts of the Spirit's work. My point is not to disparage Richard's Trinitarian theology, but to distinguish the nature of the two approaches. Richard's theology has its roots in medieval Scholastic theology; it was also no doubt influenced by Scripture passages such as 1 John 4:16, which says, "God is love," and Romans 5:5, which links the Spirit to the gift of divine love.[50]

49. Richard of St. Victor, *On the Trinity* 3.2 (pp. 248-49); 3.4-7 (pp. 250-53); 3.11-20 (pp. 256-64).

50. For example, in Book 6, Richard's discussion of Romans 5:5 follows in the path of

The approach to the Trinity in this book begins with the Pentecostal experience of the Spirit, and then moves to the biblical narratives of the Spirit to draw out the personal identity of the Holy Spirit. The reader should also note that I do not naively assume that my theology arises directly from the pages of Scripture. The theology developed here obviously has roots in contemporary theology and Pentecostal religious experience. Beginning with Pentecostal experience, and from there following the path of the biblical narrative of the Spirit, is, however, a distinct approach relative to Richard's.

Second, Richard's theology of concordant love is not ultimately a pneumatological contribution to Trinitarian theology. Although initially, or *in fieri,* it applies to the Holy Spirit, once the three forms of love are realized, all the divine persons express and receive the three forms of love. Hence, *in facto esse,* the Holy Spirit is not in any unique sense concordant love. Consider the difference between Richard's and Augustine's Trinitarian theology. The mutual-love model makes a pneumatological contribution, even if many criticize it for ultimately subordinating and obscuring the personal identity of the Holy Spirit. In the mutual-love model, the Holy Spirit has eternal identity as the mutual love of the Father and the Son and a unique place in the Godhead as the bond of love between the Father and the Son. In contrast, the Holy Spirit is not concordant love in Richard's theology.

The result is that Richard of St. Victor does not offer a Trinitarian theology based on pneumatology, but one based on a rational principle of philosophical theology: namely, the full expression of perfect goodness and love requires three divine persons. His Trinitarian theology has the impression of making a contribution based on pneumatology because it initially portrays the Holy Spirit as concordant love and as bringing divine love to full expression. However, the Spirit's identity as concordant love is transitory and is the result of Richard's logical steps — self-love, mutual love, concordant love — and not the unique personal identity of the Holy Spirit. In Richard's Trinitarian theology, each divine person fully manifests the three forms of love, and no one alone exclusively manifests and receives one form of love. Through their sharing in each type of love, nothing remains that is distinct to any one of the divine persons. In contrast,

---

Augustine and Peter Lombard by using it to support a theology of the Spirit as the gift of the Father and the Son, whom they send in grace (see Richard of St. Victor, *On the Trinity* 6.14 [p. 334]).

the Spirit's work in the biblical drama of redemption reveals the Holy Spirit as one who makes a distinctive contribution to the Trinitarian God.

I will bring this section to a close by observing that the Spirit's identity does not exclusively derive from being a procession from the Father or the Father and the Son. The Spirit plays an active role and contributes to the personal identity of the Father and the Son. Without the Spirit, God is neither a Trinity nor a community of love (as Richard argued in more philosophical categories). The Spirit plays a constitutional role, not just an instrumental one. In the mutual-love model, the Spirit is instrumental. The Spirit is the bond of love between the Father and the Son. In other words, the Spirit is the interpersonal relationship of love between the Father and the Son, but does not provide a unique and additional relational dynamic that is proper to the Spirit. In my proposal here, the Spirit is constitutional, which means that the Spirit fulfills the fellowship of the Trinitarian God by expanding the relational dynamic from mutual fellowship between two to the fellowship of the three divine persons. The Spirit does fulfill the relationship between the Father and the Son by uniting them in eternal love; but the Spirit also adds to that fellowship a truly Trinitarian relational dynamic and thus fulfills the fellowship of the *Trinitarian* God. It shares affinity with Richard's theology of concordant love, but has important differences. The Spirit's constitutional and consummative roles in completing the fellowship of the Trinitarian God derive from the revelation of the Spirit's eschatological work in the biblical drama of redemption and are not merely a step in a philosophical and logical sequence.

Contemporary Trends

In the latter half of the twentieth century, a renaissance emerged in contemporary Trinitarian theology, with Karl Barth and Karl Rahner in the vanguard.[51] Not only was the doctrine of the Trinity a renewed area of

51. Their work stimulated a host of groundbreaking works on the doctrine of the Trinity: e.g., David Brown, *The Divine Trinity* (LaSalle, IL: Open Court, 1985); David Coffey, *Deus Trinitas: The Doctrine of the Triune God* (New York: Oxford University Press, 1999); Catherine Mowry LaCugna, *God for Us: The Trinity and Christian Life* (New York: HarperCollins, 1991); Jürgen Moltmann, *The Trinity and the Kingdom: The Doctrine of God,* trans. Margaret Kohl (San Francisco: Harper and Row, 1981); Thomas F. Torrance, *The Christian Doctrine of God, One Being Three Persons* (Edinburgh: T&T Clark, 1996); Michael Welker, *God the Spirit,* trans. John F. Hoffmeyer (Minneapolis: Fortress, 1994).

study; it also became a source for the revitalization of a multitude of other areas of theology and Christian life and ministry.[52] This section engages two of these contemporary figures, John D. Zizioulas and Thomas G. Weinandy. Zizioulas, one of the key voices in Orthodox Trinitarian theology, intentionally draws on his tradition to present a Trinitarian theology that speaks to the contemporary world. Weinandy's proposal, though it gives the Spirit a unique role in the Trinity and endeavors to develop a unique model of the Trinity, remains squarely within the Western Augustinian tradition.[53] The following articulates key areas of the Trinitarianism of Zizioulas and Weinandy and offers constructive improvement on the basis of a Pentecostal Trinitarian theology.

John Zizioulas

John Zizioulas's theology played a significant role in the renewal of Trinitarian theology for at least two reasons. It taps into the historic doctrines of patristic and Eastern Trinitarian theology, and it articulates these traditional doctrines in the relational and personal values of contemporary philosophy, theology, and culture.[54] His contribution to Trinitarian theology consists of two principles. First, the Father is the personal ground of the being of God, which expresses the Cappadocian and Eastern doctrine

52. For example, Trinity and anthropology and social relations: Marc Cardinal Ouellet, *Divine Likeness: Toward a Trinitarian Anthropology of the Family* (Grand Rapids: Eerdmans, 2006); Trinity and creation: Samuel M. Powell, *Participating in God: Creation and the Trinity* (Minneapolis: Fortress, 2003); Trinity and ecclesiology: Miroslav Volf, *After Our Likeness: The Church as the Image of the Trinity* (Grand Rapids: Eerdmans, 1998); Trinity and Christian mission: John G. Flett, *The Witness of God: The Trinity,* Missio Dei, *Karl Barth, and the Nature of Christian Community* (Grand Rapids: Eerdmans, 2010); and Trinity and theology of religions: S. Mark Heim, *The Depth of the Riches: A Trinitarian Theology of Religious Ends* (Grand Rapids: Eerdmans, 2001).

53. Weinandy is also a charismatic Catholic. Moreover, his charismatic experience fostered his contribution to Trinitarian theology, a process that reflects my proposal for the theological fertility of the experience of the Spirit. However, I have treated him here because his work is known less as charismatic than Kilian McDonnell's is, whom I discuss in chapter 5 below, "Charismatic Trinitarian Theology." My judgment may seem arbitrary, and I do not hereby question in any way the sufficiency of Weinandy's charismatic credentials.

54. Whether his appropriation of Cappadocian theology is accurate is another matter, which I leave to patristic scholars such as Lucian Turcescu, "'Person' versus 'Individual', and Other Modern Misreadings of Gregory of Nyssa," in Coakley, ed., *Re-Thinking Gregory of Nyssa,* pp. 97-109.

of the monarchy of the Father. It means that the Son and the Holy Spirit derive their being from the Father. The Father begets the Son and spirates the Holy Spirit. The Father is the one God and the ground of unity of the three divine persons. From that first principle emerges the second principle: communion, or persons in relationship, is constitutive of being. The Trinity (or persons in relationship) is the most basic ontological reality.[55] Based on these two relational notions, Zizioulas develops a relational theory of human personhood in which human beings transcend individualism and attain authentic personhood through communion with the Trinitarian God and the people of God through the ministry of the church.[56] I want to deal with several implications of these two principles. I argue that his theology of the monarchy of the Father cannot sustain his communitarian ontology, but a turn to pneumatology provides the way to retain key aspects of his theology of the Father and support for his communitarian ontology.

The first issue is that Zizioulas's theology bears a fundamental contradiction. On the one hand, Zizioulas sees the Father as the ontological ground of the Trinity. He declares that the Father is the "*personal ontological* origination" and "the one ontological *arche* in the Trinity," that "the Trinity is a *movement* from the one to the three ('the monad moved to triad . . .')," and that the "relational character of the 'divine substance'" arises from the generation of the Son and the procession of the Spirit from the Father.[57] In a summary, he says the following: "The Trinity *depends ontologically on the Father* and is not in itself, that is, *qua* Trinity, the one God. If the Trinity is God, it is only because the Father makes it Trinity by grant-

55. Stanley J. Grenz calls this principle the "Zizioulas Dictum" and says that its influence in contemporary theology is comparable to Rahner's rule, which posits the symmetry between the economic and immanent Trinity (Grenz, *Rediscovering the Triune God: The Trinity in Contemporary Theology* [Minneapolis: Fortress, 2004], pp. 134-35).

56. For an extensive and worthwhile evaluation and appropriation of these ideas in Zizioulas, see Volf, *After Our Likeness.* For an introduction to the main contours of Zizioulas's Trinitarian theology and ecclesial vision of Christian personhood, see Patricia A. Fox, *God as Communion: John Zizioulas, Elizabeth Johnson, and the Retrieval of the Symbol of the Triune God* (Collegeville, MN: Liturgical Press, 2001), pp. 25-52; Grenz, *Rediscovering the Triune God,* pp. 131-47; Kärkkäinen, *The Trinity,* pp. 88-99, and *An Introduction to Ecclesiology: Ecumenical, Historical, and Global Perspectives* (Downers Grove, IL: InterVarsity, 2002), pp. 95-102.

57. John D. Zizioulas, *Communion and Otherness: Further Studies in Personhood and the Church,* ed. Paul McPartlan (New York: T&T Clark, 2006), pp. 119, 122, 150 (italics in original). Hereafter, page references to this work appear in parentheses in the text.

ing it *hypostases*" (p. 154). On the other hand, he distinguishes between the *ousia,* or the divine nature, and the *hypostases,* or the persons. Zizioulas maintains that the Father causes the hypostases of the Son and the Holy Spirit, but clarifies that this takes place "on the hypostatic or personal level, and not on that of *ousia.*" In other words, the generation of the Son and the procession of the Holy Spirit do not occur at the "level of substance" (p. 119).

If the Father is the ontological ground of the Trinity, then the movement from the one Father to the Son and the Holy Spirit is at the level of substance or nature. To deny the latter point is to deny the former one and to grant the former is to accept the latter. One cannot affirm that the Father is the ontological ground of the Godhead (as he calls it, a "Patrocentric view of divine unity" [p. 120]) and deny that the generation of the Son and the procession of the Holy Spirit occur at the level of the divine nature. One way to sort out this conundrum may be to suggest that the ontological role of the Father, as the ground of the Son and the Spirit, pertains to their status or being as persons and not to their divine nature per se. This solution would allow for the Father to be the source of the Son's and Spirit's existence as persons. This initially seems to be Zizioulas's view, since he maintains, "The Cappadocians insisted on the Father, rather than the divine *ousia,* being the *arche* of personal divine being," and the Father is the "initiator at once both of personal being and freedom, that is, of ontological otherness in the Trinity" (pp. 119, 121).[58] Nevertheless, it also subverts Zizioulas's central thesis — that the ground of all being is personal — and what he maintains at other points about the Father as the ontological source of the Trinity.[59] It does so because it drives a wedge between the ontology of the divine nature and the ontology of the divine persons. Unfortunately, uniting being and personhood is precisely what Zizioulas's claim that the generation of the Son and the procession of the Spirit from the Father take place "on the hypostatic or personal level, and not on that of *ousia*" endeavors to safeguard (p. 119). This situation is a case where one

58. The freedom of the Father is also a central conviction of Zizioulas's Trinitarian theology. The decision of the Father to create personal diversity is perfectly voluntary and under no necessity. For a discussion of this notion, see Paul M. Collins, *Trinitarian Theology, West and East: Karl Barth, the Cappadocian Fathers, and John Zizioulas* (New York: Oxford University Press, 2001), pp. 179-83.

59. See, e.g., John D. Zizioulas, *Being as Communion: Studies in Personhood and the Church* (London: Darton, Longman, and Todd, 1985), pp. 40-41, 89; see also *Communion and Otherness,* pp. 116, 160-61, 165.

simply cannot have it both ways. Either the Father is really the ontological ground of the Trinity, in which case the subsistence of the Son and Spirit are subsistences of the divine nature that are caused by the Father, or the Father is the ground of their personal subsistences, which does not entail the personal subsistence of the divine nature as such in the three divine persons.

Zizioulas endeavors to resolve this tension with the qualification that, in Cappadocian theology, "being" entails both the notions of substance or nature and personhood, but also their sharp distinction.[60] Whether or not this principle represents Cappadocian theology is unimportant, but it does set forth a sensible way of thinking about the being of God and provides a way of affirming the irreducibility of the divine persons and the divine nature. The problem is that it contradicts Zizioulas's argument that the Father causes the hypostases of the Son and the Holy Spirit, but that this takes place "on the hypostatic or personal level, and not on that of *ousia*" (pp. 119, 125-26).[61] If being is intrinsically personal, then the generation of the Son and the procession of the Spirit from the Father occur at both the levels of personhood and nature. Since the diversification of the persons from the Father is not at the level of the divine nature, the ontological ground of divine being is not the Father, which means that the ontological ground of the divine being is not personal or characterized by communion.[62]

This conclusion unhinges Zizioulas's thesis that the ground of being is persons in communion. It does so because the Father is only the ontological ground of the persons and not of the divine being. Thomas F. Torrance is closer to the mark when he argues that the Son does not proceed from the "*person* of the Father . . . but from the being of the Father."[63] Thus, while theologians can distinguish between the divine nature and the divine persons for the sake of — indeed, because of — the inherent incapac-

60. He makes this distinction in several versions: e.g., cause applies to persons, but not the substance, *hypostasis*, and *ousia*, the what (nature) and how (persons) of the divine being (Zizioulas, *Communion and Otherness*, pp. 125-30).

61. A. J. Torrance makes a similar criticism in *Persons in Communion: An Essay on Trinitarian Description and Human Participation, with Special Reference to Volume One of Karl Barth's* Church Dogmatics (Edinburgh: T&T Clark, 1996), p. 289.

62. E.g., he says: "The idea of causation is used in order to describe the *how* of divine being and avoid making the emergence of the Trinity a matter of transmission of *ousia*. What the Father 'causes' is a transmission not of *ousia* but of personal otherness" (Zizioulas, *Communion and Otherness*, pp. 129-30).

63. Torrance, *Christian Doctrine of God*, p. 141.

ity of the human mind to comprehend God, no distinction actually pertains between the nature and the persons in the Godhead. God is the Trinity of Father, Son, and Holy Spirit.

If the substance is not differentiated in the divine persons, then what are the three divine persons? As Augustine points out, God is the three divine persons.[64] The divine nature exists as the Father, the Son, and the Holy Spirit, which Zizioulas affirms when he says, the "Holy Trinity is a *primordial* ontological concept and not a notion which is added to the divine substance or rather which follows it, as is the case in the dogmatic manuals of the West."[65] It is noteworthy that Zizioulas commits the very error he attributes to Augustine and the West: he accuses Augustine of elevating "the one divine substance above or before the person of the Father."[66] However, by putting the subsistence of the persons at a level other than that of the divine nature, Zizioulas does the same thing. A riposte might be that, yes, a distinction pertains between the *ousia* and the persons; but this does not mean that the nature is before the persons. We may grant this; but if we allow this nuance for Zizioulas, we should do the same for the Western distinction between nature and persons, which obviates Zizioulas's criticism of Western Trinitarianism. This distinction still makes the one between the persons and the nature in such a way that the Father cannot be the ontological ground for the divine being per se, but only for the persons of the Son and the Spirit.

Another way of seeing this problem in Zizioulas is his construal of the options in strict binary terms: either one accepts his view of the monarchy of the Father as the ultimate ontological ground of the communion of the divine persons, or one takes the impersonal divine substance as the ultimate ontological category.[67] He makes this argument against the view that posits the Trinity as the "ultimate ontological ground in God," which, ac-

64. Augustine, *The Trinity* 15.43 (p. 428). For a contemporary treatment of Augustine's Trinitarian theology, see Lewis Ayres, *Nicaea and Its Legacy.*

65. Zizioulas, *Being as Communion,* p. 17.

66. Zizioulas, *Communion and Otherness,* p. 118.

67. For example, Zizioulas, *Being as Communion,* pp. 40-41; *Communion and Otherness,* pp. 162, 165. In a comparison and evaluation of the concept of Trinitarian personhood in Zizioulas and T. F. Torrance, Ralph Del Colle frames the debate in terms of two options: "Is the ontological ground or principle of God the person of the Father or the relational divine being itself?" I think this accurately states the alternatives as long as the "relational divine being itself" is understood as the Trinity of Father, Son, and Spirit itself. See Del Colle, "'Person' and 'Being' in John Zizioulas' Trinitarian Theology: Conversations with Thomas Torrance and Thomas Aquinas," *Scottish Journal of Theology* 54 (2001): 70-86 (esp. p. 72).

cording to Zizioulas, "does away with any idea of *ontological derivation* in divine being" (by which he means the ontological derivation of the Son and the Spirit from the Father).[68] However, the options are more numerous than Zizioulas allows.

The key issue for an interpersonal understanding of the divine persons' identities is not whether the Father is the source of the generation of the Son and the procession of the Holy Spirit. For the sake of discussion, let us grant that the Father is the source of the immanent processions. The issue for an interpersonal and genuinely reciprocal view of divine personhood is whether that processive process exhausts and is even primary for their personhood. If one adopts a relational view of personhood, which entails reciprocal and dynamic *inter*personal relationships — which Zizioulas does when he affirms that "persons are givers and recipients of personal identity" — then the identities of the Son and the Spirit cannot be informed primarily in their "ontological derivation" from the Father because such a status is decidedly nonreciprocal and thus nonrelational, at least in an interpersonal sense (pp. 142, 134-35; italics in original). The same point applies to the Father: he is the begetter and spirator, and thus his interpersonal relationships *with* the Son and the Spirit add nothing to his identity.[69]

The consequence of investing so much in the monarchy of the Father is twofold. First, the Father is the primal individual and not a person defined in communion with other persons. The Father is Father "prior" to the generation of the Son and procession of the Spirit.[70] Zizioulas says that the Father, the Son, and the Holy Spirit are "relational entities," but what

68. Zizioulas, *Communion and Otherness,* pp. 134-35. Hereafter, page references to this work appear in parentheses in the text. Miroslav Volf also critiques Zizioulas's limitation of the theological option to his own view or a unity based on substance (Volf, *After Our Likeness,* p. 79).

69. According to Thomas H. McCall, the priority Zizioulas gives to the Father derives from his concern to retain the absolute freedom or sovereignty of God. He also argues that Zizioulas's way of understanding the priority and causal origin of the Father vis-à-vis the Son and the Spirit borrows conceptually from Heidegger's philosophical categories of *unthrown* and *thrown* (see McCall, *Which Trinity? Whose Monotheism? Philosophical and Systematic Theologians on the Metaphysics of Trinitarian Theology* [Grand Rapids: Eerdmans, 2010], pp. 194-201).

70. Zizioulas maintains that "[t]here *is,* in fact, an ordering [or *taxis*] in the Trinity, since the Father *always* comes first, the Son second, and the Spirit third" (*Communion and Otherness,* p. 137). I realize that the generation of the Son and the procession of the Spirit are eternal; "priority" refers to the Father as the unbegotten source of the atemporal order of the immanent processions. See *Communion and Otherness,* pp. 116, 120-22, 137, 160.

does he mean when he refers to the Father as a "relational entity"? (p. 122) Does he mean that the Father has his identity in mutual and dynamic relationships with the Son and the Spirit? No. He means that the Father is the one who begets the Son and spirates the Spirit and only then exists in relationship to the Son (he does not say that the Father has a relationship with the Spirit). His insistence that the Father is "inconceivable without the Son and the Spirit" implies that for the Father to be the Father he must beget the Son and spirate the Spirit. However, this implication is misleading because the Father has his identity as the ontological ground of the Son and Spirit prior to begetting the Son and spirating the Spirit (pp. 122, 126).[71] The Father always exists with the Son and the Spirit; nonetheless, the Father's identity, Zizioulas says, "*always* comes first" and resides in his status as the ultimate ontological ground of the Godhead and not in his relationships with the Son and the Spirit per se (p. 137; italics in original). Thomas H. McCall highlights the problem of Zizioulas's position: "For personal properties . . . are relational properties; they are the properties that make the persons the distinct entities they are *in relation to the other persons*."[72] The personal property of the Father as ontological ground is prior to begetting the Son and spirating the Spirit.

A second consequence is that the Father does not form the persons of the Son and the Spirit relationally, but *unilaterally* — through acts of begetting and spiration.[73] The Son's and Spirit's personal characteristics indicate the nonreciprocal nature of their personal formation and identity. Their personal properties are respectively begotten and spirated. The Son and the

71. Zizioulas observes: "None of the three persons can be conceived without reference to the other two, both logically and ontologically" (*Communion and Otherness*, p. 161). This point is one that I think all Trinitarians would endorse, but it does nothing to solve the unilateral derivation of the Son's and Spirit's identity from the Father and the ultimate individualism of the Father.

72. McCall, *Which Trinity? Whose Monotheism?* pp. 200-201. Miroslav Volf says: "It is difficult not to ascribe priority to the person [i.e., of the Father] before the communion" (Volf, *After Our Likeness*, p. 80).

73. Pannenberg faults both the East and the West for an exclusive reliance on the processions and relationships of origins that minimizes the contribution of the reciprocal relationships to define divine personhood (Pannenberg, *Systematic Theology*, 1: 319). Though Pannenberg's point is correct, his Trinitarian theology falls short of a thoroughly reciprocal vision of divine personhood. The Father and Son achieve their identity through mutual relationship with each other, but neither one of them has a relationship *with* the Holy Spirit; the Spirit remains a *through whom* rather than a *with whom* they have relationship (see Pannenberg, *Systematic Theology*, 1: 316).

Holy Spirit derive their hypostases not in relationship to the Father, but in having their procession from the Father. The point of the Father's monarchy is to affirm that the Father is the source of the hypostases or personhood of the Son and the Holy Spirit, which means that their hypostatic character or identity resides in their being from the Father in a particular way; that is, the Son is begotten, and the Spirit is spirated. Mode of procession — generation and spiration — defines the Son and the Spirit, and not the interpersonal relationships with each other or the Father. Moreover, the Father's relationships with the Son and the Spirit are unilateral: the Father's relationships with the Son and the Spirit are based on what he does *to* them (i.e., begetting and spirating) and do not derive from his reciprocal relationships *with* them. Despite Zizioulas's claim that the divine persons are ontologically constituted through reciprocal relationships, his notion that the Father is the cause of the Son and Spirit subverts it (pp. 141-42).

In an effort to resolve the tension between Zizioulas's theology of the Father as the source of the Godhead and the relational nature of personhood, Miroslav Volf proposes a distinction between the constitution of the persons and their relationships. The Father constitutes the persons, or "hypostatic divinity," of the Son and the Spirit, presumably through acts of generation and procession. Yet, their "innertrinitarian form" or relational identity derives from the mutual relationships among the divine persons and not exclusively from the Father.[74] Nonetheless — and though he adopts this technique from Jürgen Moltmann — Volf's proposal is a variation of Zizioulas's own device of distinguishing between the "what" and the "how" of the divine being, according to which, what the divine nature is (i.e., divine being) is distinct from how it exists (i.e., as the three divine persons).[75] What Volf has done is separate what the persons are (i.e., subsistences of the divine nature from the Father) from their personal identities. The result is the same as in Zizioulas's proposal: a rift between being and personhood. The divine persons' "hypostatic divinity," what they are at the "constitutional level," is distinct from their "innertrinitarian form," what they are at the "relational level."[76]

What is the solution to the individualism of the Father and the unilateral formation of the Son's and the Spirit's identity or, as in the case of Volf, the separation of the constitution of the persons and their relationships with

74. Volf, *After Our Likeness*, p. 216.

75. For Moltmann's use of these distinctions, see *Trinity and the Kingdom*, p. 183.

76. Volf, *After Our Likeness*, p. 217.

each other? To overcome these problems, theology needs to recognize that divine personhood arises from interpersonal relationships and is neither something the Father has without reference to the Son and the Spirit nor only the product of the Father's acts of generation and procession. Zizioulas's emphasis on the monarchy of the Father implies the same problems for the personal identities of the Son and the Spirit as covered in the discussion of the Cappadocians, and it is a problem for traditional Trinitarian theology more generally, which conceives of the personal identities of the divine persons as products of processions. Zizioulas's theology is not different in this respect, but it accentuates an inherent problem in traditional Trinitarian theology. Though I do not reject an order of immanent processions, I do not accept that the order and acts of generation and procession fully define the divine persons. The solution is that Trinitarian personhood is not only a product of processions and origins, but also interpersonal relationships. A theology of processions can indicate relative origins of the divine persons, but it does not exhaust the personal character of the divine persons.

My thesis, based on the yield of the pneumatology and Trinitarian theology outlined in chapters 1 and 2, is that — if we accept (1) the traditional *taxis* of the processions common to both East and West of the Father, the Son, and the Holy Spirit, and (2) reciprocal relationships inform divine personhood — then the personal identities of the divine persons are ontologically completed in the full Trinitarian fellowship constituted through the Holy Spirit. If an interpersonal theory of person is accepted, which is the central thesis of Zizioulas's personal ontology, then the divine persons can only achieve their full personal identity in the subsistence of the Holy Spirit and the genuine Trinitarian and reciprocal relationships that the Spirit makes possible.[77] This relational view of the Trinity is precisely the contribution of a Pentecostal theology. The Spirit is not only a procession or a bond of love. The Spirit is the divine person who completes the triune life and personal reality of God.

Does making full divine personhood contingent on the Holy Spirit replace an overemphasis on the Father with an overemphasis on the Holy Spirit? No. On the contrary, it affirms the equal contribution and participation of each divine person in the formation of each divine person's identity. The Father, the Son, and the Holy Spirit do not experience the full flowering

77. Zizioulas expresses the personal nature of being when he declares: "*To be* and *to be in relation* becomes identical. . . . It is only in relationship that identity appears as having an ontological significance" (*Being as Communion*, p. 88; italics in original).

of their personal identities until the Spirit comes forth and completes the interpersonal and reciprocal relationships among the three divine persons. Does my proposal implicitly undermine the importance of the divine processions? No. In fact, my case for the role of the Spirit in fulfilling the fellowship of the Trinitarian God can presuppose the traditional order of processions, but it does maintain that processions, whether from the Father alone or from the Father and the Son, are not the primary source of personal identity. The Spirit's interrelationship with the Father and the Son and the fully Trinitarian fellowship the Spirit brings to the Godhead fulfill the personal identities of the divine persons. The fullness of personal identity formation is in interpersonal relationships and not processions. The Son is the eternal Son, not by being merely begotten from the Father, but by dwelling in eternal communion with the Father and the Holy Spirit. Furthermore, whether one sees the Spirit's role in the traditional way as being the intermediary of the Father and Son's relationship (e.g., the mutual-love model) or, in a more social (or Richardian) Trinitarian way, as one who has relationships with the Father and the Son (my preference), the Spirit remains the divine person who brings the Father's and the Son's eternal personal activity and identity to fullness. In this respect, the Spirit is as much a cause of the Father's and Son's identity as they are of the Spirit's. Moreover, this point is consistent with the eschatological character of the Spirit's work in the economy of redemption that I discussed in chapter 2. As the Spirit of Pentecost fulfills the work of the Son sent by the Father, so the Spirit brings to fruition the fellowship of the Trinitarian God.

Finally, why are the divine persons ontologically completed through the activity of the Holy Spirit? The reason is that the divine persons are not accidental qualities of the divine nature, but are rather the hypostatic or personal way the nature exists. Ultimately, no distinction pertains between the persons and the nature; they are one and the same thing. Consequently, what informs divine personal identity is an ontological category. If the personal characteristics are not ontological, then what are they? Accidental or nonontological? As Zizioulas insists, "The person is no longer an adjunct to a being, a category which we *add* to a concrete entity once we have first verified its ontological hypostasis. *It is itself the hypostasis of the being.*"[78] If we accept that the divine persons' identities are only complete in and through their full Trinitarian communion, then it follows that the fullness of Trinitarian identity in communion happens in and through the

78. Zizioulas, *Being as Communion,* p. 39 (italics in original).

Holy Spirit; yet, at the same time, the Spirit's personhood emerges in relationship with the Father and the Son.

Consider the following illustration. My family consists of my wife, Sheila, my daughter, Gabrielle, my son, Max, and me. If, for the sake of the illustration, we take the biblical image of children being from their fathers, it suggests that although my children derive from me, their father, their personal identities — and mine as a father — do not reside primarily in their being from me. Their personal identities as my children come to shape in our interrelationships. Moreover — and vitally important for the Spirit's role in completing the fellowship and the identities of the divine persons — Sheila's and my personal identities as parents are the product of Gabrielle's and Max's relationship with us. Therefore, our personal identities, as the Studebaker family, arise precisely from our interrelationships and not merely from relations of origins.

In summary, the relational and dynamic nature of divine personhood means that the Holy Spirit is the linchpin of the fellowship of the Trinitarian God and thus also of the divine persons' identities. The Holy Spirit does not unilaterally complete the personal identity of the Father and the Son; rather, in the subsistence of the Holy Spirit and the tripersonal relationships that follow the Spirit's subsistence, the Godhead achieves a genuine Trinitarian fellowship in which each person mutually conditions the others' personal identities. The divine persons achieve their full personal identity in and through the genuine reciprocal relationships the Spirit makes possible. Each divine person, therefore, is the basis of an ontology of communion: a communion that begins with the Father, moves to the Son, and comes to completion in full Trinitarian fellowship in the Holy Spirit. This communal vision of God arises from a Pentecostal perspective on the Trinity that emerges from the biblical narratives of the Spirit.

Thomas Weinandy

Weinandy endeavors to set forth a unique Trinitarian model based on pneumatological insights. He promises that it overcomes the Western tendency to portray the Spirit in passive terms and the problematic order of processions common to both Eastern and Western Trinitarianism. His proposal is innovative and gives the Spirit a more active role in the Trinity than does either Western or Eastern Trinitarianism; nevertheless, it remains within a Western form of Trinitarian theology. As such, Weinandy provides an important example of the problems and the potential of revising Western Trinitarianism. I will first set forth the key elements of Weinandy's theology and then interact with it from the perspective of a Pentecostal Trinitarian theology.

Weinandy critiques the Western tradition for portraying the Spirit in passive terms, which, he charges, obscures the personhood of the Spirit. Whereas the Father and the Son derive from their unique relational activities — that is, the Father begets and loves the Son, and the Son loves the Father as the only-begotten Son — the same cannot be said of the Holy Spirit, who passively subsists as their mutual love and thus does not engage in personal activity.[79] Weinandy observes: "It is therefore difficult to see why, in the Western conception of the Trinity, the Holy Spirit is a distinct person or subject — a who" (p. 8). He also critiques the East for its emphasis on the monarchy of the Father, which leaves the active roles of the Son and the Spirit — and consequently their personal identities — ambiguous, and the linear nature of the processions from the Father, which renders the *perichoresis* of the divine persons opaque (p. 9).

In addition, Weinandy inveighs against the traditional order of processions among the divine persons — Father, Son, Spirit. He attributes the theory of the processions to a penchant in the East and West to prefer philosophical notions to the revelation of Scripture. With respect to the "logical or conceptual priority of the Father over the Son and the Son over the Holy Spirit," he says:

> I regard this sequentialism molded by Platonism and reinforced by Aristotelian epistemology as detrimental to a true understanding of the Trinity. A proper understanding of the Trinity can only be obtained if all three persons, logically and ontologically, spring forth in one simultaneous, nonsequential, eternal act in which each person of the Trinity subsistently defines, and equally is subsistently defined by, the other persons. (pp. 10, 14-15, 51, 55-56)

Weinandy is thus critical of central features of historic Trinitarian theology. He finds not only its way of articulating the person status of the Holy Spirit, but also its more fundamental theology of processions, problematic.

79. Thomas G. Weinandy, *The Father's Spirit of Sonship: Reconceiving the Trinity* (Edinburgh: T&T Clark, 1995), p. 8. Hereafter, page references to this work appear in parentheses in the text.

Weinandy turns to pneumatology to remedy the weaknesses in the two traditional approaches to the Trinity.[80] His thesis is that "the Father begets the Son in the Spirit and thus that the Spirit proceeds from the Father as the one in whom the Son is begotten and so in turn proceeds from the Son as the one in whom and through whom the Son loves the Father" (p. 89). He believes that the benefit of giving the Spirit a role in begetting the Son is twofold. First, it allows Trinitarian theology to transcend the philosophical categories that have subverted traditional Eastern and Western Trinitarianism; second, it offers a way to overcome the ecumenical obstacle of the *filioque.* For the East, Weinandy secures the absolute monarchy of the Father and distinguishes the Spirit's mode of procession from the Son's. For the West, he affirms that the Spirit proceeds derivatively as the Son's love of the Father (pp. 95-96). Weinandy deserves credit for his bold agenda, which both rejects dominant features of historic Trinitarian theology and endeavors to give the Spirit a more active role in the Trinity — based on a new model of the Trinity. But is the project successful? Two questions that derive from Weinandy's goals are the following: (1) Does Weinandy succeed in giving the Spirit an active role in the immanent Trinity? (2) Does he succeed in transcending the processions as definitive of the divine persons' identities? The answer on both points is no.

First, though Weinandy endeavors to give the Holy Spirit an active role in the Trinity, the Spirit is more of an instrument through whom the Father and Son act than a person who exists in interpersonal and reciprocal relationship with the Father and the Son. In an assessment of his project, Weinandy says that "the Trinity is now transfigured and redesigned. Not only does the Holy Spirit proceed principally from the Father (the concern of the East) and derivatively from the Son (the concern of the West), the Spirit in proceeding from the Father as the one in whom the Son is begotten now actively conforms the Father to be the Father for the Son and conforms the Son to be Son for the Father" (p. 97). How this formula gives the Spirit an active role in the immanent Trinity is unclear. The Holy Spirit does not engage in activity but is the instrument through whom the Father and the Son act. The Father begets the Son *in* the Holy Spirit, but the Spirit

80. Weinandy recognizes that after he developed his proposal, he found a similar one by François-Xavier Durrwell (Weinandy, *Father's Spirit of Sonship,* p. 18). Durrwell's text is *Holy Spirit of God: An Essay in Biblical Theology,* trans. Sister Benedict Davies (London: Geoffrey Chapman, 1986).

does not beget the Son. The same point can be applied to the Son's relationship to the Father, in which the Spirit proceeds as the Son's love for the Father. The Son acts, but not the Holy Spirit; in both respects the Spirit is an act of the other two.

Weinandy's conviction that the Holy Spirit plays a role in making the Father and the Son who they are in the eternal Godhead is correct. The reason for this is that biblical redemption is the yield of the Father's, the Son's, and the Holy Spirit's work, each divine person actively contributing to the content of that redemption. For example, Christ's redemptive mission, which the Father gave him, is facilitated by the Holy Spirit — for example, conception — and completed by the Spirit as the Spirit of Pentecost. The implication of their co-constitutional redemptive work is that their personal identities come to shape through reciprocal and dynamic interrelationships. However, Weinandy's description of the Holy Spirit's relationship to the Father and the Son does not support the point.

The Father and the Son are not recipients of the Spirit's activity, but the Spirit is the one through whom they act, and thus the Spirit does not play a role in the formation of their identity in any way other than an instrumental one. The Holy Spirit remains the instrument through whom the Father first acts and then the Son acts. Indeed, Weinandy's description of the Spirit's person status as "mystery" underscores the instrumentality of the Spirit's person status. The Spirit's role in the personal formation of the Father and the Son is like the wireless network through which I talk with my wife via our cell phones. The electronic signals of the cell phones are the instrument for our conversation; but they neither contribute to our personal identity, nor are they persons. They are real and play a role, but not a personal one. They are the instruments through which we conduct our personal relationships. I agree with Weinandy's desire to give the Holy Spirit a more constitutive role in the immanent Trinity, and that thesis does point toward a more active role of the Holy Spirit in the immanent Trinity. I say "point toward" because exactly what the Spirit *does* when the Father *begets* the Son in the Holy Spirit is opaque (pp. 84, 97-98). In Weinandy's proposal, the Holy Spirit remains a passive medium through whom the Father and the Son act, much like the Spirit in the mutual-love model.

A second issue and a consequence of the instrumental nature of the Spirit is that the Spirit is not a divine person who exists in interpersonal and reciprocal relationship with the Father and the Son. Weinandy recognizes this:

> The Holy Spirit does not have a distinct name because he subsists as the one in whom the Father and the Son are named. The Father subsists in relation to the Son . . . *only in the Holy Spirit* by whom he begot the Son. The Son subsists in relation to the Father *only in the Spirit* who conformed him to be Son. The Spirit subsists as a pure relation together with the Father and the Son in that he sustains their relationship and so imparts or manifests their names. (p. 84; italics in original)[81]

In this model, the Holy Spirit, as in the mutual-love model, is the relationship of the Father and the Son with each other. Thomas R. Thompson aptly surmises that the Spirit seems to remain "a depersonalized handmaid of Father and Son."[82]

The result of conceiving of the Spirit as the relationship of the Father and the Son is that the Spirit is not a person with whom they have a relationship. The Father and the Son do not have a relationship with the Holy Spirit, but through the Spirit have a relationship with each other. The Spirit is not a divine person who exists in interpersonal and reciprocal relationship with the Father and the Son. The following question underscores the significance of this point for Weinandy's project: What is the assumption of Weinandy's claim to give the Spirit an active role in the Trinity and thereby secure the full person status of the Spirit in relationship to the Father and the Son (an assumption with which I agree)? Weinandy provides the answer when he identifies the lesson the West can learn from the East; namely, "personhood is inherently dynamic" (pp. 62-63). He clarifies this standard by saying that "[t]he Father must be the dynamic source and fount of the Son and the Holy Spirit. The Son and the Holy Spirit, in their respective personhoods, must equally be in a dynamic relationship with the Father" (p. 63). I endorse his principle that personhood is dynamic and comes to fruition through reciprocal relationships.[83] Unfortunately, only the Father and the Son — and not

81. Durrwell portrays the Spirit in a similar way — with the comment that the Spirit's "personality is entirely defined by his relationship with the Father and the Son" (Durrwell, *Holy Spirit of God,* p. 140).

82. Thomas R. Thompson, review of Thomas G. Weinandy, *The Father's Spirit of Sonship: Reconceiving the Trinity,* in *Calvin Theological Journal* 32 (1997): 195-200.

83. The relational nature of personhood is widespread in contemporary Trinitarian theology. See, e.g., Christoph Schwöbel and Colin E. Gunton, eds., *Persons, Divine and Human: King's College Essays in Theological Anthropology* (Edinburgh: T&T Clark, 1991), which explores through its essays the relational nature of human personhood in light of the relational nature of the Trinitarian persons. Amos Yong, in *Spirit-Word-Community,* p. 59, adopts the term

the Holy Spirit — achieve this measure of personhood in Weinandy's account of the Trinity. With respect to the generation of the Son, Weinandy recognizes that generation "is purely passive in nature. Is there a reciprocal act that the Son performs which equally constitutes his being the Son in relationship to the Father and so, in some sense, constitutes the Father as the Father?" (p. 66) His answer to this question is that the Son loves the Father in the Holy Spirit, which conditions the personhood of the Father as the beloved Father of his beloved Son (p. 66). Again, I agree with the principle of relational reciprocity in the formation of personal identity and with the principle that the Father's and Son's acts of love toward each other are co-constitutional; but I maintain that in Weinandy's theology the Holy Spirit does not enjoy the same level of person status.

The Holy Spirit remains the instrument through whom the Father and the Son have a relationship with each other and not a divine person with whom they have relationship. Weinandy maintains that the "one action by which the Spirit is the Spirit is then twofold. . . . The Spirit, springing forth within the Father as his love in or by which the Son is begotten, conforms the Father to the Father for the Son and concurrently conforms the Son to the Son for the Father" (p. 73). Hence, the identity of the Father is not constituted by a relationship *with* the Holy Spirit, but *through* the Holy Spirit in begetting and loving the Son. The Father's identity consists exclusively in his relationship to the Son and not in a relationship with the Holy Spirit. The same can be said of the Son's identity with respect to the Father. The result is that Weinandy does not attain his goal of giving the Spirit an active role in the immanent Trinity and thereby an equivalent person status with the Father and the Son. Moreover, the fellowship of the Trinity is the fellowship of the Father and the Son and not a fully Trinitarian fellowship between the Father, the Son, and the Holy Spirit. To be consistent with the Spirit's constitutional or eschatological role in the economy of redemption, the Holy Spirit needs to be conceived of as not only the one *through* whom the Father and Son enjoy their eternal fellowship, but also one *with* whom they enjoy fellowship.

Third, Weinandy's understanding of the Spirit's identity is not significantly different from the Spirit's status in the mutual-love model, which is

---

"symbiotic relationality," which means that mutual relationships define things in the created world and the divine reality. Stanley J. Grenz refers to the "near consensus that *person* is a relational concept" in contemporary Trinitarian theology (*The Social God and the Relational Self: A Trinitarian Theology of the* Imago Dei [Louisville: Westminster John Knox, 2001], p. 9).

only problematic because Weinandy seeks to offer a model of the Trinity distinct from the East's and West's conceptions (p. 60). Unquestionably, his assertion of the Spirit's role in the begetting of the Son is unique vis-à-vis traditional Trinitarian theology; but the end product of the processions is difficult to distinguish from the mutual-love model. Weinandy summarizes the immanent processions: "The Father spirates the Spirit in the begetting of the Son . . . the Spirit proceeds also from the Son. The Son, being begotten by the Father, is confirmed as Son by the Spirit (sonship) and so the Spirit proceeds from him as the identical Love for the Father in whom he himself is begotten" (p. 96; see also pp. 29, 46). At the culmination of the procession process, the Spirit is the love whereby the Father loves the Son and the Son loves the Father. Aside from giving the Spirit an instrumental role in the begetting of the Son, his insistence on the "identical" nature of the Father's and the Son's love — that is, the Holy Spirit — is a version of the Western doctrine of the *filioque,* and is indistinguishable from the Spirit's identity in the mutual-love model.

Indeed, in the mutual-love model, the subsistence of the Holy Spirit is more readily grasped than in Weinandy's offering. Mutual love subsists as something between the Father and Son. But in Weinandy's thought, the Spirit is spiration, which is the act through which the Father begets the Son. But in what way does that act subsist? It does not have its own proper subsistence. In traditional Trinitarian thought, at least since Aquinas, a divine person has been conceived as a subsistent relationship, and a subsistent relationship is the product or the term of a procession. The Son proceeds under the mode of generation and thus subsists as the only-begotten Word of God. The act or procession of generation terminates in the subsistence of the Son. The Holy Spirit proceeds by way of spiration. The particular term or subsistence of the Holy Spirit has always been more difficult to conceive of than that of the Son, but perhaps the most common way has been to think of the Spirit as the subsisting love — mutual love — between the Father and the Son.

In Weinandy's proposal, the Spirit has no proper subsistence or at least the Spirit's manner of subsistence is even less clear than in traditional Trinitarian theology. If the Spirit is the act of the Father (the Father begets the Son in the spiration of the Holy Spirit), the consequence is that the procession of the Spirit (the Spirit's spiration from the Father) terminates in the subsistence of the Son or is the medium for the generation of the Son. Weinandy strives to give the Spirit an active role and a clearer personal identity in the immanent identity. Nevertheless, the result is less advantageous for the Holy

Spirit's personal identity than in the traditional models, which can at least more readily portray the unique subsistence and hence personal distinction of the Holy Spirit. In Weinandy's account, the Holy Spirit is a medium for begetting the Son, but has no proper subsistence. Moreover, the act of procession, in which the Holy Spirit's personhood resides, subsists as the Son, since the Father begets the Son in the spiration of the Spirit. Though not without problems, the mutual-love model portrays the Spirit as the mutual love that subsists between and unites the Father and the Son. In the end, though, the Holy Spirit is an act *and* a distinct subsistent reality: mutual love.

Fourth, Weinandy does not succeed in transcending an immanent order of processions, though he does reconfigure them. He apparently replaces the traditional sequence of Father, Son, and Holy Spirit with Father, Spirit, Son, and Spirit. I say "apparently" because the Spirit initially proceeds from the Father as the one through whom the Father begets the Son, and then finally and derivatively as the Son's love for the Father. Weinandy tries to move beyond the order of processions with the notion of simultaneous processions. He suggests that the Spirit proceeds from the Father, and the Father begets the Son in the Holy Spirit simultaneously (pp. 72-74). By positing the simultaneous procession of the divine persons, Weinandy believes that he has vaulted the obstacle of traditional Trinitarian theology's sequential processions. The problem with this proposed solution is that traditional Trinitarian theology not only sees the processions as simultaneous from a temporal perspective, but also recognizes an ontological order — and thus the sequence of immanent subsistences in Father, Son, and Spirit.

In the end, Weinandy does not get beyond an order of processions; rather, he posits the subsistence of the Holy Spirit "prior" to the Son. Since the Spirit proceeds from the Father in the begetting of the Son, the Spirit proceeds prior to the Son. "Prior" in this context refers to the ontological, and not the temporal, order of the immanent processions. So, although the divine persons subsist eternally according to their particular mode of subsistence, they do so in a relational order: the Father as the unbegotten begets the Son in the Spirit and loves the Son in the Spirit, and the Son in turn loves the Father in the Spirit. The consequence of this form of the *filioque* is that the Spirit, in the first mode of his subsistence, is prior to the subsistence of the Son because the Spirit is the instrument that proceeds from the Father and in whom the Father begets the Son. The traditional form of the *filioque* does not have this problem because it posits the double procession of the Holy Spirit from the Father and the Son after the Father begets the Son.

Weinandy's primary modification to the structure of the immanent Trinity, the notion that the Father begets the Son in the Holy Spirit, does not overcome an order of immanent processions, but only rearranges them. The only way to move beyond an order of processions as the source of the divine persons' identities is to dispense with the processions altogether. I do not recommend this move because the order of processions is significant and has value for understanding the relationships among the divine persons. The traditional notion of processions also correlates with the macro and micro structure of biblical revelation, for example, the macro movement of God/Father, Son in Christ, the Spirit of Pentecost and the micro relationships in the Father sending the Son, and the Father and the Son sending the Holy Spirit. Yet a theology of processions needs supplementation with the Spirit of Pentecost. The Holy Spirit is the divine person who fulfills the work of redemption and thus proceeds as the one who fulfills the eternal fellowship of the immanent Trinity.

Conclusion

Have I replaced a monopoly of the Father (the East and Zizioulas) or a cartel of the Father and the Son (the *filioque* of Western Trinitarianism) with the Spirit, who corners the market on divine personhood? I do not think so, because the Spirit's personal identity also comes to shape in relationship with the Father and the Son and the unique dynamic the Spirit's relationships to them bring to the Godhead. The personal identity of the Spirit is as much a product of the Spirit's relationships with the Father and the Son as theirs is with the Spirit. In the Trinity, the divine persons' identities are mutually contingent on the others; each of them adds something to each of the other two and, in a way similar to Richard of Saint Victor's notion of shared love *(condilectus)*, they each contribute something to the Godhead that transcends their contribution to any one divine person, which in turn enriches the community of the Godhead in general and the s in particular.[84] Therefore, my point is not that the Spirit displaces her and/or the Son, but that the Spirit has an irreducible role in the tution of the personal identities of the Father and the Son and has entity in relationship with the Son and the Father.

84. Paul S. Fiddes makes a similar point when he says that the Son and the Spirit also "make the Father what he is through their self-surrendering love" (*Participating in God: A Pastoral Doctrine of the Trinity* [Louisville: Westminster John Knox, 2000], p. 79).

4 Reformed Evangelical Trinitarian Theology

One may wonder, is a chapter on Trinitarian theology within North American evangelicalism necessary? For the most part, evangelicals neglected the Trinity until they found that it could serve the cause of male authority and female submission — an unfortunate development, though exceptions exist.[1] In the mid-1990s, Donald G. Bloesch and Millard Erickson devoted significant attention to the doctrine, and more recently Stanley J. Grenz (1950-2005) made it a centerpiece of his theological project, and Allan Coppedge made it the topic of a book.[2] One may object that these figures hardly ex-

1. Wayne Grudem, *Evangelical Feminism and Biblical Truth* (Sisters, OR: Multnomah, 2004); and Bruce A. Ware, *Father, Son, and Holy Spirit: Relationships, Roles, and Relevance* (Wheaton: Crossway, 2005). For a response to this trend, see Kevin Giles, *The Trinity and Subordinationism: The Doctrine of God and the Contemporary Gender Debate* (Downers Grove, IL: InterVarsity, 2002) and *Jesus and the Father: Modern Evangelicals Reinvent the Doctrine of the Trinity* (Grand Rapids: Zondervan, 2006).

2. Donald G. Bloesch, *God the Almighty: Power, Wisdom, Holiness, Love* (Downers Grove, IL: InterVarsity, 1995) and *The Holy Spirit: Works and Gifts* (Downers Grove, IL: InterVarsity Academic, 2000); Millard J. Erickson, *God in Three Persons: A Contemporary Interpretation of the Trinity* (Grand Rapids: Baker, 1995); Stanley J. Grenz, *Theology for the Community of God* (Grand Rapids: Eerdmans, 1994) and the first two of a projected six-volume series, which was cut short by his untimely passing in 2005: *The Social God and the Relational Self: A Trinitarian Theology of the Imago Dei* (Louisville: Westminster John Knox, 2001) and *The Named God and the Question of Being: A Trinitarian Theo-Ontology* (Louisville: Westminster John Knox, 2005); and Allan Coppedge, *The God Who Is Triune: Revisioning the Christian Doctrine of God* (Downers Grove, IL: InterVarsity Academic, 2007). Kevin J. Vanhoozer, *The Drama of Doctrine: A Canonical-Linguistic Approach to Christian*

haust the boundaries of evangelical theology. Thomas F. Torrance and Colin Gunton, after all, fit in the category of "evangelical." Without presuming to determine who is in and who is out of the evangelical fold, I am using the term in its more limited, but nonetheless important, North American sense.

North American evangelicalism is the heir of New England Puritanism, the revival movements of the eighteenth and nineteenth centuries, the fundamentalism of the early twentieth century, and neo-evangelicalism that emerged in the mid-twentieth century. Influential evangelical thinkers include Carl F. H. Henry (1913-2003), Bernard Ramm (1916-1992), Francis Schaeffer (1912-1984), John Stott (1921-2011), Stanley J. Grenz (1950-2005), Clark Pinnock (1937-2010), J. I. Packer, and Millard Erickson. Beliefs that typically characterize evangelicals are the deity and virgin birth of Christ, the Trinity, the authority (i.e., inerrancy or infallibility) of the Bible, the importance of a personal conversion experience and a relationship with Jesus Christ, and premillennial eschatology.[3] As the above list of figures and broad theological positions indicate, evangelicalism is not monochromatic. At present, evangelicalism has two major groups vying to be the standard-bearer of the movement. According to Roger E. Olson, the conservatives seek to define the boundaries in terms of a "fairly aggressive form of Reformed theology." Key figures in the conservative camp are Bruce Ware, R. C. Sproul, Jon Piper, and D. A. Carson. The other group, those whom Olson calls the "Postconservatives," consists of emerging church leaders such as Brian McLaren, Doug Pagitt, Tony Jones, and Eddie Gibbs, who have been influenced by theologians such as Stanley Grenz, Clark Pinnock, and John Franke.[4]

Theology (Louisville: Westminster John Knox, 2005), makes the Trinity central to his theological hermeneutics. Thomas H. McCall, *Which Trinity? Whose Monotheism? Philosophical and Systematic Theologians on the Metaphysics of Trinitarian Theology* (Grand Rapids: Eerdmans, 2010), though less programmatic, is a fine recent study on Trinitarian theology by an evangelical theologian.

3. I have not included representatives of the Emergent Church movement, such as Brian McLaren, Doug Pagitt, Tony Jones, and Eddie Gibbs, because it remains to be seen whether the movement will have an enduring influence on — and remain within — the traditional evangelical churches (on both counts I hope it does). For accounts of evangelicalism, see Garry J. Dorrien, *The Remaking of Evangelical Theology* (Louisville: Westminster John Knox, 1998); George M. Marsden, *Understanding Fundamentalism and Evangelicalism* (Grand Rapids: Eerdmans, 1991); Mark A. Noll, *American Evangelical Christianity: An Introduction* (Oxford: Blackwell, 2001); and Roger E. Olson, *The Westminster Handbook to Evangelical Theology* (Louisville: Westminster John Knox Press, 2004).

4. Roger E. Olson, *Reformed and Always Reforming: The Postconservative Approach to Evangelical Theology* (Grand Rapids: Baker Academic, 2007), pp. 7-31.

The question remains: Why, in a book on Pentecostal Trinitarian theology, should I engage evangelical Trinitarian theology? First, though the doctrine of the Trinity has not been a central issue in evangelical theology — as the doctrine of Scripture (i.e., inerrancy vs. infallibility) has been — it is both a central historic doctrine of the Christian faith and a subject of more recent attention. Second, Pentecostalism is inextricably bound to evangelicalism — at least from a historical perspective. The Pentecostal movement emerged from the revivalist and holiness movements of the late nineteenth and early twentieth centuries.[5] After World War II, Pentecostals forged social, theological, and institutional alliances with evangelicals. Evangelicals have also been the primary conversation partners in Pentecostal academic theology, though that has been less true in the last twenty years. Third, North American evangelicalism represents a major theological bloc within Christianity. Since I am seeking in this book to make a contribution to major Christian theological traditions, it is sensible to include evangelicalism.

An interaction with evangelicalism must begin with Jonathan Edwards, one of the most prominent historical figures in the American evangelical tradition. Edwards may seem to be an unlikely starting point, since he is most known for fire-and-brimstone sermons such as "Sinners in the Hands of an Angry God." Contrary to first impressions, however, the fact is that Edwards is one of the best resources for Trinitarian theology in the evangelical tradition. From Edwards, the conversation moves to the late-twentieth-century theologians Donald Bloesch, Millard Erickson, and Myk Habets. Bloesch and Erickson are among the most prominent evangelical theologians of the late twentieth century, and Habets is an emerging creative theologian from New Zealand. An obvious question might be: Why not interact with Wayne Grudem and Stanley Grenz? Grudem's influence via his *Systematic Theology* is extensive, but he does not bring his creative energy to bear on the doctrine of the Trinity to the extent that he does in other areas of theology. The Trinity has a fundamental place in Grenz's theology, both in his *Theology for the Community of God* and *The Social God and the Relational Self*. However, he adopts a common social Trinitarian theology and then uses its relational themes to develop other areas of

5. For the Reformed and Holiness evangelical roots of Pentecostalism, see Donald W. Dayton, *Theological Roots of Pentecostalism* (Grand Rapids: Francis Asbury Press, 1987); and Walter J. Hollenweger, *Pentecostalism: Origins and Developments Worldwide* (Peabody, MA: Hendrickson, 1997), pp. 144-52, 182-200.

theology, such as theological anthropology. Developing a constructive contribution to Trinitarian theology is not Grenz's goal; rather, his goal is to apply the Trinitarian insights of figures such as Wolfhart Pannenberg, Jürgen Moltmann, John Zizioulas, and Catherine Mowry LaCugna.[6]

Jonathan Edwards

By virtue of his pastoral tenures, prodigious sermonic and literary output, and rigorous and sophisticated defense of Calvinism, Jonathan Edwards gained enduring status as one of America's premier theologians and shapers of evangelical Christianity. His writings helped define central characteristics of American evangelicalism: revivalism, conversionism, and evangelism. Less well known, however, is the role of the Trinity and pneumatology in his theology, even though some of his best theology emerges when he follows his pneumatological interests. The strength of Edwards's pneumatology resides in its integration with his Trinitarian theology. For instance, he portrays the Spirit as the principle of the hypostatic union of the human and divine natures in the incarnation of Jesus Christ and as the principle of the believers' union with Christ and each other in grace. This role of the Spirit derives directly from the Spirit's identity as the mutual love of the Father and the Son. Unfortunately, though the mutual-love model of the Trinity funds some of his best pneumatological insights, it constrains them along with his broader vision of the Trinity as well. My analysis of Edwards in what follows concentrates on the Spirit's role in Edwards's Christology and theology of grace, but first it addresses the Spirit's identity as the mutual love of the Father and the Son.[7]

6. For example, chapter 1 in Stanley Grenz, *The Social God and the Relational Self,* is a survey of the key voices in Trinitarian theology since the Enlightenment (pp. 23-57). In *Rediscovering the Triune God: The Trinity in Contemporary Theology* (Minneapolis: Fortress, 2004), Grenz more thoroughly narrates developments in Trinitarian theology over the last century.

7. For more on the way Edwards's pneumatology and Trinitarian theology shaped his Christology and doctrine of grace, see Steven M. Studebaker, *The Trinitarian Vision of Jonathan Edwards and David Coffey* (Amherst, NY: Cambria, 2011).

Edwards and the Trinity

Jonathan Edwards's doctrine of the Trinity sits squarely within the mutual-love tradition and, at the same time, relies on ideas that, though not in tension, are not always central in the history of the model.[8] Here I have in mind the communicative nature of God or the divine disposition to communicate goodness. Edwards believed that intrinsic to the divine nature is a disposition to communicate divine goodness. He believed that this disposition for divine self-communication comes to expression both *ad intra* in the eternal Godhead and *ad extra* in creation and redemption, though only the former is of concern for the present discussion.[9]

Whether consciously or not, Edwards stands in continuity with medieval theologians Richard of St. Victor (d. 1173) and Bonaventure (1221-1274). Richard maintained that the perfection of goodness and love requires an eternal community of three divine persons, who repose in eternal shared love *(condilectus)*.[10] Bonaventure believed that the Trinity is a rational predicate of divine goodness, but he augmented it with the Pseudo-Dionysian notion of the self-diffusiveness of the divine being, which means that the perfection of divine goodness necessarily implies an intrinsic and eternal communication of the divinity.[11] The link between the intrinsic interper-

8. One line of interpretation posits two distinct Trinitarian models in Edwards's theology — an Eastern, or Cappadocian, model and a Western, or Augustinian, one. For more on this perspective, see Steven M. Studebaker, *Jonathan Edwards' Social Augustinian Trinitarianism in Historical and Contemporary Perspectives* (Piscataway, NJ: Gorgias, 2008), pp. 67-107, and Studebaker, "Jonathan Edwards' Social *Augustinian* Trinitarianism: An Alternative to a Recent Trend," *Scottish Journal of Theology* 56 (2003): 268-85. In *Jonathan Edwards' Social Augustinian Trinitarianism,* I argue that Edwards's Trinitarian theology should be read in terms of the Augustinian Trinitarian tradition and eighteenth-century Trinitarian theology. My second book on Edwards's Trinitarian theology brings him into ecumenical conversation with the Catholic theologian David M. Coffey and applies their theology to two areas of contemporary evangelical theology: the nature of grace and justification and theology of religions. See Studebaker, *The Trinitarian Vision of Jonathan Edwards and David Coffey.*

9. *The "Miscellanies" (Entry Nos. 1153-1360),* ed. Douglas A. Sweeney, in *The Works of Jonathan Edwards* (hereafter *WJE*), Harry S. Stout, gen. ed., vol. 23 (New Haven: Yale University Press, 2004), no. 1266a, p. 213; no. 1218, p. 153; and Edwards, *Dissertation I. Concerning the End for Which God Created the World,* in *Ethical Writings,* ed. Paul Ramsey, *WJE,* vol. 8 (New Haven: Yale University Press, 1989), pp. 432-34.

10. Richard of St. Victor, *The Trinity,* in *Richard of St. Victor: The Twelve Patriarchs, the Mystical Ark, and Book Three of the Trinity,* trans. Grover A. Zinn, The Classics of Western Spirituality (New York: Paulist, 1979), 3.2 (pp. 374-75).

11. *The Works of Bonaventure,* trans. José Vinck, vol. 2, *The Breviloquium* (Paterson, NJ:

sonal nature of divine goodness and the disposition of the divine nature for self-communication is a centerpiece of Edwards's Trinitarianism. Edwards believed that the divine disposition to communicate goodness can find realization only in a community of three divine persons.[12]

Edwards adopted the mutual-love model as the form for the divine disposition's communication of goodness. Following his predecessors, such as Augustine, Bonaventure, and Aquinas, Edwards also used the categories of the psychological analogy to describe the divine persons' modes of procession. What is important is that Edwards articulates the processions of the divine persons in terms of the psychological analogy (i.e., acts of understanding and will) and within the framework of the mutual-love model. In doing this he was following a well-established tradition of Trinitarian theology.

The Father, as the original source of the communication of goodness, first communicates the goodness of the divine nature in begetting the Son. In this respect, Edwards adopts the traditional view that the Father is self-subsistent and unbegotten.[13] As unbegotten, the Father is the ultimate source of the processions of the Son and the Holy Spirit.[14] The Son subsists as the Word or idea of the divine essence.[15] The generation of the Son occurs as God the Father has the divine essence as the object of the eternal act of the divine understanding. As the idea of the divine essence, the Word "repeats," or subsists, as the divine nature, and consequently the Son possesses the same dynamic features of the divine nature. The Son, like the Father, possesses the ability to know and to love and to communicate being. Therefore, the Son can co-spirate the Holy Spirit as mutual love; Edwards thus affirmed the *filioque*.[16]

St. Anthony Guild, 1963), p. 36; see also *The Works of St. Bonaventure,* ed. George Marcil, vol. 3, *Disputed Questions on the Mystery of the Trinity,* trans. Zachery Hayes (St. Bonaventure, NY: The Franciscan Institute, St. Bonaventure University, 2000), pp. 254-57.

12. *The "Miscellanies" (Entry Nos. a-z, aa-zz, 1-500),* ed. Thomas A. Schafer, *WJE,* vol. 13 (New Haven: Yale University Press, 1994), no. 96, pp. 262-63.

13. Edwards, "Miscellanies," *WJE,* vol. 13, no. 94, p. 257; *Discourse on the Trinity,* in *Writings on the Trinity, Grace, and Faith,* ed. Sang Hyun Lee, *WJE,* vol. 21 (New Haven: Yale University Press, 2003), pp. 130-31; and "The Threefold Work of the Holy Ghost," in *Sermons and Discourses, 1723-1729,* ed. Kenneth P. Minkema, *WJE,* vol. 14 (New Haven: Yale University Press, 1997), p. 379.

14. Edwards, "The Threefold Work of the Holy Ghost," *WJE,* vol. 14, p. 379.

15. Edwards, "Miscellanies," *WJE,* vol. 13, no. 94, pp. 258-60; no. 151, pp. 301-2; no. 260, p. 368.

16. Edwards, *Discourse on the Trinity, WJE,* vol. 21, pp. 116, 131; "Miscellanies," *WJE,*

The Holy Spirit flows forth in the second procession of the divine nature. As the Son proceeds via the divine understanding, so the Spirit proceeds and subsists as an eternal act of the divine will, which is love.[17] Specifically, the Holy Spirit subsists as the mutual love of the Father and the Son. Edwards believed that the subsistence of the Spirit as mutual love fulfills the dispositional nature of God. But why is mutual love necessary? It is because Edwards believed that a genuine communication of love includes reciprocation, or a return of love. It is not enough for the Father to communicate goodness by begetting and loving the Son. The Son must return love to the Father to fulfill the divine nature's disposition to communicate goodness. The communication of goodness or happiness presupposes a capacity of reception and return in the recipient of love. For Edwards, the mutual sharing of love between the Father and the Son — the Holy Spirit — fulfills the disposition of the divine nature to communicate goodness.[18]

Given that, in chapter 3 above, I discussed the Western approach to the Trinity, which Edwards adopted, my interaction with Edwards's use of the mutual-love model briefly addresses two ways that it impacts pneumatology — before I proceed to more sustained interactions with his Christology and theology of grace. The Spirit's personal identity as the mutual love of the Father and the Son is minimal relative to the Father and the Son for two reasons. First, though Edwards uses the mutual-love model, he understands the modalities of the processions in terms of the psychological analogy. As Augustine earlier realized, the processions of a rational nature illustrate diversity within and without the division of a nature, but the processions are relative activities within, or subsistences in, one nature and

---

vol. 13, no. 363, p. 435; no. 370, p. 442; *Notes on Scripture,* ed. Stephen J. Stein, *WJE,* vol. 15 (New Haven: Yale University Press, 1998), no. 335, pp. 319-20. Edwards's theory of the Son as an ideal repetition of the divine nature has led critics from Horace Bushnell and Benjamin Warfield to the contemporary Oliver Crisp to charge that his theology implies modalism, tritheism, or infinite multiplication of divine persons. For details, see Steven M. Studebaker and Robert W. Caldwell, *The Trinitarian Theology of Jonathan Edwards* (Burlington, VT: Ashgate, 2012).

17. Edwards, *Discourse on the Trinity, WJE,* vol. 21, pp. 113, 116-17, 121-22; "Miscellanies," *WJE,* vol. 13, no. 94, pp. 260-61; and "Charity and Its Fruits," in *Ethical Writings,* ed. Paul Ramsey, *WJE,* vol. 8 (New Haven: Yale University Press, 1989), p. 373.

18. Edwards, *Discourse on the Trinity, WJE,* vol. 21, pp. 135, 144; "Miscellanies," *WJE,* vol. 13, no. 97, p. 264. But Edwards also believed that the divine nature possessed an intrinsic tendency for economic self-communication. See Caldwell and Studebaker, *Trinitarian Theology of Jonathan Edwards.*

not really distinct subsistences of the nature.[19] Crudely put, the Son and the Spirit appear to be the operations of God's (or the Father's) understanding and will, which clearly reduces the Son and Spirit to functions of God (or the Father) because, according to the analogy, the mind is the term of substance, and the understanding and will its relative operations.[20]

Second, Edwards articulated — and I think rightly so — a strong relational notion of love and implicitly of personhood. I say "implicitly" with respect to personhood because his discussions of reciprocity deal specifically with the nature of love and not personhood. That is, love requires giving and receiving goodness and happiness. Although the presumption is that persons are the subjects giving and receiving love, making a case for relational personhood is not his purpose per se. Furthermore, Edwards does not apply to the Holy Spirit his principle that love requires a return. He argues that love is equivalent with excellency and consent, which means that love consists of a harmonious and reciprocal relationship between persons or consenting beings. In Edwards's version of the mutual-love model, the Father and the Son manifest the fullness of goodness, excellency, and happiness in their mutual and shared love with each other.[21] However, the Holy Spirit does not participate in this form of love. The Spirit neither receives nor gives love. The Spirit is love; the Spirit is the mutual love that binds the Father and the Son in eternal fellowship. The society of Edwards's Trinity is, therefore, two divine persons united in loving communion by the third person that is identical with the mutual love between the Father and the Son. If receiving and giving love is the essence of personhood, then the Spirit does not attain it. In other respects, my perspective on Edwards's use of the mutual-love model falls in line with the assessment made in chapter 3, and therefore, rather than repeat them here, I move to areas of his constructive theology that at the outset seem to offer the most promise.

19. Augustine, *The Trinity,* trans. Edmund Hill, vol. 5 of *The Works of Saint Augustine: A Translation for the 21st Century,* John E. Rotelle, gen. ed. (Brooklyn: New City, 1991), 9.2-8 (pp. 271-75).

20. Edmund Hill, *The Mystery of the Trinity,* Introducing Catholic Theology, 4 (London: Geoffrey Chapman, 1985), p. 126; "Introduction," in *The Works of Saint Augustine,* 5: 18-59 (esp. p. 53).

21. Jonathan Edwards, "The Mind," no. 1 (pp. 336-38), no. 45 (pp. 362-65); and "Beauty of the World," p. 305, in *Scientific and Philosophical Writings,* ed. Wallace E. Anderson, *WJE,* vol. 6 (New Haven: Yale University Press, 1980).

Edwards, Christ, and the Holy Spirit

Edwards's Trinitarian theology shaped his pneumatology, which, in turn, informed his constructive improvements on his tradition's Christology and doctrine of grace. In this synergy between the Trinity, Christology, and grace, pneumatology is central. Edwards consistently connects the Spirit's immanent identity and economic activity.[22] In the following two sections I focus on the way the Trinity and pneumatology direct the development of his theological account of the two primary works in the economy of redemption: incarnation and grace.

Edwards's consideration of the incarnation of Christ led him to what today is called Spirit Christology. Contemporary Spirit Christology is an attempt to counterbalance what its proponents see as a list toward Logos Christology in traditional theology. Without jettisoning Logos Christology, the proponents seek to give the Holy Spirit a formative role in the incarnation of the eternal Son of God.[23] Edwards shares common cause with this contemporary movement. The basic content of Edwards's Spirit Christology is that the Holy Spirit creates, sanctifies, and unites the humanity of Jesus Christ with the divine Son.[24]

Edwards's Spirit Christology directly derives from his understanding of the Spirit's work as grace, but more importantly from the Spirit's iden-

22. Edwards's theory of the relationship between the immanent and economic Trinity is very close, though perhaps not identical, to Rahner's principle that the "'economic' Trinity is the 'immanent' Trinity and the 'immanent' Trinity is the 'economic' Trinity." Karl Rahner, *The Trinity,* trans. Joseph Donceel, intro. Catherine Mowry LaCugna (New York: Crossroad, 1998), p. 22.

23. For background on the Logos and Spirit Christology, see Gary D. Badcock, *Light of Truth and Fire of Love: A Theology of the Holy Spirit* (Grand Rapids: Eerdmans, 1997), pp. 266-72; Ralph Del Colle, *Christ and the Spirit: Spirit-Christology in Trinitarian Perspective* (New York: Oxford University Press, 1994); Colin J. D. Greene, *Christology in Cultural Perspective: Marking out the Horizons* (Grand Rapids: Eerdmans, 2004), pp. 33-43; Roger Haight, "The Case for Spirit Christology," *Theological Studies* 53 (1992): 257-87; Harold Hunter, "Spirit Christology: Dilemma and Promise (1)," *Heythrop Journal* 24 (1983): 127-40 and "Spirit Christology: Dilemma and Promise (2)," *Heythrop Journal* 24 (1983): 266-77; Walter Kasper, *Jesus the Christ,* trans. V. Green (Mahwah, NJ: Paulist, 1976); Philip J. Rosato, "Spirit Christology as Access to Trinitarian Theology," in *God's Life in Trinity,* ed. Miroslav Volf and Michael Welker (Minneapolis: Fortress, 2006), pp. 166-76; and Studebaker, *The Trinitarian Vision of Edwards and Coffey.*

24. Edwards, "Miscellanies," *WJE,* vol. 13, no. 294, p. 385; no. 386, p. 454; no. 487, p. 530; and *The "Miscellanies" (Entry Nos. 501-832),* ed. Ava Chamberlain, *WJE,* vol. 18 (New Haven: Yale University Press, 2000), no. 624, p. 154; no. 709, pp. 333-35; no. 767, p. 414.

tity in the immanent Trinity. Since the Spirit's primary redemptive work is to unite believers with Christ, Edwards reasons that the Spirit plays a similar function in the union of Jesus' humanity with the divine Son.[25] He draws on biblical images to support the Spirit's uniting role in the incarnation and grace. Scripture describes the Logos dwelling in the humanity of Christ as in a tabernacle and a body (1 Cor. 3:16-17; 2 Cor. 6:16). It also portrays believers as the temple of the Holy Spirit and body of Christ (John 1:14; Heb. 10:5). Edwards surmises that the Holy Spirit effects the union in both cases. The Spirit draws believers into union with Christ and the human nature into union with the divine Son.[26] What this means is that the Spirit's role in grace corresponds with the Spirit's role in the incarnation. Though the immediate source of the Spirit's role in the incarnation comes from Edwards's understanding of the Spirit's work as grace, the mutual-love model of the Trinity is the fundamental foundation of both theological insights. Having applied the logic of the Spirit as unitive love in the eternal Godhead to the Spirit's function in grace, Edwards extends it and applies it to the incarnation. The Spirit's activity in the Godhead and the incarnation mirror one another. As the Spirit is the bond of love between the Father and the Son in the eternal Godhead, so is the Spirit the love of God, expressed economically, that unites the humanity of Jesus with the Son.[27]

Edwards's integration of pneumatology and Trinitarian theology with Christology is praiseworthy, especially given its rarity within the theological tradition. Christology has often been developed with little consideration of the Holy Spirit beyond the initial creation of Jesus' humanity based on Luke 1:35.[28] Yet despite its salutary improvement, Edwards's Spirit Christology, based as it is on the mutual-love model, remains a central piece of a broader

25. Edwards, "Miscellanies," *WJE,* vol. 13, no. 487, p. 528. Ross W. Hastings also makes this observation in "'Honouring the Spirit': Analysis and Evaluation of Jonathan Edwards' Pneumatological Doctrine of the Incarnation," *International Journal of Systematic Theology* 7 (2005): 279-99 (esp. pp. 283-84).

26. Edwards, "Miscellanies," *WJE,* vol. 13, no. 487, pp. 528-29. For Edwards's use of Scripture to support the role of the Spirit in the incarnation, see Robert W. Caldwell III, *Communion in the Spirit: The Holy Spirit as the Bond of Union in the Theology of Jonathan Edwards* (Milton Keynes, UK: Paternoster, 2006), pp. 87-89.

27. Edwards, "Miscellanies," *WJE,* vol. 13, no. 466, p. 411; no. 487, p. 529.

28. For example, Millard J. Erickson's *The Word Became Flesh,* probably the most extended contemporary account of Christology by an evangelical theologian, develops the Spirit's role in the life of Jesus no further than a few comments on his conception based on Luke 1:35 (see *The Word Became Flesh* [Grand Rapids: Baker, 1991], pp. 23-24, 39).

Christocentric theology of redemption. It gives the Spirit a clearer and even a constitutional role in the incarnation, but the Spirit's role remains functionally instrumental. The work of the Spirit facilitates Christ's work, which provides redemption. Christology drives pneumatology. Edwards's pneumatological concept of grace initially seems to promise a way to transcend the functional instrumentality of the Spirit vis-à-vis Christ; but in the end it remains constrained by the Trinitarian theology that inspires it.

Edwards and the Holy Spirit as Grace

Edwards stands within the Protestant Reformation tradition — and specifically within its Reformed, Puritan, and evangelical trajectory. Central to this theological legacy is the Protestant doctrine of justification by faith. In Protestantism, justification by faith not only addresses the specific issue of "justification," but it is also the catch phrase for a comprehensive vision of grace and redemption. Moreover, it has consequences for Christology and pneumatology. Edwards's thought both reflects and reacts to the evangelical and Reformed variation of Protestant theology that accentuates judicial and legal assumptions and images. In evangelical Reformed theology, the control paradigm of salvation is the sinner before a holy God, who threatens eternal punishment unless God's holy wrath finds amelioration in a worthy penal-substitute. Jesus Christ fulfills the divine law's demand for punishment of sin and becomes the sinner's penal-substitute. His death on the cross is the objective sacrifice that appeases God's wrath and righteousness and, when imputed on the occasion of faith in his death, provides believers with righteousness that covers their sins. Through Christ, the accounts of sinners are made whole.

This theology impacts Christology and pneumatology in several ways. First, it associates Christ's work with justification and the Spirit's work with sanctification. Moreover — and in terms of importance — Christology trumps pneumatology. The real business of salvation occurs on the cross, which provides the basis for the forgiveness of sins and the imputation of Christ's righteousness. Pneumatology offers nothing essential as such to salvation. The work of the Spirit is related to the subjective application of the benefits of redemption — "sanctification" — and these benefits are, strictly speaking, subsidiary and not essential or constitutive of salvation itself. To illustrate the theological vacuity of sanctification, consider that in evangelical soteriology, salvation consists in the objective (justification) and not the subjective (sanctification) aspect of salvation. In other words, believers stand before God as righteous and thus are "saved" not on the basis of their level of personal holiness (sanctification), which is the work of the Holy Spirit, but exclusively on the basis of Christ's righteousness. Second, since Christ achieves salvation through his life of obedience and vicarious death, the only thing left for the Spirit to do is distribute the benefits of the redemption earned by and identified with the work of Christ, and to provide one of its derivative benefits — that is, sanctification.

Of course, evangelical Protestants affirm the importance of sanctification and the Holy Spirit for the Christian life. Nevertheless, the point here is not the content of evangelical rhetoric, but its theology. Theologically, sanctification and the work of the Spirit are functionally irrelevant to salvation. The critical issue for pneumatology, and the one against which Edwards objected, is that the portrayal of Christ as the one who achieves redemption, and the Spirit as the one who applies it, subordinates the Spirit's work to Christ's.[29]

In *Treatise on Grace,* Edwards was not sparing in his judgment on this aspect of traditional pneumatology:

> If we suppose no more than used to be supposed about the Holy Ghost, the honor of the Holy Ghost in the work of redemption is not equal in any sense to the Father['s] and the Son's. . . . Merely to apply to us, or immediately to give or hand to us, [the] blessing purchased after it is purchased . . . is but a little thing to the purchaser of it by the paying an infinite price by Christ.[30]

Edwards believed that construing the Spirit as the one who applies the gift of salvation wrought by another introduces an inequality in their respective roles in the economy of redemption, though he did not reject the forensic or imputational doctrine of justification.[31] Consequently, his solu-

29. I have developed this argument at further length in "Beyond Tongues: A Pentecostal Theology of Grace," in *Defining Issues in Pentecostalism: Classical and Emergent,* ed. Steven M. Studebaker (Eugene, OR: Pickwick, 2008), pp. 46-68 (esp. pp. 48-52); and in "Pentecostal Soteriology and Pneumatology," *Journal of Pentecostal Theology* 11 (2003): 248-70. For a contrary perspective, see Garry J. Williams, "Penal Substitution: A Response to Recent Criticisms," *Journal of the Evangelical Theological Society* 50 (2007): 71-86 (esp. p. 83).

30. Edwards, *Treatise on Grace, WJE,* vol. 21, p. 191.

31. Edwards retained a forensic doctrine of justification and imputation of Christ's righteousness. See Jonathan Edwards, "Justification by Faith Alone," *WJE,* vol. 19, *Sermons*

tion is a mix of continuity and discontinuity with his theological tradition. However, the focus here is Edwards's innovative pneumatological concept of grace.

Edwards's decisive contribution lies in the notion that the Spirit is the "great purchase of Christ."[32] This formulation ironically contains his continuity and discontinuity with his tradition. The legal-contractual language and conceptual framework reflect continuity. The Holy Spirit is the item purchased by Christ on behalf of human debtors. The divergence resides in shifting the nature of redemption from a conferred judicial status to the gift of a divine person. "The sum of all that Christ purchased," Edwards observes, "is the Holy Ghost."[33] Grace is thus not essentially pardon from sin, imputed righteousness, sanctification, and so on, but a divine person — the Holy Spirit. Edwards affirms that "grace . . . is no other than the Spirit of God itself dwelling and acting in the heart of a saint."[34] According to Edwards, making the Spirit the purchase of redemption brings equality to the Spirit relative to Christ. It does so because the gift of salvation (the Spirit) is equal to the value of its cost (the suffering of Christ). In both circumstances a divine person is the currency of redemption.[35] By casting salvation in terms of the gift of a divine person, Edwards at once overcomes the subordination of the Spirit in his tradition and radically alters the nature of redemption. The redefinition of redemption as the gift of the Holy Spirit achieves a pneumatological concept of grace.

Edwards also brought parity to the Holy Spirit by identifying the giving of the Spirit as the goal of the Father's and Christ's work. He developed the terminal nature of the bestowal of the Spirit in several places. The

---

and Discourses, 1734-1738, ed. M. X. Lesser (New Haven: Yale University Press, 2001), pp. 185-89. For a full discussion of Edwards's doctrine of justification and its scholarly interpretation, see Studebaker and Caldwell, *The Trinitarian Theology of Jonathan Edwards*, chap. 8; see also Studebaker, *The Trinitarian Vision of Edwards and Coffey.*

32. Edwards, "Charity and Its Fruits," *WJE*, vol. 8, p. 353; "Miscellanies," *WJE*, vol. 18, no. 706, p. 326.

33. Edwards, "Miscellanies," *WJE*, vol. 13, no. 402, p. 466; vol. 18, no. 706, p. 326.

34. Edwards, *Treatise on Grace, WJE*, vol. 21, p. 192.

35. Edwards, "Charity and Its Fruits," *WJE*, vol. 8, pp. 353-54; *Discourse on the Trinity, WJE*, vol. 21, pp. 130-31, 135-37, 142, and 144; "God Glorified in Man's Dependence," in *Sermons and Discourses, 1730-1733*, ed. Mark Valeri, *WJE*, vol. 17 (New Haven: Yale University Press, 1999), pp. 202, 207-8; "Miscellanies," *WJE*, vol. 13, no. 364, p. 436; no. 402, pp. 466-67; vol. 18, no. 706, pp. 326, 328-29; no. 755, pp. 403-4; no. 772, pp. 419-20; see also *The "Miscellanies" (Entry Nos. 833-1152)*, ed. Amy Plantinga Pauw, *WJE*, vol. 20 (New Haven: Yale University Press, 2002), no. 1062, pp. 438-40; and *Treatise on Grace, WJE*, vol. 21, pp. 188-91.

short essay *On the Equality of the Persons of the Trinity* is illustrative, where he suggests that the Father's and the Son's efforts in redemption are subordinate to the Spirit's. He declares: "His end in giving the Son is to purchase this [the "possession" of the Spirit]. The end of the Son in all his suffering is to obtain this, to purchase this. This was the great precious thing to which all that the other two do is subordinated."[36] Relativizing the work of the Father and the Son to the gift of the Spirit has intra-Trinitarian ground and indicates the systematic nature of his theology. The subsistence of the Holy Spirit as the mutual love of the Father and the Son completes the immanent self-communication of God. Since the giving forth of the Spirit as love perfects the immanent divine self-communication, it also does so in the economic self-communication of God.

Edwards was on the right course when he described the Spirit as the gift of redemption rather than making the Spirit the handmaiden of Christ. His pneumatology goes far in correcting the subordination of the Spirit to Christ that is inherent in the traditional way of relating their works. Nevertheless, his pneumatology and Trinitarian theology remain within the conceptual parameters of the mutual-love model. In the following analysis I first discuss the paradigmatic role of the mutual-love model on Edwards's pneumatology and suggest that starting with the narratives of the Spirit offers a way to transcend these boundaries. In light of these narratives, I develop a theology of the proper role of the Holy Spirit as a Pentecostal solution to the abiding instrumentality and implicit subordination of the Spirit to Christ in Edwards's use of the mutual-love model.

The prominent role that Edwards gave the Spirit has close affinities with Pentecostal theology. Yet the mutual-love model prevents his pneumatology from fully expressing the Spirit's work and identity revealed in the biblical drama of redemption. That sounds harsh. In saying that, I do not mean that Edwards's pneumatology and Trinitarian theology — and all others who use the mutual-love model of the Trinity — are unbiblical. The mutual-love model and Edwards's use of it can be supported by Scripture. Indeed, Edwards cites Scripture to support his theology of the Trinity. Yet the categories of the mutual-love model (e.g., the divine persons as products of processions) emerge more from patristic views on the nature of rational or spiritual being than from Scripture. Using extra-

36. Jonathan Edwards, *On the Equality of the Persons of the Trinity,* in *Writings on the Trinity, Grace, and Faith,* ed. Sang Hyun Lee, *WJE,* vol. 21 (New Haven: Yale University Press, 2003), pp. 146-47.

biblical categories is not problematic, and the distinction, if pressed too far, becomes an artifice, since the Bible speaks in the languages and conceptual parameters of human beings. In the end, however, the biblical narratives of the Spirit — rather than a metaphysical assumption about the nature of spiritual being — should drive pneumatology and Trinitarian theology.

The biblical narratives of the Spirit point to a proper work or mission of the Holy Spirit. The notion of a proper work needs to be understood in light of the doctrine of *appropriations.* Appropriation predicates a work to one divine person, but in fact considers the act accomplished by the three persons. So, for example, one might appropriate creation to the Father, salvation to the Son, and sanctification to the Holy Spirit. However, in traditional Trinitarian theology, this construal is somewhat fictional because all three divine persons create, save, and sanctify. The Western Scholastic tradition used the doctrine of appropriations to assign certain *ad extra* works to the divine persons, but also to retain the unity of the three persons and the efficient causality of the divine essence in the work of redemption. The classic formula for expressing this doctrine is *omnia opera trinitatis ad extra sunt indivisia,* which means that all of the acts of the Trinitarian God in the economy are undivided. Based on the unity of the divine nature, patristic and Scholastic theologians affirmed the principle that all divine activities *ad extra* are undivided; or, to put it another way, any given work of God in creation and redemption is the work of all three divine persons and, from the perspective of creation, is undifferentiated. Because of the indivisible nature of the divine essence, the divine persons cannot operate without the others. Moreover, the principle was taken to mean that personal relationships within the Godhead do not extend to anything outside of the Godhead. So, although the divine persons relate to one another on a personal level within the immanent Trinity, they do not do so to anything or anyone in the economic Trinity. In other words, created entities relate to God as one, but not individually to the divine persons. The incarnation of the Son was an exception to the doctrine of appropriations. Some theologians allowed a proper mission to the Son.

A proper mission affirms that a specific activity of God in creation-redemption is proper to one divine person. The activity *ad extra* does not merely bear a logical affinity with a specific divine person, but has a real correspondence with or is characteristic of the divine person's personal identity within the Trinitarian God. Referring to the incarnation as a proper mission of the Son means that the Son takes on humanity, but not the Father or the Spirit. The latter two remain united to the Son, thus preserving the unity of the divine nature (i.e., the principle of *omnia opera trinitatis ad extra sunt indivisia*) — but they were not incarnate. More specifically, as Rahner points out, the incarnation of the Son in Jesus Christ is not merely appropriated to the Son, but is proper to him. Granting a proper mission to the Son in the incarnation, Scholastic theology did not bestow the same favor on the Holy Spirit in grace. Even though the tradition often attributed sanctification to the Spirit, it understood it as the effect produced in the person by the unified divine nature and not as one formally related to the person of the Holy Spirit. In other words, in sanctification the believer does not experience anything that is properly unique to the person of the Spirit.[37]

Some contemporary theologians have endeavored to assign to the Holy Spirit a proper work that corresponds to the proper mission already allocated to the Son in the incarnation. Important figures in this effort are Yves Congar, Heribert Mühlen, and especially David Coffey, whose Trinitarian theology and pneumatology share strong similarities to those of Jonathan Edwards.[38] Coffey argues that the proper mission of the Spirit is grace. The value of Coffey's identification of grace as the proper mission of the Holy Spirit is that grace is essentially personal. Grace is not the effect of God operating according to efficient causality, but the presence of the Spirit operating according to the Spirit's personal character.[39]

In the remainder of this section, I want to present a Pentecostal development on Coffey's theology of the proper mission of the Spirit in order to offer an improvement on Edwards's pneumatology and Trinitarian theology. My use of Coffey is not a simple borrowing. The mutual-love model also shapes Coffey's articulation of the Spirit's proper mission. In this respect, he is much like Edwards, but his greater theological precision

37. Edward J. Kilmartin, "The Active Role of Christ and the Holy Spirit in the Sanctification of the Eucharistic Elements," *Theological Studies* 45 (1984): 225-53 (esp. pp. 237-38).

38. David Coffey, "A Proper Mission of the Holy Spirit," *Theological Studies* 47 (1986): 227-50; Yves M. J. Congar, *I Believe in the Holy Spirit*, 3 vols. (New York: Seabury, 1983); Heribert Mühlen, *Der Heilige Geist als Person* (Münster: Aschendorff, 1963). For a thorough account of the doctrine of appropriations and Coffey's modification of it, see Ralph Del Colle, *Christ and the Spirit*, pp. 3-140.

39. Coffey's theology of the Spirit as grace is available in *Grace: The Gift of the Holy Spirit*, Marquette Studies in Theology, 73 (Milwaukee: Marquette University Press, 2011). For a more thorough discussion of Coffey's theology of the proper mission of the Spirit and its compatibility with Edwards's pneumatology, see Studebaker, *The Trinitarian Vision of Edwards and Coffey.*

provides the concept of a proper mission of the Spirit that can be expanded on the basis of a Pentecostal reading of the biblical narratives of the Spirit, which portray the Spirit's work as liminal, constitutional, and consummative.

Although Edwards's pneumatological concept of grace gives the Spirit a more equal role relative to Christ than does traditional evangelical Reformed theology, it retains a subordination of the Spirit to Christ that is intrinsic to the mutual-love model. Even though the work of Christ leads to the giving of the Spirit in a sense, Christ's work is not oriented to the Spirit. The *telos* of Christ's work is not really the giving of the Spirit. The Spirit of Pentecost has an instrumental purpose. As an economic modality of mutual love, Christ's giving of the Spirit at Pentecost is his return of love to the Father. The Spirit then is given by Christ to fulfill his economic return of love to the Father; the outpouring of the Spirit simply completes the economic manifestation of the Holy Spirit as the mutual love of the Father and the Son. The redemptive function of the Spirit of Pentecost is to bring believers into union with Christ and, in doing so, to make them children of God who participate in the Son's love of the Father. Accordingly, the outpouring of the Spirit has orientation, first, to union with Christ and, second, to devotion to the Father, both of which do not have anything particular to do with the Spirit as such.

Coffey is an appropriate dialogue partner at this point because, though Edwards does not use the terminology of "proper" role or mission, his understanding of the relationship between the Spirit's immanent identity and economic work is the same as Coffey's.[40] The proper work of the Son is to become incarnate in Jesus Christ. Coffey maintains that the Spirit's proper role derives from the Spirit's identity as the mutual love of the Father and the Son. Consequently, the Holy Spirit is the Father's "descending" love that unites Jesus' humanity with the Son and the Son's returning or "ascending" love that draws him and all believers into unity with the Father through the Spirit.[41] In this respect, Christology conditions the Spirit's work, and for this reason Coffey says the title of the "Spirit of Christ" best expresses the entelechy (the intrinsic *telos*) of the Spirit.[42] However, I want to propose that Christology and pneumatology

40. I detail these continuities in Studebaker, *The Trinitarian Vision of Edwards and Coffey.*

41. David M. Coffey, *Deus Trinitas: The Doctrine of the Triune God* (New York: Oxford, 1999), pp. 60-65.

42. For his development of the Spirit as *entelechy,* see David M. Coffey, *"Did You Receive*

are mutually conditioning concepts and that the proper work of the Spirit includes a pneumatological orientation and not only a christological one, or at least that the proper work has an orientation that is not subordinate and subsidiary to christological criteria.

The liminal, constitutional, and consummative character of the Spirit's work, elaborated on the basis of the biblical narratives of the Spirit (chapter 2), indicates the proper work of the Spirit. First, the Spirit functions as the liminal agent in the region between death and life. This work parallels the Spirit's work in creation and the inception of the incarnation of the Son in Jesus Christ and later in the resurrection of Christ (Rom. 8:11). Second, the Spirit's gift of new life constitutes the renewed life of the believer. Without the movement of the Spirit, Christian faith would not have a resurrected Christ, just as there would be no Christian faith without the revivifying work of the Spirit in human persons. Third, the Spirit of Pentecost consummates redemption because the outpouring of the Spirit makes the particular history of the Spirit's work in Christ universally available to all people. The Spirit makes the life fostered in Jesus Christ accessible to every person.

Moreover, the Spirit's life-giving work is intrinsic to the person of the Spirit. The new life of the Spirit, which makes it possible to become children of God in union with the Son of God, corresponds to the Spirit's creation and union of the humanity of Jesus with the Son. One should note that this final facet of the Spirit's proper work incorporates the Spirit's role in the mutual-love model, but it does not subordinate pneumatology to Christology. In the mutual-love model, christological criteria circumscribe the Spirit's work. Even in its most robust applications, such as in Edwards's and Coffey's Spirit Christology and pneumatological concept of grace, the Spirit is the love that binds the Son to the Father, and vice versa, and believers to the Son and the Father. Nevertheless — and as the biblical account of the Spirit shows — since Christ is only the Christ through the activity of the Spirit, the work of Christ is as conditioned by the Spirit as the latter's is by the former's. Furthermore, the Spirit does not merely give something provided by Christ, but carries out a work in the believer that parallels the Spirit's work in Christ. This work, though accomplished first

the Holy Spirit When You Believed?" Some Basic Questions for Pneumatology, The Père Marquette Lecture in Theology, 2005 (Milwaukee: Marquette University Press, 2005), pp. 76, 102-3; see also Coffey, "The Spirit of Christ as Entelechy," *Philosophy and Theology* 13 (2001): 363-98.

in Christ, is unique to the Spirit and not a derivative and instrumental function of the activity of the Father and the Son.

In the mutual-love model, the Spirit is the principle of reciprocal bilateral symmetry: the Spirit is the Father's love for the Son and the Son's love for the Father. The mutual-love model posits dual *teloi.* The Father and the Son are each objects of each other's activities, though their mutual love subsists in an undivided way as the Holy Spirit. The consequence is that the Spirit is never an object and subject of love; the Spirit does not receive or give love — or anything else, for that matter. Consequently, the Spirit is not the *telos* of the activities of the Son and the Father, but the Spirit is an instrument through which the Father and Son treat each other as ends or objects of love. Therefore, the outpouring of the Spirit of Pentecost is not for the sake of the Spirit as such, but to fulfill the reciprocation of love from the Son to the Father within the economic Trinity.

My proposal is Trinitarian *teloi:* each divine person has an intrinsic *telos* that the others seek. A proper role, or intrinsic *telos,* does not mean a disparate or isolated one. For example, the proper work of the Son is to be incarnate, but the Son does not do this of his own accord or for self-seeking motivations; he comes to reveal the Father and to send the Spirit. The Son only becomes the incarnate Son when the Father sends him and the Spirit creates and unites the humanity of Jesus with him. With respect to the Father's and Spirit's work, they are both oriented to Christ. Yet their work is unique, or proper. The Father sends, the Son becomes incarnate, and the Spirit creates and unites. If we stop here, we have essentially Edwards's application of the mutual-love model to the incarnation. However, the Father and Spirit do not only have an orientation to Christ, but the Father and the Son also have an orientation to the Spirit.

Since the Spirit's creative work, the work that creates the humanity of Jesus and unites it to the Son, is proper to the Spirit, the Father and Christ desire for all people to participate in it. Christ's work finds fulfillment in the Spirit of Pentecost, because the universal access to the new life of humanity initiated supremely in Christ by the Spirit is only realized in the outpouring of the Spirit at Pentecost. In this respect, Christ sends the Spirit so that the work begun in him by the Spirit can be accomplished in all of humanity. Hence, Christ sends the Spirit not so that the Spirit can distribute his benefits, but so that all people have the opportunity to participate in the benefit of life (inception and resurrection) that Christ received from the Spirit. In sending the Spirit, Christ seeks a pneumatological end and not just a christological one: that is, to fulfill his love for the Father by completing his modality of the mutual love between him and the Father. Positing a pneumatological *telos* of the Father and Son does not dislodge pneumatology and make it float free from Christology; rather, it integrates them and treats the Spirit as a viable and equal personal end among the Trinitarian persons.

My goal is not to replace Christocentrism with pneumacentrism, nor to replace all Trinitarian models with the Pentecostal one proposed here. My goal is, on the one hand, to overcome the implicit subordination of the Spirit to Christ in traditional Trinitarian theologies and, on the other hand, to make a Pentecostal contribution to traditional Trinitarianism. The mutual-love model — and especially Edwards's use of it (as well as Coffey's) — highlights a vital aspect of redemption: that is, salvation involves being united to the Son and the Father through the Holy Spirit. Moreover, this model captures something of the Spirit's eternal role in the Godhead. When I critique the mutual-love model, I am not denying these insights; but I *am* suggesting that the biblical narratives of the Spirit provide a more expansive vision of the Spirit's work and identity. The recognition of a unique *pneumatological*, or proper, work of the Spirit, which is not defined exclusively in christological terms, does not entail the rejection of the insights of Edwards and Coffey and the role of the Spirit in facilitating the fellowship of the Father and the Son in the immanent Trinity, and believers with each other and the Father and Son in the economic Trinity. No, the goal here is ecumenical. A Pentecostal contribution to Trinitarian theology is not an attempt to supplant, but rather to supplement, other Trinitarian theologies and traditions by recognizing the unique identity and work of the Holy Spirit in the economic and immanent Trinity.

Donald Bloesch and Millard Erickson

Donald Bloesch and Millard Erickson became representative of two strands within North American evangelical theology. Bloesch's ecumenical style and his lack of interest in defining the boundaries of the movement are problematic for the gatekeepers of evangelical orthodoxy. At the same time he is too liberal for those defending the ramparts of evangelical orthodoxy, Bloesch is too conservative for the progressives sallying forth from what they perceive as the fortress of fundamentalism. According to Roger Olson, Bloesch is an exemplar for serious-minded and moderate evangelicals.[43] Bloesch is thus a mediating figure between the conservative evangelicals and the postconservatives.

Millard Erickson has been one of the most influential evangelical theologians in the past thirty years. His *Christian Theology* has been a staple for many students who have studied theology in evangelical seminaries. Comparing it to alternative standard evangelical theological textbooks, David S. Dockery declares: "There is room for improvement in Erickson's theology, but to this date there is not a finer evangelical work available."[44] Compared to some of the other representatives of conservative evangelicalism, he is less strident and more moderate in content and tone.[45] Stanley Grenz describes Erickson, without overstatement, as the successor to Carl Henry and, along with Clark Pinnock (who embodies the liberal, or postconservative, pole of evangelical theology), one of the two most important theologians of the second generation of neo-evangelical scholars.[46] Erickson provides symmetry with Bloesch, who represents the more progressive and liberal side of evangelical theology, and Erickson is a good match with Bloesch because they represent the two mature and dominant alternatives in Trinitarian theology in the late twentieth century. Erickson adopted social Trinitarianism and preferred the Cappadocians and Moltmann; Bloesch carried on with Augustinian and Barthian instincts and was less comfortable with the threeness of God.[47]

43. Roger E. Olson, "Locating Donald G. Bloesch in the Evangelical Landscape," in *Evangelical Theology in Transition,* ed. Elmer M. Colyer (Downers Grove, IL: InterVarsity, 1999), pp. 18-34 (esp. p. 31). He is also a mediating figure between fundamentalism and evangelicalism, on the one hand, and fundamentalism and liberalism, on the other hand, which is in a significant way indebted to the influence of Karl Barth on his theological approach. See Patrick M. McManus, "An Introduction to the Theology of Donald G. Bloesch," in *Donald G. Bloesch: A Research Bibliography,* ed. Paul E. Maher, ATLA Publications Series, 3 (Lanham, MD: Scarecrow, 2007), pp. 1-20 (esp. pp. 3-6, 10).

44. David S. Dockery, "Millard J. Erickson: Theologian for the Church," in *New Dimensions in Evangelical Thought: Essays in Honor of Millard J. Erickson,* ed. David S. Dockery (Downers Grove, IL: InterVarsity, 1998), pp. 17-31 (esp. p. 31).

45. Although I characterize him as conservative, he is at the center, according to his own self-assessment. See Millard J. Erickson, Paul Kjoss Helseth, and Justin Taylor, eds., *Reclaiming the Center: Confronting Evangelical Accommodation in Postmodern Times* (Wheaton, IL: Crossway, 2004).

46. Stanley J. Grenz, *Renewing the Center: Evangelical Theology in a Post-Theological Era* (Grand Rapids: Baker Academic, 2000), pp. 117-18, 128.

47. Note that the above statement is not an unintentional endorsement of the East-West paradigm. I believe that the paradigm is largely a myth of contemporary systematic theology. Nonetheless, it is one that is embraced by many theologians. The function the par-

Donald Bloesch

Reflecting on modern Trinitarian theology, Bloesch hits on several significant points that relate to theological hermeneutics, pneumatology, and Trinitarian theology, which call into question the theological hermeneutic deployed in the current project. Bloesch laments:

> The point of departure is no longer the preexistent Trinity and the hypostatic procession but the impact of the Spirit of God on the quest for justice and peace. We begin not with abstract metaphysical speculation but with human experience and the role of the Spirit in this experience. There is also a marked tendency in contemporary theology to view the Spirit as working universally in history and experience even apart from the parameters of Christian faith. . . . [Many contemporary theologians] contend that our theology of the Spirit should be shaped by experiences of the Spirit in Third World and primitive cultures that will force us to be less dependent on and more critical of our Eurocentric heritage.[48]

This passage sets forth central programmatic and navigational guides for understanding Bloesch's place in the field of contemporary Trinitarian theology.

First, this quotation shows Bloesch's critique of theological approaches "from below." But how can theology begin otherwise? The theologian has no direct access to God. Even those who contend that theology should begin "from above" agree that the "from above" data is not God *in se*, but the revelation of God especially through Christ, the Spirit-inspired testimony of Scripture, and its interpretation in the classical dogmas of the Christian faith, such as the Trinity.[49] In the end, even the "from above" method starts "from below." The distinction between theology that begins "from above" and "from below" assumes that the former is an objective

---

adigm plays in contemporary Trinitarian theology is to give theologians an orientation or starting point for their Trinitarian theology: the East starts with the three persons; the West starts with the one substance/nature. Therefore, the paradigm serves a real role in modern Trinitarian theology, despite its less than tangible basis in patristic theology.

48. Bloesch, *Holy Spirit,* pp. 262-66.

49. Donald G. Bloesch, *Essentials of Evangelical Theology,* vol. 1: *God, Authority, and Salvation* (San Francisco: Harper & Row, 1978), pp. 51-64; see also Bloesch, *God the Almighty,* pp. 27-28. Hereafter, page references to this latter work appear in parentheses in the text.

starting point of theology and the latter a subjective and experiential one. Bloesch also supposes a unilateral relationship between theology and experience. Theology shapes experience, not the other way around. Yet this theological method overlooks the historical and experiential process that produced Scripture and theology. For example, the doctrine of the Trinity did not begin as an abstract and metaphysical doctrine, but with the early Christian experience of God in Christ and the Holy Spirit. Hebrew monotheism did not start with a philosophical and metaphysical concept, but with Abraham's experience of being called to leave Ur and set out on a trek to Canaan (Gen. 12:1), and with Moses' encountering the "I am who I am" in a burning bush in the wilderness of Midian (Exod. 3:1-14). What Christian theologians now take as venerable metaphysical doctrines that float above the vicissitudes of experience did not begin that way. They emerged in the hurly-burly of the human encounter with God and human deliberation on that experience. Even Scripture is the product of the human experience of God and reflection on that experience (e.g., redactional elements), unless one accepts a strict dictation view of inspiration.

Second, Bloesch is suspicious of the efforts to draw on nontraditional theological sources. However, is the Spirit's work circumscribed by the parameters of explicit Christian witness, confession, and work, particularly its western European form? For the sake of the many who never had and do not now have access to Christian witness, one can only hope otherwise. But Bloesch's point moves beyond the ostensible issue of theology of religions. Bloesch suspects that calls to hear the voice of the Spirit in nontraditional and global movements is covert criticism of Western theology. Although some calls for drawing on a diversity of global and particularly non-Western sources is likely the theological expression of a broader and reflexive Western self-loathing characteristic of much of elite culture in North America and western Europe, it does not mean that the principle is misguided.

Consider the fact that the early Christians were perceived as pests on the fringes of Judaism. Many of the early leaders were not among the theological literati, the apostle Paul being a notable exception. To contemporary first-century Jewish ears, their views would have sounded extreme, nonsensical, and primitive. The Christian affirmation of the Father, the Son, and the Holy Spirit must have appeared as an odious lurch backward toward polytheism. The Romans also thought Christians were nutty. They referred to them as "atheists" because they did not have the good sense to recognize the traditional gods along with Jesus, and they feared that their

Lord's Supper was communal cannibalism. Yet their experience of God in Christ and the Spirit of Pentecost, and their subsequent theological reflection on that experience, yielded the traditions of Christian faith. The difference between what is fringe and respected can be a matter of historical context and cultural vantage point. Pentecostalism is a case in point. Just a few decades ago, Pentecostals were primarily known as tongues-babbling fanatics and "holy-rollers" — and not for prodigious theological works. The situation is altogether different today. Contemporary theology should neither champion the demise of Western theology nor ignore and patronize perspectives that are, from a Western point of view, new, marginal, and from the "other." John 3:8 instructs: "The wind blows wherever it pleases, but you cannot tell where it comes from or where it is going." Therefore, theologians should not ensconce themselves in a sycophantic echo chamber of traditional Western theology.

Bloesch also engages the relationship between the processions and identities of the divine persons. After describing six Trinitarian models (e.g., the Eastern procession of the Son and Spirit from the Father alone) and analogies (e.g., Gregory of Nyssa's light from light), Bloesch offers a seventh one that "shows the mutual self-giving and fundamental equality among the persons of the Trinity" (p. 202). Bloesch retains the idea that the Son and Spirit proceed from the Father but also adds that they return in a "loving response to the Father" (p. 203). Not only does the Son actively engage the Father, as in the mutual-love model, but the Spirit does, too. He sees the Son and Spirit playing active and creative roles in the Godhead. He portrays the inner Trinitarian movement in terms of a circular motion. It begins with the Father and the "Son and Spirit proceed from the Father, but they also return to the Father. The Spirit returns with the Son and the Son through the Spirit. There is not only initiation of action by the Father but also active response by the Son and Spirit" (pp. 202-3, esp. n. 94). Bloesch thus affirms that the divine persons' identities are mutually interdependent (p. 300, n. 97).

Bloesch's claim moves Trinitarian theology in the right direction. He seeks to overcome the unilateral and nonreciprocal nature of the divine persons, which are implicit to models of the Trinity that base the divine persons' identities on processions. It is significant that he extends the reciprocal notion of identity formation to the Holy Spirit. Since the mutual-love model achieves reciprocity between the Father and the Son, Bloesch's insight is most significant on the pneumatological point because it moves toward Trinitarian reciprocation. However, his proposal remains suggestive and does not develop the interpersonal nature of the formation of their identity. Furthermore, since he portrays the persons as products of processions, how can they be mutually constituted?

My proposal, in common with Bloesch's, does not reject the processions as constitutive elements in the formation of the divine persons, though I do not necessarily find the doctrine of the Father as the original source of the processions problematic, as Bloesch does (p. 203). However, I have endeavored to give a rationale for full Trinitarian reciprocation and contribution to the identity formation of the divine persons. Bloesch also comes at the issue from a predominantly christological orientation (p. 27). Christology is, without doubt, an essential source of Christian theology, but so is pneumatology. My work approaches the Trinity from a Pentecostal context and the biblical narratives of the Spirit, though it shares a common cause with Bloesch to develop a more relational Trinitarianism than what exists in the traditional theologies of the Trinity. Moreover, the notion of a proper role or mission of the Spirit that in turns informs the Spirit's personal identity and role in the Trinity should develop details on what remains a more suggestive proposal in Bloesch.

Millard Erickson

Veli-Matti Kärkkäinen notes the odd fact that Erickson's work has disappeared not only from the radar screens of theologians in general but also from those of evangelical theologians.[50] In the survey of contemporary Trinitarian theology by leading evangelical theologian Stanley Grenz, Erickson receives no substantive discussion and does not even make it into the index. The same is true of the more recent work by Allan Coppedge, who, though he is a Wesleyan, interacts with evangelicals such as John Feinberg.[51] This situation is unfortunate. Erickson has clearly been one of the premier theologians among North American evangelicals in the past three or four decades. Furthermore, he has written a Trinitarian theology — which is a rarity, as Erickson acknowledges — and in it he sides with more progressive or at least nontraditional social Trinitarianism.[52] No theologian

50. Veli-Matti Kärkkäinen, *The Trinity: Global Perspectives* (Louisville: Westminster John Knox, 2007), p. 226.

51. For Coppedge, see *The God Who Is Triune.*

52. Erickson declares that "[t]here has been no major scale doctrine of the Trinity produced for some time by persons of distinctly evangelical persuasion, despite the centrality of

can exhaustively interact with all others, but the near absence of any mention of Erickson by others is rather inexplicable given his prominent stature during the past few decades within the evangelical community.[53]

Erickson's work on the Trinity exhibits the theological genre of neo-evangelicalism. Carl F. H. Henry found the flight of the fundamentalists to the fringes unsatisfactory, and thus did he, along with many other evangelicals, launch a program of credible engagement with contemporary philosophy, theology, and biblical scholarship. In order to fulfill this agenda, figures like Henry needed to speak in the terms and the schools of thought that were popular with their liberal, or at least nonevangelical, counterparts. Erickson's work on the Trinity continues this agenda. In fact, constructive and critical engagement of nonevangelical theologians is central to his style.

Erickson draws on key spokespersons for social Trinitarianism, such as Jürgen Moltmann and Leonardo Boff, and he recommends such a Trinitarianism to evangelicals. His analytical method most often entails description, analysis, and pointing out the weaknesses and strengths from the given position of evangelical orthodoxy. The positive side of this approach is that it provides a useful evangelical commentary on contemporary Trinitarian theology and catalogs and discusses the relevant biblical passages. The negative side of this neo-evangelical style is that it does not facilitate the production of an *evangelical* Trinitarian theology. We learn that Erickson is more Moltmannian than Barthian or Rahnerian, but we do not receive an Ericksonian or an evangelical view. It will not do to protest that an evangelical Trinitarian theology is a *biblical* Trinitarian theology, since every Christian theologian believes that his or her theology articulates biblical teaching, and Erickson himself acknowledges that the Trinity is the product of both the Bible and Christian tradition (p. 33). My goal is to develop a Pentecostal contribution to ecumenical Trinitarian theology and thereby to bring a Pentecostal voice to the table.

Erickson adopts modern social Trinitarianism without its usual polemics toward the Western tradition, an admirable quality of his work in

---

the doctrine in evangelical theology" (*God in Three Persons,* p. 14). Hereafter, page references to this work appear in parentheses in the text.

53. My discussion is not exhaustive and relates to issues germane to ones brought up in the presentation of the Pentecostal Trinitarian theology of this project. I recommend Kärkkäinen's work for an assessment of Erickson that treats similar and other issues (Kärkkäinen, *The Trinity,* pp. 214-34).

general.[54] For example, he displays an amiable spirit in his criticisms of postconservative theology. Erickson prefers to start with the three persons rather than the alleged Western affinity for the one nature. He affirms that the divine persons are individual centers of thought and action, though not separate from each other, and he rejects Barth's understanding of the divine persons as modes of being. Finally, he rejects the doctrine of divine simplicity understood as numerical oneness (pp. 230-32).

Although Erickson's social Trinitarianism affirms that each divine person is a distinct center of thought and agency, it does not articulate the basis of each person's unique individuality. He does suggest a distinction on the level of the economic Trinity. He attributes creation to the Father, redemption to the Son, and sanctification to the Holy Spirit (p. 235). Yet he does not draw implications from these works for their immanent identities. Another example is the incarnation. He cites biblical language that has the Father sending the Son and the Spirit empowering and coming upon Jesus at his baptism. He affirms that, though they share a unity of action in the incarnation, the Son undergoes experiences in the incarnation that are unique to him. The Father and Spirit have not, for example, experienced temptation; nonetheless, they "have experienced Christ experiencing temptation" (p. 224). The uniqueness of their experience moves in the direction of a proper mission of the divine persons, which in turn derives from their unique personal identities but remains at the level of intimation in Erickson's treatment.

I suspect that his avoidance of drawing correlations between the divine persons' immanent identities and economic activities relates to his desire to forestall any basis of subordinationism (pp. 294-95, 300-304). Erickson shows little interest in the divine processions for two reasons: he seems to believe that concepts of "origin" within the Godhead unavoidably imply ontological subordination; in addition, evangelical theology shies away from the technicalities of the immanent processions and prefers to

54. The problem with social Trinitarianism is not its proposal on the relational nature of God, but its misinformed understanding of Cappadocian and Augustinian Trinitarian theology. (For my discussion of this point, see chapter 3, n. 18, above). Elsewhere, I have evaluated the application of the threeness-oneness paradigm to Jonathan Edwards's theology, but not the insights of social Trinitarianism per se (see the discussion in n. 8 of the present chapter). I think my critique of its historical and theological metanarrative has led some to believe that I am against social Trinitarianism — which is not the case. I affirm a dynamic and interpersonal view of the Trinity. My problem with social Trinitarianism is historical and not theological.

discuss God's foreknowledge and providence. Veli-Matti Kärkkäinen suggests that Erickson, "in opposing all kinds of notions of subordinationism in the life of God, ends up arguing against the principle of the economic Trinity being a reliable guide to the inner life of God."[55] Erickson rejects the eternal functional and personal hierarchy and subordination among the divine persons — the order of Father, Son, and Holy Spirit — promoted by his evangelical colleagues such as Wayne Grudem and Bruce Ware. The effect, however, is a failure — whether intentional or intuitive — to connect the divine persons' economic activities with their immanent identities. In contrast, I maintain that the economic activities reveal the immanent identities, though not in an exhaustive or univocal way. For this reason, the biblical narratives of the Spirit, which have been neglected in traditional Trinitarian theology and in Erickson's work as well, serve as the basis for making a Pentecostal contribution to Trinitarian theology.

Myk Habets

Myk Habets is a Reformed evangelical theologian who represents a younger voice in the evangelical tradition and who has engaged the areas of theological hermeneutics, theology of gender, the doctrine of theosis, and Trinitarian theology. He teaches systematic theology and is director of the R. J. Thompson Centre for Theological Studies at Carey Baptist College in New Zealand. Though he is not North American, his theological identity coheres with what I have described as the North American evangelical tradition, but also with the younger generation of evangelical thinkers who are engaging new areas of theology for the evangelical tradition — for example, theosis and the Trinity.

Habets's most sustained effort in Trinitarian theology is his book *The Anointed Son*, in which he endeavors to develop a Trinitarian Spirit Christology, and which promises a more thorough integration and prominent role of the Trinity and pneumatology in Christology.[56] He believes that Spirit Christology can highlight and correct the marginalization of the Holy Spirit in traditional theology. "What a Spirit Christology seeks to

55. Kärkkäinen, *The Trinity*, p. 229.

56. Myk Habets, *The Anointed Son: A Trinitarian Spirit Christology*, Princeton Theological Monographs (Eugene, OR: Pickwick, 2010). Hereafter, page references to this work appear in parentheses in the text.

achieve," says Habets, "is to bring the role of the Holy Spirit back into focus in all of the manifold expressions of his relationship to Jesus and the Father" (p. 161). Moreover, addressing the Spirit's function in Jesus Christ will lead to a more thoroughgoing Trinitarian theology (pp. 161, 173). This section first presents Habets's Spirit Christology. My goal here is not to survey Habets's entire argument for Spirit Christology, but to focus on the points of his theology that most directly deal with Trinitarian theology, the Spirit's identity, and the relationships between the Spirit and Christ and their implications for the Trinity. I then assess whether it achieves its goal to develop a Trinitarian Spirit Christology and to speak to the relationships between the Son and the Holy Spirit in redemption and the eternal Trinity.

Habets, Spirit Christology, and the Trinity

With respect to the Trinity proper, Habets adopts the theology of Thomas Weinandy. Since I have treated Weinandy at length in chapter 3, here I will mention only the main point of Habets's use of Weinandy. Habets argues that Weinandy's model overcomes the "passive" and "impersonal" implications of the Spirit's personal identity in the Western tradition and the unilateralism of the Eastern one. Habets believes that in Weinandy's model the Holy Spirit becomes a genuine and reciprocal person in the immanent Godhead (pp. 224-25). Before critically engaging his work, I will outline what Habets considers the contribution and nature of Spirit Christology.

First, Habets believes that "Spirit Christology" serves as a counterbalance to Logos Christology, which characterizes traditional Christology. According to Logos Christology, the eternal Son, or Word, becomes incarnate in the humanity of Jesus of Nazareth: the Son is the active agent of the incarnation. Logos Christology starts with the assumption of the eternal Son (Logos); it is a theological method "from above." Without rejecting Logos Christology, Spirit Christology seeks to complement it, and does so by starting not with the Son in eternity, but with Christ's life and ministry — with a special focus on the Spirit's role in the life of Jesus (pp. 4-5). According to Habets, a biblical Christology's point of departure is pneumatology. Biblical Christology begins with Spirit Christology (p. 227). The basis for the claim that biblical Christology starts with the Spirit is the conception narratives in Matthew and Luke. Since the Spirit conceives Jesus, Christology jumps off with the Spirit.

Second, Habets shows that the Spirit is at work throughout the life of Jesus. The Holy Spirit's work in Jesus begins with his conception in Mary. The Spirit is present and active at the very inception of Jesus' life (pp. 123-28). At Jesus' baptism, the anointing of the Holy Spirit reveals Jesus' messianic identity and divine sonship both to the public and to Jesus (pp. 137-38). After the public announcement, the Spirit leads Jesus into the wilderness to be tested by Satan. Unlike the infidelity that marked Israel's sojourn in the desert, Jesus resists Satan's temptation. His faithfulness to God the Father validates that the Spirit is upon him to fulfill the messianic mission (pp. 131-40). The Spirit's anointing of Jesus reaches its most powerful expression on the cross. The cross, because Jesus endures its horror in the Spirit, is also a *pneumatological crucis.* The Spirit remains and participates in Jesus' suffering and Godforsakenness (pp. 160-68).[57] After the terror of the cross, the Spirit raises Jesus from the dead. However, Jesus' relationship with the Spirit changes fundamentally in the resurrection. Up to this point, he is the Christ of the Spirit, but afterwards the Spirit becomes the Spirit of Christ. Therefore, in the exaltation or ascension, Jesus Christ becomes the one who sends the Holy Spirit upon the community of believers. Indeed, so dramatic is the change in the relationship that Habets declares, "Jesus Christ is Lord *of* the Spirit" (p. 180).

Habets convincingly shows that the Holy Spirit is a central player in the life of Jesus Christ. The Spirit's role commends Spirit Christology to supplement traditional theology's near singular focus on Logos Christology. Nevertheless, the implications for pneumatology, Christology, and the Trinity run deeper than Habets pursues them. For example, I agree with Habets that Matthew's and Luke's conception narratives recommend a Spirit Christology, but I disagree on what this means for pneumatology and the Trinity. Indeed, Habets's Spirit Christology, though it effectively highlights the Spirit's work in the life of Jesus, unfortunately carries on a traditional Christocentrism and subordination of the Spirit to Christ. In what follows, I engage Habets's theological project from a Pentecostal perspective and suggest a more prominent role of the Spirit in Jesus Christ and thereby also in the Trinity.

57. Habets draws on Jürgen Moltmann and D. Lyle Dabney for a *pneumatological cruces.* I discuss the latter in chapter 5.

Christ, the determining agent of the Spirit?

Though he does much to redress the overemphasis on Logos Christology, Habets retains a subordination of pneumatology to Christology. After charting an impressive array of ways the Spirit works in the life of Christ, and even calling Jesus "the Christ of the Spirit," Habets sees the resurrection as a turning point in which pneumatology is for the most part absorbed into Christology. After the resurrection, the Spirit's work has no unique character per se, but is entirely christological. Changes to their titles and personal relationships indicate the transition in the relationship between the Spirit and Christ. Reflecting both alterations, Habets says:

> The Spirit of God becomes the Spirit of Christ (Rom. 8:9), the Spirit of the Son (Gal. 4:6), and the Spirit of faith (2 Cor. 4:13), so that Christ becomes the determining subject of the Spirit: he sends the Spirit (John 16:7); he breathes out the Spirit (John 20:22). (p. 173)

These descriptors are, of course, biblical and characterize the Spirit. However, Habets's saying that "Christ becomes the determining subject of the Spirit" diminishes the pneumatological gains he has otherwise made. The resurrection-ascension is the pivot point of the economy of redemption for Habets. At the ascension, Jesus fully possesses the Spirit and thus becomes Lord of the Spirit. Following traditional Protestant theology, Pentecost and the Spirit become adjuncts to Christology.[58] Once Jesus ascends to the Father and becomes Lord of the Spirit, the Spirit's identity submerges under the glory of the risen Christ. Furthermore, soteriology becomes almost entirely christological. Jesus is the savior, not the Spirit. The Spirit plays a secondary and instrumental role. The Spirit enables people to express faith in Christ, and after that empowers them to follow the moral and spiritual ideals of Christ; but the Spirit contributes nothing to salvation per se. Christ is both the provider and content of salvation.

I want to engage Habets's point that Christ becomes "the determining subject of the Spirit." The problem with the idea is twofold: on the one hand, it is inconsistent with the work of the Spirit that Habets chronicles and points to as the basis of Spirit Christology; on the other hand, it is the

58. For an elaboration of this claim and a critique of the subordination of the Spirit in traditional Protestant and Pentecostal theology, see Studebaker, "Beyond Tongues," pp. 46-58.

product of an underdeveloped Spirit Christology. By limiting the Spirit's work primarily to the creation and empowerment of the humanity of Jesus and not the incarnation itself, Habets's Spirit Christology remains open to Christocentrism rather than moving toward a more mutual and reciprocal understanding of the relationship between Jesus and the Spirit. Habets's Spirit Christology is on the right track, but it needs to press on to achieve its pneumatological aspirations. The following discussion highlights the points where Habets's Spirit Christology carries with it an implicit Christocentrism and suggests a way to achieve a more thorough Spirit Christology and Trinitarian theology.

First, the Holy Spirit and the Son are codetermining agents of Jesus Christ and thus of each other. To begin with, the biblical account of the Spirit's activity in the life and ministry of Jesus suggests that christological categories do not entirely circumscribe the Spirit's personal identity. The Spirit's identity and work that emerges in the drama of biblical redemption is not finally lost in the shadow of the risen Christ. Stated in positive terms, the Holy Spirit enables and constitutes Jesus' life, death, and ministry, as the incarnate Son of God. In this respect, the Spirit is a determining agent of Jesus Christ. As Habets argues, otherwise convincingly, the Spirit is a principal player in the incarnation of the Son, the life and ministry of Jesus, and his death and resurrection. The Spirit's role in the incarnation makes the Son's work in Jesus Christ possible. The Spirit's function in creating and uniting the humanity of Jesus with the Son is not a one-time event at the conception but an abiding one. The Spirit continues to be the principle of the hypostatic union throughout the life of Jesus Christ. Based on this work, I maintain that the Holy Spirit, as the Spirit of Pentecost, retains the identity manifested in these works and is thus neither fully determined by Christ nor, as the Spirit of Pentecost, veiled behind a christological mask.

Jesus Christ is the nexus of the Son and the Spirit. What this means is that the incarnation is the confluence of the work of the Spirit and the Son. With respect to the Holy Spirit, the Spirit operates as the liminal and constituting actor in the incarnation. The Spirit initiates the incarnation. The Spirit creates, sanctifies, and unites the humanity of Jesus with the divine Son. The Holy Spirit in this sense is the principle *of the hypostatic union;* the Spirit constitutes the hypostatic union of the humanity of Jesus and the person of the Son. The Spirit also facilitates the actualization of the Son's divine Sonship and relationship to the Father in and through Jesus Christ. The Spirit's work begins with the initial incarnation of the Son and reaches its zenith in sustaining Jesus through the suffering of the cross and raising him from the dead. The Spirit emerges as the divine agent who constitutes the incarnation of the Son and thus enables Jesus Christ to fulfill his relationship with the Father.

It is important to realize that the Spirit's activity is not limited to the humanity of Jesus. Since Jesus' humanity is the concrete mediation of the Son, the Spirit's work shapes the specific way the incarnate Son acts in and through the humanity of Jesus. In other words, the horizon of what the Son does in the incarnation is pneumatological. Representative of the pneumatological context of his ministry, Jesus declares to the Pharisees in Matthew 12:28, "If I drive out demons by the Spirit of God, then the kingdom of God has come upon you." Consequently, the Spirit shapes the personal character and activities of Jesus Christ — the incarnate Son. As the foundation of the incarnation and not merely the empowerment of Jesus' humanity, the Spirit makes the Son's incarnate life possible. The Spirit's work enables the very activities carried out by the Son. Unless one posits a divide between the Son's personal identity and the activities in Jesus Christ, then the Spirit's role in shaping the Son's identity and activity can be accepted.

On the part of the Son, the Son is the subject, or primary agent, *of the activity of Jesus Christ,* because the personal identity of Jesus Christ is the Son. The Son is active in and through his union with the humanity of Jesus. Because the Spirit remains the principle of the incarnation and thus in personal union with the incarnate Son, the Son's action in and through Christ is determinative for the Holy Spirit. The Son incarnate in Jesus Christ is a determining agent of the Spirit because, as the Son acts in and through Jesus, he is acting in relationship with the Spirit. Without the reciprocal activity of the Son to become incarnate, the Spirit's work in Jesus would go unanswered. So, though the Spirit is the primary agent of the incarnation, without the reciprocal willingness of the Son to be drawn into union with the humanity of Jesus, the incarnation would not take place. In responding to the Spirit's initiative, the Son contributes to the Spirit's identity. Yet, at the same time, the Spirit shapes the Son. The Son becomes the Christ of the Spirit. Moreover, without the Son's response to the Spirit's overture, the Spirit would never become the Spirit of Christ in the second sense of the term that I have set forth in chapter 2 (i.e., the Spirit's active role in forming the personal identity and activity of Jesus Christ). The Son's activities in Christ are in and through the Spirit as much as they are in and through the human nature of Jesus. This inter-relationality of the Son and Spirit in Christ are mutually and reciprocally determining experiences.

The passion of Christ illustrates the mutual determination of the Son and the Holy Spirit in Jesus Christ. As Habets convincingly argues, the cross is not only an event of the Son, but also of the Spirit; it is a *pneumatological crucis* (pp. 160-70). Jesus presses on in faithfulness to the Father, even death and the experience of alienation, by virtue of the Spirit's sustaining power in his life. Jesus Christ, the incarnate Son, endures the cross by virtue of the Spirit's work in his life. In this sense, the Spirit is a determining agent of Jesus Christ — and thus Habets's term "the Christ of the Spirit." However, Jesus Christ is not merely passive in the passion. He persists in faithfulness to the Father to the point of suffering death. Consequently, the Son, as the proper subject and the divine person who acts in Jesus Christ, determines the Spirit, and hence the Spirit is "the Spirit of Christ" as well.

The second point I want to address is the *duration* of the Spirit and Son's reciprocal and mutual relationship. Habets recognizes that the Spirit is a determining subject of Christ up to the resurrection. However, he believes that in the resurrection a reversal occurs in their relationship. Christ makes a transition from being the one empowered by the Spirit to the one who sends the Spirit. Habets clarifies: "The resurrection represents the transition from the Christ of the Spirit to the Spirit of Christ," and "[i]t is at this juncture that the Christ of the Spirit is functionally transformed into the Spirit of Christ" (pp. 173, 161; see also pp. 146, 169). Once Christ has risen and returned to the Father, the Spirit becomes indistinguishable from Christ. The Holy Spirit is not experienced as the Spirit as such, but "the Spirit experienced by the community of believers now and forever bears the impress of Jesus Christ" (p. 173). The Spirit's identity and work morph into Christology. Since the Spirit's role in the incarnation suggests the mutual and reciprocal determination of the Spirit and Christ, why not continue this mutuality and reciprocity between them in the era of the Spirit of Pentecost? Habets goes to great lengths to substantiate that the Spirit contributes to the identity of Jesus Christ when he refers to the "Christ of the Spirit." Why, then — if Jesus' life, death, and resurrection are determined by the Holy Spirit — should all this work fall by the wayside and theology revert back to traditional Christocentrism in which the Holy Spirit's identity is lost behind a christological canvas? (pp. 162-64)

Recalling Rahner's principle of the reciprocal relationship between the economic and immanent Trinity helps to adjudicate this issue. Since the

Spirit's work in the preascension Christ flows from the Spirit's personal identity, the Spirit's postascension relationship to Christ and work will bear continuity with the Spirit's former work. Habets's treatment reveals an internal crosscurrent that is suggestive of this point. For example, he says, "the risen Christ lives from, and in, the eternal Spirit, and the divine Spirit of life acts in and through Christ" (p. 173).[59] If the risen Christ "lives from, and in, the eternal Spirit," then the Spirit certainly remains a determining subject of Christ. Regrettably, in the next paragraph, Habets abandons this insight and returns to a Christocentric theology. Indicative of this shift is his comment that the "Spirit of God becomes the Spirit of Christ . . . so that Christ becomes the determining subject of the Spirit" (p. 173). I propose, on the contrary, that Spirit Christology should be an ongoing theological category for understanding Christ and not a transient one that converts to a Christocentric pneumatology at the resurrection-ascension.

The mutual and reciprocal nature of the Spirit and the Son's relationship does not come to an end at a certain moment in the economy of redemption. The "subject" or identity of the Spirit is not now submerged under Christology. After the resurrection of Christ, the Spirit of Pentecost mediates the presence of the risen Christ, both bringing Christ to the believer and the believer to Christ. In that respect, the Spirit is the Spirit of Christ, the Spirit of faith, and the Spirit of adoption. Yet the Spirit remains the Spirit of Christ in the second sense as well (the constitutional sense of "of"). The Spirit's work of making human beings children of God through union with the risen Christ parallels the Spirit's work in making Jesus the incarnate Son of God. The Spirit thus retains a unique identity and work relative to Christ and, therefore, the Spirit's identity is not entirely "determined" by Christ, any more than is the Son's solely determined by the Spirit. The Son and Spirit's identities are mutually constituted, but they both — and the Father as well — retain unique identities and work that flow from their identities.

Third, the mutual and reciprocal relationship between the Son and the Spirit in Jesus Christ have implications for their identities in the eternal Trinity. Based on the principle that the economic Trinity reflects the im-

59. Habets also shows his inclination to see the Spirit's work in a more fundamental way, in reference to Johannine Christology: "Here we find the Johannine miraculous conception. Jesus' birth by the Spirit is substantially related to the incarnation of the Logos. Both speak, albeit in different ways, of divine origins and divine union with humanity" (*The Anointed Son,* p. 127).

manent identities of the divine persons, the mutual and reciprocal relationship between the Spirit and the Son exhibited in Jesus Christ suggests a similar pattern of relationships in the eternal Godhead. The Spirit and the Son mutually and reciprocally contribute to each other's personal identities. Since the work of the Spirit provides the horizon for the incarnate Son's life of devotion to the Father in Jesus Christ, the Spirit makes the Son's immanent fellowship with the Father possible as well. The Spirit constitutes the Son as the eternal Son by bringing him into relationship with the Father.[60] The Trinity "becomes" the Trinity in the Holy Spirit. The fellowship of the eternal Godhead crosses the threshold of dyadic relationships only through the Spirit's activity that completes and thereby fulfills the fellowship of the Trinitarian God. Moreover, the relationship between the Spirit and the Son is not unilateral. Just as the Son was not passive in Jesus Christ, but actively loved and served the Father through the incarnation, facilitated by the Holy Spirit, so the Son responds to the relational opportunity provided by the Spirit in the Trinity. The Son engages in loving relationship with the Father and in so doing shapes the personal identity of the Spirit (and the Father's too). In the immanent Trinity, if the Son did not respond to the Spirit's offer to establish his fellowship with the Father, the Spirit would not be the divine person who constitutes the fellowship of the Trinity. The life of Jesus Christ reveals a Spirit who actively facilitates the incarnation of the Son and a Son who embraces and fulfills his identity and work in Jesus Christ. Since the Spirit plays an active role in the identity and work of Jesus Christ, the Spirit has a corresponding one in the eternal Trinitarian God.

Pneumatological Hermeneutics and Transcending Christocentrism

Habets argues that the early Christians used a retroactive hermeneutic to interpret Jesus' life and ministry and that the Holy Spirit played an important role in this hermeneutical process and interpretation. His hermeneutic is a sensible understanding of the way the early Christians developed their accounts of Jesus Christ; but I think that Habets again falls into a

60. Amos Yong makes a similar point using the categories of the mutual-love model. See Yong, *Spirit-Word-Community: Theological Hermeneutics in Trinitarian Perspective* (Eugene, OR: Wipf and Stock, 2002), p. 78. For my assessment of the limitations of the mutual-love model for developing the full reciprocal and interpersonal nature of the triune fellowship, see chapter 3 above.

form of Christocentrism — though his retroactive hermeneutic contains the resources with which to recover the pneumatological gains that are otherwise lost in that implicit Christocentrism.

The retroactive hermeneutic affirms that the post-Easter believers came into an experience of the risen Jesus through the power of the Holy Spirit. The Spirit, in turn, enabled them to understand their experience of Christ in light of their remembrance of his life and teaching. The retroactive process whereby the Spirit illuminates the meaning of Christ for the church is an ongoing one. In other words, the retroactive hermeneutic affirms a symbiotic relationship between Christian experience and the understanding of Jesus' teachings. The early Christians interpreted their experiences in light of his life and teachings, and the canon of Christian Scripture is the documentation of these interpretations. The retroactive hermeneutic, therefore, affirms the theological fecundity of Christian experience and its dialogical role with the life and teachings of Jesus, which were the early Christians' remembrances of Jesus' life, ministry, and teachings. For contemporary Christians, they are the accounts of his life and ministry in Christian Scripture (pp. 103-7).

The problem is that Habets's retroactive hermeneutic subordinates pneumatology to Christology. The Spirit becomes an instrument for a christological function: the gospel is about Christ, not the Holy Spirit. Accordingly, the Spirit illuminates the "Christ event" and enables the church to be Christlike (pp. 105-6). It reduces the gospel to a christological narrative with pneumatological Cliff's notes. Though I am Pentecostal, I am not making special pleading for more theological attention to be given to the Spirit in order to legitimate Pentecostal experience. Rather, the issue is that this attenuation of the Spirit is out of step with the Spirit's role and identity that emerges in the biblical accounts of Christ, which, according to Habets, are the post-Easter interpretation of Jesus' life and ministry in terms of the post-Easter Christians' experience of Christ in and through the Holy Spirit.

The question is: Does the record of the early church's experience fit with a theology that subordinates the Spirit to Christ? If the retroactive hermeneutic is true, that Christian experience and the Word (for the post-Easter Christians in the form of remembrances of Christ and for contemporary Christians in the form of Scripture) correspond, then Habets's Spirit Christology fully pursues neither the pneumatological implications of that experience nor the biblical theology of the Spirit. In the book of Acts, the initiating event of the church is the outpouring of the Holy Spirit.

The early Christians interpreted the pinnacle of Jesus' work in pneumatological terms. They did not see the Spirit merely playing an explanatory role relative to Jesus. Jesus' life, death, resurrection, and ascension to the Father culminate in the gift of the Holy Spirit. John the Baptist declares that Jesus will baptize in the Holy Spirit, and Acts 2:1-4 is the fulfillment of that promise. The early church chose to interpret the ministry of Jesus through a pneumatological lens and to see his work concluding in the outpouring of the Spirit of Pentecost. Thus, they did not see the Spirit's work only — or even primarily — as helping them to discern the meaning of Jesus' life and ministry; but they saw Christ's life and ministry defined in a significant way in terms of the gift of the Holy Spirit. They believed that Jesus' ministry is not complete until he sends the Holy Spirit. In other words, Jesus' work is not completed on the cross or even in the resurrection, but in the eschatological giving of the Spirit. The reciprocity and mutuality of the Son and the Spirit should be kept in mind, because their activity together in Christ defines Jesus' life and ministry.

The Holy Spirit remains a creative, liminal, and eschatological agent. The Spirit works in the space between confusion and clarity, death and life, anticipation and realization, despair and hope. Illustrating this work is the similarity that marks the transition from obscurity to public ministry in the life of Jesus and the post-Easter disciples. When John the Baptist baptized Jesus, Jesus crossed a threshold from private life to public and messianic ministry. Prior to that event, he was Jesus of Nazareth; after it he was Jesus the Christ. The descent of the Spirit and the voice of the Father ratify his messianic identity and ministry. What is important for pneumatology is that the Spirit is the active agent of the anointing, and Jesus is the passive recipient of the Spirit's activity. Accordingly, the relationship between the Spirit and the Son is not unilateral. The Spirit does not exclusively do the bidding of the Son, but acts on and toward the Son — and not merely in an instrumental sense, but a constitutional one. The anointing of the Spirit elevates Jesus of Nazareth to his public ministry as Jesus the Christ. The Spirit plays a similar role in the life of the post-Easter disciples. In the upper room, the disciples are a cowering huddle of forlorn — and presumptively former — disciples of the resurrected but departed Christ. The Spirit of Pentecost arrives and empowers them to cross over into the new life of the church, the community indwelt by the risen Christ, and to become bold and effective in their witness to the gospel of Jesus Christ.

Later Christian writers record experiences and the work of the Holy Spirit that parallels the Spirit's work in the life of Jesus. Believers leave behind the sin of their former life and become God's adopted children. Paul says, "You were dead . . . in your sins," and "if anyone is in Christ, he is a new creation; the old is gone, the new has come!" (Eph. 2:1 and 2 Cor. 5:17). John says that the Christian is a child of God who is "born again" and "born of the Spirit" (John 1:13; 3:3, 8). Who is the agent of this renewal, this transformation from death to life? John links the new birth, the right to be called children of God, to the Spirit. These works of the Spirit are consistent with the liminal, constitutional, and consummational work of the Spirit that begins in the creation accounts and finds its fullest expression in the raising of Christ from the dead, coming as the Spirit of Pentecost, and giving life to the Christian community.

Finally, the Pentecostal experience of the Spirit coheres with the post-Easter interpretation of the Christian faith. The Holy Spirit is the foundation of the Pentecostal experience of God. At the same time, recognizing the prominent place of pneumatology in no way marginalizes Christology in Pentecostal experience. Christ and the Spirit have a mutual orientation. The work of the Spirit brought forth the incarnation of the Son in Jesus Christ and empowered his life and ministry. Jesus Christ fulfilled his messianic calling so that he could give the Holy Spirit and provide the way for all others to participate in the Spirit's work. The aspiration of Christ's and the Spirit's work is not self-oriented with respect to either one of them, but is Trinitarian. Their goal is to lead humans into the Trinitarian fellowship they enjoy with each other and the Father.

Conclusion

This chapter has engaged the doctrine of the Trinity in the evangelical tradition from the Puritan Jonathan Edwards to Myk Habets, a contemporary theologian from New Zealand. In Edwards we found a creative and constructive use of the mutual-love tradition, but also a pneumatology that remains confined to its conceptual parameters. Donald Bloesch and Millard Erickson provided representatives from later twentieth-century evangelicalism. Both, in different ways, wrestle with traditional Trinitarian categories, such as the doctrine of divine processions, but do not achieve a clear and constructive evangelical contribution to Trinitarian theology. In Myk Habets's Spirit Christology, we encounter a fresh and innovative effort to integrate pneumatology, Christology, and Trinitarian theology. However, relying on Thomas Weinandy's Trinitarian proposal and retaining Christocentrism leaves the project's pneumatological and Trinitarian promise unrealized. My goal throughout this chapter has been to interact with these figures from the perspective of a Pentecostal Trinitarian theology. Recognizing a proper role of the Holy Spirit both in the economic and immanent Trinity gets beyond the limits of the mutual-love model in Edwards's theology. With respect to Bloesch and Erickson, I have proposed that, since the Pentecostal tradition is a work of the Spirit, it can serve as a source for theological reflection, that a genuine theology of reciprocal personal identity in the Trinity must include a contribution from pneumatology, and that the economic work of the Spirit is a guide to the Spirit's immanent identity. Finally, rather than returning to Christocentrism with Habets, a Pentecostal Trinitarian theology recognizes the enduring contribution of the Spirit of Pentecost to the economic and immanent Trinity.

5 Charismatic Trinitarian Theology

What is the place of the Trinity in Pentecostal theology? Though a controversy over the Trinity divided the early Pentecostals in North America, the doctrine received little attention thereafter, at least by Classical Pentecostals.[1] Like evangelicals, Pentecostals are mainly confessional

1. Oneness Pentecostalism began at a camp meeting in Arroyo Seco, California (near Los Angeles), in April 1913. The key issue was a new understanding of the nature of and formula for water baptism. Based on Acts 2:38, the Oneness Pentecostals baptized in the name of the Lord Jesus Christ rather than following the Trinitarian pattern of Matthew 28:19. By 1916, the Oneness insistence on baptism and rebaptism in the name of Jesus and its nontraditional Trinitarianism led the Assemblies of God (Trinitarian Pentecostal denomination) to include a clear Trinitarian confession in its Statement of Fundamental Truths — and thereby to exclude Jesus' Name ministers and congregations. For a thorough investigation of Oneness Pentecostalism, see David A. Reed, *"In Jesus' Name": The History and Beliefs of Oneness Pentecostals* (Blandford Forum, UK: Deo Publishing, 2008).

Oneness Pentecostalism derives its name from its rejection of Nicene Trinitarian theology. Oneness theology affirms that the terms Father, Son, and Holy Spirit are titles that Scripture uses to indicate the different roles of the one God in salvation history. Trinitarian language, therefore, applies only to the distinct redemptive roles of the one God and not eternal distinctions or persons within the one God. The critical point is that the titles of Father, Son, and Holy Spirit are not names of divine persons; God has one personal identity. Consequently, the one God has one name, the name of Jesus. According to Nicene Trinitarian theology, Oneness Pentecostalism is a modalist approach to God that sees God as one eternal being without internal distinction of persons. For their part, Oneness Pentecostals see Nicene theology as a corruption of monotheism that implies polytheism or subordinationism. I favor a Nicene view. Though they are ultimately beyond human conception, the names of the Father, the Son, and the Holy Spirit refer to eternal distinctions in God. For a

Trinitarians, but not Trinitarian theologians. This is illustrated in the widely used systematic theology textbook *Knowing the Doctrines of the Bible,* by Myer Pearlman, which endorses the traditional doctrine of the Trinity but pursues no substantial reflection on it. Referring to the Athanasian Creed, Pearlman affirms one God in three persons and rejects modalism, tritheism, and subordinationism.[2] In a theological text that was later used in Assemblies of God institutions, Kerry D. McRoberts provides a similar presentation of the doctrine of the Trinity, with more detail on the biblical basis and its development in the patristic era, plus an apologetic interaction with the Oneness Pentecostal doctrine of God.[3] However, "until recently Pentecostals have not bothered themselves with formulating their doctrine of the Trinity in cohesive theological terms," says Veli-Matti Kärkkäinen. "In fact, the most important thing for Pentecostals is not the doctrine *per se,* but the experience of the Trinity."[4] More recently, Keith Warrington suggests, with respect to Pentecostals, that they are "theologically . . . Trinitarian though practically, this is less clearly defined."[5] Recognizing the deficit, Warrington's work nonetheless sets aside the pursuit of a Pentecostal Trinitarian theology and remains content to address the traditional Pentecostal discussion of the Spirit and the experience of grace.[6]

In cases where Pentecostals have pursued a constructive use of the Trinity, they have not done so in terms of a theology of the Trinity as such, but have drawn on the Trinity as a resource for rethinking other areas of theology. In this respect, Pentecostals have engaged in Trinitarian-inspired theological projects, but not a theology of the Trinity.[7] Andrew K. Gabriel

---

Oneness understanding of God, see "Oneness-Trinitarian Pentecostal Final Report, 2002-2007," *Pneuma: The Journal of the Society for Pentecostal Studies* 30 (2008): 208-24; see also Reed, *"In Jesus' Name,"* pp. 265-73.

2. Myer Pearlman, *Knowing the Doctrines of the Bible* (Springfield, MO: Gospel Publishing House, 1981 [first published in 1937]), pp. 68-77.

3. Kerry D. McRoberts, "The Holy Trinity," in McRoberts, *Systematic Theology,* rev. ed. (Springfield, MO: Logion, 1998 [first published in 1995]), pp. 145-77.

4. Veli-Matti Kärkkäinen, *Toward a Pneumatological Theology: Pentecostal and Ecumenical Perspectives on Ecclesiology, Soteriology, and Theology of Mission,* ed. Amos Yong (Lanham, MD: University Press of America, 2002), pp. 97, 103.

5. Keith Warrington, *Pentecostal Theology: A Theology of Encounter* (New York: T & T Clark, 2008), p. 30.

6. Warrington, *Pentecostal Theology,* pp. 46-130.

7. E.g., Amos Yong resources several strands of Trinitarian theology, principally Irenaean, Athanasian, and Augustinian, to develop a Trinitarian theological hermeneutics;

makes a similar assessment of Pentecostals' use of pneumatology and the doctrine of God. He argues that, while Pentecostals have produced numerous studies on the Holy Spirit and Spirit baptism, spirituality, and charismatic gifts, a pneumatology proper is rare.[8] Though Pentecostals have historically neglected the doctrine, recent figures have made important first steps toward applying Pentecostal insights to the Trinity. In order to address their contributions, I interact in this chapter with Kilian McDonnell, Frank D. Macchia, and Clark H. Pinnock, but I begin with D. Lyle Dabney's critique of and challenge to Pentecostal theologians.[9]

D. Lyle Dabney

D. Lyle Dabney grew up in a Pentecostal home, and, like many Pentecostal theologians, he was drawn to pneumatology, though he was dissatisfied

---

see Amos Yong, *Spirit-Word-Community: Theological Hermeneutics in Trinitarian Perspective* (Eugene, OR: Wipf and Stock, 2006), pp. 50-72. Pneumatology is a central category of Yong's work, but the doctrine of the Trinity has not been a major area for his constructive theology. Though the Trinity plays a significant role in *Spirit-Word-Community* (discussed in chapter 1, above), his focus in that work is theological hermeneutics and not primarily the development of a Pentecostal Trinitarian theology. Simon Chan also uses the Trinity as the basis for his Pentecostal theology of Christian spirituality; see Chan, *Spiritual Theology: A Systematic Study of the Christian Life* (Downers Grove, IL: InterVarsity, 1998), pp. 40-55.

8. Andrew K. Gabriel, *The Lord Is the Spirit: The Holy Spirit and the Divine Attributes* (Eugene, OR: Pickwick, 2011), pp. 90-91, 98-99.

9. An obvious figure left out is Veli-Matti Kärkkäinen. He is one of the most visible and prolific Pentecostal scholars. Widely published in the areas of ecumenical and systematic theology, he also has written four books related to the doctrine of the Trinity: *The Trinity: Global Perspectives* (Louisville: Westminster John Knox, 2007); *Trinity and Religious Pluralism: The Doctrine of the Trinity in Christian Theology of Religions* (Burlington, VT: Ashgate, 2004); *The Doctrine of God: A Global Introduction* (Grand Rapids: Baker, 2004); and *Pneumatology: The Holy Spirit in Ecumenical, International, and Contextual Perspective* (Grand Rapids: Baker, 2002). Nevertheless, his work has more of an explicit ecumenical orientation than a Pentecostal one. His theological work in general, and his contributions to pneumatology and the Trinity in particular, cover and introduce a variety of voices but do not develop a unique Pentecostal or charismatic theology. Kärkkäinen also characterizes his efforts as "evangelical" rather than "Pentecostal" and "charismatic" (see Veli-Matti Kärkkäinen, "Trinity and Religions: On the Way to a Trinitarian Theology of Religions for Evangelicals," *Missiology: An International Review* 33 [2005]: 159-74, esp. pp. 161, 163. The ecumenical and summative nature of his theology are not faults; however, these elements are limited in their suitability to serve as a primary dialogue partner in a chapter on constructive Pentecostal and charismatic approaches to the Trinity.

with traditional Pentecostal accounts of the Holy Spirit. He eventually earned his doctorate at the University of Tübingen, where he studied with Jürgen Moltmann.[10] Over time he became convinced that the Wesleyan theological tradition could provide better resources to foster his pneumatological interests than could the Pentecostal one. Inspired by Karl Barth's call for a turn to a theology of the Holy Spirit and Moltmann's work in pneumatology, he proposes that theology has been dominated by theologies of the first (doctrine of God the Father) and second (doctrine of God the Son) articles of the creed and should now turn to the neglected third article — the Holy Spirit.[11] Dabney believes that a shift to pneumatology is appropriate in light of its marginalization in the historic traditions, the openness to language of the S/spirit in the postmodern cultural context of the West, and the rise of the Pentecostal and charismatic movements.[12] Although he mentions the rise of the Pentecostal and charismatic movements as a reason why theology should turn to a theology of the third article, he does not see their theology as particularly helpful for his project and critiques it for falling short of fulfilling its theological promise. Though Dabney's work remains at the level of programmatic proposal set forth in several essays and articles, Pentecostal theologians should hear his challenge.[13]

The problem, according to Dabney, is that Pentecostals formulate their theological identity in the foreign categories of evangelical theology. Pentecostals are the theological manifestation of David clambering around

10. His dissertation was published as *Die Kenosis des Geistes: Kontinuität zwischen Schöpfung und Erlösung im Werk des Heiligen Geistes,* Neukirchener Beiträge zur Systematischen Theologie (Neukirchen-Vluyn: Neukirchener, 1997).

11. Barth suggested a turn to a "theology of the third article" in his 1968 "Nachwort, or Concluding Unscientific Postscript on Schleiermacher," in Barth, *The Theology of Schleiermacher: Lectures at Göttingen,* trans. Geoffrey W. Bromiley (Grand Rapids: Eerdmans, 1982), pp. 261-79 (esp. p. 278).

12. Bradford E. Hinze and D. Lyle Dabney, "Introduction," in *Advents of the Spirit: An Introduction to the Current Study of Pneumatology,* ed. Hinze and Dabney, Marquette Studies in Theology (Milwaukee: Marquette University Press, 2001), pp. 11-34.

13. E.g., D. Lyle Dabney, "Jürgen Moltmann and John Wesley's Third Article Theology," *Wesleyan Theological Journal* 29 (1994): 140-48; "Otherwise Engaged in the Spirit: A First Theology for a Twenty-first Century," in *The Future of Theology: Essays in Honor of Jürgen Moltmann,* ed. Miroslav Volf, Carmen Krieg, and Thomas Kucharz (Grand Rapids: Eerdmans, 1996), pp. 154-63; "Pneumatologia Crucis: Reclaiming *Theologia Crucis* for a Theology of the Spirit Today," *Scottish Journal of Theology* 53 (2000): 511-24; "'Justified by the Spirit': Soteriological Reflections on the Resurrection," *International Journal of Systematic Theology* 3 (2001): 46-68.

in Saul's armor.[14] Dabney can be unsparing in his assessment. With respect to the Roman Catholic and Pentecostal dialogue, he declares, "The fundamental problem faced by Pentecostals in this theological dialogue is that they have no theological account of themselves, that is, in terms of theology, they simply don't know who they are or what they are about."[15] Despite this criticism, Dabney believes that the promise of Pentecostal theology is "the possibility that Pentecostal theologians might yet throw off the dead weight of the 'might' and 'power' of [Saul's] armor and discover their own theological voice in a genuine theology of the Holy Spirit."[16] I agree with Dabney's call for Pentecostals to discern and articulate the theological substance of their experience of God's Spirit, though, as Veli-Matti Kärkkäinen warns, to avoid doing so in a divisive way.[17]

Dabney confronts and rejects the popular view that the essence of Pentecostalism is charismatic experience rather than theology.[18] Of course, charismatic experience of the Holy Spirit is central to Pentecostalism, but it is an experience with a latent theology that needs to blossom. The options for Pentecostals do not reduce to the false alternatives of defining the movement in terms of either charismatic experience or theology and doctrine. The Pentecostal movement is about being caught up in an experience of God's Spirit that transforms lives and empowers them to serve God in this world. Yet that experience of the Spirit points the way toward a Pentecostal theology. Not a theology that fractures the Christian communities, but a theological "tongue" of the Spirit of Pentecost that contributes to the richness of the Christian community. The popular view that Pentecostalism is about experience and practice and not about theology is similar to saying that, prior to AD 325, Christianity was not about the doctrine of the Trinity. Such a view is nonsense, even though prior to Nicaea a formal and endorsed doctrine of the Trinity did not exist. The doctrine of the Trinity de-

14. D. Lyle Dabney, "Saul's Armor: The Problem and Promise of Pentecostal Theology Today," *Pneuma* 23 (2001): 115-46.

15. Dabney, "Saul's Armor," p. 120.

16. Dabney, "Saul's Armor," pp. 116-17.

17. Veli-Matti Kärkkäinen, "David's Sling: The Promise and the Problem of Pentecostal Theology Today: A Response to D. Lyle Dabney," *Pneuma* 23 (2001): 147-52 (esp. pp. 150-51). Kärkkäinen is less than enthusiastic about Dabney's call for a theology of the third article for theology in general and Pentecostal theology in particular. He does not believe that pneumatology plays a leading role in either the biblical tradition or the history of Christian thought (Kärkkäinen, "David's Sling," pp. 151-52).

18. Dabney, "Saul's Armor," pp. 120-21.

veloped out of the experience of Jesus and the early church and over time in formal theological reflection that received the status of orthodoxy at the Council of Nicaea. In a similar way, the Pentecostal movement is barely a century in the making. Discerning and developing its theological traditions vis-à-vis other theological traditions will take time and patience. That the Pentecostal movement has yet to produce a clear theological tradition means neither that it has none nor that it should abandon all hope of developing one. This project joins with other Pentecostal theologians in the task of developing the emerging Pentecostal theological tradition — particularly with respect to the doctrine of the Trinity. Though Dabney's comprehensive articulation of a third-article theology has yet to emerge, his assessment of the problem and promise of Pentecostal theology is on the mark and thus provides a good starting place for an investigation of current Pentecostal work in the doctrine of the Trinity.

Kilian McDonnell

Kilian McDonnell's substantial contribution to the charismatic and ecumenical movements spans at least four decades. In 1974, he began to serve as an international liaison between the Vatican and Catholic Charismatic Renewal. This followed his appointment in 1972 to co-chair the International Dialogue between Pentecostal Churches and the Secretariat for Promoting Christian Unity, which concluded in 2001.[19] In 1985 he published a seminal article that called for a more fundamental role of pneumatology in Trinitarian theology.[20] This article was the seed for his book *The Other Hand of God,* where he argues that the Trinity is foundational not only for an adequate theology of the Holy Spirit, but also for the understanding and integration of pneumatology and Christology.[21]

McDonnell's central thesis is that pneumatology and Christology mutually condition one another (*Other Hand,* p. 61). He bases this notion on

19. In addition to ecumenical initiatives with Pentecostals, McDonnell has played official roles in dialogues between the Catholic Church and Methodist, Reformed, and Lutheran churches.

20. Kilian McDonnell, "A Trinitarian Theology of the Holy Spirit," *Theological Studies* 46 (1985): 191-227. Hereafter, page references to this work appear in parentheses in the text.

21. Kilian McDonnell, *The Other Hand of God: The Holy Spirit as the Universal Touch and Goal* (Collegeville, MN: Liturgical Press, 2003), p. 2. Hereafter, page references to this work appear in parentheses in the text.

the Pauline theology of being "in Christ" and "in the Spirit," according to which to be in Christ is to have one's life determined by the Holy Spirit ("Trinitarian Theology," p. 204; *Other Hand*, pp. 203-4). Taking Irenaeus's theology of the "two hands" of the Father, he proposes that Christ and the Spirit share equal missions in the economy of grace ("Trinitarian Theology," pp. 206-7; *Other Hand*, pp. 194-98).

The mission of the Spirit is to make Christ's mission operationally effective ("Trinitarian Theology," pp. 210-11). McDonnell uses the term "contact function" to express the idea that "the Spirit is the universal point of contact between God and history . . . [and] the point of entry into the Christological and Trinitarian mystery" (McDonnell, "Trinitarian Theology," pp. 211-12; *Other Hand*, pp. 111-20). Recovering pneumatology does not replace Christocentrism with pneumacentrism, but recognizes the important place of both Christ and the Spirit for theology (*Other Hand*, p. 206). Pneumatology plays a hermeneutical role with respect to the task of theology that correlates with the Spirit's role in the experience of grace. Through the Spirit, the believer is "in Christ." In a similar way, the Spirit is not the object of theology, but rather the divine subject who enables theology to understand God, especially the revelation of God in Christ. For this reason, McDonnell recommends a "theology in the Spirit (in contrast to a theology of the Spirit)" ("Trinitarian Theology," p. 219; *Other Hand*, pp. 213-14, 219-20, 221-24).

He suggests: "Pneumatology is, in some sense, epistemology, and to this degree determines the rules for speaking about the presence of the mystery" ("Trinitarian Theology," p. 223). In this respect, the Spirit provides the theological endeavor with christological clarity. In the end, McDonnell articulates the role of the Holy Spirit in light of the work of Christ. The result is a lingering Christocentrism.

First, McDonnell's portrayal of the Spirit's relationship to Christ in instrumental terms reveals a Christocentric Trinitarian theology. The Holy Spirit is the instrument of the revelation and redemption provided by Christ. Clarifying the relationship between Christ and the Spirit, McDonnell affirms that, "[t]hough one can say that Christ works through the Spirit, that cannot be turned around. The Spirit does not work through Christ" ("Trinitarian Theology," pp. 210-11; *Other Hand*, p. 201). That statement highlights the way McDonnell understands the Holy Spirit's role in Christian life and theology. Through the Spirit one participates in the grace of Christ and receives the knowledge of God revealed in Christ. The Holy Spirit is the medium for the revelation of God's knowledge and salvation in Christ. The work of the Spirit is not only integrated with but also circumscribed by Christology. McDonnell says: "[B]oth the revelation of the Spirit and the bestowing of the Spirit, which is uniquely the Spirit of Christ, take place only in and through Christ," and "There is no act or manifestation of the Spirit which is not through Christ" ("Trinitarian Theology," pp. 204-5). Pneumatology serves Christology: the role of the Spirit is to reveal and make effective the work of Christ. The Spirit retains a unique identity, but it is hidden because the Spirit "takes on the personality of Christ" (*Other Hand,* p. 6). The consequence is a Christocized Holy Spirit.

Though the relationship between Christ and the Spirit is instrumental for McDonnell, it is not entirely unilateral. The Son and Spirit have distinct but integrated missions. The mission of the Son is to die and provide salvation, and the Spirit's mission is "to make the mystery of the Son effective in the church" (*Other Hand,* p. 86). McDonnell's goal is to avoid two problematic tendencies. The first, which sometimes appears in the Eastern tradition of the church, is an independent mission of the Spirit. The second, characteristic of the West, subsumes the Spirit's mission under the Son's. In their place, he suggests that the Son's and Spirit's missions are mutually determined (*Other Hand,* pp. 87-88). He concentrates his attention on Western subordinationism and endeavors to evade the relegation of the Spirit to a "junior grade mission" (*Other Hand,* p. 89). Nevertheless, though McDonnell clearly integrates the Spirit's work throughout the life of Christ (e.g., the Spirit conceives and raises Jesus from the dead), he continues to give the Spirit an instrumental mission.[22] Christ is the content, or the "what," and the Spirit is the "how" of the gospel (*Other Hand,* pp. 89-90). The mission of the Spirit is to apply the work of Christ. The Spirit is the "mediation" of Christ the "mediator" (*Other Hand,* p. 206). Portraying the Spirit as the universal mediation of Christ is consistent with the Western practice of identifying the Holy Spirit as the mutual love that unites the Father and the Son. The Spirit adds nothing to the substance of redemption (the "what"), but merely applies the grace of Christ (the "how"). Extrapolated to the Trinity, the Holy Spirit is the medium (the "how") of the mutual relations (the "what") of the Father and the Son. The result is

22. I have critiqued the instrumental role and subordination of the Spirit to Christ in "Pentecostal Soteriology and Pneumatology," *Journal of Pentecostal Theology* 11 (2003): 248-70, as well as in "Beyond Tongues: A Pentecostal Theology of Grace," in *Defining Issues in Pentecostalism: Classical and Emergent,* ed. Steven M. Studebaker (Eugene, OR: Pickwick, 2008), pp. 46-68.

that the Spirit plays a constitutional role in neither the immanent nor the economic Trinity, but more narrowly facilitates the personal relationships and works of the Father and the Son.

Second, McDonnell understands the gospel in terms of christological content. He observes: "Even in the enthusiasm of the Pentecost event Luke has Peter preach a sermon (Acts 2:14-36) not about a Spirit-centered kingdom but about Jesus crucified and risen" (*Other Hand,* p. 69; he previously affirmed this point in "Trinitarian Theology," p. 205). Reinforcing the christological nature of the gospel, he affirms that "[t]he church is not the body of the Spirit" (*Other Hand,* p. 89). His point captures a fundamental aspect of the gospel, but misses an equally important one. Jesus Christ is clearly a central feature of the gospel; yet the gift of the Holy Spirit is no less significant. Acts 2:33, which is a kerygmatic formula, identifies the gift of the Holy Spirit as the apex of the reception of the gospel: forgiveness of sins, baptism, and the promise of the Father (i.e., the gift of the Holy Spirit). Moreover, though the "body of Christ" is a biblical image of the church, the "temple of the Holy Spirit" is as well. McDonnell is correct that Peter does not preach a "Spirit-centered kingdom." However, the option is not Christocentrism or pneumacentrism. The New Testament story of Jesus Christ does not end at the cross, the resurrection, or even the ascension, but at Pentecost, the outpouring of the Holy Spirit, and finally the new heaven and new earth. Moreover, the gift of the Spirit not only makes available a grace made complete by Christ, but it completes the work of redemption. Without the Spirit, no one touches redemption. Therefore, Acts 2:33 in specific, and the framing of the purpose of Jesus' ministry as baptizing in the Spirit, more broadly (e.g., John the Baptist in the Gospels and the outpouring of the Spirit in Acts 2:1-4), suggest that the gospel has christological and pneumatological content.

Third, McDonnell maintains that the object of theological reflection is Christ and not the Holy Spirit. Rather than critique the uneven treatment of the Holy Spirit relative to the Father and the Son in the history of theology, he endorses it — due as it is, he suggests, to the "ambiguous" place of the Spirit in revelation. The Holy Spirit is not to be known, but to make Christ known. Christ is the object and the Spirit the hermeneutical medium of theology ("Trinitarian Theology," pp. 223-27). The distinction between Christ as the object and the Spirit as the hermeneutical key of theology assumes that theology has more direct access to the Son than to the Spirit in the revelation of God in Jesus Christ. However, theology has no more direct access to the Son of God than to the Holy Spirit. A Christocentric approach presupposes that, because it has access to the life of Jesus, it has access to the Son; but this is not so, at least not in a direct way. The revelation of the Son is mediated through the humanity of Jesus Christ. Theology accesses the Son through the historical accounts and interpretations of Jesus Christ in Scripture ("Trinitarian Theology," pp. 223-27). Consequently, the revelation of the Son occurs principally in the life of Jesus: the life of Jesus is the Son's narrative of revelation and redemption. The revelation of the Spirit is also historically mediated. In a similar way that the narrative of Christ reveals the Son, the biblical narratives of the Spirit reveal the identity of the Holy Spirit, which include the Spirit's role in the incarnation of the Son and the life of Jesus Christ. For this reason, the Holy Spirit is a legitimate object of theology. The Son and Spirit do different things in the life of Jesus, but that difference does not entail the claim that the content of pneumatology is Christology, or, as McDonnell puts it, that the Spirit "takes on the personality of Christ" (*Other Hand*, p. 6).

Though McDonnell attributes mutual roles to Christ and the Spirit, he carries on the Western Trinitarian tradition's tendency toward Christocentrism. The Spirit remains an instrument for accessing a christological revelation and redemption. The Spirit interprets the work of Christ and is the medium ("contact function") for relation or union with Christ ("Trinitarian Theology," pp. 208-12). Since the Holy Spirit's role is to reveal Christ, pneumatology is not a distinct area of sustained theological reflection. Though McDonnell is correct that the Holy Spirit has an ambiguous status in the theological traditions, the biblical narratives of the Spirit provide pneumatological content and a theology of the Holy Spirit that is integrated with Christology and not simply an instrument for revealing Christology. Recognizing the identity of the Spirit in these narratives and their implication for the Trinity is the basis of a Pentecostal contribution to the other traditions of Trinitarian theology.

Frank Macchia

Frank Macchia is a leading theological voice from within Classical Pentecostalism. Though not likely a strict Classical Pentecostal, his recent works mount a case for recovering the central place of the doctrine of Spirit baptism for the movement, though his view of Spirit baptism is not necessarily a "Classical" one. This project began with his seminal *Baptized in the Spirit* (2006). Against the popular trend that characterizes Pentecostalism in terms of charismatic experience and doctrinal diversity, he argues that Spirit baptism is the distinctive doctrine of Pentecostalism. Macchia does not rehash the exhausted arguments of the past. He articulates the doctrine from the perspective of the Trinity and shows its implications for ecclesiology and the entire Christian life. By doing so, he frees the doctrine from the cramped corridors of the Classical view, which defines Spirit baptism as a second experience of grace evidenced by speaking in tongues.[23] His *Justified in the Spirit* (2010) extends and applies the vision of the previous book to the doctrine of justification by faith.[24] He proposes a Pentecostal theology of justification that moves beyond the traditional Catholic view of moral transformation and the Protestant emphasis on a forensic declaration of righteousness. Justification consists in Spirit baptism, which brings a renewal of life and an inclusion into the divine *koinonia.* His goal is not the development of a Pentecostal Trinitarian theology per se, but a Trinitarian interpretation of justification.

With respect to the Trinity, Macchia draws on Athanasian and Augustinian theology. Macchia turns to the Athanasian notion of the "mutual dependence" of the divine persons (p. 303). Mutual dependence means that the Father is the Father only in relationship to the Son, and the Son in relationship to the Father. Applied to the Spirit's work in justification, Macchia argues that the Spirit opens up to the world the love enjoyed and shared between the Father and the Son. He also adopts Augustine's view of the Spirit as the mutual love of the Father and the Son with an important qualification. He recognizes that thinking of the Spirit as a "bond" of love can depersonalize the Spirit. To avoid this danger, he assigns the Spirit an active role in the economy of grace. The Spirit justifies people through Spirit baptism and includes them in the *koinonia* of God (p. 302). However, he is reluctant to articulate the way this economic activity of the Spirit corresponds to or derives from the Spirit's role as mutual love in the immanent life of the Trinity.

In fact, his discussion of the relationship between the economic and immanent Trinity reveals a tension. On the one hand, he affirms the reciprocal relationship between the immanent and economic Trinity because Spirit baptism is a metaphor that points to the "interdependent dynamism

23. Frank D. Macchia, *Baptized in the Spirit: A Global Pentecostal Theology* (Grand Rapids: Zondervan, 2006).

24. Frank D. Macchia, *Justified in the Spirit: Creation, Redemption, and the Triune God* (Grand Rapids: Eerdmans, 2010). Hereafter, page references to this work appear in parentheses in the text.

of divine love within God and from God in redemptive history" (p. 305). So here the Spirit as the love that unites the Father and the Son is the basis of the Spirit as the love poured out in Spirit baptism that draws believers into the communion of the Father and the Son. On the other hand, he follows Pannenberg and Moltmann's criticism of the traditional doctrine of eternal origins and thus sees the sendings or processions of the Son and the Spirit described in John's Gospel as economic relationships and not as revelations of their immanent identities (pp. 304-5). He supports Simon Chan's recommendation that theology should look to the eschatological purpose of the sending of the Son and outpouring of the Spirit rather than to their relations of origins (p. 305). Yet, why posit discontinuity between two approaches — origins versus eschatological — to thinking about the relationships of the divine persons? Though I have critiqued traditional theology's overreliance on origins for understanding the divine persons and have recommended that the eschatological work of the Spirit can contribute to Trinitarian theology, I have not at the same time rejected the theology of origins and processions, based so clearly as it is on the economic pattern of the sending of the Son and the Spirit. If the economic activities are indicative of immanent identities, then we should expect to find a corresponding relationship between these domains of theological reflection. Moreover, if no connection pertains between the economic and immanent relationships, theology is futile speculation.

While noting this issue in Macchia's discussion of the Trinity, I suggest that his purpose is not to develop a Pentecostal Trinitarian theology, but to develop a Pentecostal and Trinitarian — and particularly a pneumatological — theology of justification. Macchia's use of the Trinity is a creative integration of Augustinian and Athanasian Trinitarian theologies for the purpose of constructing a Pentecostal theology of justification. In the end, though, Macchia's Trinitarian theology primarily remains within the structure of the Augustinian tradition and focuses more on the Spirit's role in the economic work of justification and less on the Spirit's identity and role in the Trinity.

Clark H. Pinnock

In the final section of this chapter I discuss Clark Pinnock, who has written extensively on the doctrine of the Trinity from a charismatic perspective. Pinnock personifies much of Pentecostal theology. Forged by North

American evangelical theology, the trajectory of his theological development and Christian experience eventually led to a tenuous relationship with it. Pinnock's theological contributions have been surveyed, analyzed, and critiqued by a host of scholars.[25] With this in mind, I will seek to avoid traveling terrain that is ably covered by others, and will highlight his contribution to Pentecostal theology — especially his theology of the Holy Spirit and Trinity. I pursue this goal by charting two ways that Clark Pinnock's theology reflects and contributes to Pentecostal theology and then by analyzing his pneumatology and Trinitarian theology.

A Charismatic Theologian

Though he was, strictly speaking, a Baptist rather than a Pentecostal theologian, Pinnock can be counted a charismatic, or "renewal," theologian and is important to Pentecostal theology for several reasons.[26] Pinnock's Pentecostal experience occurred mostly within the charismatic movement and the Third Wave (Toronto Airport Vineyard Christian Fellowship).[27] Consequently, neither his experience nor his understanding of Spirit baptism and speaking in tongues match the Classical Pentecostal view.[28] Pinnock's spiritual and theological journey also has parallels with the history of North American Pentecostalism. Like Pinnock, Pentecostalism has a clear kinship with evangelicalism. Many of the early Pentecostals came from Reformed revival and Wesleyan-Holiness movements of the late-nineteenth and early-twentieth centuries. The early Pentecostals largely adopted evangelical theology and added on the Pentecostal doctrine of Spirit baptism and spiritual gifts.[29] Robert P. Menzies maintains that, as Spirit baptism is a

25. A number of treatments that track Pinnock's theological career are available. The most thorough is Barry Callen, *Clark H. Pinnock: Journey toward Renewal; An Intellectual Biography* (Nappanee, IN: Evangel, 2000).

26. For a fuller treatment of Pinnock's identity as a charismatic and his contribution to Pentecostal theology, see Steven M. Studebaker, "Clark Pinnock: A Canadian Charismatic Pilgrim," *Canadian Journal of Pentecostal-Charismatic Christianity* 1 (2010): 1-29.

27. Clark H. Pinnock, *Flame of Love: A Theology of the Holy Spirit* (Downers Grove, IL: InterVarsity, 1996), p. 240.

28. E.g., Clark H. Pinnock and Grant R. Osborne, "A Truce Proposal for the Tongues Controversy," *Christianity Today* 8 (Oct. 1971): 6-9; Clark H. Pinnock, "The New Pentecostalism: Reflections by a Well-Wisher," *Christianity Today* 14 (Sept. 1973): 6-10; Clark H. Pinnock, "Charismatic Renewal for the Radical Church," *Post-American* (Feb. 1975): 16-21.

29. For just a few criticisms of this tendency, see Matthew S. Clark, Henry Lederle, et al.,

donum superadditum to the salvation provided by Christ, so traditional Pentecostal theology has been a *donum superadditum* to conservative evangelical theology.[30] Pinnock's efforts to expand evangelical theology also parallel much of the Pentecostal theology of the past several decades. Pentecostal theology has been searching for its own theological voice(s) that does not so much repudiate evangelical theology as it discerns the categories of thought appropriate to its own history and experience of God. Pinnock, like Pentecostalism more broadly, retained a strong association with evangelicalism, but also sought to move beyond both its experiential and theological frameworks. As a charismatic-evangelical, Pinnock has been a catalyst and a role model for Pentecostal theologians who endeavor to develop unique contributions to theology, which are free from the cloister of conservative evangelical theology.

In addition to shaping his Christian experience, Pinnock's participation in the charismatic renewal has given a new orientation to the style and content of his theology. Barry Callen observes: "Pinnock is probably the most prominent pioneer of a fresh mood, maybe even fresh movement in contemporary North American evangelical theology."[31] Pinnock has traveled on a theological odyssey, from being a strident apologist for conservative Reformed neo-evangelicalism to an irenic, ecumenical, postconservative, and charismatic theologian. In a recent autobiographical essay, he described his theological journey in the following way: "Mine is the story of a man's theology which . . . began in the 'conservative-evangelical' camp with the scholastic tendency and is finishing up (it appears) in the 'post-conservative' camp with the pietists and pentecostals."[32] The charismatic movement provided a

---

What Is Distinctive about Pentecostal Theology? (Pretoria: University of South Africa, 1989), p. 100; Dabney, "Saul's Armor," pp. 115-17; Donald W. Dayton, "The Limits of Evangelicalism: The Pentecostal Tradition," in *The Variety of American Evangelicalism*, ed. Donald W. Dayton and Robert K. Johnston (Downers Grove, IL: InterVarsity, 1991), pp. 36-56 (esp. p. 48); Walter J. Hollenweger, *Pentecostalism: Origins and Developments Worldwide* (Peabody, MA: Hendrickson, 1997), p. 19; David R. Nichols, "The Search for a Pentecostal Structure in Systematic Theology," *Pneuma* 6 (1984): 57-76 (esp. p. 57); Pinnock, *Flame of Love*, p. 240; and Russell P. Spittler, "Suggested Areas for Further Research in Pentecostal Studies," *Pneuma* 5 (1983): 39-56 (esp. p. 43).

30. Robert P. Menzies, *The Development of Early Christian Pneumatology, with Special Reference to Luke-Acts*, Journal for the Study of the New Testament Supplement Series, 54 (Sheffield, UK: Sheffield Academic Press, 1991), p. 48.

31. Callen, *Clark H. Pinnock*, p. 5.

32. Clark H. Pinnock, "Confessions of a Post-Conservative Evangelical Theologian," *Dialog: A Journal of Theology* 45 (2006): 382-88 (esp. p. 382). For Pinnock's theological trajec-

pathway for Pinnock to diverge from his rationalist and doctrinaire practice of the Christian faith and pursue a piety of the heart.

Pinnock's theological pilgrimage led him to pneumatology. He has encouraged Pentecostals to break loose from their inherited scholastic approach to theology, which reflects their habit of relying on traditional neo-evangelical approaches to theology, and to pursue a method and content for their theology that is more reflective of their experience of the Holy Spirit.[33] On the content of his theology, Pinnock made contributions to Pentecostal theology in the areas of the doctrine of God, pneumatology, ecclesiology, and theological hermeneutics.[34] Indeed, he describes his major text on pneumatology, *Flame of Love*, as "charismatic in celebrating Pentecostalism as a mighty twentieth-century outpouring of the Spirit."[35] In addition to Pinnock's contributions, Pentecostal theologians have drawn on his theology to assist their approaches to certain areas of theology, such as theology of religions and Spirit Christology.[36] I now turn to two areas of his theology that bear on the Trinitarian theology I am pursuing in this book.

---

tory, see "From Augustine to Arminius: A Pilgrimage in Theology," in *The Grace of God and the Will of Man*, ed. Clark H. Pinnock (Minneapolis: Bethany, 1989), pp. 15-30.

33. Clark H. Pinnock, "Divine Relationality: A Pentecostal Contribution to the Doctrine of God," *Journal of Pentecostal Theology* 16 (2000): 3-26 (esp. p. 22). In the decade after Pinnock's call for Pentecostals to develop a Pentecostal theology, notable advances have been accomplished: e.g., Macchia, *Baptized in the Spirit;* Warrington, *Pentecostal Theology;* Amos Yong, *The Spirit Poured Out on All Flesh: Pentecostalism and the Possibility of Global Theology* (Grand Rapids: Baker Academic, 2005); and the new Pentecostal Manifestos Series coedited by James K. A. Smith and Amos Yong (published by Eerdmans).

34. For the doctrine of God, see Pinnock, "Divine Relationality," pp. 3-26. On ecclesiology, see Pinnock, "Church in the Power of the Holy Spirit: The Promise of Pentecostal Ecclesiology," *Journal of Pentecostal Theology* 14 (2006): 146-65. For the responses, see Frank D. Macchia, "Pinnock's Pneumatology: A Pentecostal Appreciation," *Journal of Pentecostal Theology* 14 (2006): 167-73; Terry L. Cross, "A Response to Clark Pinnock's 'Church in the Power of the Holy Spirit,'" *Journal of Pentecostal Theology* 14 (2006): 175-82; R. Hollis Gause, "A Pentecostal Response to Pinnock's Proposal," *Journal of Pentecostal Theology* 14 (2006): 183-88. For theological hermeneutics, see Clark H. Pinnock, "The Work of the Spirit in the Interpretation of Holy Scripture from the Perspective of a Charismatic Biblical Theologian," *Journal of Pentecostal Theology* 18 (2009): 157-71, and "The Work of the Holy Spirit in Hermeneutics," *Journal of Pentecostal Theology* 2 (1993): 3-23.

35. Pinnock, *Flame of Love*, p. 18.

36. Amos Yong has constructively drawn on Pinnock to develop a Pentecostal theology of religions in *Beyond the Impasse: Toward a Pneumatological Theology of Religions* (Carlisle, UK: Paternoster; Grand Rapids: Baker Academic, 2003), pp. 32-33. I have engaged with Pinnock's Spirit Christology in Steven M. Studebaker, "Integrating Pneumatology and Christology: A Trinitarian Modification of Clark H. Pinnock's Spirit Christology," *Pneuma* 27 (2006): 5-20.

Pentecostal Experience and Theology

Pinnock urges that Pentecostal experience should shape Pentecostal theology. This call is more fundamental than simply a contribution to one area of Pentecostal theology; it is also within the context of Pinnock's advocacy for the Pentecostal movement as a catalyst for church renewal. Pinnock's understanding of the critical issue for church revitalization shifted. Early in his career he believed that a recovery of conservative-evangelical doctrinal fidelity and a high view of Scripture (i.e., the doctrine of biblical inerrancy) would renew the church. During this period, he was a leading figure in moving the Southern Baptist Convention back to a conservative theological posture.[37] The focus on biblical inerrancy and doctrine for church renewal coincided with his tenure at New Orleans Baptist Theological Seminary (1965-1969) and Trinity Evangelical Divinity School (1969-1974). However, he gradually came to the conviction that doctrinal reformation and purity alone were insufficient for the vitality of the church. Pinnock began to see the Pentecostal and charismatic movements as sources for church renewal. Influenced by his charismatic experience, he also based this belief on theological grounds. "Theologically," he said, "the basis for seeking renewal is the simple fact that, according to the New Testament, the church is a charismatic community. It exists by God's grace and functions as the gifts of the Spirit manifest themselves in people. The normal Christian experience involves a lively faith in the Spirit as the pivotal reality in human lives."[38] Pinnock's point has ramifications for Pentecostal ecclesiology in particular, and Pentecostal theology in general.

Pinnock recognizes that Pentecostals should have a *Pentecostal* theology and that the Pentecostal way of experiencing God should shape the content of their theology. He warns Pentecostals to avoid walking down the path of conservative evangelicalism — with its rationalistic approach

37. Pinnock's first publications illustrate this phase of his career: *A Defense of Biblical Infallibility* (Philadelphia: Presbyterian and Reformed, 1967); *A New Reformation: A Challenge to Southern Baptists* (Tigerville, SC: Jewel Books, 1968).

38. Pinnock, "Baptists and the 'Latter Rain': A Contemporary Challenge and Hope for Tomorrow," in *Costly Vision: The Baptist Pilgrimage in Canada,* ed. Jarold K. Zeaman (Burlington, ON: Welch, 1988), pp. 255-72 (esp. p. 266); he also makes this point later in "Church in the Power of the Holy Spirit," p. 157. In a response to Pinnock, Terry Cross recommends that the doctrine of the Trinity should ground a Pentecostal ecclesiology rather than relying exclusively on pneumatology (see Cross, "A Response to Clark Pinnock's 'Church in the Power of the Holy Spirit,'" pp. 176-77).

to theology. He declares: "Pentecostals are now in a strong position to make contributions to theology, distinctive contributions reflecting their own ethos and experience."[39] At the heart of this recommendation is Pinnock's conviction that Pentecostal experience has theological implications.[40] Concurring with Pinnock, Terry Cross remarks that "Pentecostals insist that 'theology follows experience, not the other way around.' . . . Because we know and experience God in the existential reality of our lives, we are prepared to construct our theological understanding of God with this experiential reality in mind."[41] Reflecting the connection between Pentecostal experience and theology, Pinnock suggests that the dynamic God of "open theism" coheres better with the way Pentecostals experience God than with God conceived "as an unblinking cosmic stare or metaphysical iceberg," assumed in conservative and "paleo-Calvinist" evangelical theology.[42] I agree with Pinnock and Cross, not primarily because I am a partisan for Pentecostal theology, but because I believe it reflects the historical relationship between religious experience and doctrine (though, as I have acknowledged in chapter 1, the relationship is reciprocal and not exclusively unilateral). For example, the disciples did not encounter the Son of God first in terms of the doctrines of the *homoousios* and the hypostatic union, but as Jesus Christ, who called them to follow him and whose teachings often clashed with their religious and doctrinal assumptions.

Pentecostals have intuitively sensed the interrelationship between their experience and theology, but they have not always effectively identified its theological rationale or thought through its theological implications. Indeed, many Pentecostals deny that the movement can be defined in theological terms and must rather be understood in terms of some category of religious experience — for example, charismatic spirituality.[43]

39. Pinnock, "Divine Relationality," p. 4.

40. Clark H. Pinnock, "The Holy Spirit as a Distinct Person in the Godhead," in *Spirit and Renewal: Essays in Honor of J. Rodman Williams*, ed. Mark W. Wilson (Sheffield, UK: Sheffield Academic Press, 1994), p. 34.

41. Cross, "The Rich Feast of Theology: Can Pentecostals Bring the Main Dish or Only the Relish?" *Journal of Pentecostal Theology* 8, no. 16 (2000): 24-47 (esp. pp. 30, 33-36).

42. Pinnock, "Response to Daniel Strange and Amos Yong," *Evangelical Quarterly* 71 (1999): 349-57 (esp. p. 353); "Divine Relationality," p. 25. Cross is less sure that "open theism" is palatable to Pentecostals (Cross, "The Rich Feast of Theology," pp. 39-46).

43. E.g., Warrington, *Pentecostal Theology*, pp. 18-27; see also Allan Anderson, *An Introduction to Pentecostalism: Global Charismatic Christianity* (New York: Cambridge University Press, 2006), pp. 9-15, 60.

However, as Pinnock points out, the community of believers is a manifestation of the work of the Spirit; the "church is a charismatic community."[44] The notion that the church is a charismatic community, a community whose life is a product of the Holy Spirit's activity, provides a theological foundation for drawing on Pentecostal experience in the effort to construct Pentecostal theology. Pentecostals should follow Pinnock's advice to let their experience of God inform their theology, because their experience is an experience of the Holy Spirit.

Intimating a Pentecostal Trinitarian Theology

This section charts Pinnock's charismatic Trinitarian theology and investigates it from the perspective of a Pentecostal Trinitarian theology based on the Pentecostal experience of the Spirit and the biblical narratives of the Spirit. Pinnock strives to develop Trinitarian theology from the perspective of pneumatology. Others have engaged this task as well, such as D. Lyle Dabney; but what makes Pinnock unique is that he pursues this task as a charismatic Christian. Despite his charismatic instincts, however, in several ways Pinnock's Trinitarian theology remains within traditional Trinitarian thought patterns.

First, Pinnock's Trinitarian theology bears a residual Christocentrism. He affirms that the triune life of God is grounded in the history of Jesus.[45] The life of Jesus no doubt informs the Christian understanding of the Trinitarian God, but what about the history of the Spirit? Especially since the history of Jesus is also the history of the Spirit. Pinnock uses the biblical language of Romans 8:9, which has the Spirit raising Jesus from the dead, but he does not draw on the Holy Spirit in a substantial way to inform the doctrine of the Trinity (p. 29). The Holy Spirit's unique contribution to Pinnock's Trinitarian theology remains unclear.

Second, the Spirit's identity and role in shaping the identity of the Father and the Son remain elusive. Pinnock's identification of the relationships that define the Father and the Son are clear. The Father is the Father in relationship to the Son; the Son is the Son in relationship to the Father; however, the Holy Spirit does not have a relationship with the Father or

44. Pinnock, "Baptists and the 'Latter Rain,'" p. 266.

45. Pinnock, *Flame of Love*, p. 29. Hereafter, page references to this work appear in parentheses in the text.

the Son. Pinnock suggests that the "Spirit is the Spirit as he glorifies the Father in the Son and the Son in the Father" (p. 31). The Spirit appears as an agent who facilitates the glory of the Father and the Son. Reflecting traditional Trinitarianism, Pinnock's theology leaves the personal identity of the Spirit ambiguous. He also follows the Western tendency to describe the Holy Spirit as the mutual love of the Father and the Son, and thus to portray the Spirit as the relationship between the Father and the Son rather than as a divine person with whom they have interrelationships, or as one who has relationships with them.

Additionally, the enigmatic identity of the Spirit is not accidental. According to Pinnock, "the Son became visible and renders the Father visible, while the Spirit remains invisible and not as easily known" (p. 36). Though the identity of Jesus of Nazareth is accessible in the Gospel narratives, does it really make the identity of the Father and the Son an open book? John's description of the preincarnate Son as the Logos and the tradition's tendency to explain that in terms of an eternal and self-referential symbolic representation of the divine being (i.e., procession of the Word) takes no small effort to comprehend in personal terms. My point is not to cast doubt on the revelation of the triune God, nor to demur with the assumed easier grasp of the Father's and the Son's identity. Nevertheless, though the names "Father" and "Son" sound more personal than does "Holy Spirit," it does not mean that theology actually has more access to the identity of the Father and the Son than it does to the Holy Spirit. The thesis of this book is that the Holy Spirit's identity, just like the Father's and the Son's, derives from the Spirit's activities in the economy of redemption. For example, Pinnock observes: "Father and Son have a face. We can picture them, thanks to the narrative of salvation. Does the Spirit have a profile too? . . . Revelation drops only hints about the Spirit's identity, and what can be said is limited" (pp. 35-36). Why has theology found it easier to apprehend the person of the Logos from texts such as John 1:1 and John 1:14 than it apprehends the Holy Spirit from texts such as Luke 1:35 and Matthew 1:18-25, both of which portray the Spirit as an active and creative agent?

Theology more readily grasps the identity of the Son because Scripture records the life and history of the Son in Jesus Christ. However, Scripture also describes the Christ constituted, led, and empowered by the Holy Spirit. The ministry of Christ ultimately leads to the outpouring of the Spirit. Christology is not simply about the Son; Christology pursued without pneumatology is not biblical Christology. The life of Christ that leads to the outpouring of the Spirit of Pentecost is the nexus of the work of the

Son and the Holy Spirit and, therefore, revelatory of the Son and the Spirit, and the Father as well. "Christology" is thus informative but not exhaustive for understanding God — or even Christ.

Third, Pinnock's theology oscillates between the Trinitarian theology of Richard of Saint Victor and Saint Augustine. He describes the Holy Spirit, on the one hand, as the mutual love of the Father and the Son and, on the other hand, as one with whom the Father and the Son share their love (pp. 37-38). He affirms:

> It is fruitful to see the Spirit in this way, as the bond of the divine relationship and as the principle of the divine unity. The identity of the Spirit is best located in the communion of Father and Son, as the mutual and reciprocal love that flows between them. The Spirit can be seen as the love that they share and even to constitute the *condilectus,* the channel, of their loving. . . . [S]o Father and Son perfect their love by sharing it with the Spirit. (p. 38)

Pinnock embraces a social Trinitarian model, following the example of contemporary theologians such as Jürgen Moltmann and Colin Gunton, and he understands Richard of Saint Victor as an early representative of it (pp. 33-34). He also recognizes the strain caused by his adoption of the mutual-love model, which he admits runs the risk of reducing the Spirit to an impersonal bond of love, and a social Trinitarian model, which sees the Spirit as a giver and receiver of love along with the Father and the Son (pp. 40-42). Still, the tension remains unresolved.

Alternating between Trinitarian models reflects the strength and weakness of Pinnock's Trinitarian theology. Positively, it illustrates his eclectic, ecumenical, and effervescent style. A plenitude of sources and images inspire his theology. He does not rely on a rigid theological model. Though his style can be frustrating for readers preferring logical consistency, it makes his writings rich and exciting to read, because one never knows where he will go next. Pinnock seems to follow and take up the theological ideas that unlocked the mysteries of the faith, regardless of whether he could fit all the pieces together in a tightly locked logical synthesis. Yet these tensions, like his use of social and Augustinian models, prevent the development of a consistent and more comprehensive Trinitarian theology.

Pinnock's instincts, more than the substance of his Trinitarian theology, point the way toward a Pentecostal Trinitarian theology. In content, his Trinitarian theology is an eclectic fusion of rich sources and traditions. However, toward the end of his treatment of the Trinity, he wonders:

> It may be that we should seek the face of the Spirit in the face of the community, God's dwelling and the place where love is being perfected (1 John 4:12). As the Son reveals the Father's face and the Spirit reveals the Son's face, perhaps the place where the Spirit's is seen is in the faces of believers (Rev. 22:4). (p. 41)

Pinnock's intuition of finding the face of the Spirit in the life of the Christian community is correct, though the biblical narratives of the Spirit are foundational, too. The methodological and epistemological starting point of this project is that the Pentecostal experience of the Spirit is informative for a Pentecostal Trinitarian theology, and not only a Trinitarian theology for Pentecostals but also one that can contribute to the historic traditions of Trinitarian theology. However, the Pentecostal experience of the Spirit is only the starting point for a process of theological reflection that engages Scripture with a desire to acquire the biblical narratives of the Spirit and thereby the Spirit's identity in the Trinity. A Pentecostal Trinitarian theology emerges from this movement of the experience from the Spirit to the Spirit's role in the biblical drama of redemption and finally to the Spirit's identity in the triune God.

Conclusion

Pentecostal and renewal theology has made important first steps on the way toward a Pentecostal Trinitarian theology. They are, however, preliminary and still largely function within the received traditions of Trinitarian theology. The goal of this project is neither to contribute a unique theology simply for the sake of being unique nor to dismiss the traditional forms of Trinitarian theology. The purpose is to discern the theological implications of the Pentecostal experience of the Spirit in conjunction with the biblical narratives of the Spirit in order to join the ecumenical and global conversation on the doctrine of the Trinity with a Pentecostal voice. To that end, I have in this chapter sought to frame the theological proposal of this volume in light of other charismatic and Pentecostal contributions to Trinitarian theology.

6 The Spirit of Pentecost and Theology of Religions

In North America today, encounters with people of other religions are common. Interfaith interactions happen at school activities, children's sporting events, the workplace, the local coffee shop, and in our neighborhoods. The fact of religious pluralism is not new, but the experience and visibility of it in North America is. Various forms of religious diversity touch and run through our personal relationships and families. Consider my extended family. It includes a variety of religious identifications: Filipino Catholic, Swedish Lutheran, former Episcopalian now charismatic, American Catholic, ex-Catholic now agnostic, Pentecostal, atheist, faith in a generic God — and others who don't think too much about religion. Though no one represents a non-Christian religion per se, differences and mutual antagonisms can characterize relationships between Christians, on the one hand, and atheists and agnostics, on the other hand, no less than they do between Christians and Muslims. I teach at McMaster Divinity College, located on the campus of McMaster University in Hamilton, Ontario. The university has a student population of more than 20,000. Walking to the student center for lunch is a cross-cultural and interreligious experience. One encounters people from all around the world and student groups representing all the major world religions.

The experience of religious diversity should remind us that we are dealing with real people and not merely a set of abstract beliefs. They have hopes and dreams, worries and fears, just as we do. I believe that when we think about Christianity's relationship to other religions and whether salvation is available in non-Christian religious contexts, we should keep the personal nature of the issue in mind. How should we understand the religious aspirations and activities of people? Are people who do not practice Christianity, such as the Muslim student who invited me to a Muslim-Christian dialogue on the campus, outside the redemptive work of God in the world? In this chapter I wish to reflect on a theology of religions based on the pneumatology and Trinitarian theology developed in the previous chapters.

Pentecostal mission usually proceeds on the assumption that there is no salvation outside of explicit faith in Jesus Christ — or at least very little. Indeed, the zeal of early Pentecostal missionaries assumed that the world beyond the domains of explicit faith in Christ was in spiritual darkness. Amos Yong suggests that Pentecostals tend to contrast their *faith* with other *religions* along the following lines: Pentecostal faith is a divinely given means of salvation that provides for a genuine relationship with God, whereas other religions are human rituals contrived to attain salvation at best and demonic distractions to authentic faith at worst.[1] Accordingly, Pentecostal mission mainly presupposes a negative theology of religions. Non-Christian religions are thus not only misguided but also very likely serious impediments to salvation. However, is the traditional negativism toward a theology of religions out of step with the Spirit of Pentecost, whose mission — from creation to Pentecost — is not only to breathe life into all human beings but also to draw them into the fellowship of the Trinitarian God?

In this chapter I present a theology of religions based on the Trinitarian theology presented in the previous chapters. Though I frame its contribution in terms of the broad contours and options in the discourse on the theology of religions, direct engagement with the myriad particular thinkers is beyond my scope. Overall, I approach the theology of religions from the perspective of the Spirit of Pentecost. I seek to develop a pneumatological and Trinitarian theology of religions that both integrates Christology and transcends Christocentric approaches. With respect to the religions, I do not see the other religions as part of a divine program in the sense that God designed them (contra Raimundo Panikkar).[2] However,

1. Amos Yong, "From Azusa Street to the Bo Tree and Back: Strange Babblings and Interreligious Interpretations in the Pentecostal Encounter with Buddhism," in *The Spirit in the World: Emerging Pentecostal Theologies in Global Contexts*, ed. Veli-Matti Kärkkäinen (Grand Rapids: Eerdmans, 2009), pp. 203-26 (esp. pp. 215-16).

2. Raimundo Panikkar, *The Trinity and the Religious Experience of Man: Icon — Person — Mystery* (Maryknoll, NY: Orbis, 1973).

unlike traditional inclusivism, such as that of Gavin D'Costa, I suggest that the religions can be understood as the context for and response to the grace of the Spirit.[3] Moreover, I propose that all those who participate in redemption will share in the everlasting kingdom, in contrast to S. Mark Heim's proposal of a diversity of religious ends.[4]

I will proceed here in three steps: first, I present the current status of the theology of religions in Pentecostal theology; second, I set forth the mission of the Spirit of Pentecost as it relates to a theology of religions; third, I articulate the implications of the mission of the Spirit of Pentecost for a theology of religions. Foundational to the theology of religions that I present in this chapter is a twofold pneumatological and Trinitarian thesis: (1) that the Spirit of Pentecost, from creation to the eschatological event of Pentecost, is a liminal and constitutional agent within the history of redemption, and (2) that the Spirit of Pentecost is the nexus of human religious activity and redemptive relationship with the Trinitarian God.

Pentecostals and Theology of Religions

In the past several decades Pentecostal and charismatic scholars have tended to shift away from exclusivism toward inclusivism. Some key Pentecostal contributors include Amos Yong, Tony Richie, Tony Moon, Clark Pinnock, and Veli-Matti Kärkkäinen. Two points characterize the current state of the theology of religions among Pentecostals. First, except for Yong, the Pentecostals have embraced inclusivism but have retained a negative theology of religions. In other words, although they embrace hope that the unevangelized can participate in God's grace, they do not see the religions playing a meaningful role in this experience of grace: in other words, members of other religions can be saved *in spite* of their religious beliefs and practices. Second, Christocentric concerns still dominate Pentecostal theology of religions, with Yong's work again the exception.

3. Gavin D'Costa, *The Meeting of Religions and the Trinity,* Faith Meets Faith Series, Paul Knitter, gen. ed. (Maryknoll, NY: Orbis, 2000), pp. 99-138.

4. S. Mark Heim, *The Depth of the Riches: A Trinitarian Theology of Religious Ends,* Sacra Doctrina: Christian Theology for a Postmodern Age, Alan G. Padgett, gen. ed. (Grand Rapids: Eerdmans, 2001), pp. 1-11, 168-207.

Pentecostals, Inclusivism, and Theology of Religions

Sometimes willing to countenance the possibility that members of non-Christian religions may receive God's grace, provided they have never heard the gospel, Pentecostals overall remain less enthusiastic about the role of the religions. Veli-Matti Kärkkäinen believes that the Holy Spirit is at work in the religions and they contain elements of truth that can instruct Christians; nevertheless, he retains an essentially negative theology of religions with respect to their promise for serving as the conduits and manifestations of saving grace.[5] He affirms that the religions play an important role in helping the church arrive at a deeper understanding of God, but he denies that that they are "salvific as such."[6]

However, a critical question is this: If the Spirit of God is at work in the religions of the world and this activity reveals divine mysteries, then why are they not acceptable means to experience the Spirit's redemptive work? Moreover, if the religions are not manifestations of the grace of the Spirit, then how can they instruct Christians "into the divine mystery"?[7] If the world religions can instruct Christians about the Christian God, this is because they are in some way authentic human responses, whether in some of their doctrinal teachings or in their moral principles and practices, to the grace of the Spirit. On this point, Amos Yong concludes: "The potentiality of the Spirit's presence and activity in the religions and their adherents means both that the religious traditions of humankind are redeemable for the glory of God and that the gospel can be communicated . . . even found manifest in new ways, in the other faiths."[8] If the religions can instruct Christians, they also can lead their practitioners closer to God. In other words, if one acknowledges "the gifts of God in other religions by virtue of the presence of the Spirit" and if one, on that basis, is open "to-

5. Veli-Matti Kärkkäinen, *An Introduction to the Theology of Religions: Biblical, Historical and Contemporary Perspectives* (Downers Grove, IL: InterVarsity, 2003); see also Kärkkäinen, *Trinity and Religious Pluralism: The Doctrine of the Trinity in Christian Theology of Religions* (Burlington, VT: Ashgate, 2004).

6. Kärkkäinen, *Trinity and Religious Pluralism*, p. 179.

7. Kärkkäinen, "'How to Speak of the Spirit among the Religions': Trinitarian Prolegomena for a Pneumatological Theology of Religions," in *The Work of the Spirit: Pneumatology and Pentecostalism*, ed. Michael Welker (Grand Rapids: Eerdmans, 2006), pp. 47-70 (esp. p. 66). For similar remarks, see Kärkkäinen, *Trinity and Religious Pluralism*, p. 179.

8. Amos Yong, *The Spirit Poured Out on All Flesh: Pentecostalism and the Possibility of Global Theology* (Grand Rapids: Baker Academic, 2005), p. 247.

ward other religions," then why not see those gifts as providing ways for the members of the non-Christian religions to enter into relationships with God?[9] After all, are these gifts of the Spirit found in the other religions only useful for Christians? It seems a plausible conclusion, then, that if they can teach Christians, they can do the same for people within non-Christian religious communities. Kärkkäinen is not alone in this hesitancy about the religions. Clark H. Pinnock, who was one of the more robust charismatic and evangelical inclusivists, hesitated to call the non-Christian religions "vehicles of grace and salvation."[10] I will return to this issue below when I discuss Amos Yong's work. But here I suggest that the view of Kärkkäinen and Pinnock is representative of Pentecostal inclusivists: they are hopeful about the fate of the unevangelized and believe that interreligious dialogue can help Christians learn from the other religions; but they maintain that the religions as such are not conduits for the experience of grace and do not help their adherents relate to God.

Pentecostals, Theology of Religions, and Christocentrism

Known for its charismatic experience and emphasis on Spirit baptism, Pentecostalism is no less a Jesus-centered form of Christianity. Consider the Christocentrism of the fourfold gospel, or Full Gospel, which many take to be the heart of at least the early Pentecostal movement.[11] The fourfold gospel consists of this: Jesus saves, baptizes in the Holy Spirit, heals, and will soon return. Pentecostals may be baptized in the Holy Spirit, but it is Jesus who baptizes them. The result is that efforts to develop a theology of religions follow this tendency to think in Christocentric categories.

A case in point is the lively debate between Tony Richie and Tony Moon over the extent to which the early Pentecostal Holiness church leader J. H. King was an inclusivist.[12] Richie suggests that King opened the door to the

9. Kärkkäinen, "'How to Speak of the Spirit,'" p. 66.

10. Clark H. Pinnock, *Flame of Love: A Theology of the Holy Spirit* (Downers Grove, IL: InterVarsity, 1996), p. 207.

11. For the classic historical case for this point, see Donald W. Dayton, *Theological Roots of Pentecostalism* (Grand Rapids: Francis Asbury, 1987); for a more recent use of the paradigm for constructive systematic theology, see Kenneth J. Archer, *A Pentecostal Hermeneutic: Spirit, Scripture, and Community* (Cleveland, TN: CPT, 2009).

12. For the dialogue on J. H. King between Tony G. Moon and Tony Lee Richie (listed in chronological order), see Richie, "Azusa Era Optimism: Bishop J. H. King's Theology of Reli-

possibility that some people participate in the grace of Christ without being conscious of Christ or having explicit knowledge of Christ.[13] King's statement that "there may be those who have the essential Christ that know nothing of the historic Christ" lends support to Richie's suggestion.[14] Moon finds Richie's reading of King far too optimistic. Given King's habitual description of the non-Christian religions in terms of "heathen," "darkness," and "demonic," the most one can say is that his theology shows a "significant optimistic, inclusivist *element* with respect to hope for the unevangelized."[15] Despite nuances in interpretation, Richie and Moon disagree on the degree and not the substance of King's inclusivism. King affirmed the universal availability of Christ's saving work and was hopeful that some come to salvation without explicit knowledge of Christ.

Furthermore, Richie and Moon agree that King's ruminations on inclusivism were Christocentric.[16] Saving grace and revelation come only through the work of Christ. They both also believe that pneumatology can help with the articulation of a contemporary Pentecostal theology of religions.[17] More recently, Kärkkäinen's theology of religions stands in continuity with King's Christocentrism. Though working toward a Trinitarian theology of religions, Christology retains theological preeminence. He maintains that, "[i]n Christian theology in general and trinitarian theology in particular, Christology plays a criteriological function."[18] Regard-

---

gions as a Possible Paradigm for Today," *Journal of Pentecostal Theology* 14 (2006): 247-60; Moon, "J. H. King's Theology of Religions: 'Magnanimous Optimism'?" *Journal of Pentecostal Theology* 16 (2007): 112-32; Richie, "A Moderate Move or Missing the Point? A Response to Tony Moon's 'J. H. King's Theology of Religions: "Magnanimous Optimism"?'" *Journal of Pentecostal Theology* 16 (2008): 118-25; Moon, "Richie Misses the Point: A Reply to Tony Richie's 'A Moderate Move or Missing the Point?'" *Journal of Pentecostal Theology* 17 (2008): 110-32; Richie, "Getting Back to the Heart of the Matter: The Way Forward and a Final Response to Tony Moon," *Journal of Pentecostal Theology* 18 (2009): 141-49; and Moon, "'Getting Back to the Heart of the Matter': A Brief Rejoinder to Tony Richie," *Journal of Pentecostal Theology* 18 (2009): 312-18.

13. Tony Richie, "Azusa-Era Optimism: Bishop J. H. King's Pentecostal Theology of Religions as a Possible Paradigm for Today," in Kärkkäinen, ed., *The Spirit in the World,* pp. 227-44 (esp. p. 250).

14. J. H. King, *From Passover to Pentecost,* 4th ed. (Franklin Springs, GA: Advocate, 1976 [first published, 1914]), p. 101.

15. Moon, "J. H. King's Theology of Religions," pp. 113-16.

16. Richie, "Azusa-Era Optimism," p. 251; Moon, "J. H. King's Theology of Religions," pp. 128, 130.

17. Richie, "Azusa-Era Optimism," pp. 7-8.

18. Kärkkäinen, *Trinity and Religious Pluralism,* pp. 171-72.

less of what one takes away from the Richie-Moon debate on King, Richie's advice should be followed. On the one hand, he warns Pentecostals to avoid assuming and borrowing a "pessimistic" theology of religions from another theological movement, usually the adoption of evangelical exclusivism. On the other hand, he urges Pentecostals to search their Pentecostal theological heritage for the resources to develop a Pentecostal theology of religions that can effectively serve Pentecostal mission in the twenty-first century.[19]

Beyond Christocentrism and Toward a Pneumatological Theology of Religions

Amos Yong's work is unique among Pentecostals because it represents an effort to develop a positive theology of religions and overcome Christocentrism, which he argues has prevented the contribution of pneumatology to the theology of religions. Yong has also produced the most sustained body of work on a Pentecostal theology of religions. His first book, *Discerning the Spirit(s),* proposed a pneumatological approach to theology of religions.[20] *Beyond the Impasse* extended and clarified the pneumatological theology of religions that he presented in *Discerning the Spirit(s).*[21] His latest work on this subject, *Hospitality and the Religious Other,* proposes a theology and framework of practices for interacting with people from non-Christian religions according to a Trinitarian vision of the hospitality of God.[22]

Yong's most controversial thesis is that a pneumatological theology of

19. Richie, "Azusa-Era Optimism," p. 255, and "Getting Back to the Heart of the Matter," pp. 143-45. For Richie's analysis of Parham's inclusivist theology, see "Eschatological Inclusivism: Exploring Early Pentecostal Theology of Religions in Charles Fox Parham," *Journal of the European Pentecostal Theological Association* 27 (2007): 138-52.

20. Amos Yong, *Discerning the Spirit(s): A Pentecostal-Charismatic Contribution to Christian Theology of Religions,* Journal of Pentecostal Theology Supplement Series, 20 (Sheffield, UK: Sheffield Academic Press, 2000).

21. Amos Yong, *Beyond the Impasse: Toward a Pneumatological Theology of Religions* (Carlisle, UK: Paternoster; Grand Rapids: Baker Academic, 2003).

22. Yong has also published numerous articles on this subject, as well as the recent book edited with Clifton R. Clarke, *Global Renewal, Religious Pluralism, and the Great Commission: Towards a Renewal Theology of Mission and Interreligious Encounter,* The Asbury Theological Seminary Series in World Christian Revitalization Movements in Pentecostal/Charismatic Studies, 4 (Lexington, KY: Emeth, 2011).

religions should proceed, at least initially, with functional independence from Christology.[23] I use "functional" to underscore the fact that theologically he recognizes that pneumatology and Christology ultimately cohere under the theological category of the Trinity. In other words, functional independence does not mean ultimate theological independence. Drawing on the Irenaean view of the relationship between the Word and the Spirit (two hands of God), Yong says: "It is sufficient to grant that there is relationship-in-autonomy between the two divine missions. For heuristic purposes, however, we will seek to investigate the religious dimensions of the Spirit's economy with the intention that Christological issues will not be discarded forever."[24] Yong opposes what might be called a christological Borg: that is, a tendency in traditional theology, especially evangelical theology, in which all resistance to assimilate theology to Christocentric categories is futile. Yong wants to recognize pneumatology as a theological arena in its own right. His goal is to articulate criteria for recognizing both the presence and absence of the work of the Spirit among the religions and their adherents. Yong's work should be understood as an effort to posit the integrity of the domain of pneumatology, but not its total independence from Christology or other areas of Christian theology. Yong's effort makes common cause with that of other inclusivists. His unique contribution is that he pursues pneumatological criteria for discerning the work of the Spirit among non-Christian religions.

My work has much in common with Yong's, but it has a different focus. I agree that the discipline of pneumatology has theological integrity and should not be reduced to the pursuit of Christology by other means. However, whereas Yong's work explores the providential place of the religions and the implications for interreligious dialogue (e.g., *Discerning the Spirit[s]*) and interrelationships (e.g., *Hospitality and the Religious Other*) from the perspective of pneumatology, my approach is more concerned with soteriology. In other words, his question is not: Are people who practice non-Christian religions saved? He believes that beginning there neces-

23. For an example of a critic who misreads Yong's theological strategy, see James Merrick, "The Spirit of Truth as Agent in False Religions? A Critique of Amos Yong's Pneumatological Theology of Religions with Reference to Current Trends," *Trinity Journal* 29 (2008): 107-25. In a more sustained analysis, Todd L. Miles overlooks the ultimate unity of the economies of the Spirit and Christ and, based on a Christocentric hermeneutic, rejects Yong's pneumatological approach. See Miles, *A God of Many Understandings: The Gospel and a Theology of Religions* (Nashville: B & H Academic, 2010), pp. 230-46.

24. Yong, *Discernment of the Spirit(s)*, pp. 58, 70; see also *Beyond the Impasse*, pp. 43-44.

sarily means starting with Christology and circumventing pneumatology.[25] For the sake of developing his approach to thinking about the religions, he treats theology of religions and soteriology as distinct spheres of theological reflection.[26] Yong's work also concentrates on the hermeneutical dimension of the theology of religions. He strives to construct a rationale for coordinating or "discerning" the thoughts and practices found in the religions with those in Christianity. I want to contribute to this discussion by focusing on the soteriological issue in a way that does not lapse into Christocentrism. What is the theological — indeed, the pneumatological — basis for not only an inclusive soteriology, but also for seeing the religions as the liminal space for the work of the Spirit of Pentecost? My goal is to answer this question on the basis of Pentecostal and Trinitarian theology.

The Mission of the Spirit of Pentecost

David Bosch's *Transforming Mission* charted the shift from ecclesiological to theological notions of mission, for example, *missio Dei.*[27] Jürgen Moltmann underscores that perspective when he says that "[i]t is not the church that has a mission of salvation to fulfill to the world; it is the mission of the Son and the Spirit through the Father that includes the church, creating a church as it goes on its way."[28] Mission, therefore, is fundamentally an activity of the Trinitarian God in which the church participates; it is not primarily a subsidiary function of the church. Historically, missions were front and center among Pentecostals. Spirit baptism, the distinctive doctrine of Pentecostalism, was intrinsically missional. Believers received Spirit baptism so that they could preach the gospel to the ends of the earth (Acts 1:8) — even though this traditional view of mission was implicitly ecclesiocentric and Christocentric. The Spirit of Pentecost empowers

25. Yong, *Beyond the Impasse,* pp. 17 and 27.

26. For example, in *The Spirit Poured Out on All Flesh* (p. 250), he affirms that since the Spirit is universally active and the purpose of the Spirit is to bring about the kingdom of God, the Spirit is active in the religious sphere of human activity.

27. David J. Bosch, *Transforming Mission: Paradigm Shifts in Theology of Mission* (Maryknoll, NY: Orbis, 1995), pp. 368-93.

28. Jürgen Moltmann, *The Church in the Power of the Spirit: A Contribution to Messianic Ecclesiology,* trans. Margaret Kohl (New York: HarperCollins, 1991 [first published in 1977]), p. 64.

Christians to preach the gospel of Jesus Christ to those who are otherwise in spiritual darkness. Without discarding this role of the Spirit, I want to advance a more comprehensive view of the Spirit's mission, which can provide a pneumatological horizon for a theology of religions.[29] Bearing that in mind, we can turn to consider what the reach and nature of the Spirit's mission is.

Most basically, the Spirit's mission is to bring creation to its proper way of participating in redemption: fellowship with the Trinitarian God. The narrative path of the Spirit's mission begins with creation and reaches its apex in the incarnation and Pentecost. Therefore, the Spirit's mission encompasses all of salvation history and does not begin in Acts and the establishment of the Christian church. When we consider "mission and evangelism," we may think of the scope of the Spirit's redemptive work and mission in compartmental ways: for example, the Spirit is at work here in Christian religious and mission contexts and not there in non-Christian religious and mission contexts. However, the mission of the Spirit of Pentecost is universal and perennial. There has never been and never will be a person outside the mission and redemptive activity of the Holy Spirit. The Spirit of Pentecost's mission is to fulfill the creative-redemptive work of the Spirit charted in the biblical drama of redemption (see chapter 2).

On the Day of Pentecost, Peter identifies the outpouring of the Holy Spirit as the inauguration of the promise of Joel 2:28 — that "I will pour out my Spirit on all people" (Acts 2:17). The key qualifier for the scope of the Spirit's mission is the "all" of the promise. "All" means all.[30] The Spirit of Pentecost has been poured out on all people. Perhaps to reinforce the inclusive nature of the promise, Luke concludes Peter's Pentecost quote of Joel 2:32 with "everyone who calls on the name of the Lord will be saved," and drops the ending of the verse that spotlights "for on Mount Zion and in Jerusalem there will be deliverance."

The promise of the Spirit's outpouring on all people, with the exclusion of the Jerusalem qualifier, draws attention to the fact that people within one faith community often intuitively believe that people in an-

29. I prefer the term "mission of the Spirit" (Spirit's mission) to "Spirit of mission" because the latter term portrays mission as an instrumental function of the Spirit rather than as something intrinsic to the Spirit. Moreover, "mission of the Spirit" highlights that mission is fundamentally theological and pneumatological and not ecclesiastical. The Spirit is not merely the power supply for the church to fulfill *its* mission.

30. F. F. Bruce, *The Book of Acts,* rev. ed., New International Commentary on the New Testament (Grand Rapids: Eerdmans, 1989), p. 61.

other one are either bereft of the presence of God or, at the very least, do not have the same favors and benefits of God as they possess. The inclusive delineation of "all" in Joel 2:28-32 and quoted by Peter in Acts 2 presupposes the assumption of privileged status before God. That is why the Joel passage instructs the reader that "all" really means all. Whether Joel specifically envisioned an outpouring of the Spirit that transcended Israel or meant more minimally that all the people of Israel, regardless of social status, would receive the Spirit is an important issue. The historical context suggests that he had the people of Israel, specifically the people of Jerusalem, in mind. However, Douglas Stuart points out that the outpouring of the Spirit in Joel is a promise "for a covenant people" — and not only the people of Jerusalem or Israel.[31] Regardless of how the original audience understood Joel 2:28, in Acts "all people" clearly transcends Israel and includes people from "every nation" (Acts 2:5). One might object by saying that these people from "every nation" were Jews and converts to Judaism. That is correct. However, the subsequent expansion of the gospel beyond Jerusalem to Samaria and throughout the Mediterranean, especially the stories of Peter and Cornelius and the Jerusalem Council, not to mention Paul in Antioch, shows that the gift of the Spirit is without regard to either ethnic or ritual association with the Jewish religion.

The book of Acts narrates not only the historical instances of the outpouring of the Spirit on all people, but also the early Christians' difficulty in embracing that truth. Indeed, though Peter declared the fulfillment of Joel's promise of an outpouring of the Spirit, he probably thought of Jews as its primary recipients and did not grasp its comprehensiveness, which was indicated in his later struggle with inclusion.[32] Peter's inhibitions were common. When the Samaritans received the gospel, the suspicious Jerusalem church dispatched Peter and John to vouchsafe it (Acts 8:4-17). Later, when the Gentile household of Cornelius received the Holy Spirit, it required a council of the church to ratify it (Acts 10–11; 15:1-35). The obvious point of Acts is that the outpouring of the Spirit transcends ethnic boundaries and is available to all people — it is for Jew and Gentile.

The theological point I want to make is the following. The outpouring of the Spirit is not only available to all, but has been received by all. This

31. Douglas K. Stuart, *Hosea-Jonah,* Word Biblical Commentary (Waco, TX: Word, 1987), pp. 261-62.

32. Darrell L. Bock, *Acts,* Baker Exegetical Commentary on the New Testament (Grand Rapids: Baker Academic, 2007), pp. 118-19; Bruce, *Acts,* p. 61; Ajith Fernando, *Acts,* New International Version Application Commentary (Grand Rapids: Zondervan, 1998), p. 101.

suggestion immediately raises the specter of universalism. I hope that Rob Bell is correct that "Love Wins"; but given the depth of human depravity and the freedom God gives human beings to engage or reject the Spirit, I have doubts.[33] I affirm that the Spirit has been poured out on all people and ever works to bring them into the fellowship of the triune God, but I do not believe all people respond to the Spirit and, therefore, I am not adopting universalism with respect to salvation. Below I will make a distinction between the universal outpouring of the Spirit and the particular participation in the Spirit of Pentecost, but here I want to consider this question: "What is this Spirit doing who has been poured out on all people?"

The preceding question brings the discussion to the mission of the Spirit of Pentecost. The mission of the Holy Spirit is for all people to participate in the Spirit as the Spirit of Pentecost. The work of the Spirit in Christ (the Spirit of Christ) illuminates the nature of the universal work of the Spirit of Pentecost. The Spirit established the union of Jesus' humanity with the eternal Son of God and empowered his relationship with the Father as the incarnate Son. In a similar way, the Spirit unites believers with Christ and draws them into the ambit of the Trinitarian fellowship. The work of the Spirit finds its fullest historical mediation in the incarnation of the Son of God. Though the Spirit's work in Christ is *sui generis* with respect to the hypostatic union, it is paradigmatic for the Spirit's universal work that spans all of history and touches every human being. The Spirit of Pentecost is present with all persons, drawing them toward union with the triune God. The outpouring of the Spirit of Pentecost is but the full revelation of the Spirit's mission, as the Spirit who ever breathes life into all human beings (Genesis 2:7 and Acts 2:1-4 are thus coordinate events).

Returning to the distinction between universal outpouring and particular participation: the universal outpouring of the Spirit means that the Spirit is universally present with and working in all people as the Spirit of Pentecost. That theological affirmation, however, needs an important qualification: although all people have *received* the Spirit of Pentecost, not all people have *yielded* and *participated* in the Spirit of Pentecost. When people yield to the Spirit's work or participate in the Spirit of Pentecost, they cross a Pentecostal or pneumatological threshold that draws them into union with the Trinitarian God, and that makes them children of God (John 1:12). The Spirit's mission as Spirit of Pentecost is, therefore, consis-

33. Rob Bell, *Love Wins: A Book about Heaven, Hell, and the Fate of Every Person Who Ever Lived* (New York: HarperOne, 2011).

tent with the liminal and constitutional creative-redemptive work of the Spirit charted in the biblical narratives of the Spirit, which begin with creation, proceed through the history of the people of Israel, and conclude with the incarnation and Pentecost.

One may wonder how I can say that the Spirit has been poured out on all people when the book of Acts portrays people receiving the Spirit, people who beforehand apparently did not have the Spirit. This affirmation rests on the following argument: the Holy Spirit is present as the source of life in all human beings; the Spirit's role in giving life is not distinct from the Spirit's work in redemption, which the Spirit's work in Christ and as the Spirit of Pentecost fully reveals; therefore, continuity characterizes the Spirit's creative-redemptive work. The Spirit breathes life into human beings so that they may live a Spirit-baptized life, which finds its highest expression in Jesus Christ. So, when I say, "'all' means all people," I mean nothing more than that the Spirit creates and sustains human life (all life, for that matter). In this sense, all people have received the Spirit. Moreover — based on the unified nature of the Spirit's creative-redemptive work — the Spirit who gives life also acts as the Spirit of Pentecost. The Spirit gives life for no other reason than to bring human beings into the experience of Spirit-baptized life. Yet not all people have experienced what Acts calls Spirit baptism. How, then, can I interpret "all" so literally with respect to the outpouring of the Spirit of Pentecost?

Acts 2 is a phenomenological description of the outpouring of the Holy Spirit. Consider the fact that the Holy Spirit was already present in the upper room on the day of Pentecost before the disciples were baptized in the Spirit; indeed, the Spirit was present in them as their ongoing source of life and was always working to actualize a Spirit-baptized life in them. The Spirit creates and sustains human life for no other purpose. Taken literally, the outpouring of the Spirit makes no sense, because the Spirit was already there and within them. Yet the account accurately describes their evolving experience of the Holy Spirit. Suddenly they tapped the dynamic power of the Spirit that would enable them to fulfill their mission to preach the gospel "to the ends of the earth" (Acts 1:8).

At an ontological level, the Spirit is ever present as the source of life and at the same time as the Spirit of Pentecost. If one accepts the unity of the Spirit's creative-redemptive work (which is based on the reciprocity between the Spirit's identity and role in both the immanent and economic Trinity), this principle becomes self-evident. In the ontological sense, the Spirit dwells in all people. At the phenomenological and experiential level, not all people have participated in the Spirit of Pentecost because they have not all responded and yielded to the Spirit. In this respect, they have not been baptized in the Spirit. Spirit baptism, as described in Acts, refers to the manifestation of the Spirit in a willing heart. Thus, as Acts says, "I will pour out my Spirit on all people . . . [a]nd everyone who calls on the name of the Lord will be saved" (Acts 2:17 and 21). Notice that faith (i.e., "calling on the name of the Lord") is not the condition of the outpouring of the Spirit, but only of salvation. The promise is for a universal outpouring of the Holy Spirit. Based on this gift, all who call on the name of the Lord are saved. The Spirit who becomes known as the Spirit of Pentecost in salvation is not an outsider; rather, the Spirit is the intrinsic agent and source of human life and redemption.

Also important is that Acts is not primarily describing an *ordo salutis* for individual salvation. It narrates a dramatic threshold in God's universal redemptive plan. Therefore, we should take care in reading off its pages a paradigm of individual salvation. Yes, God cares for and saves the individual. But the focus of Acts is grander than me and my personal relationship with Jesus. Acts sets forth the eschatological realization of a universal story of redemption that began in Genesis 1. Finally, the outpouring of the Spirit is not a one-off event in either the history of God's people or the individual. The Christian life is an ongoing journey in the baptism of the Spirit. Spirit baptism — participation in the Spirit of Pentecost — is the threshold and the horizon of life lived in fellowship with God and God's world (see, e.g., Eph. 5:18).[34]

Throughout the previous chapters I have maintained that a parallel relationship pertains between the Spirit's work in the biblical narratives and the Spirit's identity in the Trinity. Here I affirm the same corresponding relationship between the Spirit's mission and identity. In the Trinity, the Spirit plays an active role in constituting the fellowship of the Trinitarian God. The Spirit is the liminal agent in which the divine being "becomes" the Trinity. The interpersonal work of the Holy Spirit is the threshold for the constitution of the eternal fellowship of the triune God. The mission of the Spirit in creation-redemption bears the same nature. Since the Spirit is the nexus for the fellowship of the divine persons, the Spirit is the liminal space for relationships between human persons and the Trinitarian persons. Since the eternal life of God consists in the fellowship of

34. Graham H. Twelftree, *People of the Spirit: Exploring Luke's View of the Church* (Grand Rapids: Baker Academic, 2009), pp. 72, 95.

the Father, the Son, and the Holy Spirit, human redemption — in its most fundamental sense — is participation in that reality. The "all" of the Spirit of Pentecost derives from the continuity between the Holy Spirit's identity and work. Everywhere the Spirit is, the Spirit works as the Spirit of Pentecost. Because the Spirit has been poured out on all people, the threshold of participation in the Spirit of Pentecost is universal and not restricted to the formal boundaries of the Christian church and ministry.

The Spirit of Pentecost and Theology of Religions

The mission of the Spirit has two key facets: (1) the universal scope of the outpouring of the Spirit, and (2) the universal opportunity to participate in the Spirit of Pentecost. Assuming these two points, what are the implications for the theology of religions? In other words, how do the religions, and especially those who embrace and practice them, relate to the two dimensions of the mission of the Spirit? The remainder of this chapter proposes four answers to those questions: (1) the religions are not an insuperable barrier to the Spirit's work; (2) the Spirit is at work in all people regardless of their religion; (3) the religions can be the context for faith; and (4) certain elements of the religions can be partial and progressive ways to participate in the Spirit of Pentecost.

The Spirit of Pentecost and Religious Boundaries

The Spirit of Pentecost is at work in every person regardless of his or her posture toward a particular religion. The Spirit of Pentecost is present with and active in the atheist, the Muslim, the Christian — all human beings. Certainly, not everyone responds to and yields to the Spirit. But where sin abounds, grace does much more (Rom. 5:20), which in this context implies that resistance to the Spirit does not lead to the abdication of the Spirit. The universal work of the Spirit of Pentecost opens the possibility for universal access to grace and redemption. It does not imply universalism (the actualization of universal salvation), but it does mean that the opportunity to participate in grace and redemption is universal. A consequence of the universal scope of the Spirit's work is that the mission of the Spirit of Pentecost always precedes Christian mission. Indeed, as Kirsteen Kim points out, if the Spirit were not operative outside the visible boundaries of the church, mission would be impossible.[35] We need to remember that when Christians do missions work, they do not bring the Spirit of Pentecost to a place where the Spirit otherwise was absent.

I recognize that this point is contrary to what Kim describes as the traditional tendency to locate and largely limit the Spirit's work to the institutional and sacramental functions of the church and/or individual spirituality (e.g., the Spirit reveals truth and sanctifies the inner dimensions of the person).[36] It also stands in tension with the traditional role of the Holy Spirit and the experience of Spirit baptism within Pentecostalism. Pentecostals normally see the Spirit empowering Pentecostal missions rather than enabling people to participate in salvation outside the scope of Christian mission initiatives.[37] Notwithstanding these traditional tendencies, the Spirit of Pentecost *working as* the Spirit of Pentecost in the lives of people always precedes the Christian mission task and is unbounded by explicit Christian mission activities.

The Spirit of Pentecost, Religion, and Culture

Understanding the cultural embeddedness of religion can open up space to consider the religions as places where the Spirit is at work and ways that people authentically respond to the Spirit. The view that an acceptable response to God can only happen in a Christian setting rests on an erroneous assumption. It assumes that the "Christian" religion — or at least biblical revelation — is reified and acultural, but this is not the case. For example, in Acts the Holy Spirit is manifest in terms of wind and "tongues of fire." "Wind" and "fire" have no intrinsic ontological connection to the Holy Spirit; that is, the Spirit is not inherently "wind" and "fire." The visible manifestation of the Spirit takes the form of wind and fire probably because it has clear precedent in the religious tradition of Israel (e.g., creation narratives, flood, exodus, burning bush, pillar of fire, and fire on the altar in the tabernacle), which in turn resonated with religious ideas com-

35. Kirsteen Kim, *The Holy Spirit in the World: A Global Conversation* (Maryknoll, NY: Orbis, 2007), p. 140.

36. Kim, *Holy Spirit in the World*, pp. 4-7.

37. See Allan Anderson, *Spreading Fires: The Missionary Nature of Early Pentecostalism* (Maryknoll, NY: Orbis, 2007), pp. 212-15; Veli-Matti Kärkkäinen, "Pentecostal Pneumatology of Religions: The Contribution of Pentecostalism to Our Understanding of the Work of God's Spirit in the World," in Kärkkäinen, ed., *The Spirit in the World*, pp. 163-66.

mon in the Ancient Near East (ANE). The association of divine presence with wind and fire was common in the Near Eastern religions (see chapter 2). For instance, as Greeks attributed the storm (wind) that sunk the Persian fleet at Chalkis (480 BCE) to divine activity, so the Hebrews escaped annihilation from Pharaoh's army by a wind from God that divided the sea. The point is not that the Old Testament borrows or co-opts popular religious thought in a cut-and-paste manner, with merely a change in the names of the deities and circumstances, but rather that it describes the revelation and work of God in ways that were sensible to people living in the ANE. They lived in a world that associated divine activity and presence with the wind and the storm and other natural phenomena. The Old Testament association of God and God's Spirit with wind and fire is the provision of redemption and revelation through religious forms that were common in the ANE, including the Hebrew religious tradition.

With respect to a Pentecostal theology of mission: if we first begin with the assumption that the gospel that we preach in missions is the pure and culturally transcendent gospel, we have already in a sense distorted biblical revelation. The Bible and the epoch of divine deliverance contained in it are not acultural categories dropped from heaven. The categories through which the God of the Bible spoke and acted were contextual revelations and redemptive activities. Of course, the biblical traditions transform — and at times even demythologize — the ANE religious categories, but the point is that they use them, too (e.g., the creation narratives draw on ANE cosmic myths, but they also demythologize those myths).

Second, the assumption of an acultural gospel also carries with it an "us"-to-"them" missions posture: "We" bring the truth of the gospel to "them," who are otherwise bereft of God's redemptive activity. The "us"-to-"them" posture is unstable for at least two reasons. Initially, it assumes that our (the Western) view of the gospel is without cultural trappings, that it is timeless and noncontextualized, and thus that "our" version of the gospel is *the* form of the gospel for all people. The "us"-to-"them" posture presupposes that all authentic articulations and expressions of the gospel will mirror ours. This attitude is perhaps the religious parallel of other Western and modernist "universalisms."

Furthermore, as the biblical narratives illustrate, the revelation and manifestation of the Holy Spirit for salvation happens in terms of indigenous cultural and religious expectations. The manifestations of the Spirit on the Day of Pentecost in terms of fire and wind were not timeless and "biblical"; rather, they were situated in a cultural and religious context that made them sensible. It is my guess that most of us have not experienced the Spirit in terms of fire and wind, but we have nonetheless had authentic experiences of the Spirit. The point is that the Spirit of God encounters and speaks to human beings in terms they can comprehend. The Spirit's redemptive work bears transcendent continuity, but it can occur in diverse religious and cultural contexts.

Two biblical examples illustrate that access to grace is not contingent on holding certain religious beliefs and observing specific religious rites of the "biblical" community of faith. Amos 9:7 declares: "Are not you Israelites the same to me as the Cushites? . . . Did I not bring Israel up from Egypt, the Philistines from Caphtor, and the Arameans from Kir?" These are staggering statements. Israel is God's special covenant people, and God's deliverance of them from Egypt is the epic event in which God establishes Israel as a nation and provides them with the covenant. Nevertheless, Amos suggests that neither are exodus kinds of acts of deliverance exclusive to the people of Israel, nor is Israel an exclusive recipient of God's compassionate affection ("Are not you Israelites the same to me as the Cushites?"). To think that the Cushites, Philistines, and the Arameans all adopted the religious thought and practices of Israel as either the precondition or consequence of God's redemptive work among them strains credulity.

The Ninevites' repentance at hearing the warning of Jonah is another example of people experiencing God's redemptive activity, or at least the withholding of judgment, without adopting Israel's approved set of religious beliefs and activities. It also illustrates the difficulty people who perceive themselves to be God's special group (e.g., Jonah) have with accepting that God can and does work in people outside the "special-privileges" club. The Ninevites expressed their repentance by "declaring a fast," covering themselves with sackcloth, and "giving up their evil ways and violence" (Jonah 3:5-8). Their acts of religious contrition were not unique to Israel, but common in the ANE. The text gives no indication that they gave proper covenant-sanctioned sacrifices to Yahweh, abandoned polytheism, and destroyed their idols. In fact, Douglas Stuart notes that the text does not even make it clear whether they directed their repentance to Yahweh or to one of the deities in the Assyrian pantheon.[38] The hard restrictivist or exclusivist position seems to be the contemporary version of Jonah's fear: "O Lord, . . . you are a gracious and compassionate God, slow to anger and abounding in love, a God who relents from sending calamity" (Jonah 4:2).

38. Stuart, *Hosea-Jonah,* p. 494.

But Yahweh's requirements for the people of Israel were far more specific. Perhaps the specificity related to the fact that they had received fuller revelation and not to delineating exclusive channels of grace. The repentance of the Ninevites shows that God is not miserly with grace and does not narrowly restrict authentic religious response among people in order to receive that grace.

The Amos and Jonah texts suggest that we can expect God to work within and through religious and cultural expectations of people whom we seek to evangelize, and this is true whether we are engaged in domestic or foreign missions. We should expect the Spirit to speak and act in ways that people will understand. We also should expect the Spirit to contradict and transform those elements of people's religious expectations that are inconsistent with the revelation and activity of the Spirit we find in the biblical traditions. Recognizing the contextual nature of divine activity and the Spirit's manifestation in the Bible does not relativize the Spirit, but it calls into question a facile rejection of culture and non-Christian religions as graceless and devoid of divine activity. Furthermore, recognizing the cultural-contextual nature of biblical revelation opens up the space to consider the religions of the world as possible places where the work of the Spirit of Pentecost achieves concrete manifestation in the lives of people.

The Spirit of Pentecost and the Religions

The universal work of the Spirit of Pentecost opens up at least two possibilities for a Pentecostal theology of religions. The first one is that some people have responded and participated in the Spirit of Pentecost, which suggests an inclusive soteriology. Inclusivism can affirm that people who respond to the Spirit, and do so in a way that is authentic to the Spirit of Pentecost and not necessarily to "our" way, have received grace and redemption. Just as Abraham expressed faith in God in a way that was sensible to him and authentic to the work of the Spirit in his life, so may people in non-Christian religions today do so, too. Consider that Abraham's experience of God as a flaming pot (Gen. 15:17) bears little or no correspondence to the religious experience of most North American Pentecostals; however, that does not impugn the legitimacy of their experience of God in any way. Essential for a theology of religions are two interrelated notions: if the Spirit of Pentecost is at work in all people, then people can respond to the Spirit's work; and this affirmation leads to a further one —

that some of the concrete ways people respond to the Spirit of Pentecost can be manifestations of grace.

The first possibility implies the second, namely, that some non-Christian religious thought and activity are a response to the Spirit of Pentecost. This point suggests a positive theology of religions. As I have observed earlier, Pentecostals have held a negative one.[39] Even if they are open to the idea that those who have never heard the gospel might receive grace and be judged on the light available to them (agnostic inclusivism), Pentecostals tend to deny that the religions are potential avenues and expressions of grace. A case in point is the final report of the Roman Catholic–Pentecostal Dialogue. The Pentecostals expressed reticence at considering redemptive elements in the religions and preferred to limit the Spirit's work therein to preparing people for hearing the gospel.[40] One reason for defaulting to a negative theology of religion is that Pentecostals, following the logic of evangelical exclusivism, assume that inclusivism conflicts with their commitment to missions.[41]

As Amos Yong insists, however, pragmatism and consequentialism should not be the exclusive drivers of Pentecostal theology.[42] Moreover, pure negativism on this issue conflicts with the universal work of the Spirit of Pentecost, who lays a foundation for a positive theology of religion. Although that is not traditional within the Pentecostal movement, Pentecostal theology should follow its pneumatological instincts. A positive theology of religion means that the religions in certain ways *may be* (1) legitimate ways for people to respond to the Spirit of Pentecost and (2) sacramental means

39. Anderson, *Spreading Fires,* p. 221; Veli-Matti Kärkkäinen, *Toward a Pneumatological Theology: Pentecostal and Ecumenical Perspectives on Ecclesiology, Soteriology, and Theology of Mission* (Lanham, MD: University Press of America, 2002), pp. 229-30; 231-34; Yong, *Discerning the Spirit(s),* pp. 185-87, 189.

40. See "Evangelization, Proselytism, and Common Witness: The Report from the Fourth Phase of the International Dialogue (1990-1997) between the Roman Catholic Church and Some Classical Pentecostal Churches and Leaders," *Pneuma* 21 (1999): 11-51 (esp. p. 16).

41. Other Pentecostals who come to similar conclusions include Kärkkäinen, "Pentecostal Pneumatology of Religions," pp. 170-71; Amos Yong, *Hospitality and the Other: Pentecost, Christian Practices, and the Neighbor,* Faith Meets Faith Series (Maryknoll, NY: Orbis, 2008), p. 72; Amos Yong and Tony Richie, "Missiology and the Interreligious Encounter," in *Studying Global Pentecostalism: Theories and Method,* ed. Allan Anderson, Michael Bergunder, André Droogers, and Cornelius van der Laan (Berkeley: University of California Press, 2010), pp. 245-67 (esp. pp. 251-53).

42. Yong, *Beyond the Impasse,* p. 26.

for the work and experience of the Spirit.[43] These two points raise the controversial question: Is there a biblical basis for seeing non-Christian religions as possible conduits, points of contact, and expressions of the Spirit and means of experiencing the Spirit? To put it another — and more personal — way: Is there a biblical rationale for seeing people in non-Christian religions as participating in God's grace? I suggest that the answer to that question is yes, for the following reasons.

First, and rather uncontroversial, the Spirit and grace can operate in non-Christian religious contexts. The Spirit is omnipresent and always at work as the Spirit of Pentecost. Second, the Spirit always works through sacramental means such as language, cultural assumptions, and religious ideas. Third, the work of the Spirit in practitioners of non-Christian religions can transform them, insofar as they yield to it. Because of the reciprocity between the Spirit's identity and work, the Spirit always works as the Spirit of Pentecost. In other words, the Holy Spirit always desires and seeks to draw human persons into the fellowship of the triune God. Jesus Christ is the Spirit's most stellar achievement of the reality in a concrete human being. Therefore, the Spirit's transformation of people, regardless of their particular religious affiliation, has a Christological character. Fourth, the transformation of the Spirit comes to concrete expression in people's lives in terms of thought and action, and these are "fruits of the Spirit." Fifth, the concrete manifestations of the Spirit in certain people can be the (sacramental) way for others, in turn, to yield to the Spirit calling them to faith. Sixth, people codify their responses to the Spirit in religious traditions over time, and this can function sacramentally as the means for others to yield to the Spirit of grace.

This last point does not mean that every element of a religion represents a tradition of authentic response to the Spirit, for even Christianity does not attain such a level of endorsement. This last point is the controversial one because it not only affirms that the Spirit and grace may be at work in the lives of non-Christians, but also that this may occur in the context of their religious activities. Though it may seem a theological bridge too far, the step from the position that grace is available to non-Christians to the one that their religion is the context for the work of grace

43. "Sacramental" means that something can both signify and serve as the means for participation in God and grace. The text of Scripture signifies, for example, the content of the gospel. Moreover, when people read Scripture, the text becomes the conduit for their apprehension of the gospel and taking part in grace; in other words, God communicates grace to people through the text of Scripture, and in this respect the text is sacramental.

is not as large as it seems. An interaction with Roman Catholic Gavin D'Costa, who affirms the former and denies the latter, illustrates the point.

Gavin D'Costa's Trinitarian theology of religions goes to great lengths to uphold the operation of grace and elements of truth in the non-Christian religions and to reject the religions as structures that mediate grace. Based on the Second Vatican Council and postconciliar documents, he argues that the presence of the Spirit in other religions is "intrinsically trinitarian and ecclesiological." Nevertheless, with respect to the Spirit's work in the other religions, he remarks that "all these actions of the Spirit cannot facilitate a theology of religions which affirms the various religious quests as authentic in themselves, apart from Christ, the trinity, and the Church."[44] However, we should neither simply accept en masse the religions nor assume that they are, in all their aspects — and especially the people who practice them — apart from Christ. In a summary of the insights of Pope John Paul II's *Crossing the Threshold of Hope,* D'Costa continues:

> It is also clear that the grace encountered in non-Christian religions is viewed as a *preparatio evangelica,* though *not* in terms of a division between the grace of creation and the grace of salvation, or natural and supernatural grace, but only because within the historical church is this grace finally properly ordered toward its eschatological fulfillment.

He further argues that "silence, indeed refusal, to acknowledge other religions, *per se,* as possibly being salvific structures, indicates that pluralism and inclusivism are not sanctioned by the Conciliar and post-Conciliar documents."[45]

Whether D'Costa's understanding accurately represents statements of Catholic doctrine is beside the point; but his affirmation that grace is present in the non-Christian religions and his rejection of the salvific structure of the religions needs consideration. He wants to retain Christianity as the normative religious structure, which he thinks requires denying other religions a role in salvation. However, one can hold both the normative status of Christianity and the operation of grace in other religions. If, as D'Costa accepts, the grace at work in the non-Christian religions and through the church is the same grace of the Spirit ("intrinsically trinitarian and ecclesiological"), then the operation of that grace in a non-Christian religion can-

44. D'Costa, *Meeting of Religions,* pp. 110, 106-7.

45. D'Costa, *Meeting of Religions,* pp. 108-9.

not be abstracted from the structure of that religion any more than it can from the Christian religion. Furthermore, the Spirit can work precisely through those structures to actualize grace in people (e.g., the Ninevites). Anyone who receives the grace of the Spirit in a non-Christian religion has Christ, participates in the fellowship of the Trinity, is being formed in the image of Christ, and is a member of the church even if only in a covert way.

This theology of religions helps to explain why one can sometimes find people with no association with Christianity who, nonetheless, appear to be more Christlike than some Christians. I do not think that we want to credit these examples to mere human moral purity and fortitude. The Spirit no doubt uses concrete events, people, and experiences as occasions for the operation of grace in human lives — and to elicit an implicit faith response from them. Although certainly not all non-Christian religions and their practices are places of the Spirit's work (just as not all Christian practices are means of the Spirit — in fact, they may at times get in the way of the Holy Spirit), religious activities seem a rather obvious place for such an operation of the Spirit and experience of grace to occur.

If some moral and religious beliefs and practices are authentic human responses to the redemptive work of the Spirit, then it follows that those thoughts and practices may be ways for others to come into redemptive participation in the Spirit. That is, they may be conduits for the Spirit's *summons* and the person's *answer* to the Spirit. This is true because people experience the universal presence of the Spirit in culturally specific ways. For instance, if the heavens declare the glory of God (Ps. 19:1-6), then reflection on the beauty of creation may be the occasion for people to have a faith response to the Spirit's work. The same logic applies to human religious and moral expressions. As part of creation and as potential manifestations of the Spirit, they can provide the occasion for people to yield to the Spirit, who always moves them to union with God — just as the beauty of creation can. The presence and work of the Spirit comes to tangible expression on the horizon of human experience through sacramental means: grace is always mediated in a sacramental way. Ideally, this occurs through the sacramental rites of the church, for example, the written and preached Word, baptism, and the Eucharist. However, the Spirit is not restricted to the traditional sacraments, but is free to work grace through a variety of means. Since the operation of the Spirit in non-Christians occurs through something, why not through their religion? *Insofar* as elements within a religion represent genuine human responses to the Spirit's presence, the Spirit can use them to facilitate a faith response in people.

Consider the case of Christian evangelism, compared to the religious activities of people in other religions. Some Christian efforts at evangelism are actually an impediment to the Spirit of Pentecost. An in-your-face, combative, confrontational, and judgmental approach has no doubt won a few to Christ, but it has turned away scores more, since it appears to come from a sense of moral superiority and spiritual self-righteousness rather than from love and mercy toward others. More often Christian witness springs forth from a genuine gratitude to God and love for others. These activities are undoubtedly authentic responses to the Spirit and the means of the Spirit to touch the lives of others. Nevertheless, even the best Christian witness is never unalloyed with the imperfection of the human condition. In a similar way, perhaps the religious devotion of some people and certain elements in other religions are the result of the Spirit's diligence to bring grace to all people and become the doorways for others to open their lives to the Spirit of Pentecost.

Recognizing the Spirit's work in and through the religions does not mean that all religious practices are authentic responses to the Spirit and are expressions of faith. Some religious practices are not responses to and avenues of the Spirit. In some respects, if one operates from a normative Christology and pneumatology, according to which redemption derives from participating in their mutual work, no religion — not even Christianity — saves anyone. However, Christians affirm that God mediates grace in conjunction with the preached gospel, the sacraments, and the ministries of the church. Therefore, the Christian traditions typically affirm that salvation derives exclusively from Christ; but they also grant that humans appropriate it in various ways. My argument here is that all legitimate manifestations and human responses to the Spirit, whether those by individuals or formalized in religious traditions, can be ways that people concretely express their faith response to the Spirit. Salvation is participation in the fellowship of the Trinitarian God. Religion can be an avenue for coming into, and a way of embodying, that redemptive relationship.

Carl F. H. Henry argues that, considered as a whole, non-Christian ethical systems are not true, but that structural elements within them may be consistent with Christian moral truth.[46] This ethical distinction is similar to the one I make with respect to the religions. Religions, taken as comprehensive systems, are not simply equivalent with Christianity as paths to

46. Carl F. H. Henry, *Christian Personal Ethics* (Grand Rapids: Eerdmans, 1957), pp. 146-47.

God. Before becoming complacent, however, we should remember that practicing one of the various expressions of the Christian religion is not the same thing as participating in redemption. No religion saves anyone. Salvation is renewed life from God's Spirit and communion with the Trinitarian God. The question remains: How does religion help or get in the way of participating in God's redemption?

I am not a religious pluralist because I believe that the various forms of Christianity, as comprehensive systems, declare the gospel and as such offer a sure way to God. The Lutheran dialectics of law and gospel are helpful here. According to this view, anything contrary to the free grace of the gospel is a religion of the law (salvation based on human merit). In this perspective, the critical question is not, What religion am I a member of? Rather, it is, Do I trust the gospel? No religion is one and the same with the gospel. They are all, including the various forms of the Christian religion, a mix of law and gospel. Therefore, the difference between Christianity and other religions is one of degree and not kind. Here is where I disagree with Carl Henry. Based on the distinction between general and special revelation, Henry believes that Christianity (i.e., its ethical system/s) is unique because it is based on special revelation. I think this distinction misses the continuity in divine revelation. All revelation has the purpose of drawing human beings into relationship with the triune God. With respect to the religions, Christianity is based on the revelation of God in Jesus Christ and the outpouring of the Holy Spirit, where the non-Christian religions are not. But insofar as they are responses to God's revelation in other venues, they are different from Christianity in degree and not kind.

I also think it is worth remembering that neither Jesus nor the Spirit of Pentecost revealed a religion. God did not send a religion to earth; God sent his Son and Spirit. They offered the opportunity to share in the life and fellowship of the triune God, and their offer extends to all people, irrespective of their religious practice. Consider again the example of Jonah and the Ninevites. The structural elements of the religion of Israel revealed a clearer path to a relationship with God than the religion practiced by the Ninevites. Nevertheless, the Ninevites were closer to the kingdom than Jonah. Jonah practiced the right religion, but his heart was far from the God revealed in that religion. The Ninevites, who practiced the wrong religion, nonetheless responded in the right way to what God was doing in their lives. Relationship with God often comes to concrete expression in terms of religious practices, but the substance of redemption lies deeper in the depths of humans and their response to the work of God in their lives. But what — without minimizing the concrete acts of religious devotion — is the deeper theological basis of religion? From whence does human religious desire and activity arise, and how should we understand the human religious response?

The Spirit of Pentecost, Faith, and Religion

The articulation of a theology of religions requires a fundamental understanding of faith. "Faith" is, in the Christian traditions, the most profound and essential basis of the human being's relationship with God. Pentecostals ordinarily adopt a content-rich view of faith. To have faith is to believe certain things about the person and work of Jesus Christ. In Pentecostal and evangelical churches, the normative conversion paradigm is the repetition of the "sinner's prayer," after which the new believer attends to various forms of piety, such as daily Bible and prayer devotions and participation in church activities and ministries, all of which are understood as the pursuit of Christlikeness. For Pentecostals, faith has a concrete christological expression.

Although the christological emphasis is certainly correct, it can get in the way of sounding out a deeper theological appreciation of the nature of faith. But before I discuss the nature of faith, I want to address the relationship between the faith with which a person believes *(fides qua)* and the faith that is believed *(fides quae)*. This distinction probes the relationship between the subjective and objective aspects of faith. Is there a bare minimum of doctrinal truth that must be believed in order for someone to receive grace? If so, what is the truth yardstick of *fides quae?* Is it ten, three, two points — or one point — of doctrine? In Pentecostalism and evangelicalism, for example, the necessary *fides quae* has been to believe that one is a sinner who is separated from God and who can only through faith and a personal relationship with Jesus Christ receive forgiveness of sins and peace with God. In this view, christological content is necessary for genuine faith: the *fides quae* must include explicit knowledge of Christ. The parable of the sheep and the goats, however, suggests that the truth embraced in salvation has less to do with the cognitive content of faith than the faith of living in the way of Jesus. The basis for being declared a sheep is not a propositions checklist. What mattered was the relationship of the sheep with Christ, which was manifested in the way they treated other people (Matt. 25:31-46). Living in the way of Jesus is not salvation by works. Living in the way of Jesus indicates that a person has embraced the truth of

Christ or, in other words, lives by faith in Jesus Christ. In a similar way, the goodness of the Good Samaritan is completely unrelated to the intellectual content of his faith. Jesus taught that the way to "eternal life" is to love God and your neighbor (Luke 10:25-37). Knowledge is not unimportant, but ultimately the faith that is believed has more to do with loving God and neighbor than confessing a doctrinal statement.

What is faith? As indicated above, the immediate answer is likely: Believe in Jesus Christ. While believing in Jesus is certainly an act of faith, such a description does not deliver a theological account of the act and subsequent life of devotion called faith. The traditional Pentecostal and evangelical emphasis on the doctrinal data of faith masks what happens at the fundamental theological level between a person and God, and that Christian salvation ultimately depends on a divine presence and overture and not on a human intellectual or moral response, though the latter are certainly involved. Harry R. Boer makes this point when he says, "The gospel is not the story of Man's search for God, but the story of God's seeking and claiming and finding Man."[47] At a basic and theological level, faith is a human person's affirmative reply to the Spirit of Pentecost. Faith is the response to and relationship with God that takes place in the most intimate depths of a person's life.

Faith, whether it is thought of as the initial act of the religious life or the ongoing way of spiritual life, begins with God's initiative. No human being, from wells of moral and spiritual goodness, decides to believe and live a saintly life. God's Spirit originates and sustains the human capacity for a relationship with God and its direction in a life of devotion to God and to the neighbor in this world. God's Spirit is not an amorphous phantom, but the Holy Spirit of the eternal Trinity. Moreover, given the continuity between identity and work, the Holy Spirit present and active in all humans seeks to do for them what he does in the Trinity. Within the Trinity, the Holy Spirit constitutes the eternal triune life and community of God; in the Trinity, the Spirit's identity and activity are inseparable. In the economy of redemption, the same continuity pertains. The consequence for the Spirit's work in human beings is that the Spirit endeavors to draw all people into the life and fellowship of the Trinitarian God. Whether understood as an act or process (or both), yielding to the stirrings of the Spirit and thereby participating in the Spirit of Pentecost is faith.

47. Harry R. Boer, *An Ember Still Glowing: Humankind as the Image of God* (Grand Rapids: Eerdmans, 1990), p. 121.

A qualification is in order at this point. Faith is simultaneously and mysteriously the product of divine providence and human freedom. A person's activities are the concrete ways he or she manifests that theological reality. People in non-Christian religions who accept the drawing of the Spirit participate in a category of spiritual response that is essentially the same as the person in a Pentecostal or evangelical church who responds to a call of salvation by going forward to pray at the altar. The difference lies in the way they manifest their response and not the nature of the response itself. For the person in the church, the expression of faith takes place in reciting the "sinner's prayer" or an alternative Christian initiation rite — for example, baptism. For the people in another religion, their response will occur in terms of, and at times in contrast to, their religion. Nevertheless, both responses can be, at a deeper level, their way of responding to the Spirit.

Theologically, faith is a dynamic pneumatological, anthropological, and Trinitarian process. It begins with the Spirit's invitation to participate in the Trinitarian life of God. This invitation is to all people. The invitation comes with the grace that enables human beings to embrace the call, and when they do so, they participate in the Spirit of Pentecost and thereby share in the Trinitarian communion constituted by the Holy Spirit. What is common to the human religious quest, therefore, is ultimately not anthropological but theological, more specifically pneumatological. By placing the Spirit at the base of human religious expression (this does not mean all religious activity is from the Holy Spirit), this theology of religions avoids the risk, as Christoph Schwöbel warns, of basing an "understanding of the religions . . . on some supposedly universal anthropological constant such as an alleged 'religious a priori.'"[48] The religious a priori is the Holy Spirit. Moreover, the essential human religious response to the Spirit of Pentecost is faith, which is humans' saying yes to the Spirit's work in their lives. Salvation is by faith. Whether one defines the inner seat of the person in the traditional category of the soul or the more contemporary emergent and nonreductive physicalist view, faith is the human being's response to and participation in the Spirit of Pentecost. If the root of faith is the Spirit of Pentecost, how does the ongoing life of faith relate to the Holy Spirit?

48. Christoph Schwöbel, "Particularity, Universality, and the Religions: Toward a Christian Theology of Religions," in *Christian Uniqueness Reconsidered: The Myth of a Pluralistic Theology of Religions,* ed. Gavin D'Costa, Faith Meets Faith Series (Maryknoll, NY: Orbis, 1996), pp. 30-46 (esp. p. 39).

Progressive and Partial Participation in the Spirit of Pentecost

The narrative arc of the Spirit of Pentecost begins with creation, moves to incarnation, and then to thematic climax on the Day of Pentecost. What this shows is an incremental and progressive revelation and experience of the Holy Spirit. In a similar way, the experience of the Spirit by people, regardless of their religious tradition, can be incremental and progressive. Tony Richie intimates that the early Pentecostal leader J. H. King's progressive doctrine of salvation could be applied to a theology of religions when he says:

> King does not directly relate his pneumatology and soteriology at this point to theology of religions, [b]ut it seems a small step to apply his dynamic and progressive Pentecostal pneumatology and soteriology beyond the pale of conventional Christianity.[49]

I want to take that step.

A key theological principle is that the work and identity of the Holy Spirit is always in continuity. This point means that the redemptive work of the Spirit is the same, regardless of time and space. Though the nature of the Spirit's work is progressively revealed in the history of biblical redemption and in ways appropriate to cultural circumstances, it has fundamental continuity. For example, what God was doing in Abraham and at Pentecost shares commonality. Jesus Christ is the fullest concrete revelation of God's redemptive work. The Spirit's work in Christ is the paradigm for what the Spirit seeks to do in every person — past, present, and future.[50] Applied to people in other religions, the Holy Spirit endeavors to draw them into union with the Son and the Father so that they can share in the fellowship of the triune God. This theology of the Spirit supports the proposition that perhaps people in other religious traditions can concretely experience God in a way (1) that is sensible to their cultural and religious context and (2) that is authentic to the Spirit of Pentecost.[51]

49. Richie, "Azusa-Era Optimism," p. 234.

50. Graham H. Twelftree highlights the fact that the Spirit's work in redeeming human beings parallels what the Spirit did in Christ. See Twelftree, *People of the Spirit,* pp. 31-32.

51. Amos Yong makes a similar proposal using the parable of the Good Samaritan. For the first-century Jew, the Samaritan was the religious other, a heretic bereft of salvation. Nevertheless, Jesus presents him as one who loves God and neighbor. In other words, he fulfills the law and qualifies for inheriting eternal life (Luke 10:25-37). Yong raises this question:

The test of authentic manifestation and experience of the Spirit is whether the experience and the practice it sponsors are consistent with the nature of the Spirit as revealed in Scripture; for example, does it lead people to act justly and with mercy (cf. Matt. 25:31-46). This applies not only to people in non-Christian religions, but to Christians as well. Pentecostals do not typically believe that religion saves anyone; Christianity, per se, does not save a person.[52] People participate in salvation when they participate in the Spirit as the Spirit of Pentecost, the Spirit of Christ. Participation in the Spirit means that people yield and respond in their lives to the Spirit's transformative work, which is the essence of faith.

Religion is both the work of the Spirit of Pentecost and the human attempt to bring the Spirit of Pentecost to an authentic expression; as such, religion is a "mixed bag" (again, this is true of Christianity as well).[53] Anthea Butler is on the mark when she suggests that Pentecostalism includes practices that can be characterized as the good, the bad, and the ugly.[54] Religion can be a work of the Spirit because the Spirit is always seeking to initiate people into and develop in them a fuller experience of the Spirit of Pentecost. Religion also is the effort, never perfect and sometimes defunct, of human beings to respond in authentic ways to the Spirit. Moreover, just as other religions may detract and obscure the manifestation of the Holy Spirit's work, so too may certain forms of Christian thought and practice, which the story of the Jerusalem Council in Acts 15, Paul's struggle against the "Judaizers" (Gal. 5:1-12), and John's critique of Gnostic permutations of the gospel (2 John 7) demonstrate. As Amos Yong urges, the "unfinished character of Christian identity" supports openness on the part of Christians to learn from alternative religious traditions.[55]

The Christian doctrine of sanctification assumes that redemption is an incremental experience — hence the ongoing need to "be filled with the

---

Since the Samaritan, as the religious outsider, embodies an authentic relationship with God, is it not possible that members of other religions do so today? See Yong, *The Spirit Poured Out on All Flesh,* pp. 243-44.

52. Tony Richie argues that the early Pentecostal J. H. King "ascribed saving efficacy to 'the religion of Christ,' not to the Christian religious system per se," and that this opens the door to a more positive Pentecostal theology of religions (Richie, "Azusa-Era Optimism," p. 236).

53. Richie, "Azusa-Era Optimism," p. 239.

54. Anthea Butler, "Pentecostal Traditions We Should Pass On: The Good, the Bad, and the Ugly," *Pneuma* 27 (2005): 343-53.

55. Yong, *Spirit Poured Out on All Flesh,* p. 240.

Spirit" (Eph. 5:18). Since Christians grant allowance for their progressive (indeed, often oscillating up and down) experience of sanctification, they should extend the same courtesy to others who may be, at a deep spiritual level, responding to the Spirit of God's work in their lives. The idea of a partial participation in grace bears similarities with Wesley's theology of prevenient grace. For Wesley, the process of salvation does not begin with justification and the new birth, but in the earlier movement of the person to moral awareness, recognition of the need for repentance, a yearning for God, and, most importantly, the presence of God's Spirit as the divine source of these renewed abilities.[56] Though salvation proper occurs when the person receives justification and the process of sanctification begins, this work is in continuity with prevenient grace. The intended outcome of prevenient grace is the reception of justification and sanctification.[57] Kenneth J. Collins describes such people as "accepted" by God and "on *the way* of salvation . . . [b]ut they are not yet justified and born of God."[58] Prevenient grace is a grace that prepares a person to receive the gospel, but by itself it does not seem to provide access to the gospel and salvation.

Salvation comes through "converting and sanctifying grace," which specifically enable repentance and faith in Christ.[59] Wesley trusted God's mercy to deal justly with people who never hear the gospel but who have otherwise responded to the overture and work of God's Spirit in their lives. The primary difference between what Wesley suggests and what I propose here is that I think we can affirm that, if people outside the reach of the gospel respond to the Spirit of the Pentecost, then they receive the grace of

56. John Wesley, "The Scripture Way of Salvation," in *John Wesley's Sermons: An Anthology,* ed. Albert C. Outler and Richard P. Heitzenrater (Nashville: Abingdon, 1991), pp. 372-80 (esp. pp. 372-73); see also Wesley, "On Working Out Our Own Salvation," in *John Wesley's Sermons,* pp. 486-92.

57. Randy L. Maddox, *Responsible Grace: John Wesley's Practical Theology* (Nashville: Kingswood, 1994), pp. 83-90.

58. Kenneth J. Collins, *John Wesley: A Theological Journey* (Nashville: Abingdon, 2003), p. 226.

59. Randy L. Maddox, "Karl Rahner's Supernatural Existential: A Wesleyan Parallel?" *Evangelical Journal* 5, no. 1 (1987): 3-14 (esp. p. 11). Wesley used "salvation" in two senses: one to refer to the comprehensive process of grace, which begins with prevenient grace and concludes with final salvation in the *eschaton,* and the other to refer to salvation proper, which is the reception of the grace of justification and sanctification. The point is that participation in prevenient grace is not necessarily to receive the grace of salvation proper, though no one receives the latter without the former. See also Harold Lindström, *Wesley and Sanctification: A Study in the Doctrine of Salvation* (Grand Rapids: Francis Asbury, 1980), pp. 105-6, 113-14.

redemption. But a caveat is in order. Discerning the Spirit of Pentecost is important. I think we need to recognize that some religious traditions and practices simply are not and cannot be authentic manifestations of and responses to the Holy Spirit. Human sin and evil are real, and sometimes in human systems they obviate the Spirit's redemptive work. However, in some cases, just as in Christianity, human religious thought and practices are a mixture of genuine and aberrant responses to — and even rejection of — the Spirit.

Conclusion

I think it is a fair generalization that many Pentecostals and evangelicals — perhaps the majority of them — have inclusivist tendencies with respect to those who have not heard the gospel. The theological Rubicon is: Do the religions play any role, and can they be the context for the grace of God's Spirit and salvation? I think most Pentecostals and evangelicals would answer with a definitive no. In this chapter I have invited you to reconsider a no with a yes — or at least a maybe. Moreover, I do so for reasons that are intrinsic to, not foreign to, the Pentecostal theological tradition. The work of the Spirit of God begins with creation and reaches its thematic and canonical culmination as the Spirit of Pentecost. Although often understood as distinct works, the Spirit's work within creation and redemption is unified. The scope of the creative-redemptive work of the Spirit of Pentecost is universal. The Spirit is always seeking to initiate people into and to develop in them a fuller experience of the Spirit of Pentecost. The universal outpouring of the Spirit of Pentecost provides a theological basis for a theology of religions and mission as participation in the Spirit of Pentecost. Specifically, it recommends first that religion can be both the work of the Spirit of Pentecost and the human attempt to bring the Spirit of Pentecost to authentic and concrete expression. Second, it suggests that Christian mission is a way that Christians participate in the Spirit's mission. The Spirit's mission is to bring all people to participate in the outpouring of the Spirit as the Spirit of Pentecost. When Christians engage in missions, they join in the mission of the Spirit to help a person or group of people to begin or to progress in their participation in the Spirit of Pentecost and the fellowship of the Trinitarian God.

7 The Spirit of Pentecost and Creation

I grew up in the Pacific Northwest with a love and appreciation for the outdoors. I spent a significant amount of my teenage years fly-fishing for trout, salmon, and steelhead all across the state of Oregon, a passion that I would later pursue in Washington, British Columbia, Alaska, the Boundary Waters Canoe Area, Quetico Provincial Park, Georgia, Ontario, and upstate New York. Though I did not grow up in a religious home, I remember having a mystical, enrapturing sort of experience. I was casting flies in Gales Creek. Through breaks in the trees, I caught glimpses of the surrounding Coast Range Mountains. The fast water, interrupted here and there by small pools, masked the rumble of the infrequent car passing on the Wilson River Highway. At the time, I lacked the religious vocabulary to articulate the experience, but I had a profound sense that something beyond what I could see made my surroundings sacred.

At the age of nineteen, I became a Christian through a men's Bible study sponsored by a local Assemblies of God church. I learned to see God at work in my life when I prayed, read the Bible, and engaged in what are called the spiritual disciplines and church ministries. The rest of the world and those parts of my life not clearly connected to spiritual pursuits were secular. I was warned that skipping church during the peak of the salmon run might be a sign of backsliding. The world was something that could be enjoyed, but always with the recognition that it is not really our home and that it should not get in the way of more important spiritual matters. My love for outdoor activity, especially fly-fishing, had not waned; but my worldview had changed. The world was no longer a place of mystical enchantment. To get that experience, I went to church.

What accounted for this alteration in my outlook? I can identify two features of Pentecostal and evangelical theology. The first is dispensational and premillennial eschatology. Following evangelicalism, Pentecostal eschatology has not been world-affirming. On the contrary, it foresees a world that is destroyed in a cataclysmic end-time conflagration.[1] From this perspective, environmental calamities can be seen as a sign of the "end times" and creation care as antithetical to God's eschatological program.[2] The second is a dualistic and hierarchical worldview that pits spiritual issues over worldly ones. This latter perspective is the more fundamental one because it gets to the theology of creation presupposed in both viewpoints. Though highlighting theological sources, I do not lay the proclivity of humans to despoil the planet solely at the feet of the Western Christian tradition, since the modernist worldview and good old-fashioned greed account for much of it. Nevertheless, as Lynn White has concluded,

> Despite Darwin, we are not, in our hearts, part of the natural process. We are superior to nature. . . . To a Christian a tree can be no more than a physical fact. The whole concept of the sacred grove is alien to Christianity and to the ethos of the West. For nearly two millennia Christian missionaries have been chopping down sacred groves, which are idolatrous because they assume spirit in nature.[3]

1. Peter Althouse argues that early Pentecostals held a more positive "Latter Rain" eschatology and did not co-opt the more evangelical premillennialism until the mid-twentieth century. See Althouse, "'Left Behind' — Fact or Fiction: Ecumenical Dilemmas of the Fundamentalist Millenarian Tensions within Pentecostalism," *Journal of Pentecostal Theology* 13 (2005): 187-207. For his fuller engagement with Pentecostal eschatology in dialogue with the theology of Jürgen Moltmann, see *Spirit of the Last Days: Pentecostal Eschatology in Conversation with Jürgen Moltmann,* Journal of Pentecostal Theology Supplement Series, 25 (London: T&T Clark, 2003).

2. R. J. Berry, "Part I: Rationale," and Ron Elsdon, "Eschatology and Hope," in *The Care of Creation: Focusing Concern and Action,* ed. R. J. Berry (Leicester, UK: InterVarsity, 2000), pp. 13-16, 161-66 (esp. pp. 14, 161).

3. Lynn White, Jr., "The Historical Roots of Our Ecological Crisis," *Science* 155 (1967): 1203-7. White may invest Christianity with too much cultural influence; nevertheless, as Theodore Hiebert remarks, the "problem with White's critique of the Bible was not so much that it lacked good exegetical method — which it did — but that it so closely mirrored the result of the best biblical scholarship on nature, a scholarship which, as I wish to argue here, needs some serious rethinking." See Hiebert, "Rethinking Traditional Approaches to Nature in the Bible," in *Theology for Earth Community: A Field Guide,* ed. Dieter T. Hessel, Ecology and Justice Series (Maryknoll, NY: Orbis, 1996), pp. 23-30 (esp. p. 25).

The Christian tradition, however, is not so monolithic. Albert Hernández shows that a strand of medieval theology and spirituality emerged that integrated Christian pneumatology with the nature spiritualities of pre-Christian Celtic Europe.[4] Yet these movements, as Hernández recognizes, were contrarian to the "official" Augustinian pneumatology of the Western church.[5] Thus, though it is not absent, an ecological ethic has not been a driving force in the church's vision of the Christian life. Reflecting this tradition, Pentecostals and evangelicals have been satisfied to save souls, not trees. Though Pentecostals and evangelicals have recently begun to embrace environmental stewardship (e.g., the Evangelical Environmental Network and Restoring Eden: Christians for Environmental Stewardship), they mostly still inhabit a two-tiered spiritual and natural world, which leaves creation care with an ambiguous place in the Christian life and the church's cultural engagement.

I started this chapter with a personal reflection because theology should engage the real world. It should address the world of our lives. If talk of the Trinity, the Son, and the Holy Spirit is nothing more than a flight into the surreal that never speaks to the specific circumstances of contemporary life, why bother? In point of fact, we are already shaped by theology(ies) and worldview(s). The question is: What kind of theology is it? Does the way we think about the world emerge from the history and expectation of God's redemptive works? Furthermore, as Peter Scott points out, most of the problems facing human beings today are political and social.[6] The global financial crisis of 2008 was not a natural disaster. An earthquake, hurricane, or new super virus did not precipitate it; it was the result of corrupt collusion between financial and political elites. The consequences, of course, reached far beyond Wall Street and Pennsylvania Avenue. The looming debt crisis of the United States, due to both official national debt and the unfunded liabilities of programs like Social Security and Medicare, is our own creation.[7] De-

4. Albert Hernández, *Subversive Fire: The Untold Story of Pentecost,* Asbury Theological Seminary Series in World Christian Movements in Medieval and Reformation Studies, 1 (Lexington, KY: Emeth, 2010), pp. 29-50.

5. Hernández, *Subversive Fire,* p. 84.

6. Peter Scott, *Political Theology of Nature* (Cambridge: Cambridge University Press, 2003), p. 6.

7. For an excellent description of the structural financial problem with Social Security and Medicare, see Laurence J. Kotlikoff and Scott Burns, *The Coming Generational Storm: What You Need to Know about America's Economic Future* (Cambridge, MA: The MIT Press, 2005).

cades of political dithering, false promises, demagoguery, incompetence, and indolence — along with a complacent electorate that either gullibly believes there is such a thing as a free lunch or indulges a crass sense of self-entitlement with a seemingly unending array of social programs at the expense of future generations — is the source of the crisis.

On the ecological front, regardless of whether one believes the apocalyptic prognostications of the climate-change prophets of doom, our world seems to be facing severe environmental distress.[8] Most of which is our own doing. The activity of human beings can even compound the effects of natural disasters. Japan's March 2011 earthquake, tsunami, and aftershocks triggered the nuclear meltdown at the Fukushima Reactor plant. More locally, the tradeoff for fertilized green lawns in Rochester, New York, is a potential dead zone in Lake Ontario's Irondequoit Bay.

The United States House of Representatives passed (May 12, 2011) the bill "reversing President Obama's Offshore Moratorium Act." The bill, though rejected by a three-vote margin in the Senate (May 19, 2011), would have opened up to offshore oil drilling, among other places, the Bristol Bay Region of Alaska.[9] Currently, the Pebble Partnership (a multinational conglomerate comprised of Northern Dynasty Minerals, Rio Tinto, Anglo American, and Mitsubishi Corporation) seeks to open Pebble Creek gold and copper mines in the Bristol Bay watershed in southwestern Alaska. Plans include locating two mines, a massive open pit and an underground mine, near Lake Iliamna in the headwaters of two major Bristol Bay drainages, the Nushagak and Kvichak rivers.[10] The operation also would include a mill, the largest earthen dam on the planet (spanning over four miles and reaching 700 feet in height) to contain billions of tons of waste, and a 100-mile road through pristine wilderness to transport the ore yield to Cook inlet.[11] Bill Sherwonit raises the following questions:

8. Christian environmental ethicist Michael S. Northcott says that "global warming is the earth's judgment on the global market empire, and on the heedless consumption it fosters" (Northcott, *A Moral Climate: The Ethics of Global Warming* [Maryknoll, NY: Orbis, 2007], p. 7).

9. Clearly a process of political posturing and theater, it nonetheless shows that the environmental threat to these areas is real.

10. Details on the proposed mine are available at Alaska Department of Natural Resources, Division of Mining, Land, and Water, "Pebble Project": http://dnr.alaska.gov/mlw/mining/largemine/pebble/.

11. According to a recent report (May 3, 2011), Pebble Partnership will conduct a $91 million initiative to create a "detailed project description" that will serve as the basis for re-

> Can a vast industrial project — which might include a two-mile-wide open pit mine and a dam, hundreds of feet high and up to four miles long, to hold tailings and acid wastes — be constructed in a wild, seismically active zone without leading to an environmental catastrophe? And, ultimately, will the mining of this vast mineral wealth irreparably harm the natural wealth that defines Bristol Bay — its salmon?[12]

If past performance is indicative of future results, the answers to those two questions are no to the first and yes to the second. To believe in the proposition that the Pebble Creek mines will have no deleterious environmental impact requires a level of faith beyond that of the most holy Christian saint.

The biblical creation story begins in a garden, fecund and vibrant. It paints a picture of a thriving and harmonious world. God commands his human charges to care for creation. After the call to be fruitful, God's first command to human beings is not to build a temple and perform a rigorous routine of religious calisthenics, but to be stewards of his creation — to cultivate and care for the earth (Gen. 1:28). As a Pentecostal, I want to explore how a theology of creation, informed by a theology of the Holy Spirit and the Trinity, can shape a Christian perspective on creation care. Many Pentecostal and evangelical Christians may embrace environmentally friendly lifestyles, but they find it difficult to see these efforts as an arena of the Spirit's work and as a part of their Christian life. Why should they? Is there a biblical and theological basis to consider the care and preservation of the earth as part of discipleship? I think there is.

Scripture presents an expansive and earthly vision of the Spirit's work. The Spirit who fosters and renews human life is also at work throughout the cosmos and will ultimately "liberate creation from its bondage to decay" and usher in the New Heaven and the New Earth (Rom. 8:21; Rev. 21:1). Creation care, no less than the traditional disciplines of Christian formation, is a way that the Holy Spirit enables Christians to foreshadow and participate in the ultimate renewal of creation. In the report "God, Creation, and Climate Change," the Lutheran World Federation called for

---

ceiving permits (Becky Bohrer, "Alaska: Pebble Mine Taking Step toward Permitting," *Bloomberg Businessweek* (no pagination): http://www.businessweek.com/ap/financialnews/D9MVV0KG0.htm.

12. Bill Sherwonit, "Alaska's Pebble Mine: Fish Versus Gold," *Yale Environment 360: Opinion, Analysis, Reporting and Debate* (Sept. 2008): http://e360.yale.edu/feature/alaskas_pebble_mine_fish_versus_gold/2062/

a theology of creation that is Trinitarian and pneumatological (rather than primarily Christocentric) and that integrates nature into God's redemptive program. This chapter works toward those two goals, along with a third goal: articulating a vision of creation care as Christian formation. The resource for this task is the pneumatology and Trinitarian theology of the previous chapters. By engaging in this effort, I endeavor in this chapter to make a contribution both to a Pentecostal theology of creation and the wider ecumenical project of contemporary theology. The first step, however, is to examine the theological source — the traditional distinction between common and special grace — of the impoverished view of creation that characterizes not only Pentecostal and evangelical but most of Christian thought as well.[13] The second and third sections show that pneumatology and Trinitarian theology can fund a Christian theology of creation that (1) overcomes the stark dualisms of secular and sacred and common and special grace and (2) attains a unified and comprehensive vision of God's grace, which in turn supports the practice of creation care as an important dimension of Christian discipleship.[14] The fourth section presents

13. My interaction with "evangelicalism" does not dismiss the diversity within the movement, but recognizes that overall it has tended to embrace a conservative theological and social posture. Nevertheless, within the evangelical movement one can find figures, churches, and organizations interested in environmental issues, e.g., the 1994 *An Evangelical Declaration on the Care of Creation,* and its 2004 sequel, *The Sandy Cove Covenant and Invitation:* http://www.earthcareonline.org/evangelical_declaration.pdf.

14. Additional contributions to the relationship between theology, science, and creation by Pentecostal and charismatic scholars include: Augustinus Dermawan, "The Spirit in Creation and Environmental Stewardship: A Preliminary Pentecostal Response toward Ecological Theology," *Asian Journal of Pentecostal Studies* 6 (2003): 199-217; Andrew K. Gabriel, "Pneumatological Perspectives for a Theology of Nature: The Holy Spirit in Relation to Ecology and Technology," *Journal of Pentecostal Theology* 15 (2007): 195-212; Clark H. Pinnock, *Flame of Love: A Theology of the Holy Spirit* (Downers Grove, IL: InterVarsity, 1996), pp. 49-77; James K. A. Smith and Amos Yong, eds., *Science and the Spirit: A Pentecostal Engagement with the Sciences* (Bloomington: Indiana University Press, 2010); Amos Yong, ed., *The Spirit Renews the Face of the Earth: Pentecostal Forays in Science and Theology of Creation* (Eugene, OR: Pickwick, 2009); and Yong, *The Spirit of Creation: Modern Science and Divine Action in the Pentecostal-Charismatic Imagination,* Pentecostal Manifestos, James K. A. Smith and Amos Yong, gen. eds. (Grand Rapids: Eerdmans, 2011); the three essays on ecological issues by Michael Wilkinson, A. J. Swoboda, and me in *A Liberating Spirit: Pentecostals and Social Action in North America,* ed. Michael Wilkinson and Steven M. Studebaker, Pentecostals, Peacemaking, and Social Justice Series (Eugene, OR: Pickwick, 2010), pp. 213-63; and the section, with seven essays, "Pentecostal Voices in the Theology-Science Conversation," *Zygon: Journal of Religion and Science* 43 (2008): 875-989.

a case for seeing creation care as a pneumatological and proleptic participation in the *eschaton* and, as such, as a dimension of Christian formation and sanctification.

Common and Special Grace

Traditional Pentecostal theology for the most part shares evangelicalism's theology of creation.[15] Indicative of this commensurability is their assumption and view of common grace and general revelation and special grace and revelation.[16] The distinction between common and special grace parallels the one between the doctrines of general and special revelation. Common grace refers to the various ways God influences the lives of people in a nonsalvific way. Common grace restrains sin, provides the moral sense that keeps human societies more or less civil, and funds cultural pro-

15. I focus on the Pentecostal traditions that were influenced more by Reformed evangelicalism than by Wesleyan theology. Wesleyan-Holiness Pentecostals, however, also adopted elements of the relationship between nature and grace discussed in this section. See the references to R. Hollis Gause and French L. Arrington, who are both Wesleyan-Holiness Pentecostals. Furthermore, the Dutch Reformed tradition has a more developed theology of the relationship between common and special grace. A key figure in this tradition is Abraham Kuyper. Kuyper also addressed the relationship between common and special grace in terms of pneumatology. The distinction between common and special grace arises from a Reformed view of election. God gives common grace to all people, but only special grace, the grace of regenerated life, to the elect. So, though Kuyper has a robust theology of common grace that fosters the purposes of the created order (e.g., human cultural production and social organization), it remains distinct from the grace of salvation. This distinction is precisely the problem. My proposal is that God's purposes for creation are ultimately unified: to bring all creation to its proper way of participating in the divine life. For an introduction to Kuyper's theology of common grace and its relationship to Christian participation in society, see Vincent E. Bacote, *The Spirit in Public Theology: Appropriating the Legacy of Abraham Kuyper* (Grand Rapids: Baker Academic, 2005), esp. pp. 96-107. For Kuyper's understanding of the relationship between the Holy Spirit and the orders of common and special grace, see Kuyper, *The Work of the Holy Spirit,* trans. Henri De Vries, intro. Benjamin B. Warfield (Grand Rapids: Eerdmans, 1946 [first printed in 1900]), pp. 45-46, 288-91, 295, and 310-13.

16. Illustrative of the above point is John R. Higgins's chapter entitled "God's Inspired Word," which primarily bases its description of general and special revelation on the work of Bruce Demarest, Millard Erickson, and Carl F. H. Henry. See John R. Higgins, "God's Inspired Word," in *Systematic Theology,* ed. Stanley M. Horton, rev. ed. (Springfield, MO: Logion, 1995), pp. 61-81. For additional examples, see Larry D. Hart, *Truth Aflame: Theology for the Church in Renewal,* rev. ed. (Grand Rapids: Zondervan, 2005), pp. 42-49; and William W. Menzies and Stanley M. Horton, *Bible Doctrines* (Springfield, MO: Logion, 1993), pp. 20-26.

duction. Similarly, general revelation, a more specific manifestation of common grace, provides knowledge of God's existence, character, and moral expectations that is available through the natural world, history, and various dimensions of human experience.[17] Special grace, or saving grace, is the unique operation of God that inspires faith and empowers the Christian life. Special revelation gives the knowledge of God necessary for salvation, which usually has a specific and detailed christological content.[18] Because special revelation occurs through specific supernatural acts, such as the incarnation of Jesus Christ and the inspiration of Scripture, it is not universal but limited, at least initially, to the target community of faith — for example, Israel and the Christian church. Because common grace and special grace are more comprehensive terms, I will ordinarily use them to refer to the pairs of ideas.

What is significant for the present discussion is that common grace and special grace, although not opposed, are discrete divine programs.[19] The key to the difference is that none of the effects of common grace has anything to do with the order of special grace. A person can participate fully in common grace, but never touch special grace. In other words, common grace and general revelation are not for the purpose of salvation. Salvation derives from the second order of grace — special grace and revelation.[20] Although common grace is categorically distinct from special grace, the terms relate to each other: they render people guilty before God and subject to divine wrath.[21]

17. Millard J. Erickson, *Christian Theology* (Grand Rapids: Baker, 1985), pp. 153-54.

18. Bruce A. Demarest, *General Revelation: Historical Views and Contemporary Issues* (Grand Rapids: Zondervan, 1982), pp. 13-14, 228, 233, 250; see also his later essay "General and Special Revelation: Epistemological Foundations of Religious Pluralism," in *One God, One Lord: Christianity in a World of Religious Pluralism,* ed. Andrew C. Clarke and Bruce W. Winter, 2nd ed. (Grand Rapids: Baker, 1992), pp. 199, 205. For examples in Pentecostal theology, see Higgins, "God's Inspired Word," pp. 75-76; see also Menzies and Horton, *Bible Doctrines,* p. 21.

19. For example, even though Terrance L. Tiessen sees both common and special grace as benefits of Christ's atoning work, he still maintains that common grace is nonsalvific. See Tiessen, *Who Can Be Saved? Reassessing Salvation in Christ and World Religions* (Downers Grove, IL: InterVarsity, 2004), pp. 100-101, 396-400, 416, 418, 422-23.

20. Demarest, *General Revelation,* pp. 247-53; Erickson, *Christian Theology,* pp. 153-54; Wayne Grudem, *Systematic Theology: An Introduction to Biblical Doctrine* (Grand Rapids: Zondervan, 1994), pp. 658-63. For Pentecostals endorsing this view, see Higgins, "God's Inspired Word," pp. 75-76; and Menzies and Horton, *Bible Doctrines,* pp. 20-21.

21. Todd L. Miles offers an alternative to this traditional evangelical view. He argues that general revelation conveys a number of important items, such as God's moral will, divine attributes, and a comprehension of the world, but that it was never intended to be sepa-

The traditional set of beliefs about the relationship between common grace and special grace, accountability, and faith that tends to characterize evangelical and Pentecostal theology is problematic for four reasons.

The Extrinsic and Intrinsic Modalities of Common and Special Grace

The common-special grace distinction assumes an extrinsic-intrinsic notion of the Spirit's work in human beings.[22] Prior to conversion, the Spirit's work is extrinsic. The Spirit episodically acts on the person in the mode of common grace. In conversion, the Spirit regenerates the person from within and thus becomes an intrinsic agent of grace.[23] Assuming these modalities, Daniel Strange contrasts the impartation of the Spirit in regeneration and sanctification — that is, special grace — with the universal presence of the Spirit in creation — that is, common grace.[24]

---

rated from special revelation. From the creation of Adam and Eve it required God's illumination. Furthermore, its purpose never included communicating the message of salvation. Miles rejects the view that it is for condemnation. He nonetheless maintains that general revelation has no salvific value. Salvation depends on special revelation, which alone brings the message of salvation. See Miles, *A God of Many Understandings: The Gospel and a Theology of Religions* (Nashville: B & H Academic, 2010), pp. 330-34.

22. My focus is on how this dualistic and hierarchical view of grace impacts a Christian theology of creation and how pneumatology and Trinitarian theology can help overcome it. For other ways that traditional Christian theology fosters indifferent and sometimes even hostile attitudes toward nature, see the Lutheran World Federation's "God, Creation, and Climate Change: A Resource for Reflection and Discussion," in *God, Creation, and Climate Change: Spiritual and Ethical Perspectives*, ed. Karen L. Bloomquist, Lutheran World Federation Studies (Geneva: Lutheran University Press and Lutheran World Federation, 2009), pp. 13-26.

23. The extrinsic-intrinsic logic informs Grudem's argument that regeneration is the work of the Holy Spirit *in* the believer (*Systematic Theology*, pp. 699-702). For Pentecostals, see Hollis R. Gause, *Living in the Spirit: The Way of Salvation* (Cleveland, TN: Pathway Press, 1980), pp. 15-24; Daniel B. Pecota, "The Saving Work of Christ," in Horton, ed., *Systematic Theology*, pp. 325-73 (esp. pp. 364-65); French L. Arrington, *Encountering the Holy Spirit: Paths of Christian Growth and Service* (Cleveland, TN: Pathway Press, 2003), pp. 41-43, 55. Arrington says: "[S]o, from conversion on, the Spirit takes up residence in the believer," which indicates a transition from an extrinsic to an intrinsic relationship between the Spirit and the believer (p. 62).

24. Daniel Strange, *The Possibility of Salvation Among the Unevangelized: An Analysis of Inclusivism in Recent Evangelical Theology* (Eugene, OR: Wipf and Stock, 2002), p. 259.

Scripture, however, indicates that the Spirit is the intrinsic principle at the inception of human life and is the divine presence that enables human beings to participate in fellowship with God (Gen. 2:4-7; 6:3; 7:15, 22). The coalescence of the human becoming a living being and one who stands in relationship to God with the gift of the Spirit is never emendated, but reiterated and affirmed (Job 33:4 and Ps. 104:29-30). Consequently, the Spirit remains interior to human existence even in the post-Fall condition. Therefore, the Spirit is never primarily an extrinsic agent to the human person; the Spirit calls and works not from the outside *(extra nos)* but from within the depths of human life and consciousness.

The Discontinuity between Common and Special Grace

The categories of common and special grace sunder Scripture's unified vision of redemption. Creation and redemption are distinct in the sense that God redeems creation, but not in their economic program and end. The economic order is one: the redemption of creation. This conviction prompted George S. Hendry to point out that "since everything that God has created, including the world of nature, is good, everything is destined to participate in the consummation."[25] In Scripture, therefore, creation and redemption are not two separate orders, spheres, or modalities of divine activity, but one program. God's acts of redemption redeem creation.[26] The unity of creation and redemption does not deny a conceptual distinction between them, but it does set aside a dichotomy that implies that they are separate economic orders. For example, at the moment that God creates a human life, God does so for no other purpose than to nurture in that person loving patterns of life and relationship with creation, other humans, and the triune Godhead. Moreover, whatever people do in and through their lives more or less either contributes to or detracts from the actualization of God's creative purpose for their lives. Conceptually, a distinction can be drawn between God's act of creating a human person and the purpose for that creation. However, the distinction is more logical and abstract than illuminative of separate divine programs.

25. George S. Hendry, *Theology of Nature,* The Warfield Lectures 1978 (Philadelphia: Westminster Press, 1980), p. 220.

26. Sallie McFague, *The Body of God: An Ecological Theology* (Minneapolis: Fortress, 1993), pp. 179-82. McFague makes a case for creation as the place of salvation using the metaphor of the universe as the body of God.

The Hierarchy of Common and Special Grace

The discontinuity between common and special grace results in a hierarchical way of understanding their interrelationship.[27] Bruce Demarest reflects a hierarchical worldview when he seeks to relate general to special revelation, but subordinates the former to the latter.[28] He portrays the relationship in a pyramid diagram, in which general revelation forms the base and special revelation the pinnacle. The order of special grace is more important than and ultimately discontinuous with common grace for it has to do with salvation and the eventual everlasting kingdom of God. The problem with this view is that common grace has little to do with God's ultimate redemptive purposes. Other than keeping human beings from being as bad as they otherwise might be, its chief service is to provide sufficient knowledge to condemn them.

The common-special grace paradigm also divides the Holy Spirit's work into distinct domains. Clark H. Pinnock similarly critiques traditional evangelical theology when he says: "The effect of neglecting these activities ['the cosmic and creational role of the Spirit'] is to break creation and redemption into separate spheres and to draw a line between them."[29] Common and special grace segregates the Spirit's activities. For evangelical Calvinists like Wayne Grudem, not only are those separate spheres, they

27. For example, see Tiessen, *Who Can Be Saved?* p. 396. Although affirming the intrinsic value of common grace, Richard J. Mouw otherwise trades on the traditional distinctions between the orders of common and special grace (*He Shines in All That's Fair: Culture and Common Grace* [Grand Rapids: Eerdmans, 2001], pp. 31-51). The critique that Christianity is prone to construe the relationship between God and the world, the human and the world, and the spirit and the body in hierarchical and dualistic terms is common. Examples include Ian Barbour, *Nature, Human Nature, and God* (Minneapolis: Fortress, 2002), pp. 128-29; Elizabeth Johnson, *Women, Earth, and Creator Spirit* (Mahwah, NJ: Paulist Press, 1993), pp. 10-31, 58-60, and *Quest for the Living God: Mapping New Frontiers in the Theology of God* (New York: Continuum, 2007), pp. 181-90; McFague, *Body of God*, pp. 131-50, and *Life Abundant: Rethinking Theology and Economy for a Planet in Peril* (Minneapolis: Fortress, 2001), pp. 133-55. Mark I. Wallace advocates a biocentrism that overcomes hierarchical dualism by binding together the life of the universe and God. See Wallace, *Fragments of the Spirit: Nature, Violence, and the Renewal of Creation* (New York: Continuum, 1996), pp. 133-48.

28. Demarest, *General Revelation*, p. 251.

29. Pinnock, *Flame of Love*, p. 54. Amos Yong identifies a similar problem in the common distinction between natural and supernatural gifts. He suggests that the gifts of the Spirit permeate and enable the entire range of human activity in the world and are not restricted to ecclesial contexts. See Yong, *The Spirit Poured Out on All Flesh: Pentecostalism and the Possibility of Global Theology* (Grand Rapids: Baker Academic, 2005), pp. 294-96.

are unrelated as well. Salvation is not an experience that arises gradually along a continuum of grace, but comes from the immediate work of regeneration. For faith to arise, a person must receive the initial act of special grace, the regenerating work of the Holy Spirit. The doctrine of prevenient grace in Wesleyan theology avoids this separation and offers a more integrated view of grace. In prevenient grace, the Holy Spirit prepares and leads humans to receive saving grace by restoring the abilities (1) to discern God through reason and reflection on creation; (2) to comprehend morality and act morally; and (3) to respond to the overtures of divine grace. The advantage of Wesleyan prevenient grace over evangelical Calvinism is that it sees prevenient grace and saving grace as distinct movements on a continuum of grace.[30]

Ecology and the Hierarchy of Common and Special Grace

The traditional hierarchy of common and special grace presents a problem for an ecological concern. The earth and the human activities related to it fall within the realm of common grace, and if they are not properly subordinated to spiritual matters, they can be a distraction to the activities pursued under the category of special grace. A consequence of this theology for the Christian life is, for example, that evangelism is an activity of special grace, whereas the more mundane effort to preserve a wetland falls within the sphere of common grace. Evangelism promises to have eternal value, whereas environmental action will not outlast a world that is passing away. Wise Christians, according to this perspective, give their energies to things of eternal consequence and not to those of this ephemeral world. Tending the earth is not the concern of special grace, Christian ministry, and the kingdom of God. The affairs of creation — and thus efforts to save the earth — are not the context for the saving work of Christ; therefore, they should not be the place where Christians seek to "work out [their] salvation with fear and trembling" (Phil. 2:12). Saving trees and preserving wetlands distract Christians from saving souls, building the church, and supporting the approved moral and social issues.

Privileging spiritual over material reality takes root in the intellectual landscape of common and special grace. The result is an anthropocentric

30. Randy L. Maddox, *Responsible Grace: John Wesley's Practical Theology* (Nashville: Kingswood, 1994), pp. 83-90.

theology of creation that not only gives human beings preeminence among creatures, but also, with respect to their possession of a spiritual soul, places them in an altogether higher realm of creation. Human beings are not at home; they are aliens in this world. The ancient Hebrews had a much more grounded anthropology and theology of creation. Indeed, they understood that human life comes from the same soil as other living things. They possessed a profound sense of dependence and interrelationship with their environment that "is not so natural in a highly specialized modern culture in which our dependence on the environment has been largely obscured by our technology . . . [and] our Western idealistic theological tradition, which has taught us to divide the spiritual from the material."[31] The biblical creation accounts recognize that humans have a unique capacity for a relationship with their Creator and role within creation. Moreover, they see human uniqueness not as a reason to escape this world, but as a basis for a distinctive relationship with God and for living in a particular way within this world.

A hierarchy of concerns is not problematic per se. For example, humanitarian relief takes precedence over preserving wetlands (but, as indications in the aftermath of Hurricane Katrina suggest, the two efforts can be interrelated). Christian theology can recognize a hierarchy that distinguishes between relative levels of value, embraces activities within its strata as participating in a unified redemptive program, and sees all redemptive activities, whether directed specifically toward human or environmental welfare, as proleptic participations in the everlasting kingdom of God. Moreover, the hierarchical worldview presupposes that "spiritual" reality is superior to the "natural" world. Certainly, God grieves more over the death of a child from malnutrition than over a bug killed by lawn pesticides. However, it is not that the former is a "spiritual" being and the latter a "natural" one in an ontological sense; rather, their difference lies in their distinct capacity for a relationship with their Creator. I get mildly frustrated when the rabbits eat the young plants in my garden (in other words, they destroy something I had a part in creating); but I get apoplectic when another kid does something to hurt one of my children. Hence, we can make distinctions between relative levels of relational importance between God and creation, and also between humans and the rest of creation, without falling into a dualistic hierarchy of spiritual and natural being. The following sections of this chapter provide the theological rationale for a per-

31. Hiebert, "Rethinking Traditional Approaches," p. 29.

spective that enfolds all of creation in a cosmic vision of redemption — and thereby provides a theological basis for creation care.

The Trinitarian Spirit of Creation

Before arguing for the unity of the Spirit's work in creation and grace, I want to address the Trinitarian basis for a pneumatological theology of creation. To do so, I draw on David Coffey's adaptation of the Augustinian mutual-love model of the Trinity. Coffey's theology is one of the most refined and constructive articulations of Augustinian Trinitarian theology: his Spirit Christology and theology of the Spirit as the grace of Christ gives the Spirit a more visible and dynamic role than is commonplace in the Western theological tradition. Yet his understanding of the Holy Spirit as "the Spirit of Christ" retains a degree of Christocentrism because Christ is the *entelechy*, or the fundamental driving orientation, of the Holy Spirit.[32] Here I revise my previous appropriation of Coffey's theology for a theology of creation based on the pneumatology and Trinitarian theology proposed in chapter 2.[33] In short, where Coffey has Christ as the entelechy of the Holy Spirit, I suggest the fellowship of the Trinity as the entelechy of the Holy Spirit.

The Mutual-Love Model of the Trinity and the Entelechy of the Holy Spirit

In the theology of Karl Rahner and David Coffey, an entelechy is an internal force or principle that drives a being toward its destiny.[34] The philo-

32. Colin E. Gunton also works toward a Trinitarian theology of creation with an integral pneumatology, but retains a christological orientation. See Gunton, *The Triune Creator: A Historical and Systematic Study,* Edinburgh Studies in Constructive Theology (Grand Rapids: Eerdmans, 1998), pp. 168-71.

33. Steven M. Studebaker, "The Spirit in Creation: A Unified Theology of Grace and Creation Care," *Zygon: The Journal of Religion and Science* 43 (2008): 943-60; see also Studebaker, "Creation Care as 'Keeping in Step with the Spirit,'" in Wilkinson and Studebaker, eds., *A Liberating Spirit,* pp. 248-63.

34. Rahner's use of the term differs from its traditional Aristotelian sense, according to which *entelechy* denotes something having perfection. See David Coffey, "A Trinitarian Response to Issues Raised by Phan," *Theological Studies* 69 (2008): 852-74.

sophical term "entelechy" helps to express the theology of the biblical description of the Holy Spirit as "the Spirit of Christ."[35] Rahner nuanced entelechy in two ways: in the first sense, the Holy Spirit is the entelechy of the history of revelation and salvation — that is, the Holy Spirit is the intrinsic principle that directs revelation and salvation history; in the second sense, Christ, inclusive of the incarnation, cross, and resurrection (and the actualization of his grace in humans), is the entelechy of the Holy Spirit.[36] In this second use of entelechy, Rahner understands the Christ event as the final cause (the goal or end of an activity that determines the operation of efficient causality) of the Spirit's efficient work in the world. Since Christ is the final cause of the Spirit's work, Christ is the entelechy of the Spirit. The Christ event governs the Spirit's direction of the history of revelation and salvation. The two senses in which Rahner uses entelechy are distinct, but coherent. However, the second use (Christ as the entelechy of the Spirit) is foundational (theologically primary) because it guides the first (the Spirit as the entelechy of salvation history). The Holy Spirit is "the Spirit of Christ" because the entelechy of the Spirit's work is Christ. Coffey's contribution is to give Rahner's notion of the entelechy of the Spirit Trinitarian articulation in terms of the mutual-love model.

The mutual-love model posits that the Father from eternity generated the Son and that the Holy Spirit proceeds and subsists as the mutual love that unites the Father and the Son.[37] Coffey maintains that although the Holy Spirit subsists as the mutual love of the Father and the Son, the Spirit as the Father's love that rests on the Son is the most basic component.[38] In

35. David Coffey, "The Spirit of Christ as Entelechy," *Philosophy and Theology* 13 (2001): 365-70.

36. Karl Rahner, *Theological Investigations,* vol. 17: *Jesus, Man, and the Church,* trans. Margaret Kohl (New York: Crossroad, 1981), p. 46.

37. Denis Edwards and Mark Wallace both use the notion of the Holy Spirit as the divine love between the Father and the Son, but they do not develop the Spirit's identity as such and its informative power for the Spirit's work in creation within the Augustinian framework. Although appreciating the Western insight of Augustine, Edwards draws on the Trinitarian theology of Basil of Caesarea (Edwards, *Breath of Life: A Theology of the Creator Spirit* [Maryknoll, NY: Orbis, 2004], pp. 120, 148-57). Wallace's interests lie in the performative truth function of pneumatology; that is, the ability of a pneumatological image to inform an environmental ethic that is consistent with love of neighbor (Wallace, *Fragments of the Spirit,* pp. 145 and 168).

38. David M. Coffey, *"Did You Receive the Holy Spirit When You Believed?" Some Basic Questions for Pneumatology,* Père Marquette Lecture in Theology (Milwaukee: Marquette University Press, 2005), pp. 97-98.

other words, the Holy Spirit's primary personal identity is the Father's love for the Son. The Father has priority of order in the relationship because the Son is *from* the Father. The reciprocal love of the Son for the Father that completes their mutual love presumes the Father's initial love.[39] The consequence is that the Spirit's orientation — entelechy — to the Son is primary in the Spirit's personal identity.[40] The entelechy of the Spirit, then, is to be the one who unites the Father to the Son and thus the divine person who always seeks and rests on the Son.[41]

The entelechy of the Spirit, as the Father's love for the Son, provides the theological basis for understanding the Holy Spirit as "the Spirit of Christ." Coffey specifies the concrete form of the Holy Spirit as "the Spirit of Christ" in terms of a Spirit Christology and a pneumatological concept of grace. According to Coffey's Spirit Christology, the incarnation is an event in which the Father bestows love on humanity by sending the Holy Spirit (i.e., the expression of his love) and through that sending achieves the creation, sanctification, and radical union of the humanity of Jesus Christ with the divine Son.[42] Since the Father's bestowal of love in the Holy Spirit inevitably terminates on the Son, Jesus Christ is the entelechy of the Spirit. This dynamic also applies to the Spirit's role in grace. When the Father economically directs his love as the communication of the Spirit to human persons, his love still has the Son as its ultimate term or goal. The Spirit then seeks to bring humans into communion with the Spirit's proper, or original, term — which makes them children of the Father. Believers experience union with Christ by participating in the Spirit as "the Spirit of Christ," that is, by participating in the entelechy of the Spirit as "the Spirit of Christ."[43] In the economy of redemption, therefore, the Holy Spirit is always "the Spirit of Christ."[44]

39. The sequence of the Father loving the Son, who then returns love to the Father, refers to the immanent and not a temporal order of relations.

40. Coffey, *"Did You Receive?"* p. 98.

41. Coffey's integration of the entelechy of the Spirit with the Spirit's personal identity in the immanent Trinity gives the notion its Trinitarian rationale that is not found in Rahner.

42. David M. Coffey, "Spirit Christology and the Trinity," in *Advents of the Spirit: An Introduction to Pneumatology,* ed. Bradford E. Hinze and D. Lyle Dabney, Marquette Studies in Theology, 30 (Milwaukee: Marquette University Press, 2001), pp. 315-38; see also Coffey, "The Theandric Nature of Christ," *Theological Studies* 60 (1999): 405-31 (esp. pp. 425-30).

43. Coffey, *"Did You Receive?"* p. 34; Coffey, *Grace: The Gift of the Holy Spirit,* Marquette Studies in Theology, 73 (Milwaukee: Marquette University Press, 2011), p. 182.

44. For a fuller development of Spirit Christology, see Steven M. Studebaker, "Inte-

The Trinity as the Entelechy of the Holy Spirit

Although the Holy Spirit plays a significant role in establishing the fellowship of the Father and the Son, the mutual-love model preserves an instrumental role for the Spirit. The Spirit facilitates the mutual relationship of the Father and the Son. In the economy of redemption, the result is a pneumatology in the service of Christology, with the christological view of the entelechy of the Spirit the key indicator (though Coffey's theology of a proper role of the Holy Spirit goes a long way toward overcoming the endemic subordination of the Spirit in traditional Western theology).[45] In place of the Christocentric entelechy of the Spirit, I propose a Trinitarian one. The defining feature of the Spirit's personal identity is not as the Father's love for the Son or even as the mutual love of the Father and the Son, but as the divine person who completes the Trinitarian fellowship of the Father, the Son, and the Holy Spirit.[46] Without the Holy Spirit, there is no Trinity. Since the Spirit's activity is to bring the being of God to full Trinitarian communion, the Spirit's entelechy is the Trinity. The motivating dynamism of the Spirit is not the Son but the communion of the Trinity. The Spirit's identity and work is always oriented to constituting the fullness of the triune God.

Transposed to the economy of redemption, the entelechy of the Holy Spirit is also Trinitarian. The Spirit seeks to actualize the Trinitarian life

---

grating Pneumatology and Christology: A Trinitarian Modification of Clark H. Pinnock's Spirit Christology," *Pneuma* 27 (2006): 5-20.

45. David M. Coffey, "A Proper Mission of the Holy Spirit," *Theological Studies* 47 (1986): 227-50.

46. Sigurd Bergman points out that Gregory of Nazianzus has the Holy Spirit playing a consummational role in the history of redemption as well. Though Bergman gives an excellent exposition and appropriation of Nazianzus for a contemporary theology of creation, Nazianzus's view differs from the one that I propose here. Nazianzus seems to have conceived of the relationship between the works of Christ and the Spirit in terms of Trinitarian dispensations. The era of the incarnate Christ has come to a close, whereas the time of the Spirit, which "carries on the incarnate Son's work of liberation," has commenced. There is continuity between Christ and the Spirit, but a chronology, too. My goal is to affirm continuity and temporal or economic interpenetration rather than economic phases or eras that appear to characterize Nazianzus's way of relating the works of the Son and the Spirit. Moreover, the Spirit's orientation toward the future and consummation is defined specifically in Trinitarian terms. See Bergman, *Creation Set Free: The Spirit as Liberator of Nature*, Sacra Doctrina: Christian Theology for a Postmodern Age, Alan G. Padgett, gen. ed. (Grand Rapids: Eerdmans, 2005), pp. 81, 159-60, 167, 169-70, 318.

and fellowship of God in creation. The highest expression of the Spirit's economic work occurs in Christ, but the Spirit's work in Christ is fundamentally Trinitarian and not christological per se. The Spirit's purpose, through the particular humanity of Jesus of Nazareth, is the realization of the fullest communication of the triune life of God in creation. In Jesus Christ, the Spirit facilitates the most sublime manifestation of the Trinity in the economy of redemption. The Holy Spirit is the principle of the hypostatic union of Jesus' humanity with the eternal Son of God.[47] The incarnate Son of God's relationship with the Father, his life and ministry, comes to expression in a pneumatological horizon. The critical point is that Jesus' life and ministry is none other than the Son's incarnate relationship with the Father, and he actualizes this relationship through the agency and ministry of the Holy Spirit. The Spirit, therefore, economically realizes the fellowship of the Trinitarian God in Jesus Christ, just as the Spirit does for the Son and Father in the immanent Trinity. "The Spirit of Christ" thus applies to the Holy Spirit most importantly in the second way I used the term in chapter 2, not as the one who is sent by Christ, but as the one who facilitates the fellowship of the Trinitarian God both in eternity and in the work of redemption. The Spirit's work as "the Spirit of Christ" achieves the manifestation of the Trinitarian God in the economy of redemption.

How does the entelechy of the Spirit relate to a theology of creation? In "Creation Care as 'Keeping in Step with the Spirit,'" I adapted Coffey's theology of the Spirit's entelechy as "the Spirit of Christ" to propose that the Holy Spirit is the intrinsic principle of cosmic history that brings creation to its particular mode of participating in the everlasting kingdom.[48] However, I conceived of this entelechy of the Spirit within a christological framework: the Spirit's lodestar was Christ. The proposal here is that the Trinity is the motivating force of the Spirit's activity within creation. The Spirit ever seeks to bring the diversity of life in creation to its particular mode of participation in the overflowing life and vitality of the Trinitarian God. Though pneumatological, a Christian theology of creation is also christological. Christ provides the clearest glimpse of the manifestation of the triune life in the economy of redemption. Having established the pneumatological and Trinitarian groundwork for a theology of creation,

47. For a further development of this idea, see Studebaker, "Integrating Pneumatology and Christology," pp. 5-20.

48. "Creation Care as 'Keeping in Step with the Spirit,'" pp. 248-63.

the next step is to revisit the unified nature of creation and redemption and the pneumatological content of a Trinitarian theology of creation.

The Spirit and Creation

A unified theology of creation and redemption depends on the integration of the traditional distinctions between common and special grace. But what is the basis of this unification? The coordination of the Holy Spirit's identity and work provides the principle to synthesize these traditional categories. The Holy Spirit fulfills the fellowship of the triune God and thus seeks to fulfill creation's participation in that fellowship. This correspondence consolidates the Spirit as the breath of life (i.e., common grace) and Spirit as the agent of redemption (i.e., special grace). The yield is a unified and pneumatological theology of creation and cosmic vision of redemption. The following first resolves the problematic nature of the common-special grace hierarchy and then articulates the unified and cosmic nature of the Spirit of Pentecost's work in this world.

The Spirit and the Unity of Creation and Grace

A pneumatological and unified theology of creation and grace overcomes the hierarchical and extrinsic-intrinsic view of the Spirit's work in the common-special grace paradigm. First, it does not conceive of the Spirit's work in grace in extrinsic and intrinsic categories. The Spirit cannot be, on the one hand, the intrinsic principle of life for all creation and, on the other hand, the episodic extrinsic agent of common grace. If the Spirit is present with all living creatures as their source of life, then the Spirit's work always comes from within the very depths of their life. Hence, the Spirit's work is never only from the outside.

Second, since the Spirit's work always reflects the Spirit's identity as the person who constitutes loving fellowship, the Spirit's work always has a redemptive orientation. The Spirit never works in contradistinction to the Spirit's identity. Consequently, the Spirit does not have a common operation vis-à-vis a special operation with the latter taking precedence to the former. The Holy Spirit, who is present everywhere as the Spirit of life, is at the same time ever and everywhere the Spirit of redemption, or Spirit of Pentecost. In other words, the Spirit's work as breath of life is inseparable from the Spirit's work of redemption.[49] The Spirit does not have two orders within the economy of redemption, one common and the other special. The Spirit has a singular focus. The Spirit breathes life into creation for no other purpose than to facilitate the manifestation of the triune life of God in creation and the participation of creation in the fellowship of the Trinitarian God. The Spirit always seeks the particular eschatological end of all created life forms. Thus, rather than separated and ranked, the Spirit's work — in what are often called creation and grace — is one.

Scripture illustrates the unity between creation and grace. One way is the corresponding pattern of activities and images that describe the Spirit's work in creation and redemption.[50] The Spirit of God is the foundation for the horizon of the days of creation in Genesis 1:1-2. The same Spirit is the life-breath that animates the dirt person, so that the human can live in fellowship with the Creator and the earth in Genesis 2:4-9. The work of the Spirit, in what is traditionally referred to as grace, parallels the creative work of the Spirit in Genesis 1 and 2. For this reason, Moltmann observes: "In both the Old and the New Testaments, the words used for the divine act of *creating* are also used for God's *liberating* and *redeeming* acts."[51] The Spirit, who is the breath of life, is the Spirit-wind unleashed at Pentecost (Acts 2:1-4) that created and sustained the early Christian communities. The Spirit, who was the divine presence hovering over the primordial cosmos and who was the vivifying energy that created an earth teeming with life, is the Spirit who is the living water and the source of rebirth in the Gospel of John (John 3; 4; and 7). These images support the coordination of the traditional categories of the Spirit as breath of life and Spirit as agent of redemption in a unified theology of grace that overcomes the dialectical and hierarchical structure of common and special grace.

The Spirit and the Cosmic Scope of Redemption

The work of the Spirit throughout creation has a Trinitarian entelechy. All work of the Spirit, therefore, ultimately has an orientation to draw cre-

49. Sigurd Bergman draws a similar conclusion from the theology of Gregory of Nazianzus (Bergman, *Creation Set Free*, pp. 142 and 155).

50. For fuller details on the unity of creation and grace, see chapter 2, above, under "Spirit of Creation as Spirit of Redemption."

51. Jürgen Moltmann, *The Spirit of Life: A Universal Affirmation*, trans. Margaret Kohl (Minneapolis: Fortress Press, 1992), pp. 8-10, 177-79.

ation to its particular mode of participation in the life of the Trinitarian God. Scripture extends redemption to all of creation and does not restrict it to the "spiritual" dimension of the human.[52] Romans 8:21 promises that "the creation itself will be liberated from its bondage to decay." Moreover, that passage correlates the suffering of creation with the human yearning for eschatological renewal: "We know that the whole creation has been groaning as in the pains of childbirth right up to the present time. Not only so, but we ourselves, who have the first fruits of the Spirit, groan inwardly as we wait eagerly for our adoption as sons, the redemption of our bodies" (Rom. 8:22-23). The groaning of creation parallels that of the Christian community for final redemption. Moreover, as Dale Moody notes, this text links the groaning of creation and the children of God with the sighs of the Spirit.[53] The Spirit who cries out from the breast of every forlorn human also groans within creation and yearns for the same eschatological redemption. Human disregard for the life of other creatures for the sake of its own is environmental sin. The suffering of the Spirit is to endure giving life to those who disregard and destroy the life the Spirit gives to other living things.[54] Scripture exhorts us: "Do not grieve the Holy Spirit of God" (Eph. 4:30). Living at odds with the Spirit of life grieves and evokes the groans of the Spirit within creation. When the gift of life becomes the instrument of suffering and death, sin abounds.[55]

The passage from Romans 8 also casts the longing for cosmic redemption in pneumatological terms. The verses 23 and 26-27 suggest that the human yearning for final redemption arises from the sustaining presence of the Spirit. The inference seems appropriate that if the human "groans" for redemption arise from the Spirit, then so do creation's moans for its emancipation from its current ordeal. The reciprocal travail of the Spirit in humans and the rest of creation derives from the biblical affirmation that the Spirit, who is the breath of life and who redeems humans, is the same

52. Barbour, *Nature,* p. 126.

53. Dale Moody, *The Word of Truth: A Summary of Christian Doctrine Based on Biblical Revelation* (Grand Rapids: Eerdmans, 1981), p. 135.

54. A more extensive development of this notion is available in Jane E. Linahan, "Breath, Blood, and the Spirit of God: The Kenotic Cost of Giving Life," in *God, Grace, and Creation,* ed. Philip J. Rossi, Annual Publication of the College Theology Society, 55 (Maryknoll, NY: Orbis, 2010), pp. 107-23 (esp. p. 116).

55. This point does not imply that all death is evil. Life and death is an environmental process. The suffering and death I have in mind is the excess of ecological decay and death created by the perfidiousness of human waste and self-indulgence.

Spirit who breathes life into all living creatures (Gen. 6:17; 7:15, 22). In this respect, humans share an earthy and pneumatic union with all of creation because they come from the dust; that is, they are created from the stuff of creation and, like all other creatures, ultimately receive life from the same Spirit of life.[56] Moreover, the Spirit promises to redeem all of creation and not only the human "soul."

The renewal of creation is also contained in the promise of Pentecost. Though Acts 2:17-21 cites only Joel 2:28-32, the preceding context frames the outpouring of the Spirit in terms of the renewal of the people and land of Israel. The refreshing of the Lord will restore the green fields, the vine and the wine, the bountiful harvest, and will banish locusts, want, and scarcity.[57] Moreover, the Spirit of Pentecost is at the same time "the Spirit of Christ" (1 Pet. 1:11). The Spirit leads all of creation not only to union with Christ but to participation in the everlasting life, love, and kingdom of the Trinitarian God. Constituting the fellowship of the Trinitarian persons and consummating creation's participation in that divine community of life is the Holy Spirit's entelechy. To be sure, pine trees and rainbow trout will not participate in the *eschaton* in the same way that human beings will; nonetheless, in some way, God promises to redeem creation and it will thus share in the everlasting kingdom in a way appropriate to its varied forms.

To sum up this section: Scripture uses similar imagery to portray the work of the Holy Spirit in the traditional categories of creation and redemption. This symmetry allows Pentecostal theology (and Christian theology in general) to conceive of the work of the Spirit in terms of one order of grace or a unified theology of the salvific-economic mission of God. The Spirit's work does not have two orders — creation *and* redemption — but one, the redemption *of* creation. Moreover, the redemption of creation encompasses all of creation and thus is not limited to the human soul. Creation and redemption are distinct in the sense that creation is the sphere of divine redemptive activity, but not in the sense that there are dimensions of creation that are purely "natural." Pure nature does not exist. The apostle Paul recognized the sacredness of creation when he quoted Epimenides the Cretan's poetic phrase, "For in him we live and move and have our be-

56. George T. Montague, *The Holy Spirit: Growth of a Biblical Tradition* (New York: Paulist, 1976), pp. 5-9.

57. For a discussion of Pentecost in terms of Joel and the covenant of creation, see Margaret Barker, *Creation: A Biblical Vision for the Environment* (New York: T&T Clark, 2010), p. 183.

ing" (Acts 17:28).[58] The rejection of creation and redemption as discrete spheres and modes of divine activity renders untenable the notions of common and special grace. With the theological rationale for a unified and cosmic pneumatological theology of graced creation established, the discussion turns to the application of this theology to creation care.

The Spirit and Creation Care

Many Christians have little trouble considering their religious and moral activities of prayer, Bible study, and fasting as empowered by the Spirit and acts of Christian formation. Yet few Pentecostal and evangelical Christians consider creation care as an arena of the Spirit's work and, much less, as a form of sanctification and path of discipleship. However, creation care, no less than the traditional disciplines of Christian formation, is a way that Christians can "keep in step with the Spirit" (Gal. 5:25). In other words, buying organic fair-trade coffee and turning the heat down may be just as much a way "to work out your salvation with fear and trembling" as praying, attending church, and fasting (Phil. 2:12). Based on a pneumatological and Trinitarian theology of creation, this final section maintains that creation care is a participation in the eschatological Spirit of Pentecost.

The Spirit of Pentecost, Redemption, and Christian Formation

Pentecostals often think of salvation in very evangelical terms, easily adopting the language of salvation as a personal relationship with Jesus Christ and a born-again experience.[59] Without dismissing the importance of those, a Pentecostal account of redemption should give the Holy Spirit a central role. The Trinitarian theology outlined earlier provides a theological framework to do just that. From a Trinitarian and Pentecostal perspective, redemption is to be caught up in the Spirit's renewal of life and to par-

58. F. F. Bruce, *The Book of the Acts,* New International Commentary on the New Testament (Grand Rapids: Eerdmans, 1988), pp. 338-39.

59. There is good reason for this kinship, as Pentecostalism, at least in North America, grew out of Reformed and Wesleyan-Holiness revival movements of the late nineteenth and early twentieth centuries. Yet, though I recognize the historical heredity, throughout this project I have argued that the Pentecostal experience of the Spirit carries with it important theological implications.

ticipate in the consummation of the triune God's redemptive mission. Redemption is a foretaste of the everlasting kingdom; it is an hors d'oeuvre from the great banquet feast of the coming kingdom of God. In the following sequence, I highlight three features of the Trinitarian and eschatological nature of the Christian life.

First, the Trinity is the entelechy of the Holy Spirit. The Holy Spirit brings the life and community of the divine being to completion, which is the "eschatological" character of the Spirit in the Trinity. The Spirit's identity and role as the divine person who constitutes the fullness of the Trinitarian God comes to clearest expression in the Spirit's work as the eschatological Spirit of Pentecost. The Spirit who hovered over creation and brought about the manifestation of the triune life in Jesus Christ is now revealed as the one who makes that possible for all of creation.

Second, Christian formation is a participation in the entelechy of the Spirit. Christian formation is embracing what the Spirit seeks to do in and through human life. A more specific way of saying this is that Christian formation is the convergence of the Spirit's work as Spirit of Pentecost in the life of the believer with the Spirit's work in the world as the same. The Spirit is ever at work to communicate and realize the life of the Trinitarian God in creation. Christian sanctification is the dynamic process in which believers embrace and participate in the Spirit's work in the world. The focus here on the Spirit does not sideline Christ. The Spirit's identity and work as "the Spirit of Christ" and Spirit of Pentecost are not dissimilar but coherent ones. Believers receive the Spirit of Pentecost so that they may be transformed into the image of Christ; thus is the Christian called to be Christlike. The invitation to be Christlike is much more profound than taking up some spiritual and moral habits inspired by the life of Jesus. Being Christlike is to be what Christ was in the sense that the Holy Spirit does in believers what the Spirit did in Christ. The Spirit begins to actualize and enable believers to share in the fellowship and vibrant life of the Trinitarian God. The Holy Spirit seeks to foster ever more intimate union between believers and Christ and to empower patterns of life that reflect the reality that they have become God's children. Christian formation is the process in which human activity in all its manifold dimensions participates with the Spirit in facilitating the flourishing of all life. Christian formation is to embrace the Spirit's work and thereby "keep in step with the Spirit" (Gal. 5:25).

Third, the eschatological character of the Christian life means that Christian formation is a proleptic experience of that future redemption in the sense that it *anticipates* and *participates* in a future reality. The apostle Paul recognizes the proleptic nature of the Christian life when he says that "we ourselves, who have the first fruits of the Spirit, groan inwardly as we wait eagerly for our adoption as sons, the redemption of our bodies" (Rom. 8:23). He suggests the proleptic nature of the Christian life when he refers to it as an experience of the "first fruits" of a full harvest that remains outstanding; though the Spirit now "testifies with our spirit that we are God's children" (Rom. 8:16), our full adoption as God's children awaits the final resurrection of our bodies. So, for instance, when believers experience the renewal of their lives in this life, they both receive in part their future full redemption and anticipate that future redemption. Or, when believers experience physical healing, they receive a foretaste of their resurrection in the everlasting kingdom of God. How does Christian formation as a participation in the eschatological Spirit of Pentecost relate to creation care?

The Spirit of Pentecost, Christian Formation, and Creation Care

Creation care is a pneumatological participation in the coming kingdom because the scope of redemption extends to all of creation, and the Holy Spirit is the intrinsic divine presence that leads all of creation to its eschatological consummation. The Spirit who works in Christians and fosters their participation in the eschatological new creation is the same Spirit at work throughout the cosmos. Denis Edwards aptly remarks that "the story of the Spirit . . . is coextensive with the *total* life of the universe."[60] The principal question for Christian formation is: Where is the wind of the Spirit moving and going to foster life, and are we being caught up with it?

When Christians engage in traditional ministries of preaching the gospel and caring for those in need, they join with the Spirit's work. They do so because the work of the Spirit in their lives corresponds to the Spirit's work in the lives of others. For example, when a church engages in social-justice ministries, their ministry connects with what the Spirit seeks for the lives of people that society has left behind and marginalized. The correlation is not abstract, in the sense that ministry corresponds to the will of God in some theoretical sense, but direct and concrete. The work of the Spirit *in* the lives of Christians meets the work of the Spirit *in* the lives

60. Edwards, *Breath of Life,* p. 33.

of those to whom they minister. Framing this relationship in terms of the Spirit's Trinitarian identity means that the Holy Spirit is the nexus where human beings meet as mutual participants in ministry. The relationship should not be understood only in terms of those who give and receive ministry. When people come together in and through the Spirit, there are no mere givers and receivers. The ministry and formation process that occurs in the Spirit is reciprocal. As people encounter one another in the communion of the Spirit, those who receive ministry shape people who "do" ministry. The "givers" become receivers as they encounter the Spirit of God in and through the lives of others. Since the Holy Spirit brings the dynamic interpersonal relationships and life of the Trinitarian God to full expression, people who encounter one another in and through the Holy Spirit are reciprocally transformed and sanctified.

In a similar way, since the Spirit's redemptive work encompasses all of creation and is not limited to the "spiritual" dimension of human beings, when Christians engage in creation care, the work of the Spirit in them meets the work of the Spirit in creation.[61] Again, this convergence is not theoretical but concrete and specific. The Spirit present and working in the Christian abides in and seeks the well-being of every part of creation. Christian formation is the process in which the Spirit's work in the lives of believers meets the presence and work of the Spirit throughout creation, both in its human and nonhuman dimensions. Jane E. Linahan notes that the "Spirit not only gives life, but also empowers all things to live the life that is distinctively and authentically their very own."[62] The Christian life can then be understood as a process of reciprocal and mutual fulfillment. Individual persons fulfill their lives in and through their relationships and activities that enhance the life of other people and the whole community of creation. Furthermore, this activity is empowered by and accomplished in the Holy Spirit. Jesus promised, "I have come that they may have life, and have it to the full" (John 10:10). The life he received and lived through the Holy Spirit is available to all people through the Spirit of Pentecost.

The inherent connection between human sin and redemption and the

61. Carol J. Dempsey articulates the Old Testament prophetic tradition's promise of the eschatological renewal of life that takes in all of creation. See Dempsey, "Hope Amidst Crisis: A Prophetic Vision of Cosmic Redemption," in *All Creation Is Groaning: An Interdisciplinary Vision for Life in a Sacred Universe,* ed. Carol J. Dempsey and Russell A. Butkus (Collegeville, MN: Liturgical Press, 1999), pp. 269-84.

62. Linahan uses *kenosis* as a metaphor to express the Spirit's role in creation ("Breath, Blood, and the Spirit of God," p. 112).

suffering and renewal of creation highlights the relationship between creation care and Christian formation. Carol Dempsey notes that the Israelite prophetic tradition ties human sin to environmental degradation and therefore links their redemption.[63] She argues that the prophetic eschatological promise envisions the restoration of "harmonious relationships between God, ourselves, and the natural world."[64] The connection, on the one hand, between human sin and environmental suffering and, on the other hand, between human redemption and environmental deliverance indicates that when humans experience liberation from sin, it leads to the renewal of the land and its creatures.

The interrelationship between sin and ecological problems is obvious. From the corporate greed that fuels the voracious drive for more and more production and consumption to the indifference and/or indolence of individual consumers who refuse to recycle their trash, these patterns of behavior harm and jeopardize the well-being of our world. Moreover, the symbiosis between redemption and a healthy environment is clear. The Spirit, who breathes life into all living creatures and who breathes new life into Christians, empowers patterns of behavior that foster the flourishing of all life.[65] It seems plausible that the Spirit working redemptively in humans will lead them to behave in ways that are commensurate with the Spirit's life-giving work in other creatures. The Spirit's redemption of Christians from an overconsumptive lifestyle and indifference toward the earth promises to reduce environmental degradation and to "renew the face of the earth" (Ps. 104:30). Sigurd Bergman offers the perspective that since the "*totality*" of nature participates in God's work of salvation, the well-being of nature can function as a measure of our relationship to God.[66] Laurie J. Braaten maintains that, in the Old Testament prophets, "[e]arth's mourning is a sign that something is wrong, and it behooves humans to find out what, and take measures to correct it."[67] When the envi-

63. Dempsey, "Hope Amidst Crisis," pp. 270, 276, 279.

64. Dempsey, "Hope Amidst Crisis," p. 270.

65. Note: The above is not an endorsement of a radical biocentric model in which all life, from virulent viruses and bacteria to plants, animals, and humans, receives equal regard. For instance, protecting humans from the Ebola virus and indigenous trees from invasive and destructive insects would be considered acts of creation care.

66. Bergman, *Creation Set Free,* p. 143.

67. Laurie J. Braaten, "Earth Community in Joel: A Call to Identify with the Rest of Creation," in *Exploring Ecological Hermeneutics,* ed. Norman C. Habel and Peter L. Trudinger (Atlanta: Society of Biblical Literature, 2008), pp. 63-74 (esp. p. 68).

ronment is sick due to human malfeasance, it tells us that we are not right with God. To claim to love the Creator and not care for creation is perhaps to take "the name of the Lord thy God in vain" (Exod. 20:7, KJV). The Spirit of creation and Pentecost cannot be separated, nor can the Spirit's work in creation and redemption.

Although the case for creation care as a way to fulfill the command to love our neighbor as ourselves is perhaps an easy one to make, I want to promote creation care for a theological reason and not only for the sake of human benefit (though that is certainly to be encouraged).[68] The theological rationale for creation care is that the triune God's redemptive mission extends to all of creation and not just to the human "soul" and to traditional "spiritual" pursuits. This expansive vision means that all of our activities, whether directed toward the traditional "spiritual" dimensions of soul care or creation care, can be ways to participate in the Spirit's redemptive and eschatological work — and thus to pursue Christian formation. A vision of the mission of the triune God that comprehends all of creation thus enables Christians to see creation care as a dimension of their Christian formation and sanctification.

If creation care is Christian formation, what are the practical implications? How might we participate in the Spirit's renewal of creation? For me it has meant energy conservation in our home, an effort to get involved with the local chapter of Trout Unlimited, cleaning up garbage along stream banks when fishing, a conscious effort to fix and reuse rather than throw away and replace, and, since I am a seminary professor, researching and teaching on the issue. Churches can consider including environmental impact in their architectural and land use designs; partnering with community groups and public agencies to restore and preserve threatened habitats; making creation care a regular topic of discussion in teaching ministries; and promoting sustainable development. For example, churches often protest new adult entertainment and gambling venues near them. Why not also protest energy-inefficient office buildings near them and the suburban sprawl that degrades the environment? The key is to embrace activities such as these as ways to serve and worship God just as much as the

68. As Steven Bouma-Prediger observes, "An adequate ecological theology must acknowledge the link between ecological degradation and social injustice, and correlatively, ecological wholeness and social justice." See Bouma-Prediger, *The Greening of Theology: The Ecological Models of Rosemary Radford Ruether, Joseph Sittler, and Jürgen Moltmann*, American Academy of Religion Series, Barbara A. Holdrege, gen. ed., 91 (Atlanta: Scholars Press, 1995), p. 268.

traditional practices of spiritual formation because they are concrete manifestations of the Spirit of life and redemption that presage the eschatological renewal of all life.

Conclusion

This chapter proposed a pneumatological and Trinitarian theology of creation that supports creation care as a form of Christian formation. The first step was to outline the distinctions between the orders of common and special grace, a key theological source of the tendency toward environmental neglect in Pentecostal theology. In place of this traditional view, grace does not have two orders, but one. The basis of this synthesis is the Holy Spirit. The Spirit's eschatological identity and work in the Trinity shapes the Spirit's work in creation. Just as the Spirit brings to fullness the fellowship of the Trinitarian God, so the Spirit brings all of creation to its proper participation in the triune life. Christian formation is the Christian's participation in the Spirit's eschatological renewal of creation in all its varied forms.

Epilogue

The complaint in contemporary theology about the neglect of pneumatology and the call for a recovery of the doctrine of the Trinity may have become clichés. Nonetheless, these areas of theology remain vital areas for constructive efforts in the emerging Pentecostal theological tradition — and established ones as well. This volume is an effort to contribute not only to Pentecostal theology in general and to its Trinitarian theology in particular, but also to the other theological traditions. It began with the conviction that the charismatic experience of the Holy Spirit is a defining feature of the Pentecostal movement and has theological significance. It is not a turn to a fickle subjective theology but is an affirmation that at the root of this experience is the Holy Spirit, and thus this feature should be taken seriously in a Pentecostal theology, as well as having something to say to other theological traditions. It then turned to Scripture, and the central place of the Pentecostal experience of the Spirit found corroboration with the Spirit's climactic role in the biblical drama of redemption.

The investigation of the biblical narratives of the Spirit suggests that the Holy Spirit is an active divine person who consummates the fellowship of the Trinitarian God and plays a co-constitutional role in the formation of the personal identities of the Father and the Son. The ecumenical yield of a Pentecostal Trinitarian theology is to supplement the traditional tendency to treat the Spirit as a passive and derivative procession from the Father — or from the Father and the Son — with a more active and complementary role of the Holy Spirit in the Trinity. This theology not only supports the person status of the Holy Spirit, but also the reciprocal nature of the personal identities of the Father and the Son. The Holy Spirit contributes to the identities of the Father and Son no less than *they* to the Spirit's. Theology should also engage issues vital to the contemporary world. With this in mind, in the final two chapters I addressed the theology of religions and creation. Christians in North America now know firsthand the reality of living in a religiously plural world. How does the work of the Holy Spirit in the world relate to people of other faiths? The universal work of the Spirit of Pentecost provides a basis for hope that they participate in the redemptive work of the Spirit. Many Christians embrace the need to pursue lifestyles that are environmentally responsible, but they struggle to understand how that fits into their life of faith. The cosmic work of the Spirit, which includes all of creation in its redemptive mission, provides the pneumatological and Trinitarian basis for seeing creation care as a dimension of the Christian's relationship with God.

My hope is that this effort to develop a Pentecostal Trinitarian theology advances the growth of the Pentecostal theological tradition. Charismatic experience is a defining feature of Pentecostalism, but I am convinced that this experience has theological implications and assumptions that need to be mined. I also nurture the aspiration that this project, as it joins with the emerging and diversifying Pentecostal theological undertakings, will speak not only to Pentecostals but also to the wider ecumenical family of Christian theology. Pentecostals can learn much in conversation with other Christian traditions, but they have something to offer at the ecumenical table as well. Christian theology is one of the gifts of the Spirit of Pentecost. May this volume reflect a tongue of that Spirit that opens up a deeper understanding and experience of that Spirit.

Index of Names

Index of Subjects